THE COMPLETE GUIDE TO EMPLOYEE STOCK OPTIONS

Everything the Executive
and Employee Need to Know
About Equity Compensation Plans

FREDERICK D. LIPMAN

PRIMA VENTURE
A Division of Prima Publishing
3000 Lava Ridge Court • Roseville, California 95661
(800) 632-8676 • www.primalifestyles.com

To my wife, Gail

PRIMA PUBLISHING and colophon are trademarks of Prima Communications Inc., registered with the United States Patent and Trademark Office. PRIMA VENTURE and colophon are trademarks of Prima Communcations Inc.

This publication is designed to provide accurate and authoritative information (as of December 2000, except as otherwise noted) in regard to the subject matter covered. It is sold with the understanding that neither the author nor the publisher is engaged in rendering legal, accounting, or other professional service. If legal advice or other expert assistance is required, the services of a competent professional person should be sought.

> **—From a Declaration of Principles Jointly Adopted by a Committee of the American Bar Association and a Committee of Publishers and Associations.**

Library of Congress Cataloging-in-Publication Data on file.

ISBN 0-7615-3382-6

01 02 03 04 05 HH 10 9 8 7 6 5 4 3 2 1
Printed in the United States of America

How to Order

Single copies may be ordered from Prima Publishing, 3000 Lava Ridge Court, Roseville, CA 95661; telephone (800) 632-8676 ext. 4444. Quantity discounts are also available. On your letterhead, include information concerning the intended use of the books and the number of books you wish to purchase.

Visit us online at www.primalifestyles.com

CONTENTS

ACKNOWLEDGMENTS

I want to acknowledge the work of my coauthors Robert M. Broder (chapter 14) and Harry T. Lamb (chapter 15) of the Philadelphia office of Blank Rome Comisky & McCauley LLP, and Joseph T. Gulant (chapter 18) of the New York office, all of whom are tax law specialists. Helpful comments on Chapter 10 were also provided by my partner Gregg W. Winter, a tax law specialist in our Philadelphia office. Cory G. Jacobs of our Philadelphia office was kind enough to read the entire manuscript for any glaring errors. I take full responsibility for any errors in this book.

The National Center for Employee Ownership (*www.nceo.org*) and the National Association of Stock Plan Professionals (*www.naspp.com*) were both kind enough to permit me to use some of their valuable materials in this book. In addition, the international accounting firm of BDO Seidman LLP graciously permitted me to reprint their proprietary material on FASB Interpretation 44 in appendix 8 of this book.

Stephen P. Crane of the Philadelphia office of Ernst & Young was helpful in explaining to me certain aspects of FASB Interpretation 44.

Our librarians, Manny Paredes, Rebecca Stanley, and Alison T. Husted, were very helpful in researching portions of this book. Leily Ebraheimzadeh, a paralegal in our firm, helped proofread the manuscript.

Finally, I want to acknowledge my secretary, Herkita Trueheart, who was able to type and retype my manuscript at the same time she was performing all her other responsibilities, which permitted me to continue my law practice. Valerie Smith was also helpful in typing one of the appendices of this book.

CHAPTER 1

WHY EQUITY INCENTIVES FOR PRIVATE COMPANIES?

When eBay went public on September 24, 1998, the eBay employees in San Jose reportedly abandoned their cubicles and formed a giant conga line, a snake of conjoined, joyous, singing, delirious adults that wound through the office. These joyous eBay employees were celebrating not merely their company's initial public offering but the fact that many of them had become wealthy from their stock options.

Microsoft Corp. is estimated to have created 5,000 millionaires among its employees, thanks to stock options.

The newspapers have been full of stories about employees who have become instant millionaires as a result of stock option grants before an IPO, particularly if they sold their stock before it crashed. The lure of stock options has made it difficult for "old economy" (i.e., non-Internet) private companies, including family-owned businesses, to attract and retain key employees. Old economy employees suffer from wanderlust as they see their own compensation and future limited because of the lack of equity incentives.

Even unions have gotten into the act. The strike of Verizon Communications, Inc., by the Communication Workers of America resulted in a settlement requiring a one-time grant of stock options to approximately 210,000 hourly, salaried, and part-time employees to buy a total of 55 million shares. The option grants started at a minimum of 100 shares and rose depending on the employee's position and level of responsibility.

Companies such as Texas Instruments, Dell Computer, Cisco, and Akamai Technologies are reported to be offering temporary summer interns stock options. The vesting provisions entice the students to return to the company after graduation because the internship counts towards the vesting.

The recent cooling off of the dot-com IPO parade, with the meltdown of major Internet businesses, has helped bring a dose of reality to these employees. However, many key employees still see a brighter future in employment with a company offering stock options.

Although most companies offering stock options are publicly traded, a tight labor market has caused old economy private companies to reconsider their compensation packages. This is particularly true of old economy companies transforming themselves into new economy companies ("bricks and clicks" companies) by developing Internet marketing and delivery systems, either within the organization or within subsidiaries intended for spin-off in IPOs.

However, increasing cash compensation for key employees of private companies has definite limits. The company must still have cash flow sufficient to pay bank loans and to support the owner's cash needs.

The purpose of this book is to assist entrepreneurs and business owners of private companies as well as public companies in structuring equity incentives to their key employees.

There is no reason that an old economy private company cannot also adopt a stock option plan or other equity incentives. Stock options properly structured do not affect either the cash flow of the private company or its profitability for accounting purposes. Nor do properly structured stock options make it inevitable that your business will wind up with pesky minority shareholders.

Many owners of private companies have never precisely thought through their own personal objectives. Without understanding your personal objectives, it is difficult to create equity incentives that would align the interests of your key employees with your own. As a result, many equity incentive plans do not work.

Although most public companies have stock option plans, there are some that either have no equity incentive plan or have adopted the wrong stock option plan.

The major choices for equity incentive plans discussed in this book are as follows:

- Stock option plans
- Phantom stock plans payable in cash
- Restricted stock bonus or award plans
- Employee stock purchase plans

THE PURPOSE OF EQUITY INCENTIVES

An entrepreneur should not provide stock options or other equity incentives to employees unless it is in the entrepreneur's interest to do so. The dilution of the entrepreneur's own equity caused by such equity incentives must be outweighed by the benefits to the entrepreneur.

The following are situations that justify the use of equity incentives:

- Your business is unable to attract or retain key employees because competitors provide equity incentives in their compensation packages.

- Your business is losing key employees to non-competitors, such as dot-com start-ups, which provide generous stock option plans.
- Your business does not have the cash flow to pay competitive cash compensation.
- You wish to foster an ownership culture among key employees to align their interests with your own.
- You intend to sell the business in the next five years and need to motivate key employees with equity incentives to grow the business to achieve a high sale valuation.
- You are planning for an initial public offering (IPO) in the next five years, and you want to motivate key employees toward that goal and reward yourself with options to reduce the IPO dilution of your own equity caused by the IPO.

INCREASED CASH FLOW

The major advantage of equity incentives is that they do not affect your cash flow. This contrasts with cash bonus plans or similar cash-based plans. For example, stock options do not require any cash outlay other than the initial cost of establishing the plan. If and when the option is exercised, the company receives the exercise price. The option can require that the exercise price be paid in cash, thereby further increasing your cash flow. Companies sometimes permit the exercise price to be paid in other company stock (including stock acquired under the same option) or with promissory note, but that is your choice.

If the option that is exercised is not an incentive stock option, the company generally obtains a federal income tax deduction for the option profit, which also increases the company's cash flow. If your company is a Subchapter S corporation, this tax benefit flows directly to your personal federal income tax return. Even if the option is an incentive stock option, if the optionee sells or otherwise makes a disqualifying disposition of the stock within one year of exercise or two years of original grant, the company receives a similar federal income tax deduction and increased cash flow.

Ultimately, a stock option can cost you cash. For example, if the options are exercised and thereafter your company is sold, your personal interest in the sale consideration is proportionately reduced. However, you have received the benefit of employees' services prior to the sale without the necessity of paying large cash bonuses to motivate your employees.

EMPIRICAL STUDY

Rutgers University School of Management and Labor Relations released a study in 2000 that included 490 companies that had broad-based stock option plans (i.e., a majority of the full-time employees actually received stock option grants over a reasonable time period). The results show that such companies had statistically higher productively levels and annual growth rates compared to non–broad-based stock option companies in general and among their peers.

One interpretation of the findings is that the performance of firms using broad-based stock options appears to equal or exceed the equity dilution that these plans initially would have caused. However, it is difficult to prove that productivity increases were actually due to a broad-based stock option plan. The study can be found at *www.neco.org / library / optionreport.html*.

EXIT EVENT OPTIONS

Many entrepreneurs of private companies are reluctant to give up equity or to face the problem of having minority shareholders. They do not wish to be responsible to minority shareholders for their actions. Nor do they want to be obligated to reveal sensitive compensation information to their minority shareholders. However, these same entrepreneurs are less concerned about the employee becoming entitled to equity if there is an exit event (i.e. either a sale of the company or an IPO). Although technically an IPO is not an exit event but rather a liquidity event, an occurrence that may permit the subsequent sale of some of the owner's stock, in this book we will refer to an IPO as an exit event.

Stock option and other equity incentive plans can be structured so that the employees never actually own stock unless and until there is an exit event. For example, a stock option, which we will call an "exit event option," can be granted to key employees that cannot be exercised *unless and until* the company is sold or has an IPO, and the employee has remained with the company for some time period after the sale or IPO. *Until an exit event stock option is exercisable and has in fact been exercised, the employee has no rights as a shareholder.*

Merely holding an exit event option to purchase stock does not entitle the employee to any rights as a shareholder. If an employee leaves employment prior to the exit event, he or she will lose the right to exercise the option. Likewise, if the option expires (generally in ten years) before the exit event, the option terminates, and the employee never becomes a shareholder.

The idea behind an exit event option is to align the interest of the employee with that of the employer only if an exit event develops and, in the meantime, to offer incentives to the employee to help realize the exit event.

Exit event options are not appropriate for companies that are not intended to be sold or to engage in an IPO (such as family-owned businesses). An option that vests over time or upon satisfying certain performance objectives is more appropriate for family-owned businesses, as described later. Likewise, exit event options may not be appropriate for start-up companies or companies that use options instead of current cash compensation (e.g., dot-com companies), also discussed later.

With regard to public companies, the exit event would be limited to a sale. However, time-vested options are more common for public companies—that is, options that automatically vest after the employee has been employed for certain time periods, regardless of any sale or other exit event.

Exit Event Options As a Sale Motivator

Exit event options are an important tool in motivating key employees toward a sale. A sale of your company, in contrast to any IPO, creates insecurity among your key employees. They are uncertain as to whether the buyer will need their services. They are also uncertain as to whether the buyer will provide the same job growth potential that they enjoyed under your leadership.

It is not unusual for key employees to leave the company on the eve of a sale because of these uncertainties. Yet, you will need your management team to help you obtain the highest price from your proposed buyer. Defections on the eve of a sale, particularly to competitors, can be devastating to the sale value of your business.

Exit event options act as a bonus to motivate key employees to remain with you throughout the sale process. Since key employees benefit from the increase in the sale value of your business through their stock options, their interests are aligned with yours.

Disadvantages of Exit Event Options

Exit event options have two main disadvantages, each of which can be remedied:

- Upon a sale or IPO of the company, there will be an accounting charge.

> **Remedy**: If there is a concern about the accounting charge upon the sale or IPO, make the option exercisable at some point in time (e.g., nine years and ten months, provided it is likely that the optionee will still be employed at that time) regardless of whether there is a sale or IPO, but accelerate the exercisability date if there is a sale or IPO before that date (e.g., if there is a sale or IPO before nine years and ten months, the option may be exercisable earlier). In most cases, a company should not worry about an accounting charge if the transaction is a sale, particularly in view of the pending abolition of pooling accounting for buyers. Even in the event of an IPO, the accounting charge will only affect the fiscal quarter in which the IPO occurs. Appendix 1 contains an exit event option that is exercisable in nine years and ten months, but it can be exercised at an earlier date in the event of a sale or IPO and will generally avoid an accounting charge.

- If too much option profit is earned by an optionee upon the sale of a company, the profit may be subject to a substantial federal excise tax under the "golden parachute" rules of the Internal Revenue Code.

Remedy: The "golden parachute" rules are not applicable to private companies if there is shareholder approval (after adequate disclosure) by shareholders holding more than 75 percent of the voting power or if the company issuing the stock option is a "small business corporation" as defined in Section 1361(a) of the Internal Revenue Code (has no more than seventy-five shareholders and meets most of the requirements for Subchapter S elections). The optionee (whether employed by a public or private company) can also avoid the federal excise tax by voluntarily agreeing before the sale takes place to limit the amount of the option profit to a figure that does not trigger federal excise tax (in general, not more than three times annualized compensation for a five-year base period).

Exit event options should only be used by private companies if there is a reasonable prospect that you will sell or have an IPO within ten years from the grant date. Ten years is the typical term for a stock option, even though the option will usually expire earlier if the employee ceases to be employed by your company prior to the ten-year period.

Likewise, exit event options should only be used by public companies if there is a reasonable prospect of a sale within ten years from the grant date.

Obviously, a company cannot guarantee its employees that an exit event will occur within ten years of the grant date. However, it is advisable to at least have a good faith intention of an exit event within the ten-year period. If you know that you will not exit within ten years, you should consider time-vested options with call rights, which are discussed in the next section.

FAMILY-OWNED BUSINESSES

Exit event options are inappropriate if you do not ever plan to exit from your business. Many family owned businesses are intended to be left to the next generation and the owners do not expect either to sell the business or to go public. Such family-owned entities should not use exit event options.

However, they can use options that are exercisable over time (time vested) but that require that any stock acquired under the option must be resold to other family members or to the corporation at its then fair market value on the resale date. This approach permits the executive of a family-owned business to realize equity appreciation of the stock, but it prevents the stock from ultimately leaving family ownership. To achieve this objective, the executive would be required to execute a shareholders' agreement, as a condition of option exercise, that would give the family-owned business or its nominee a "call" on the stock at its then fair market value.

The "call" price can be payable over several years. Fair market value can be determined by a formula in the shareholders' agreement, by the board of directors' discretionary determination, or through the use of outside appraisers. Typically, valuation formulas include (among other things) book value based formulas and formulas that require a multiplier of EBITDA (i.e., earnings before interest, taxes, depreciation, and amortization) as adjusted for the owner's salaries and perquisites less debt.

An alternative to this type of option is a *phantom stock plan*. This plan provides a cash payment to the executive based on appreciation of the stock value during the measurement period (e.g., five years). However, a phantom stock plan produces ordinary income for the executive (generally deductible by the company) and also causes a quarterly or annual accounting charge.

If the executive can receive an incentive stock option, thereafter purchase stock at the option exercise price (based on the fair market value on the grant date), and then sell the stock back to the corporation or a family member as a result of the "call" feature one year or more after exercise, the executive would realize long-term capital gains on the stock appreciation (assuming the two-year holding period after the grant date and the continuous employment requirements, to be described in chapter 3, were satisfied).

OPTIONS FOR START-UP COMPANIES

Exit event options may also be inappropriate for certain risky start-up companies that use options instead of paying competitive cash compensation. For example, many dot-com companies are sufficiently risky that they need equity incentives to attract key employees. Likewise, many start-ups do not pay competitive salaries and instead grant options to their key employees. The options are intended as a complete or partial substitute for current cash compensation.

Options granted by companies that do not pay competitive cash compensation should generally become exercisable as the services are rendered. For example, a portion of the option could become exercisable every week or month of employment. This permits the employee to obtain vesting (i.e., exercisability) as the services are performed.

Exit event options are typically not exercisable if the employee is not still employed at the time of the exit sale or IPO. If the employee is foregoing some or all of his or her current compensation to work in the business, it is difficult to convince this individual that he or she should receive no reward whatsoever if employment ceases prior to a sale or IPO.

However, if the employee voluntarily or involuntarily terminates employment with the start-up, the shareholders' agreement should give the company a "call" to repurchase the shares previously acquired under the former employee's option. The call price can be a formula, a price determined by the board of directors, or a price calculated by outside appraisers.

It is essential that the start-up company retains the right to "call" (repurchase) the stock of former employees for a substantial period of time after employment terminates. The start-up company may lack the necessary capital to exercise the call for many years. However, it is important to be able to repurchase the stock from an ex-employee who may turn into a hostile minority shareholder or join a competitor.

GIFTS OF STOCK

Some entrepreneurs believe that they can merely make gifts of their stock to employees to provide equity incentives. Unless the employees are also family members, these so-called "gifts" will be viewed as stock bonuses and can produce unfavorable tax results to the employee.

The IRS views a gift to employee as a compensatory transaction. As a result, the employee will realize taxable income equal to the fair market value of the gift, and the company is generally entitled to a federal income tax deduction in the same amount. For example, if you give $100,000 worth of stock to an employee and the employee is taxed at a combined federal and state income tax rate of 42 percent, the employee will owe $42,000 in income taxes as a result of your "gift." This is true whether the gift comes from the company or from your personal stock holdings in the company. Moreover, the company will be required to immediately collect federal income withholding taxes on the gift of up to 28 percent, or $28,000, which is credited against the 42 percent.

Unless you are prepared to lend the employee $42,000 with which to pay federal and state income taxes, the employee may not be grateful for your "gift."

Restricted stock bonus grants can be used to postpone taxes, but they have other disadvantages, discussed in chapter 18.

Gifts to family members, including employees of your company who are family members, are generally respected as gifts by the IRS. However, gift tax returns may be required to be filed, and gift taxes paid, depending on the size of the gift to your family member.

In contrast to stock gifts, stock options granted to employees do not result in any income taxes to the employee on the date of the option grant. The only exception is for options that are readily tradable in an established market. This is rarely, if ever, the case.

SELLING STOCK AT BARGAIN PRICES

If the employee is taxed at the 42 percent combined federal and state income tax rate, the employee must be paid 42 percent of the excess.

If you sell stock to your employee and the purchase price is less than the fair market value on the date of the grant, the excess of the fair market value of the stock over the purchase price is ordinary income to your employee. This excess is also subject to immediate federal income tax withholding (which is credited against the 42 percent) at a rate up to 28 percent.

For example, suppose you sell 3 percent of your stock to a key employee and charge her $30,000. If the IRS determined that the fair market value of that stock was really $130,000, your employee would have received

$100,000 ($130,000 less $30,000) of ordinary income as a result of the sale). The income tax result is the same as if the $100,000 worth of stock was a stock bonus or stock "gift."

FEDERAL INCOME TAX RATES

The federal income tax rates used in this book are based on the federal income tax law in effect in December 2000. Consult your tax adviser for the effect of changes enacted in 2001 or thereafter.

OVERVIEW OF EQUITY INCENTIVES FOR KEY EMPLOYEES

If you want to grant equity incentives only to key employees, you have five major choices:

1. Stock options—either incentive stock options or nonqualified stock options (with or without stock appreciation rights)
2. Stock appreciation rights payable in stock or cash
3. Performance share plans payable in stock or cash
4. Restricted stock bonus and award plans
5. Phantom stock plans payable in cash

The term *phantom stock plans* is used in this book to refer to a wide variety of *cash* bonus plans, including so-called performance share/unit plans that are keyed to the increases in the value of the stock or other performance goals.

Table 1.1 provides a comparison of equity incentive plans that can be limited to key employees of your company.

TABLE 1.1

Incentive Stock Options	Nonqualified Stock Option Plans	Stock Appreciation Rights	Performance Share/Unit Plans	Restricted Stock Plans	Phantom Stock Plans
Description					
A right granted by employer to an employee to purchase stock at a stipulated price during a specified period of time in accord with Section 422 of Internal Revenue Code.	A right granted by employer to purchase stock at stipulated price over a specific period of time.	A right granted to employee to realize appreciation in value of specified number of shares of stock. No employee investment required. Time of exercise of rights is at employee's discretion.	Awards of contingent shares or units are granted at beginning of specified period. Awards are earned out during the period that certain specified company performance goals are attained. Price of company stock at end of performance period (or other valuation criteria) determines value of payout.	Shares of stock are subject to restrictions on transferability with a substantial risk of forfeiture, and shares are granted to employee without cost (or at a bargain price).	Employee is awarded units (not representing any ownership interest) corresponding in number and value to a specified number of shares of stock. When units vest, they are revalued to reflect the current value of the stock.

TABLE 1.1 (*continued*)

Incentive Stock Options	Nonqualified Stock Option Plans	Stock Appreciation Rights	Performance Share/Unit Plans	Restricted Stock Plans	Phantom Stock Plans
Characteristics					
• Option must be granted within ten years of adoption or shareholder approval, whichever is earlier, and granted options must be exercised within ten years of grant. • $100,000 limitation on total amount that first becomes exercisable in a given year (measured on date of grant). • Previously acquired stock may be used as payment medium for the exercise of incentive stock options.	• May be granted at price below fair market value. • Option period is typically ten years. • Vesting restrictions are typical. • Previously acquired company stock may be used as full or partial payment for the exercise of nonqualified stock options. • May be granted to nonemployees.	• May be granted alone or in conjunction with stock options. • A specified maximum value may be placed on amount of appreciation that may be received. • Distribution may be made in cash or stock or both in amount equal to the growth in value of the underlying stock. • May be granted to nonemployees.	• Awards earned are directly related to achievement during performance period. • Performance periods are typically from three to five years. • Grants usually are made every one to two years as continuing incentive device. • Payments are made in cash or stock or combination. • May be granted to nonemployees.	• Shares become available to employee as restrictions lapse, generally upon completion of a period of continuous employment. • Individual has contingent ownership until restrictions lapse. • Dividend equivalents can be paid or credited to the employee's account. • May be granted to nonemployees.	• Award may be equal to value of shares of phantom stock or just the appreciation portion. • Dividend equivalents may be credited to account or paid currently. • Benefit can be paid in cash or stock or both. • May be granted to nonemployees.

- Written approval of shareholders (within twelve months before or after adoption).

Employer

• No tax deduction allowed to employer on exercise.	• Tax deduction in the amount, and at the time, the employee realizes ordinary income.	• Tax deduction in the amount, and at the time, the employee realizes ordinary income.	• Tax deduction in the amount, and at the time, the employee realizes ordinary income.	• Tax deduction in the amount, and at the time, the employee realizes ordinary income.	• Tax deduction in the amount, and at the time, the employee realizes ordinary income.

Accounting Considerations

• Generally, no accounting expense under current FASB 25 rules is required upon grant or exercise of incentive stock options. • There is a possible dilution as the number of outstanding stock options is considered in calculating earnings per share.	• Generally, no accounting expense under current FASB 25 rules is required if option price equals or exceeds market value on date of grant. • There is a possible dilution as the number of outstanding stock options is considered in calculating earnings per share.	• Estimated expense is accrued quarterly from date of grant to date of exercise. Expense generally is equal to the amount of appreciation during each year. Restrictions on exercise may affect the amount of accrual.	• Estimated expense is accrued quarterly by amortizing the initial value of the awards and subsequent appreciation over the earn-out period based on performance against goal.	• Estimated expense is accrued annually equal to difference between stock's market value on date of grant and price paid (if any) by employee.	• Estimated expense is accrued quarterly by amortizing the initial value of the awards and/or subsequent appreciation over the maturity period. • Payment or crediting of dividend equivalents is expensed at the time of payment or credit.

If you are prepared to provide equity incentives to all of your employees on a nondiscriminatory basis, you can also consider a tax-qualified employee stock purchase plan or an employee stock ownership plan (ESOP). An employee stock purchase plan is discussed in chapter 20, and you will have to read another book to learn about ESOPs.

CHAPTER 2

COMMON MISTAKES AND AN ALMOST IDEAL PRIVATE COMPANY PLAN

We have all heard about the business owner who tried to increase his sales revenue by giving his salespersons a percentage of new sales that they booked. Sales bookings increased dramatically, but unfortunately most of the sales were unprofitable. The business owner then changed his incentives to be a percentage of the sales that are booked at a minimum profit margin. That worked for a while until the business owner discovered that his business was selling to a lot of deadbeats who did not pay their bills or only paid a portion of their bills. Finally, the business owner changed the incentive plan so that salespersons were only entitled to a commission when the profitable sales were in fact collected in full from the customer.

The business owner's mistake in this example was in failing to think through his own objectives before establishing the incentive plan. However, many other incentive plans produce undesirable results for the same reason. The following are a few examples:

- A plan that rewards increases in revenues, so employees are given incentives to obtain high-volume customers, even though your profit margins are thin or nonexistent on these customers.

- The business owner properly offers incentives to his key employees with cash or stock but fails to obtain legally enforceable noncompete agreements with them. As a result the employees leave on the eve of the sale of the business and take customers with them.

- The business owner motivates his key employees to increase his profits, and they do so by having the company make bank loans to finance large capital expenditures. Ultimately, bank loans reduce the sales price of the business to the owner, since the loans must be repaid out of the sale price.

- An incentive plan is established that causes the peak incentives to occur one year before he intends to sell the business. As a result, the valuation of the business is impaired at the time of sale since the business appears to be going backward or at least plateauing.

- The business owner is planning for an IPO and offers incentives to employees to grow the portion of his business that has the lowest multiplier for purposes of valuing the business in the IPO.

- The business owner has an unrealistic valuation for his business and motivates his key employees to increase the EBITDA (earnings before interest, taxes, and depreciation/amortization) by paying them a higher multiplier of EBITDA than the business owner would actually receive upon his sale or IPO.

- Stock awards are made/given to key employees who become disgruntled because they must pay their own federal and state income taxes on the stock awards out of their own pockets (see chapter 18).

- Key employees are given stock awards subject to restrictions, which may cause their forfeiture if certain business objectives are not satisfied, but they fail to make tax elections (Section 83[b] elections) which would permit the future appreciation to be taxed at long-term capital gains rates for federal income tax purposes (see chapter 18).

- The business owner establishes a stock option plan that quickly vests employees with rights to exercise their stock options whether or not there is a sale or IPO, and the business owner winds up with unhappy minority shareholders.

The purpose of this book is to help you avoid these or other mistakes in plan design.

IDEAL EQUITY INCENTIVE PLAN

Suppose you were to create the ideal equity incentive plan for your key employees. For many entrepreneurs, the plan would have the following characteristics:

- Your plan should permit you to discriminate among your employees so as to provide benefits only to your key employees and, if you so wish, none at all to other employees. *Note:* Stock option and stock bonus plans permit discrimination. Tax-qualified employee stock purchase plans and employee stock ownership plans do not permit discrimination.

- The plan would give employees incentives to work harder and more effectively from the date it was established. *Note:* The stock option plan in which the option exercise price equals or exceeds the fair market value of your stock on the grant date achieves this objective. The employee only profits if there is appreciation in the value of your business after the grant date. In contrast, stock bonus plans reward employees even if your company never appreciates after the stock bonus grant date. The stock bonus rewards the employee for past growth in the business, whether or not the employee played a role in that growth. However, a restricted stock bonus which prevents vesting unless and until your company's valuation increases can, in part, achieve similar objectives to a stock option plan.

- The equity incentive would not vest until after you had exited through a sale or IPO. Conversely, if you did not exit, the equity incentive would never vest.

- Your employee could not become a shareholder until all vesting conditions are satisfied and therefore would not be entitled to the rights and privileges of shareholders.

- The plan would not affect the accounting earnings that your business would show to a potential buyer or in an IPO or to your banker.

- The plan would have a minimal cost to you compared to the revenue and profit growth it generated. *Note:* An exit event option plan is inexpensive to establish. If the plan does not result in the growth of your business, the employee will not profit from the option since the option price equals the fair market value on the grant date.

- There is no federal or state income tax payable by your employees until they have received cash from the equity and any gain from the equity is taxable as long-term capital gains.

- The plan should contain clauses that motivate key employees to remain with your company for a reasonable time after an IPO or sale and restrict their solicitation of your customer or employees for a reasonable time after they leave you.

- The plan should permit you to reward outside directors of your company and important consultants to your company as well as key employees.

- The plan should help facilitate your IPO or sale exit by aligning the interest of your key employees with your own.

THE ALMOST IDEAL STOCK OPTION PLAN

Appendix 1 contains a private company exit event stock option plan, except that the option will become exercisable in any event after nine years and ten months of employment. This provision permits the plan to avoid an accounting charge as discussed in chapter 16, provided it is likely that the optionee will remain employed at that time. Appendix 2 presents a private company exit event stock option that is never exercisable unless there is a sale or other Change of Control.

Appendix 1 should be used when the company is unsure whether the exit strategy will be an IPO or sale. Appendix 2 should be used if the company is certain that an IPO is not in their future. If there is no IPO in the future, you have no reason to worry about an accounting charge on the vesting of options upon a sale or other Change of Control; therefore, you have no reason to require that the options be exercisable in nine years and ten months.

These plans, while not meeting all of the requirements for an ideal plan, come fairly close. The plans permit you to discriminate among your employees. The
equity incentive does not vest until after you have exited
through a sale or IPO (assuming, if you use appendix 1,
that you have a sale or IPO before nine years and ten
months). Conversely, if you do not exit, the equity incentive would never vest (unless, in the case of appendix 1,
the employee remains with you for nine years and ten
months). The optionee could not become a shareholder
until all vesting conditions are satisfied. The appendix 1
plan should not affect your accounting earnings since the
optionee can exercise the option after nine years and ten
months (provided it is likely that the optionee will remain
employed at that time) regardless of whether there is a
sale or IPO. If a sale or IPO occurs before nine years and
ten months, the right to exercise the option accelerates
until one year *after* the sale or IPO.

No federal income tax is payable by your employees,
who receive options under the appendix 1 or appendix 2
plans until they have received cash from the equity, with
one possible exception. Alternative minimum tax may be
applicable upon the exercise of incentive stock options
granted under the plan (see chapter 3). The gain from the
sale of the stock would be taxed at long-term capital gains
rate if certain holding period and employment requirements are satisfied. If these requirements are not satisfied for federal income tax purposes, the gain is taxed as
ordinary income to your employee, and your company
would in most circumstances be entitled to a federal
income tax deduction in the same amount.

The plan contained in appendix I does not permit
vesting for one year after an IPO or sale and also prevents newly hired employees from full vesting within
three years of their start date. In the event of an IPO, this

provision helps ensure that the employee has the incentive to remain with your company for a sufficient period of time after the IPO to help you partially exit in a secondary or follow-on offering that occurs within one year after the IPO.

This provision also makes your business more valuable to a buyer. The buyer has some assurance that all of your key employees will not leave your company immediately after the sale closes and will assist the buyer in the transition for a one-year period to obtain the benefit of option vesting.

The plan also restricts the optionees from soliciting your customers or other employees for a reasonable time after the optionee's employment terminates. However, what is a "reasonable time" (two years in the appendix I plan) will not work in every state and every context. Consult your attorney on this issue.

The appendix 1 and appendix 2 plans also permit you to grant nonincentive options to your employees and to nonemployee directors and outside consultants. Nonincentive options granted to your employees and certain outside directors at an exercise price equal or greater than the fair market value of your stock will not normally result in an accounting charge. However, options to nonemployee consultants will result in a charge to your accounting earnings (see chapter 16).

The appendix 1 and 2 plans can also be amended to include suppliers and customers as option recipients. Such option grants will cause an accounting charge, but they are useful as a method of financing a start-up business or in giving your customers an equity stake in your future success. Care should be taken in granting options to suppliers and customers in properly accounting for the cost of such options (see chapter 7) and in complying with federal and state securities laws (see chapter 17).

CHAPTER 3

INTRODUCTION TO STOCK OPTION PLANS

The National Center for Employee Ownership (*www.nceo.org*) estimates that in 2000 between seven and ten million employees actually received stock options from their companies, up from one million in 1992. Companies are offering equity incentives to a broader cross section of their workforces to encourage and develop long-term employee ownership.

Employee stock option plans are almost universal among publicly traded companies. However, a growing number of private companies are using equity incentives as well, particularly exit event options.

It is no accident that stock option plans are so universally popular. A stock option plan, whether for a private or public company, has the following advantages if the option exercise price is equal or greater than the fair market value of the stock on the grant date:

- Generally no accounting charge is made to your reported earnings on the grant or exercise of the option by an employee and certain nonemployee directors. Options and tax-qualified stock purchase plans are the only forms of compensation capable of avoiding an accounting charge.

- Your employees have no rights as shareholders until the option becomes exercisable and is in fact exercised.

- No federal income tax is paid by the employee on the grant date.

- No federal income tax is paid by the employee on the exercise date, provided the option qualifies as an incentive stock option (ISO) under Section 422 of the Internal Revenue Code (hereafter referred to as "the Code"). *Note:* The caveat is that if there is a large gain on the option, alternative minimum tax could apply.

- If the option does not qualify as an ISO (a "non-ISO"), your company is entitled to a federal income tax deduction upon exercise of the option on the option profit (i.e., the fair market value of the stock on the exercise date less the option exercise price), and your employee realizes the taxable income on the option profit (a non-ISO is also called a *non-qualified* or *nonstatutory stock option*). *Note:* If vesting conditions remain after exercising a non-ISO, the tax is postponed until the vesting conditions are satisfied (unless a Section 83[b] election is made; see chapter 18).

- If the option qualifies as an ISO, the appreciation on the sale is taxed at long-term capital gains rate at the time of sale, provided certain holding periods and employment requirements of the Code are satisfied. This means that your employees would pay a top federal income tax rate of 20 percent instead of 39.6 percent (assuming they were not subject to alternative minimum tax). If the holding period and employment requirement are not satisfied, the appreciation is taxed as ordinary income, and your company is generally entitled to a deduction of this same amount.

- Since the option exercise price can be (and must be in the case of an ISO) not less than at the current fair market value of your stock, your employee only profits if the value of your stock increases after the grant date.

- The stock option grant can encourage the employee to continue his or her employment with your company by requiring a minimum number of years of employment or an exit event (or both) before the option becomes exercisable.

- The option grant can be coupled with an agreement by the employee not to compete and not to solicit your customers or employees after they leave your company.

- A properly structured plan (see appendix 1 or appendix 2) can give incentives to employees to remain with your company until a time period has expired after an IPO or sale.

DISADVANTAGES OF STOCK OPTION PLANS

The following are the disadvantages of an incentive stock option plan:

- You will have to obtain an appraisal of the fair market value of your stock so as to set an option exercise price equal to or higher than such appraised amount. The appraisal can cost anywhere from $5,000 to $25,000 or higher, depending on whom you use as an appraiser. *Note:* A similar appraisal is also required if you adopt a nonincentive stock option plan to demonstrate that the option exercise price is equal or greater than the fair market value of the stock in order to avoid an accounting charge. Likewise, an appraisal would be required with a stock bonus plan and other equity incentive plans for income tax purposes.

- If the option grantee is to realize long-term capital gains on the stock appreciation after the grant date, the grantee must satisfy certain holding and employment requirements; otherwise, the appreciation is taxed as ordinary income for federal income tax purposes. In addition, there is a limit on the amount of long-term capital gains that can be achieved with an ISO and a possibility of alternative minimum tax upon exercise of an ISO for a grantee who has a significant gain on his or her ISO. *Note*: Alternative minimum tax can be avoided on an ISO exercise by making a sale or other disqualifying disposition in the year of exercise; however, this will result in a disqualifying disposition of the ISO stock and produce ordinary income to the optionee and a deduction for the employer.

- Only corporations can issue ISOs. Limited liability companies and limited partnerships do not qualify (see chapter 15).

- To avoid having stock option grants reduce your accounting income, you must comply with certain complex accounting rules, including a requirement that the option must at some point become exercisable, and that the optionee must be likely to be employed at that time, regardless of whether or not there is a sale in IPO.

- If the employee obtains long-term capital gains on the stock appreciation, the company loses an income tax deduction for that appreciation.

If your option plan is very successful, you could wind up with unmotivated employees. At Dell Computer, for example, they talk about employees who "call in rich," which means that their options are worth so much, they no longer have to work.

VALUING A PRIVATELY OWNED BUSINESS

Incentive stock options (ISOs) and options that do not result in an accounting charge must have options exercise prices that are at least equal to the fair market value of your stock on the grant date. To determine this "fair market value of a private business," you should use an outside appraiser to value your business. The overall business valuation of the outside appraiser is then divided by the number of your outstanding shares of common stock before the common stock option grants to determine the "fair market value per share" of your common stock.

Obviously, if your company's stock is already publicly traded, you do not need an appraiser. You can use the publicly reported last sale price before the date of option grant as the fair market value.

Hiring an Appraiser

To obtain the overall value of your private business, you should have an outside appraiser. Appraising the business yourself is not a good idea. The formal appraisal from the reputable independent appraiser will be much more persuasive to the IRS and your accountant that your options were granted at an exercise price that was not less than the fair market value on the grant date. If you have an IPO within one year of the grant date, the outside appraisal will not be persuasive to the SEC, who has its own appraisal methods.

In general, you want to retain the least expensive appraiser that you can find who will provide a competently prepared and fully reasoned, detailed appraisal report. If the cheapest appraiser you have located will only provide a single-page conclusion, keep looking. A one-page conclusion report will not be persuasive to either the IRS or possibly even your own accountant. Your own accountant may be able to provide you with an appraisal if he or she is a member of the Institute of Business Appraisers.

Look for an appraiser who belongs to a recognized appraisal group that requires an examination. The prestigious American Society of Appraisers and the somewhat newer Institute of Business Appraisers (typically certified public accountants) are examples of such groups. The Institute of Business Appraisers does not require any specific valuation experience, in contrast to the more rigorous requirements for the American Society of Appraisers, which requires five years of experience for the designation "accredited senior appraiser" and two years for the "accredited member" designation. These different professional requirements usually are reflected in the cost of the appraisal, with members of the American Society of Appraisers generally charging significantly higher fees.

If you use members of the Institute of Business Appraisers, you should be able to obtain an appraisal for as little as $5,000 to $10,000. Select the appraiser by reputation and personal recommendation. If you have special circumstances (e.g., you are under constant IRS audit), you may want to obtain an appraiser with greater prestige, such as a member of the American Society of Appraisers or even a Wall Street investment banker.

Most entrepreneurs prefer the lowest reasonable appraisal figure for the business so that they can confer low option exercise prices on options granted to their key employees and to themselves or other relatives in their business.

Appraising your stock is an art and not a science. Section 422(c)(1) of the Code provides protection in good-faith attempts to value your stock that result in an option price below its actual fair market value as defined by the IRS.

DISCOUNTS

The fair market value per share is the lowest option exercise price that the grantee of options on your common stock can receive if you wish to grant ISOs or receive favorable accounting treatment.

For example, suppose the appraiser decides that your private business is worth $5 million and you have 1,000 shares of common stock outstanding. Each share would then have a fair market value (ignoring discounts for minority interests, marketability, blockage, and other restrictions) of $5,000.

It is arguable that a minority interest in your private company should be discounted, since a minority stock position normally confers no control over the company. A minority discount of 20 percent to 33$^{1}/_{3}$ percent is within a normal range, but the amount of the discount varies with each company. If you wish to provide your employees with the benefit of a minority discount of 20 percent, the option price would be reduced from $5,000 per share to $4,000 per share. It is unclear whether the IRS will accept a minority discount in establishing the exercise price for an ISO; therefore, you should carefully check with tax counsel before using minority discounts.

If you are the majority shareholder of your private company, your exercise price should not have a minority discount, and, it can be argued, a control premium should be attached to your option shares. Consequently, it may be better to ignore the minority discount for your employees so as to avoid having the IRS raise the specter of a control premium in setting the exercise price for your own incentive stock option.

Other discounts that may be available with respect to the value of the stock of a private company include discounts for lack of marketability, blockage, and restrictive agreements. Any discount that you offer to your employees should be supported by a well-reasoned appraisal report.

STOCK SPLITS

Since an option exercise price per share of $5,000 may seem high to your employees, you may decide to lower it to exercise price per share. This can be done by a stock split. In the prior example, if you split your stock 1,000 for 1, you would have one million shares of common stock outstanding before the option grants, and the fair market value per share would be reduced from $5,000 to $5.

A stock split is also important to increase the absolute number of shares subject to each stock option that you grant. For example, if you only have 1,000 shares of common stock outstanding, an option for 3 percent of your outstanding stock would only be thirty shares. An option for thirty shares may not seem like a significant option to an employee because of the tendency of employees to look at the absolute number of shares subject to their option, rather than their percentage interest.

If you effectuate a 1,000-for-1 stock split, you would have one million shares outstanding, and an option for 3 percent of your outstanding stock would cover 30,000 shares. An option for 30,000 shares is much more impressive to many employees than an option for thirty shares, even though there is no economic difference between the two. I am aware of situations of even very sophisticated key employees, directors, officers, and attorneys who received individual stock options and never asked how many shares in total were outstanding!

A stock split is easy to accomplish. If your corporate charter (called the *articles of incorporation* or *certificate of incorporation* in most states) authorizes you to issue the additional common stock necessary to create the 1,000-for-1 stock split, your corporation adopts a resolution of its board of directors declaring a 1,000-for-1 stock split payable in the form of a stock dividend out of the authorized but unissued common stock.

If your charter does not currently authorize a sufficient number of shares for the stock split, you can change the charter. Charter changes in most states require a resolution of your board of directors and, in some states, approval by your shareholders. If your business only has a few shareholders, you can in most states use unanimous consent resolutions signed by all of your shareholders to approve the charter change, instead of holding a shareholder meeting.

The approved charter change must be properly filed with your state of incorporation, together with a nominal filing fee, to make the charter change effective.

Establishing Two Classes of Stock and Voting Trust Agreements for Private Companies

If your option plan will permit your employees to exercise options before your exit date (sale or IPO), you should consider creating a nonvoting or low voting class of stock of your private corporation and grant stock options solely with respect to the class. A nonvoting class of common stock is permitted in regular corporations ("C" corporations) under the Code, and Subchapter S corporations permit two classes of common stock if the *only* difference between the two classes is their voting rights.

The advantage of granting options for a nonvoting class of common stock is that the employee and other persons who exercise stock options will not dilute your voting power. This could be important to you if you do not currently own all of your company's stock and the votes of the option grantees who exercise their options could take control away from you if combined with the votes of other shareholders.

Another method of maintaining control is a voting trust or voting agreement. Some state laws limit the duration of voting trusts or impose fiduciary duties on the voting trustee. If you opt for a voting agreement, the options could require the grantee, as a condition to exercise, to execute an agreement which will bind the grantee to vote shares as you direct (see appendix 3 for an example).

Unlike voting trusts, of which you are the trustee, voting agreements have to be specifically enforced by a court order if the option grantee decides to breach the voting agreement.

I believe that a second class of nonvoting or low voting stock is the better method of ensuring your control, rather than a voting trust or voting agreement.

If you use two classes of stock to maintain control, it is helpful if you recapitalize your corporation so that you receive a majority of each class of common stock, including the nonvoting or low voting class of common stock. The reason for this precaution is that certain charter changes in the future might trigger a requirement for a vote of the nonvoting or low voting class. Many state laws contain requirements for a class vote if a proposed charter amendment has an adverse effect on the holders of a nonvoting or low voting class of stock. Therefore, it is better to retain control over both the nonvoting or low voting class as well as the high voting class.

An ISO plan requires a shareholder Internal Revenue Code. In addition, six states require shareholder approval of stock option plans (subject to certain exceptions), excluding New York, which abolished this requirement in October 2000.

SHAREHOLDERS' AGREEMENT FOR PRIVATE COMPANIES

If your options are exercisable before you exit (e.g., sale or IPO), you will want to condition their exercisability on the grantee executing a shareholders' agreement. Some option plans require the employee to execute a separate shareholders' agreement at the time of the option grant, rather than at exercise. Some option plans incorporate the provisions of the shareholders agreement into the option plan.

My preference, as reflected in appendixes 1 and 2, is to require the shareholders' agreement to be executed as a condition of option exercise, rather than upon grant or incorporated into the option plan.

Requiring the employee to execute a separate and usually complex shareholders agreement at the time of option grant, or incorporating a complex shareholders' agreement into the option plan, undermines the exhilarating effect of the option grant on the employee. The employee is forced to read page after page of legalese in the shareholders' agreement. If the shareholders' agreement provisions are incorporated into the option plan, the option plan becomes even longer and more complex and less easily understood by the employee.

The shareholders' agreement should typically contain the following provisions:

- If the grantee, after exercising the option, leaves your employment, your company should have the option (a "call") to buy back the stock. If appropriate, the repurchase price should be payable in installments. The repurchase price should be based on a formula set forth in the agreement or on a board of director determination of fair market value, or it should be determined through the use of outside appraisers. Some companies create a repurchase right one year or more after option exercise, which is exercisable whether or not the optionee remains employed by the company.

- If the grantee, after exercising the option, dies, becomes disabled, or retires, your company should also have the option to repurchase the shares. Some companies give a grantee who dies the right to require the company to repurchase the shares. Some companies also extend the mandatory repurchase option to grantees who become permanently disabled or retire.

- The grantee should not be permitted to transfer the shares acquired under the option without giving a right of first refusal to the company and to its shareholders.

- The grantee should not be permitted to pledge the shares.

- If your company is a Subchapter S corporation or intends to become a Subchapter S corporation, provisions should be included that require the grantee to make and maintain the Subchapter S election if requested and to do nothing to disqualify the corporation from continuing as a Subchapter S corporation.

- If appropriate, a voting trust or voting agreement in which the grantee agrees to vote the stock as directed by you.
- A noncompetition clause or nonsolicitation of customer and employee clause if the option form does not contain these provisions (see chapter 8).
- A so-called "drag along" clause, which means if you decide to sell your stock, the optionee will be required to sell his or her stock on the same terms.
- If an IPO underwriter required a lockup on the shares, the optionee should be required to enter into a lockup agreement.
- The optionee should be required to abide by federal and state securities laws in selling or otherwise disposing of the stock.
- The share certificates should be appropriately legended.

An example of a typical shareholders' agreement is contained in appendix 3. This example gives the company the right to repurchase the shares at their fair value at any time after one year from the option exercise date (whether or not the optionee continues as an employee) but permits the "call" to be exercised before one year if the optionee's employment terminates earlier.

TIME-VESTED OPTION PLANS

Appendix 4 contains an option plan for a private company that vests over time. This means that the employee will have the right to exercise the option if he or she remains employed for certain time periods, regardless of whether an exit event has occurred. In addition, appendix 5 presents a time-vested option plan for a public company.

Each of these plans contains a nonsolicitation of customer and employee provisions designed to prevent option holders from exercising their vested stock options and shortly thereafter soliciting your customers or employees for a competition.

COMPARISON WITH STOCK BONUS GRANTS

Although stock bonus grants may be simpler to effectuate, they have significant disadvantages compared to incentive stock options:

- The stock bonus is taxable to the employee on the grant date unless there are vesting conditions (versus a stock option that is not taxable on the grant date unless there is an established trading market for the option).
- The employee receiving a stock bonus becomes a shareholder immediately and is entitled to the rights and privileges of a shareholder.
- Stock bonuses may reward employees who have not contributed to the past growth of the company (e.g., new employees); in contrast, an ISO only rewards employees for stock appreciation that occurs *after* the option grant date.
- The grant of the stock bonus increases issued and outstanding stock and basic earnings per share, which is an important figure for publicly held companies (versus unexercised stock options, which are only reflected in diluted earnings per share— less important to securities analysts of publicly held companies).

The advantages and disadvantages of the stock bonus plans are discussed more fully in chapter 18.

TAX REQUIREMENTS FOR AN INCENTIVE STOCK PLAN

To qualify as an "incentive stock option," an option must satisfy complex requirements set forth in Section 422 of the Internal Revenue Code of 1986. Sections 422 through 424 of the Internal Revenue Code are contained in appendix 6. These requirements include the following:

- The grantee must receive the option for a reason connected with his or her employment by the corporation and may be granted by the employer corporation or its parent or subsidiary corporation to purchase stock in any of these companies.
- The option must be granted pursuant to a plan that includes the aggregate number of shares that may be issued under options and the employees (or class of employees) eligible to receive options.
- The plan must be approved by the stockholders of the granting corporation within twelve months before or after the date the plan is adopted by the board of directors.
- The option must be granted within ten years from the date the plan is adopted by the board of directors or the date the plan is approved by the stockholders, whichever is earlier.
- The option by its terms must not be exercisable after the expiration of ten years from the grant date.
- The option price must not be less than the fair market value of the stock on the grant date. *Note:* An option price will not fail this test, even if it is below fair market value, if there was a good-faith effort to value the stock.
- By its terms, the option must not be transferable by the optionee other than by will or laws of descent and distribution, and it must be exercisable during the optionee's lifetime only by the optionee.

- If an optionee who owns or is deemed to own more than 5 percent of the company's stock receives an option under the plan, the option price must be equal or greater than 110 percent of the fair market value of the stock on the grant date, and the option may not expire more than five years after the grant date. An optionee is deemed to constructively own stock owned, directly or indirectly, by or for his brothers and sisters (whether full or half), spouse, ancestors, and lineal descendants. Stock owned, directly or indirectly, by or for a corporation, partnership, estate, or trust, is considered as being owned proportionately by or for its shareholders, partners, or beneficiaries.

- The option must not contain any provision stating that it should not be treated as an incentive stock option.

- Options that exceed the Section 422(d) limitations (discussed in the next section) will not qualify.

The option and option plan do not by their terms have to state specifically the treatment of persons who own or are deemed to own more than 5 percent of the stock. Only certain provisions that the Code requires to be specifically stated in the option (e.g., ten year, maximum term, nontransferability) must be specifically stated in the option.

Even if the option qualified as an incentive stock option, the employee cannot obtain the benefit of long-term capital gains on the stock appreciation unless certain holding periods and employment requirements are satisfied. The holding periods require that the employee not sell or make another disqualifying disposition of the stock for at least two years after the grant date and at least one year after the exercise date. If the holding periods are violated, the stock appreciation is taxed at ordinary income rates, and the company is generally entitled to a tax deduction equal to the income realized by the employee. In addition, the employee must remain an employee at all times from the grant date (subject to certain minor exceptions) and may not exercise the option more than three months after he or she ceases to be an employee.

If the employee dies or incurs certain disabilities, the three-month period is extended until one year. Again, if these periods are not satisfied, the only "penalty" is that the stock appreciation is taxed at ordinary income rate, and the company receives a deduction in the same amount as the employee.

Note that directors of your company, as such, are not entitled to receive incentive stock options. They may only receive nonincentive stock options. However, if your director was also an employee, they could qualify for an incentive stock option. This is true even if your director was only a part-time employee.

Likewise, nonemployee consultants to your company are not entitled to receive incentive stock options. They are only entitled to receive nonincentive stock options. However, if the consultants were also part-time employees, they could qualify.

Some states and local jurisdictions may tax stock option gains. Therefore, you will need the advice of a tax lawyer or accountant prior to establishing your plan.

LIMITATIONS ON LONG-TERM CAPITAL GAINS

Section 422(d) of the Code limits the amount of long-term capital gains that an employee can receive on an incentive stock option. The limitation is measured each calendar year by multiplying the option price of the incentive stock options received by the optionee by the number of option shares that first become exercisable during that calendar year. To the extent that this multiplication exceeds $100,000 in any calendar year, the excess number of shares are not entitled to long-term capital gains investment.

For example, suppose a key employee has an option granted on January 1, 2001, for 50,000 shares, at an option exercise price of $12 per share, 20 percent of which is exercisable cumulatively each calendar year starting January 1, 2002. In 2002, when 10,000 shares first become exercisable, the multiplication of 10,000 × $12 equals $120,000 and therefore exceeds $100,000. As a consequence, only 8,500 shares of the 10,000 shares qualify for long-term capital gains on the appreciation prior to exercise. The appreciation on the remaining 1,500 shares does not qualify.

This does not mean that the key employee is only entitled to $100,000 in long-term capital gains for 2002. Indeed, the 8,500 shares may ultimately have over $1 million of appreciation when ultimately sold by the employee and the entire $1 million is all taxed as long-term capital gains if the required holding periods and employment requirements have been satisfied.

Note that it is the first exercisability date that counts under Section 422(d). The date of *actual* exercise is irrelevant.

The Section 422(d) limitation can be avoided by spreading the first exercisability dates. This is accomplished by permitting no more than 8,500 shares per year to be first exercisable in each year or portion thereof during the term of the option, at the exercise price of $12 per share (or a total of $100,000 per year). Thus, on January 1, 2002, 8,500 shares (instead of 10,000 shares) would first become exercisable. An additional 8,500 shares would vest (i.e., first become exercisable) on January 1, 2003, 2004, 2005, and 2006, and the balance of 7,500 shares would first become exercisable January 1, 2007.

Theoretically, up to $1,100,000 of option exercise price could be sheltered from the Section 422(d) limitations. This could be accomplished by having up to $100,000 of the option exercise price become first exercisable in each year of the ten-year option. Since a ten-year option can span a total of eleven calendar years (i.e., an option granted January 31, 2001, that expires January 31, 2011, has a total of eleven calendar years during its term), a maximum of $100,000 of exercise price can first become exercisable in each of the eleven calendar years.

The disadvantage to the employee of spreading the exercisability dates is that if his or her employment is terminated before the option was fully exercisable, the employee could lose a portion of the option. This result could be avoided by accelerating the vesting in the event of employment termination. However, it is likely that the acceleration of the vesting to the year of employment termination would violate Section 422(d) for the year in which the acceleration occurs and result in the accelerated portion not being treated as the exercise of an incentive stock option.

Chapter 4

ISOs Versus Non-ISOs[1]

The advantage of an incentive stock option (ISO) is that it permits the key employee to achieve long-term capital gain treatment on the appreciation of the stock after the grant date, provided two requirements are satisfied:

- The stock is not sold or otherwise disposed of in a "disqualifying disposition" for two years after the option grant and for one year after the exercise date.
- The option holder is an employee of the company at all times from the grant date until three months prior to the exercise of the stock option (one year in the case of death or "disability" as defined in the Internal Revenue Code).

---

1. The tax rates and tax concepts used in this book are based on the federal income tax law in effect in December 2000. Consult your tax adviser for the effect of changes enacted in 2001 or thereafter.

Let's consider an example. Say Joe received an ISO grant on January 1, 2002, for 5,000 shares of common stock, at an exercise price of $5 per share. The option becomes fully vested in five years and expires in ten years. Joe continues to be employed by the company until January 2, 2007, when he exercises his fully vested option on February 1, 2007, at the price of $5 per share. Joe sells the stock on February 2, 2008, at the price of $25 per share. Joe would treat the $20-per-share gain as long-term capital gain for federal income tax purposes and be taxed 20 percent (assuming long-term capital gains rate remain the same as year 2000). If Joe had sold the stock on February 2, 2007, at $25 per share, the $20-per-share gain would be treated as ordinary income, because Joe sold the stock within one year after exercise.

If Joe qualifies for long-term capital gains by selling on February 2, 2008, your company does not obtain a federal income tax deduction for this $20 gain per share. If Joe receives ordinary income treatment because he sold on February 2, 2007, your company would obtain a federal income tax deduction for the $20 per share due to the ordinary income recognized by Joe.

If your company is a "C" corporation in the 34 percent federal income tax bracket, your company loses a deduction which would lower its federal income taxes by $6.80 per share. If your company is an "S" corporation and you are in a federal income tax bracket of 39.6 percent, you lose a tax deduction worth $7.92 per share to you (39.6 percent × $20).

The cost of giving Joe long-term capital gains in this example is the *loss* by your company or you of federal income tax savings of anywhere from $6.80 per share to $7.92 per share. The answer remains substantially the same if we factor in state income taxes.

How much does Joe benefit by having long-term capital gains on the appreciation? Well, a lot less than your company or you lose. If Joe would have paid federal income tax of 39.6 percent had the $20 gain been ordinary income, and instead he pays a 20 percent long-term capital gain on the $20 gain, Joe saves only 19.6 percent of $20, or $3.92 per share.

You must decide if it is worthwhile for your company for you to give up a federal income tax deduction of $6.80 to $7.92 per share so that Joe can save $3.92 per share. The answer is probably no. For this reason, many public companies grant non-ISOs instead of ISOs. This point is illustrated in Table 4.1, supplied by the National Association of Stock Plan Professionals (NASPP) *(www.naspp.com)* based on a survey of public companies. However, that is not the end of the story.

The Advantage of ISOs

Most employees, like Joe, will not satisfy the one-year holding period on ISOs. Joe most likely cannot afford to hold the stock for one year after paying the exercise price. Whether Joe can afford to hold the stock for one year after option exercise, experience indicates that he probably won't.

Therefore, by granting an ISO, the company can give Joe the *potential* of long-term capital gains treatment, but in most cases not the reality. When Joe makes a sale or other disqualifying disposition of the stock within one year after option exercise, the company and you will generally obtain the same income tax deduction as if Joe originally received a non-ISO.

Moreover, if Joe receives a non-ISO and exercises it, your company will have to withhold on the exercise date an amount sufficient to pay Joe's federal income tax withholding and Joe's share of other payroll taxes on the $20 per share appreciation (unless the shares are subject to

TABLE 4.1
Depth of U.S.-Based Employee Granting Practices by Employee Combinations

	Total Companies Currently Granting[1]	Senior Management Only		Senior and Middle Management Only		Senior Management, Middle Management, and Other[2] Exempt		All Employees (Including Non-Exempt)	
		Cos.	%[3]	Cos.	%[3]	Cos.	%[3]	Cos.	%[3]
Stock options	345	12	3.5%	78	22.6%	105	30.4%	150	43.5%
Incentive stock options	214	6	2.8%	47	22.0%	66	30.8%	95	44.4%
Nonqualified stock options	329	11	3.33%	74	22.5%	101	30.7%	143	43.5%
Tandem SAR (with option)	57	3	5.3%	16	28.1%	23	40.4%	15	26.3%
Freestanding SAR (without option)	48	2	4.2%	14	29.2%	17	33.4%	15	31.3%

1. "Currently granting" is defined as company has a specific granting frequency and/or company has granted options to the employee group in the last three years.
2. May include some or all "other exempt" positions.
3. Percents based on the number of companies currently granting each type of stock option.

vesting conditions, in which case the tax is postponed until the vesting conditions are satisfied or a Section 83[b] election is made; see chapter 18). Using an ISO avoids this result, since there is no withholding tax upon Joe's exercise of the ISO.

I generally recommend that ISOs be issued to employees, rather than non-ISOs, because they give the employee at least the potential of long-term capital gains treatment. Even though the employee will in most cases not achieve that potential because of personal sale decisions made by the employee, the ISO is generally viewed as a more valuable option by knowledgeable employees and the employee avoids all federal withholding on option exercise.

NON-ISOS WITH TAX REIMBURSEMENT

Some companies have opted to grant non-ISOs with tax reimbursement to Joe. The tax reimbursement assists Joe in paying the federal income tax withholding upon exercise of the non-ISO. However, withholding is due on the tax reimbursement itself, so the tax reimbursement must be sufficient to permit Joe to pay withholding on both the exercise of the non-ISO and the tax reimbursement.

In the previous example, suppose Joe received a non-ISO that he exercised on January 2, 2007, and there was appreciation of $20 per share. Assume further that the required federal income tax withholding was 28 percent, or $5.60. Under these circumstances, Joe should receive tax reimbursement of approximately $7.78 per share, which after tax withholding of 28 percent of that amount, would result in Joe receiving $5.60 per share. The $7.78 tax reimbursement to Joe would ordinarily be deductible by the company. The net after tax benefits to you as sole shareholder of a Subchapter S Corporation (assuming a federal income tax rate for you of 39.6 percent on the non-ISO exercise), after subtracting tax reimbursement, would be $3.22 per share, computed as follows:

$7.92	Federal income tax benefit of non-ISO tax deduction (39.6 percent × $20 per share)
+ 3.08	Federal income tax benefit of tax reimbursement (39.6 percent × $7.78 per share)
$11.00	
− 7.78	Less cash cost of tax reimbursement
$3.22	Net cash federal income tax benefit to you if your company is a Subchapter S corporation

Thus, as the sole shareholder of a Subchapter S Corporation, you save $3.22 per share using a non-ISO in this example, *even after reimbursing Joe's federal income tax withholding*. If we factor in state income taxes, the answer remains substantially the same.

There is a slight difference in the tax result between ISO stock prematurely sold and a non-ISO. If on the exercise date of an ISO the appreciation is $20 per share, and Joe sells the stock the next day at a price that produced a gain of $19 per share (the market value dropped $1), the company's federal income tax deduction and Joe's ordinary income tax is limited to the $19 gain per share. However, if Joe receives a non-ISO, Joe is taxed on the $20-per-share gain on the date of exercise, and the sale of $1 less produces a short-term capital loss for Joe for federal income tax purposes. In this case, the company's federal income tax deduction equals the $20 recognized by Joe on the date of exercise of the non-ISO.

A federal income tax reimbursement provision only works if your company (or you, if your company is a Subchapter S Corporation) pays federal income taxes. If your company has losses or loss carryovers, there is no current federal income tax savings from the exercise of a non-ISO. The tax deduction from the exercise of the non-ISO would only increase your loss carryovers.

In addition, a tax reimbursement provision will prevent your company from obtaining favorable accounting treatment of the stock option, and you will be stuck with variable stock option accounting (see chapter 16).

If Joe is given an ISO and violates the one-year holding period, your federal income tax savings as the sole shareholder of a Subchapter S Corporation (using a 39.6 percent federal rate) is even greater than $3.22 per share and equals $7.92 per share (39.6 percent × $20). This is the same tax benefit as if you gave Joe a non-ISO without any tax reimbursement whatsoever.

The Tax Benefit to Your Company

Your company receives a federal income tax deduction equal to the amount of income realized by your employees when they exercise a non-ISO or when they sell or make another disqualifying disposition of stock previously acquired within one year after exercising an ISO. These savings can be quite substantial. If your company is a Subchapter S corporation, these tax deductions accrue to your personal benefit (assuming you have sufficient tax basis in your stock).

According to the following article by Gretchen Morgenson, which appeared in the *New York Times* on June 13, 2000, these tax deductions eliminated all of the federal income tax of both Microsoft and Cisco Systems.

The Consequences of Corporate America's Growing Addiction to Stock Options[1]

Microsoft and Cisco Systems, two of the nation's most profitable companies, are well on their way to owing nothing in federal income taxes on the money they have made so far this year.

How can powerful companies like these, reporting billions in income to shareholders, owe nothing in taxes? It is all thanks to the wonder of employee stock options.

Stock options have made many Americans wealthy beyond their wildest dreams over the last decade. Less understood is how much stock options have benefited the companies that offer them. But when stock prices stop rising, some economists and investors warn, companies and their shareholders will find themselves paying a heavy price for something they thought was a free lunch.

Consider how options help eliminate a company's income tax bill. Under I.R.S. rules, employees pay ordinary income taxes on the gain they receive when they exercise their options, even if the gain is only on paper. When they exercise their options, their company receives a tax deduction equal to the gain.

With the stock markets soaring and many employees cashing in, the taxes the employees pay on their gains have meant deductions that greatly reduce and in some cases even wipe out some companies' current tax bills. This does not mean the federal government is reaping less in taxes. It simply means that the tax burden has shifted from corporations to individuals, most of whom willingly pay because the taxes are so much less than the gains.

Microsoft's options-related tax deduction of roughly $11.4 billion in the first nine months of this fiscal year, for example, saves the company $4 billion in taxes. The size of that deduction, which shows up only on the company's tax returns, exceeds the $10.6 billion in pretax income

---

1. © 2000 by the New York Times Company. Reprinted with Permission.

that the company reported to shareholders. So while Microsoft may escape taxes this year, its employees will presumably pay tax on that $11.4 billion at ordinary rates.

Tax breaks are not the only benefit to corporations. Options can also significantly cut companies' labor costs as employees, eager to get rich off their options, demand less in cash compensation. Lower labor costs. Lower taxes.

What more could a company ask?

"Stock options have become as American as motherhood and apple pie," said Patrick S. McGurn, a vice president at Institutional Shareholder Services, an investment advisory firm in Rockville, Md. "It has all been fueled by this notion that options have no cost and that there is an unlimited supply of them. It's like the government and its printing press. But ultimately the market is going to suffer. The day of reckoning will come."

When that day comes is, of course, unclear. But when stocks stop soaring—and many have done so this year—the equations upon which option mania is based changes. Employees exercise fewer options and companies' tax bills will rise. And as worried employees begin to demand more of their compensation in cash, companies' labor costs rise.

Desperate to appease employees, many companies will issue even more options. After Microsoft's stock tumbled on the prospect of a breakup by the government, the company issued $1.9 billion in new options in April to supplement those issued last year that are worthless. This comes on top of the $69 billion in outstanding Microsoft stock options as of last June.

Trouble is, the more options there are, the less valuable the stock becomes.

Options carry significant costs. One is that companies must buy back millions of their own shares to offset the stock they have dispensed to employees at much lower prices in option programs. If they do not repurchase stock, there will be so many shares on the market that the company's earnings, on a per-share basis, will plunge. This is known as dilution.

In the last three years, for example, Dell Computer has bought back $3.6 billion worth of stock to reduce share dilution. In the period, Dell's net income totaled a little over $4 billion. The money Dell put into buybacks might have gone into research and development.

Dell is not alone in stock repurchases. A 1999 study by J. Nellie Liang and Steven A. Sharpe, researchers at the Federal Reserve Board, found that in 1998 the 140 largest nonfinancial companies in the United States expended 40 percent of their earnings to buy back shares, up from 17 percent of earnings used to do so in 1994. The study noted that large companies have borrowed money or run down financial assets to finance repurchases.

The upside of stock options has been well-chronicled in recent years. They allow cash-poor start-up companies to attract talented employees and help established companies keep the workers they have.

And options reward hard-working employees and give them the benefit of ownership in their enterprise.

All to the good. But corporate America has played down the costs associated with options. As a result, what began as a dalliance threatens to become an addiction.

The number of employees receiving stock options in the United States has grown to as many as 10 million from about one million in the early 1990's, according to the National Center for Employee Ownership. About one-third of companies have programs offering options to lower-level workers as well as executives, according to Pearl Meyer & Partners, an executive compensation consulting firm in New York. Last year, 200 of the nation's largest companies granted equity incentives—mostly options—to employees that represented 2 percent of the companies' shares outstanding, on average, the firm said. Ten years earlier, the so-called grant rate was about half that.

Now that many share prices are falling, options will harm the value of a company's shares even more than they did when stocks were higher, Mr. McGurn of Institutional Shareholder Services said. That is because executives' option grants are typically based on a dollar figure, say $2 million, rather than on a number of shares. A falling stock price means more shares dispensed to the executive in an option grant.

As managers' compensation has depended more on stock options, keeping the share price rising—and options in the money—has become paramount.

Walter P. Schuetze, former chief accountant for the enforcement division of the Securities and Exchange Commission, says the prevalence of accounting gimmickry at many American companies is in part a result of the increasing popularity of options.

"The amount of management compensation tied to the stock price is huge," Mr. Schuetze said. "And it is driving corporate managers to make their numbers so the compensation gets even larger."

An academic study by David Aboody, assistant professor of accounting at the University of California at Los Angeles, and Ron Kasznik, associate professor at Stanford University's business school, found that executives manage the disclosures of corporate news to increase the value of their options. The study will be published in the *Journal of Accounting and Economics.*

Studying option grants made between 1992 and 1996 at 1,264 public companies that make awards on fixed schedules, Professors Aboody and Kasznik found that companies had significantly lower returns in the period before the award than in the period immediately after it. This confirmed to the professors that executives delayed announcing good news until after the award dates and rushed out with bad news before the options were awarded.

"Such a disclosure strategy," the professors wrote, "ensures that decreases in the firm's stock price related to the arrival of bad news occur before, rather than after, the award date, while stock price increases related to the arrival of good news occur after, rather than before, the award."

Indeed, stock options have become so crucial to executives today that some economists say if stock prices tumble, managements interested in maximizing the value of their compensation plans would have an even greater interest in driving down their stocks' prices to guarantee future gains on options issued at rock-bottom levels.

Andrew Smithers, founder and economist at Smithers & Company, an investment advisory firm in London and the co-author with Stephen Wright of *Valuing Wall Street: Protecting Wealth in Turbulent Markets,* said: "If the market were to fall, the interests of management would cease to be driving up the stock price. It would be driving it down so the next round of options are at a lower price."

Even now, some companies' option grants are at odds with shareholder interests. A 1999 study of 900 companies by Ira Kay, a practice partner at the Watson Wyatt Worldwide consulting firm, found that companies with the greatest percentage of shares outstanding represented by unexercised options produced lower returns to shareholders than those with a smaller percentage of option grants hanging over them.

While Mr. Kay said that many companies produce good returns for shareholders in spite of the so-called option overhang, he added, "It's a scarce and very valuable resource that needs to be optimally allocated by the board of directors."

If the use of options were limited to a handful of companies, the overall market impact would not be great. But many companies have joined the option game recognizing that they are at a disadvantage to companies spreading the option wealth.

Laurence A. Tisch, co-chairman of the Loews Corporation, has for years refused to make options a part of its executive compensation plan because of their future costs to shareholders. Last year, however, he succumbed to the pressure and now hands out a tiny portion of options to managers. "I'm against options and we haven't had options at Loews in 25 or 30 years," Mr. Tisch said. "But it was a problem with some executives. Whether we needed it or didn't need it, we thought we needed it."

One of the biggest arguments for options is that they help companies retain good workers and provide an incentive for employees to increase their productivity. John Connors, chief financial officer at Microsoft, said: "We very much continue to believe strongly in the direct linkage to our employees being shareholders and creating long-term shareholder value. Both shareholders and employees would look at this program as being an integral part of the success of our company."

Microsoft said it was impossible to predict what its tax bill would be in 2000 since the year is not yet over. The company confirmed that its options-related tax deduction exceeded its taxable income as reported to shareholders so far this year, but said that there were many different elements that go into figuring the company's taxes that are not available to the public. Microsoft declined to make its tax returns available.

Mr. Connors acknowledged that his company's happy experience with stock options had come in a bull market. It remains to be seen, he said, whether options will keep employees happy if their company's stock price falls.

For the moment, options maintain their allure. Even Washington is convinced that they are good for all. Rather than fretting about the decline in corporate tax receipts, some lawmakers want to give employees a tax break as well.

John Boehner, the Ohio Republican who is chairman of the House Subcommittee on employer-employee relations, has written legislation that would create a new "superstock option." It would allow employees to pay taxes on the options at capital gains rates rather than higher ordinary income rates.

The new options would still provide a tax deduction for the companies issuing them. This would almost certainly reduce Treasury receipts.

Mr. Boehner said the legislation would help workers "share in the tremendous growth of today's economy in a way that benefits them, their employers and the entire economy." To qualify for the tax treatment, companies would have to offer options to at least half of their employees. Democrats on the subcommittee are hardly objecting—they are just insisting that companies make them available to 90 percent or more of employees to qualify.

But the cost of making options more attractive than they already are is high. "If you believe in the free market system you have to have a scorecard that works," said Bill Parish, a former accountant and auditor who is an independent investment adviser in Portland, Ore. "The scorecard has been completely corrupted and the biggest way it has been corrupted is through the issuance of watered stock. And the average person doesn't know about it."

CHAPTER 5

DESIGNING AN EXIT EVENT OPTION PLAN

Obtaining an outside appraisal for a private company as discussed in the prior chapter typically takes several months and sometimes longer. Although appraisals can be done in as little as two to three weeks, this is unusual for a private company. The outside appraiser will need a significant amount of information from the private company to complete the appraisal, and many private companies do not have this information readily available.

During the time that the appraisal process is ongoing, the company should start considering major design questions concerning the exit event option plan or whatever other type of option plan the company desires. These major questions, which are applicable to both private and public companies, are as follows:

- What percentage of the company's outstanding stock will be authorized under the plan for the issuance of stock options? This subject is answered in this chapter.

- What percentage of the shares authorized under the plan will be granted initially, and what percentage will be reserved for future grants to existing employees or new hires? This subject is answered in this chapter.

- Which particular employees of the company will be entitled to receive an initial option grant, and what percentage of the total grants will be received by each such employee? (See chapter 6.)

- Should incentive stock options or nonincentive stock options be issued under the plan? (This subject was covered in chapter 4.)

- Who will administer the stock option plan? (See chapter 8.)

- What is the duration of options granted under a plan? (See chapters 7 and 13.)

- When do options vest after an exit event has occurred (i.e., after a sale or IPO), how long must the employee wait until the option can be exercised? (See chapter 12.)

- If employment terminates (whether voluntarily or involuntarily, including death, disability, and retirement), what rights does the employee have to exercise the option? (See chapter 7.)

- Will employees be permitted to exercise options only for cash, or can they use other company stock or notes to pay the exercise price? (See chapter 13.)

- If other company stock can be used as the exercise price, will pyramiding be permitted (i.e., using shares purchased under the option to further exercise the option)? (See chapter 13.)

- Will the employee be required to execute a non-competition agreement or nonsolicitation of customer and employee agreement in consideration of the grant of the option to such employee? (See chapter 8.)

- Should options be made transferable? (See chapter 14.)

Percentage of Stock Authorized Under an Option Plan

There is no universal rule as to what percentage of your common stock should be authorized for issuance under your stock option plan. The higher the percentage, the greater the potential reward to your employees, and the greater the dilution to your personal equity interest.

If your employees are not being paid a competitive salary, then a larger percentage of your stock should be authorized for issuance under options. However, if your employees are already paid a competitive salary, the number of shares authorized for issuance should be a function of what is necessary to achieve your personal objectives.

If your personal objectives include motivating employees to assist you through a sale or IPO process, you must provide a meaningful reward to them if the process is successful. If your exit is a sale, the reward should be sufficient to induce them to stay with you through the trauma of a sale and the uncertainty to the employee of his or her future prospects with a new owner.

A meaningful figure to most employees who are paid a competitive salary is a minimum of 50 percent of their normal compensation. Since at the time of option grant it is difficult to predict what the future potential option profit will be after a sale or IPO, an educated projection is required to determine the number of options to be granted to an individual that will produce at least a 50 percent bonus.

The key to determining the number of options to be granted to each key employee is to figure out what option number will make key employees believe that they have a significant economic stake in the ultimate success of the sale or IPO.

What is a reasonable amount of dilution for a private company considering an IPO? Although there is no single answer to this question, a rule of thumb is 20 percent dilution pre-IPO. Assuming that the IPO involved the sale of approximately 33⅓ percent of your post-IPO stock, the 20 percent pre-IPO option dilution would be reduced to approximately 13 percent post-IPO option dilution. Very few underwriters would object to a 13 percent post-IPO option dilution.

Much higher option dilution has appeared in many IPOs. For example, the November 9, 1999, IPO of Webvan Group, Inc., led by Goldman Sachs and Co. as managing lead underwriter, had option dilution of approximately 23 percent of the pre-IPO shares (as diluted for the conversion of preferred stock) and option dilution of approximately 21 percent of the post-IPO shares. In that IPO, the weighted average option exercise price was $3.88 per share, and the IPO shares were sold to the public at a price of $15 per share.

As a general rule, a potential dilution of 20 percent for all authorized options under the plan would be a reasonable starting point. This means that if you have one million shares of common stock outstanding (either currently or as a result of stock splits discussed in the prior chapter), 200,000 shares would be authorized for issuance under the stock option plan.

RESERVES FOR NEW HIRES AND FOR YEARLY GRANTS

Whatever number of shares are authorized for issuance under the stock option plan, a number of options should be held in reserve to be issued in the future for new hires. At least 3 percent to 5 percent of the outstanding stock should be held in reserve for new hires. Thus, if you decide to have an option plan authorizing options for up to 20 percent of your outstanding shares, your initial option grants should be no greater than 15 to 17 percent of your outstanding stock.

In addition, if you desire to give yearly grants to your existing employees at hopefully higher valuations and exercise prices each year as the company grows, a reserve should be made for such yearly grants. The practice of yearly grants, versus one-time large grants, is discussed in chapter 6.

After computing the number of shares to be held in reserve, you should then determine the number of shares to be initially granted to your key employees, including options to be granted to you if you are an employee of the company. This subject is discussed more fully in chapter 6.

WHO SHOULD RECEIVE A STOCK OPTION AND HOW OFTEN?

There is no universal rule to help you decide who should receive a stock option among your employees. At a minimum, you should determine who are the obvious key employees to your business and make certain that they are rewarded with stock options.

Some entrepreneurs provide stock options to all of their management employees. Other entrepreneurs provide stock options to all of their employees, both management and nonmanagement, down to the janitor. They merely provide less options to the lower-level employees than to the more important employees.

The National Center for Employee Ownership conducted a survey in 2000 of stock option plan practices. The companies that responded range in size from a start-up company with no annual sales and three employees to a Fortune 500 company with $23 billion in annual sales and more than 150,000 employees. The respondents came from a variety of industrial sectors and from across the United States.

In its 2000 survey, the National Center for Employee Ownership asked for the number of options allocated under the most recent grant and then calculated a "value" for those options based on the share price at the date of grant. For instance, the average number of options allocated to middle managers and hourly employees was 5,500 and 1,800, respectively, and the value (determined by multiplying the number of option shares by the exercise price per share) was $59,400 and $8,600, respectively.

Table 6.1 provides average allocation amounts for all respondents for ongoing stock option grants.

It is unusual to provide stock options to unionized employees. The Verizon Communication strike settlement in which options were provided was a recent exception.

Tables 6.2 and 6.3 were the results of surveys conducted in 1998 by the National Center for Employee Ownership. They show the actual eligibility and allocation of

TABLE 6.1
ALLOCATION TABLE—ONGOING STOCK OPTION PLAN

Position	Average Number of Options
Executives	29,000
Senior managers	10,300
Middle managers	5,500
Salaried technical	4,100
Salaried nontechnical	3,300
Sales	4,600
Hourly	868
International employees	4,500

n = 126

TABLE 6.2
ELIGIBILITY AND ALLOCATION (BY EMPLOYEE CATEGORY AND TYPE OF PLAN): ONGOING/PERIODIC GRANTS

| | Management | | | Nonmanagement (ongoing/periodic grants) | | | | |
	Senior Executives	Executives	Senior Managers	Supervisors	Professionals	Technical	Administrative	Other
Eligibility (e.g., 100 percent of respondents make senior executives *eligible* for options and 100 percent actually *grant* options)								
Eligible for options	100%	100%	92%	84%	100%	100%	94%	18%
Actually receive options	100%	99%	91%	82%	100%	100%	92%	18%
Allocation method (e.g., 13% of respondents use percentage of pay as a guide for allocating options to senior executives; columns may total more than 100% due to multiple responses)								
Percentage of pay	13%	14%	12%	14%	13%	12%	11%	13%
Co./group performance	16%	14%	10%	10%	13%	13%	13%	17%
Promotional grant	13%	14%	12%	11%	10%	9%	10%	10%
Merit	46%	47%	45%	45%	54%	53%	51%	48%
Discretionary	47%	46%	49%	49%	46%	47%	46%	38%
Other	9%	9%	10%	6%	13%	12%	14%	15%
Average percentage of pay allocated when percentage of pay is used as a guide for allocating options								
Percentage	82%	43%	25%	15%	27%	27%	27%	27%
			n = 92					
Average value of most recent option award (stock price × number of options); excludes awards based on percentage of pay								
Value	$1,408,231	$417,877	$211,447	$91,814	$37,516	$40,881	$12,499	$12,475
								n = 79

TABLE 6.3
ELIGIBILITY AND ALLOCATION (BY EMPLOYEE CATEGORY AND TYPE OF PLAN): ONE-TIME GRANTS

	Nonmanagement (one-time grants)				Nonmanagement (new hire grants)			
	Professionals	Technical	Administrative	Other	Professionals	Technical	Administrative	Other
Eligibility (e.g., 100% of respondents make professionals *eligible* for options and 100% actually *grant* options)								
Eligible for options	100%	100%	94%	84%	100%	100%	88%	68%
Actually receive options	100%	100%	94%	84%	100%	100%	86%	65%
Allocation method (e.g., 20% of respondents use percentage of pay as a guide for allocating options to professionals; columns may total more than 100% due to multiple responses)								
Percentage of pay	—	6%	—	—	20%	17%	17%	18%
Co./group perfomance	28%	18%	13%	25%	30%	30%	30%	36%
Discretionary	33%	35%	44%	25%	—	—	—	—
Other	39%	41%	44%	50%	50%	52%	54%	46%
Average percentage of pay allocated when percentage of pay is used as a guide for allocating options								
Percentage	—	—	—	—	100%	100%	100%	100%
Average value of most recent option award (stock price × number of options); excludes awards based on percentage of pay								
Value	$8,340	$21,490	$6,237	$7,328	$56,972	$56,394	$13,997	$15,547
				n = 18				*n* = 46

stock options within management by the following job titles:

- Senior executives
- Executives
- Senior managers
- Supervisors

The tables show the eligibility and actual allocation between management and nonmanagement employees. Nonmanagement employees are classified as follows:

- Professional
- Technical
- Administrative
- Other

Table 6.2 survey respondents used ongoing periodic grant plans, as opposed to one-time grant plans reflected in table 6.3. The breakdown of public and private companies are as follows:

Public: 91 percent

Private: 9 percent

OPTIONS TO THE OWNER

Even though you may own 100 percent of the stock of your corporation, you are also entitled to recover incentive stock options if you are either a full-time or part-time officer or other employee of the corporation. Even if you are not an officer or other employee, you can award yourself nonincentive stock options in your capacity as a director or consultant to the corporation. The option plans in appendixes 1 and 2 permit the grant of such options.

Why grant stock options to yourself if you already own 100 percent of the stock of your corporation? If you are the key employee of your company, you are entitled to receive options in this role just like any other key employee. The fact that you are also an owner does not mean that you cannot be separately compensated for your role as a key employee.

If your company is sold, many buyers will assume the options. You, as an employee of the company, may be requested to play some role after the sale. The buyer may be willing to assume your options as well as the options of other key employees.

Suppose the buyer refuses to assume your option? The worse that can happen to you is that you will have to cancel your options. The cancellation of the options does not usually produce any adverse tax consequences and can be viewed as a contribution to the capital of your company.

Assume that you have an IPO. Most underwriters do not consider reasonable option dilution in valuing your company. If you have options for 200,000 shares at the exercise price of $1 per share and your company's stock is priced at $11 per share in an IPO, you have option appreciation of $2 million. After the IPO, you can sell stock in a secondary or follow-on offering at the public trading price (less underwriter discount) and replace the stock sold with option stock that you have purchased at $1 per share.

GRANT FREQUENCY

Some compensation consultants recommend yearly grants of stock options based on performance during the prior year. Some compensation consultants recommend less frequent grants, such as every three to five years.

Frequent grants pose a basic problem. If after an option grant the employee's performance results in an increased stock value, the employee is penalized for this performance, since his or her new incentive stock option grant will have a higher option price equal to the increased stock value.

An argument can be made for a single large one-time grant that vests over a lengthy period of time. With a single large one-time grant, the employee receives the benefit of the growth of stock value for the entire stock option grant and is not penalized by a higher exercise price under the frequent grant practice.

The practice in this area varies, and a chart showing different vesting options for both ongoing grants and one-time grants appears in chapter 12.

LEGAL CONSIDERATIONS

Entrepreneurs can get themselves in legal trouble when they promise stock option grants to existing employees or new hires. Any verbal or written promise of a stock option grant should include a copy of the actual stock option or, alternatively, a reference to your specific option plan, together with an offer to provide a full copy to the employee or new hire on request.

If you do not have a stock option plan at the time you promise a stock option, your letter should make it clear that the stock option will be subject to such terms and conditions as will be set forth in the plan once it is developed. Any offer letter should be either reviewed by your lawyer or be on a format previously approved by your lawyer. See chapter 9 for suggested language.

A casual letter promising a stock option grant that does not specify all of the vesting terms resulted in a lawsuit, described here, against a company called COREStaff. Even though COREStaff won the lawsuit, you would not have wanted to pay their legal bills.

Ekedahl v. COREStaff, Inc.
No. 98-7119, 1999 U.S. App. LEXIS 17927
(D.C. Cir. July 30, 1999)[1]

Ekedahl, a District of Columbia resident, left her position as a vice president with a competitor to become senior vice president of COREStaff after receiving an offer letter that included a stock option provision stating that 15,000 shares would be "granted immediately." After starting with COREStaff, which is headquartered in Texas, Ekedahl received employment and option letter agreements stating that the option would vest annually in three equal installments. She refused to sign the letters, stating that she had been promised immediately vested options.

Ekedahl testified that she would never have left her well-paying job and options at her prior employer without an agreement for immediate vesting and that the absence of any mention of vesting in the offer letter had been the "turning point" in her decision to accept the offer. COREStaff testified that delayed vesting was an integral part of its option plan and that it generally did not offer immediately vested options.

The Court of Appeals overturned a jury verdict in favor of Ekedahl and granted summary judgment for COREStaff. The court noted that the party asserting the existence of an enforceable contract has the burden of proving a "meeting of the minds" on all material terms. The court held that the offer letter was not an enforceable contract, since there was no meeting of the minds on vesting.

1. Reprinted with permission from the NASPP's 1999 Annual Conference Materials.

CHAPTER 7

ANALYSIS OF A
PRIVATE COMPANY EXIT
EVENT OPTION PLAN

A ppendix 1 contains an exit event stock option plan that can be used by private companies that want to vest options (i.e., make them exercisable) if there is sale or IPO. Appendix 2 has an exit event option that can be used by a private company that wants to vest options only if there is a sale. The plan is drafted from the company's viewpoint and not the optionees'.

The following discussion presents excerpts, and corresponding analysis, of the provisions of the appendix 1 form. The appendix 2 form is substantially similar except where noted in this chapter.

> 200,000 shares of the Company's Common Stock shall be the aggregate number of shares which may be issued under this Plan. Notwithstanding the foregoing, in the event of any change in the outstanding shares of the Common Stock of the Company by reason of a stock dividend, stock

split, combination of shares, recapitalization, merger, consolidation, transfer of assets, reorganization, conversation or what the Committee (defined in Section 4[a]), deems in its sole discretion to be similar circumstances, the aggregate number and kind of shares which may be issued under this Plan shall be appropriately adjusted in a manner determined in the sole discretion of the Committee. Reacquired shares of the Company's Common Stock, as well as unissued shares, may be used for the purpose of this Plan. Common Stock of the Company subject to options which have terminated unexercised, either in whole or in part, shall be available for future options granted under this plan.

An incentive stock option must be issued pursuant to a plan approved by shareholders with at least two provisions:

- The number of shares authorized to be issued under the plan
- The class of employees eligible to receive options

The 200,000 shares of common stock authorized for issuance under the plan represented 20 percent of the total outstanding shares of common stock (as adjusted for a prior stock split). If further stock splits or stock dividends occur, the number of authorized shares is proportionately adjusted.

All officers and key employees of the Company and of any present or future Company parent or subsidiary corporation are eligible to receive an option or options under this Plan.

If an optionee leaves employment before full option vesting, the option will terminate. The shares subject to the lapsed option will be available for reoption to other employees.

As noted earlier, an incentive option plan must set forth the class of employees eligible to receive options. The employees who are actually awarded the options are determined by the board of directors or a committee. There is no requirement in the plan that employees receiving option awards be full-time employees. The company is afforded the flexibility of being capable of rewarding key part-time employees with incentive stock options. An important consultant who would otherwise not be entitled to an incentive stock option because he is an independent contractor could become a part-time employee and receive the potential tax benefits of an ISO.

All directors of, and important consultants to, the Company and of any present or future Company parent or subsidiary corporation are also eligible to receive an option or options under this Plan.

The plan contemplates that directors and important consultants to the company, who are not employees, will also be eligible to receive options under the plan. As noted, only non-ISOs can be given to persons who are not employees.

It is important to a company considering an IPO to be able to attract outstanding individuals to its board of directors prior to the IPO. Many of these individuals do not want cash compensation and would prefer a stock option. Many cash-strapped companies would prefer to grant stock options to its outside directors rather than pay them in cash.

The plan also permits nonemployee consultants to receive stock options. In today's job market, many valuable consultants are not interested in becoming employees but would consider providing consulting services in exchange for stock options and cash. The ability to grant stock options to independent consultants should reduce the amount of cash (if any) that has to be paid to these individuals.

I have created stock option plans that also permit suppliers of goods and services to be paid with stock options. Start-up companies have typically used this form of option to conserve cash.

Care must be taken in granting a large number of options to employees, directors, consultants, and suppliers to be certain that securities laws are complied with (see chapter 17).

Prior to the registration of the Company's Common Stock under Section 12 of the Securities Exchange Act of 1934, this Plan shall be administered by the Company's Board of Directors and, after such registration, by an Option Committee ("Committee") appointed by the Company's Board of Directors. The Committee shall consist of a minimum of two and a maximum of five members of the Board of Directors, each of whom shall be a "Non-Employee Director" within the meaning of Rule 16b-3(b)(3) under the Securities Exchange Act of 1934, as amended, or any future corresponding rule, except that the failure of the Committee for any reason to be composed solely of Non-Employee Directors shall not prevent an option from being considered granted under this Plan. The Committee shall, in addition to its other authority and subject to the provisions of this Plan, determine which individuals shall in fact be granted an option or options, whether the option shall be an Incentive Stock Option or a Non-Qualified Stock Option (as such terms are defined in

> Section 5[a]), the number of shares to be subject to each of the options, the time or times at which the options shall be granted, the rate of option exercisability, and, subject to Section 5 hereof, the price at which each of the options is exercisable and the duration of the option.

Prior to an IPO, the plan is administered by the board of directors. After a public offering, SEC rules under Section 16(b) of the Securities Exchange Act of 1934 (short-swing profits rule) permit that the plan be administered by either the board of directors or a committee of the board of directors composed of two or more persons who qualify as "nonemployee directors." The SEC rules also permit options to be approved or ratified by shareholders (which is generally unworkable) and provide an exemption for options held for a period of six months.

I prefer to use a committee of nonemployee directors after a public offering, rather than the full board of directors, to permit options to be granted to principal shareholders who are also executives of the company. In the public market place, it is cosmetically preferable to use nonemployee directors if options are to be granted to such executives to avoid the appearance of self-dealing.

Rule 16(b)(3) under the Securities Exchange Act of 1934 contains a definition of who is considered a nonemployee director for this purpose. In general, an individual cannot be an officer or employee or receive more than $60,000 per year for services as a consultant (excluding director's fees), cannot have a material interest in certain transactions with management and others, and cannot be involved in certain material business relationships with the company.

If no public offering is contemplated (as in appendix 2), there is no need to refer to nonemployee directors, and the plan can be administered at all times by the board of directors or by a committee of the board, depending on the desire of the principal shareholders.

The option price for options issued under this Plan shall be equal at least to the fair market value (as defined below) of the Company's Common Stock on the date of the grant of the option.

Under the Internal Revenue Code, an ISO can only be issued with an exercise price equal to or greater than the fair market value of the stock on the grant date. Non-ISOs are not restricted by the Internal Revenue Code in this manner. However, any option issued with an exercise price less than fair market value on the grant date will subject the company to an earnings charge. Therefore, the plan requires non-ISOs as well as ISOs to have exercise prices that are at least equal to the fair market value of the stock on the grant date.

At the time of the grant of an Incentive Stock Option hereunder, the Committee may, in its discretion, amend or supplement any of the option terms contained in appendix I for any particular optionee, provided that the option as amended or supplemented satisfies the requirements of Section 422(b) of the Code and the regulations thereunder.

The plan contained in appendix 1 contains three option forms:

- A form for ISOs granted to employees (appendix I of the plan)
- A form for non-ISOs granted to employees (appendix II of the plan)

- A form for non-ISOs to be awarded to directors of the company who are not also employees and to important consultants who are independent contractors (appendix III of plan)

This provision permits the company to award options that vary from the option forms attached to the plan. For example, if the company wanted to hire a high-powered CEO, the company might be required by the CEO to permit earlier vesting of his option than appendix I of this plan permits. This flexibility may be very important in attracting a key employee.

The Board of Directors reserves the right at any time, and from time to time, to amend or supplement this Plan in any way, or to suspend or terminate it, effective as of such date, which date may be either before or after the taking of such action, as may be specified by the Board of Directors; provided, however, that such action shall not affect options granted under the Plan prior to the actual date on which such action occurred. If an amendment or supplement of this Plan is required by the Code or the regulations thereunder to be approved by the shareholders of the Company in order to permit the granting of "Incentive Stock Options" (as that term is defined in Section 422[b] of the Code and regulations thereunder) pursuant to the amended or supplemented Plan, such amendment or supplement shall also be approved by the shareholders of the Company in such manner as is prescribed by the Code and the regulations thereunder. If the Board of Directors voluntarily submits a proposed amendment, supplement, suspension, or termination for shareholder approval, such submission shall not require any future

amendments, supplements, suspensions, or terminations (whether or not relating to the same provision or subject matter) to be similarly submitted
for shareholder approval.

This provision affords broad flexibility to the company's board of directors to change the plan without further shareholder approval of the change. If you are the
sole shareholder of the company, this provision is irrelevant. However, if your company has a number of shareholders, this provision may avoid the necessity of
soliciting their consent to a plan change or of holding a
shareholders meeting.

As noted, a change in either the number of shares
authorized under an ISO plan or the class of employees
eligible for such options would require shareholder
approval under the Internal Revenue Code.

This Plan shall become effective on the date of its
adoption by the Company's Board of Directors,
subject however to approval by the holders of the
Company's Common Stock in the manner as prescribed in the Code and the regulations thereunder. Options may be granted under this Plan prior
to obtaining shareholder approval, provided such
options shall not be exercisable until shareholder
approval is obtained.

This provision permits an option to be granted subject to shareholder approval. This could be important if
the stock has a depressed fair market value on the grant
date and could rise in value by the time shareholder
approval is obtained (e.g., because of a large new contract
you expect to receive). Despite this provision, care should
be taken to obtain shareholder approval *before* granting

options if avoiding an accounting charge is important to you (see chapter 16).

> Neither the Company nor any of its current or future parent, subsidiaries, or affiliates, nor their officers, directors, shareholders, stock option plan committees, employees, or agents shall have any liability to any optionee in the event (i) an option granted pursuant to Section 5(b) hereof does not qualify as an "Incentive Stock Option" as that term is used in Section 422(b) of the Code and the regulations thereunder; (ii) any optionee does not obtain the tax treatment pertaining to an Incentive Stock Option; or (iii) any option granted pursuant to Section 5(c) hereof is an "Incentive Stock Option."

This clause, which appears in Section 5(d) of the plan, is intended to limit the liability of the company and its officers, directors, shareholders, and so forth, in the event the option does not qualify for the tax benefits of an ISO.

> This option shall terminate and is not exercisable after ten years from the date of its grant (the "Scheduled Termination Date"), except if terminated earlier as hereafter provided.

Ten years is the maximum period for which an ISO may be granted. In general, it is preferable to grant the option for the maximum ISO period since most entrepreneurs are not certain as to their exact exit date for either an IPO or a sale. If employment terminates earlier than ten years, the option would also terminate earlier than ten years. The option plans contained in appendixes 1 and 2 of this book have the option to terminate three months after employment termination (whether voluntary or not) and one year after death or certain disability terminations.

If the ISO is to be granted to an individual who owns or is deemed to own stock of more than 10 percent of the total combined voting power of all classes of stock of the employer corporation or of its parent or subsidiary corporation (typically the entrepreneur), the ISO term cannot exceed five years from the grant date, and the option price must be at least equal to 110 percent of the fair market value of the stock subject to the option on the grant date. The Internal Revenue Code provides that a person is deemed to own stock owned, directly or indirectly, by or for his brothers and sisters (whether whole or half-blood siblings), spouse, ancestors, and lineal descendants. For example, if your brother works for the company, he is deemed to own your stock; therefore, his ISO cannot exceed a five-year term and is subject to the 110 percent rule.

Stock owned, directly or indirectly, by or for a corporation, partnership, estate, or trust, is considered as being owned proportionately by or for its shareholders, partners, or beneficiaries. Thus, if you own outright 5 percent of your company's stock and an additional 6 percent through your proportional interest in an estate or trust, you will be subject to the five-year, 110 percent rule.

Your option may first be exercised on and after nine years and ten months from the date of grant, but not before that time, unless there is an Acceleration Event (as hereafter defined), in which case this option shall become immediately exercisable, except as hereafter provided. An "Acceleration Event" refers to a date which is one year (or such earlier time as the Committee determines) after the earlier of the following: (a) the first closing date for the IPO of the Common Stock of the Company (or of a parent corporation) in which the Company (or such parent corporation) raises at least $15 million, or (b) the date of a "Change of Control" (as defined below).

This provision permits the employee to exercise the option after nine years and ten months of employment after the grant date. However, if there is an IPO or Change of Control before that time, the option may be exercised at an earlier date—namely, one year after the IPO or Change of Control.

The plan contained in appendix 2 of this book only permits an earlier exercise date if there is a Change of Control. The term *IPO* is defined to refer to an initial public offering of either the company or a parent corporation in which $15 million is raised. There is nothing magical in the $15 million figure. It could have been $5 million or $30 million as well.

The importance of the dollar threshold is to be certain that sufficient capital is raised by the company (or its parent) to permit a liquid trading market in the stock. The purpose of requiring a liquid trading market is to assist the owner in the secondary or follow-on offering when a portion of the owner's stock is sold. This provision also ensures that options will not accelerate from an inadvertent public offering, such as a sale to several investors that inadvertently does not qualify as a private placement. In general, a $5 million IPO will not create a liquid trading market. A minimum of $15 million to $30 million will usually be required to create a liquid trading market.

Even if a qualifying IPO or a Change of Control takes place, the option does not accelerate until one year after those events have occurred.

A "Change of Control" shall be deemed to have occurred upon the happening of any of the following events:

1. If John Doe (or in the event of his death, a representative of his estate or his heirs) ceases to be a director of the Company or a successor to the Company by merger or other form of acquisition;

2. If John Doe (or in the event of his death, a representative of his estate or his heirs) ceases to own at least 10 percent of the stock of the Company or a successor to the Company by merger or other form of acquisition; or

3. Any other event deemed to constitute a "Change of Control" by the Committee.

The term "Change of Control" is intended to refer to a variety of situations in which there is a "sale" of the company, as the term is typically used by business persons.

The reference to "John Doe" is intended to refer to the owner or owners of the company. If the owner dies, that is not a Change of Control, unless the Option Plan Committee or the board of directors determines it to be a Change of Control. If a representative of a deceased owner's estate or heirs ceases to be a member of the board of directors, that is a Change of Control.

A typical sale involves all of the stock or assets of the company. However, many sales occur that do not involve a sale of all of the stock or assets of the company. For example, many financial buyers want the seller to retain a small percentage of the company to obtain the benefits of recapitalization accounting (which is similar pooling accounting). Under the above provision, a Change of Control occurs only if the percentage ownership of the entrepreneur goes below 10 percent. The 10 percent figure is arbitrary since some accounting firms permit recapitalization accounting to occur with as low as 5 percent retained ownership.

The Change of Control event is designed to give the Stock Option Plan Committee or board of directors discretion to deem an event to be a Change of Control.

Even if there is a Change of Control, the option is not accelerated until one year after it has occurred. Obviously, this provision can be changed at the time of negotiating the sale if the buyer is satisfied with three months or six months. Any such material change would probably disqualify the option from being an incentive stock option; however, most employees will not care at that point since they will be obtaining a portion of the sale proceeds upon completion of the three- or six-month period of employment after the sale closes.

Notwithstanding the foregoing, if on the date of an Acceleration Event, you have not been employed by the Company for a total of at least three (3) years, this option will not be exercisable in full on the date of an Acceleration Event, but instead shall be exercisable as follows: (a) if on the date of an Acceleration Event you have been employed by the Company for a total of two (2) or more years, this option will be exercisable for two-thirds of the total number of shares then subject to this option, and the remaining one-third of the total number of shares then subject to this option will become exercisable after you have been employed by the Company for a total of three (3) years; (b) if on the date of an Acceleration Event you have been employed by the Company for a total of one (1) year or more and less than two (2) years, this option will be exercisable for one-third of the total number of shares then subject to this option and an additional one-third each of the total number of shares then subject to this option shall become exercisable when you have been employed by the Company for two (2) years and three (3) years, respectively; (c) if on the date of an Acceleration Event you have been employed by the Company for a total of less than one (1) year, this option will not be exercisable until you have been employed by the Company for a total of one (1) year, at which time this option will be exercisable for one-third of the total number of shares then subject to this option and an additional one-third each of the total number of shares then subject to this option shall become exercisable when you have been employed by the Company for two (2) years and three (3) years, respectively.

An "acceleration event" occurs one year after a qualifying IPO or Change of Control. Some owners prefer to limit the acceleration to employees who have been with the company for a significant period of time. This clause is designed to require employees who have been employed by the company for a minimum of three years before the acceleration event to be fully vested one year after the qualifying IPO or Change of Control. If they do not satisfy this requirement, there is phased in vesting after the acceleration event until the three-year requirement has been satisfied.

This provision is particularly helpful in preventing an employee from joining the company shortly before an IPO, becoming an instant millionaire after only one year of employment with the company after the IPO, and then leaving the company and selling his or her stock.

The option plan contained in appendix 2 of this book ("Sale Exit Only") does not contain this provision since a sale would ordinarily bail out the owner at the closing date. This contrasts with an IPO where the owner will typically not be able to sell any stock for at least six months. However, if the company is likely to be sold with an "earnout" provision or it is likely that the purchase price is not otherwise paid in full at the closing, retention provisions such as those given earlier should be considered for inclusion in the option.

> You may exercise your option by giving written notice to the Secretary of the Company on forms supplied by the Company at its then principal executive office, accompanied by payment of the option price for the total number of shares you specify that you wish to purchase. The payment may be in any of the following forms: (a) cash, which may be evidenced by a check and includes cash received from a stock brokerage firm in a so-called "cashless exercise"; (b) (unless prohibited by the Committee) certificates representing shares of Common Stock of the Company, which will be valued by the Secretary of the Company at the fair market value per share of the Company's Common Stock (as determined in accordance with the Plan) on the date of delivery of such certificates to the Company, accompanied by an assignment of the stock to the Company; or (c) (unless prohibited by the Committee) any combination of cash and Common Stock of the Company valued as provided in clause (b). The use of the so-called "attestation procedure" to exercise a stock option may be permitted by the Committee. Any assignment of stock shall be in a form and substance satisfactory to the Secretary of the Company, including guarantees of signature(s) and payment of all transfer taxes if the Secretary deems such guarantees necessary or desirable.

This provision permits the employee to exercise the option using either cash or stock. However, to avoid the possibility of an excessive charge to accounting earnings, the Stock Option Plan Committee or board of directors is given discretion to prohibit the use of stock as the exercise price. They might exercise this discretion if showing large accounting earnings was important to the company. This would occur typically if the company's stock was publicly traded at the time of the exercise or the company was on the verge of going public.

The provision permits the use of both cashless exercise (only available for publicly traded companies) and the attestation method of exercise discussed in chapters 9 and 13.

Your option will, to the extent not previously exercised by you, terminate three months after the date on which your employment by the Company or a Company subsidiary corporation is terminated (whether such termination be voluntary or involuntary) other than by reason of disability as defined in Section 22(e)(3) of the Internal Revenue Code of 1986, as amended (the "Code"), and the regulations thereunder, or death, in which case your option will terminate one year from the date of termination of employment due to disability or death (but in no event later than the Scheduled Termination Date). After the date your employment is terminated, as aforesaid, you may exercise this option only for the number of shares which you had a right to purchase and did not purchase on the date your employment terminated. Provided you are willing to continue your employment for the Company or a successor after a Change of Control at the same compensation you enjoyed immediately prior to such Change of Control, if your employment is involuntarily terminated without cause after a Change of Control, you may exercise this option for the number of shares you would have had a right to purchase on the date of an Acceleration Event. If you are employed by a Company subsidiary corporation, your employment shall be deemed to have terminated on the date your employer ceases to be a Company subsidiary corporation, unless you are on that date transferred to the Company or another Company subsidiary corporation. Your employment shall not be deemed to have terminated if you are transferred from the Company to a Company subsidiary corporation, or vice versa, or from one Company subsidiary corporation to another Company subsidiary corporation.

This provision permits employees whose employment is terminated (whether voluntarily or not) to exercise the option for a period of three months thereafter. There is no requirement that an ISO by its terms must be exercised within three months after employment terminates; however, the Internal Revenue Code provides that if the option is not in fact exercised within such a three-month period, the optionee does not obtain the federal income tax benefits of an ISO.

Some companies provide that the three-month period in which to exercise the option does not apply if the employee is terminated for cause. If you use such a provision, great care should be exercised in terminating an employee for cause, since it is likely the company will be sued. My personal preference is not to include this provision since it encourages a race between the employee and the company, with the employee winning if the option exercise notice is received before the official time of termination. This type of provision also tends to lead to expensive lawsuits.

This provision also makes it clear that upon the sale of the stock of a subsidiary corporation, the employees of that subsidiary are deemed to have terminated their employment with the parent company. If this provision is omitted, the option becomes ambiguous if this event occurs. Chapter 13 contains a litigation on this very subject. If the employee is fired without cause after a Change of Control, the employee is permitted to exercise the option as if the employee had remained for the full one year period after the Change of Control. This provides the employee with some protection that the option will be exercisable after the sale of your business if the employee is terminated without cause by the new owners before the one-year period has expired.

In the event of any change in the outstanding shares of the Common Stock of the Company by reason of a stock dividend, stock split, combination of shares, recapitalization, merger, consolidation, transfer of assets, reorganization, conversion, or what the Committee deems in its sole discretion to be similar circumstances, the number and kind of shares subject to this option and the option price of such shares shall be appropriately adjusted in a manner to be determined in the sole discretion of the Committee.

This provision is an antidilution clause. It is typical for a company considering an IPO to have a stock split shortly before the filing date of the registration statement with the Securities and Exchange Commission. The stock split is designed to increase the number of outstanding shares sufficiently so that the stock sold to the public in the IPO can be priced between $10 and $20 per share.

For example, suppose the company grants Joe, an employee, an option to purchase 1,000 shares of common stock at $50 per share. In anticipation of an IPO, the company has a 5-for-1 stock split. This clause would result in Joe obtaining a proportional adjustment in the number of shares subject to the option and the option price per share. After the adjustment, Joe would have an option to purchase 5,000 shares of common stock of the company at an option price of $10 per share.

It is also possible that a company not considering an IPO might have a stock split or a stock dividend or some other form of recapitalization.

The provision gives broad discretion to the Stock Option Plan Committee and the board of directors to determine what events trigger the antidilution clause and the nature of the adjustment to the option.

> In the event of a liquidation or proposed liquidation of the Company, including (but not limited to) a transfer of assets followed by a liquidation of the Company, or in the event of a Change of Control (as previously defined) or proposed Change of Control, the Committee shall have the right to require you to exercise this option upon thirty (30) days prior written notice to you. If at the time such written notice is given this option is not otherwise exercisable, the written notice will set forth your right to exercise this option even though it is not otherwise exercisable. In the event this option is not exercised by you within the thirty (30) day period set forth in such written notice, this option shall terminate on the last day of such thirty (30) day period, notwithstanding anything to the contrary contained in this option.

One method of selling the company is to sell the assets of the company and distribute the sale proceeds that are left after paying off the liabilities to the shareholders in a liquidation. Upon liquidation of the company, it would be difficult to determine how much should be set aside out of the liquidation proceeds to pay to option holders, who may have many years left in the term of their options. The option holders could argue that they were not only entitled to the pro rata share of the liquidation proceeds based on the number of shares subject to their options but should also be compensated for the option privilege that they would be requested to surrender.

The purpose of this provision is to permit the Stock Option Plan Committee or the board of directors to force the option holders to exercise their options. This permits a pro rata distribution of the net liquidation proceeds from the sale (inclusive of any option price paid) to such optionees as shareholders.

The provision forces the option holder to exercise his or her option by terminating the option if the option holder fails to exercise the option within thirty days after written notice is given.

This provision could also be useful in a situation in which all of the company's stock is to be sold to a buyer. If the buyer does not wish to have employee stock options outstanding after the purchase of all of the outstanding stock, the Stock Option Plan Committee or the board of directors can send out a written notice to the option holders requiring them to exercise their option within the thirty-day period, or their option will terminate. To protect their option rights, the option holders would have to exercise their options (even though not otherwise exercisable) before the termination date, and the shares could then be purchased by the buyer as part of the purchase of all of the outstanding stock of the company.

As noted later, any optionee who exercises the option must, as a condition to exercise, execute a shareholders' agreement requiring this person to join in any sale of a majority or more than the majority or all of the outstanding stock of the company.

Notwithstanding anything to the contrary contained herein, this option is not exercisable until all the following events occur and during the following periods of time:

(a) Until the Plan pursuant to which this option is granted is approved by the shareholders of the Company in the manner prescribed by the Code and the regulations thereunder;

(b) Until this option and the optioned shares are approved and/or registered with such federal, state, and local regulatory bodies or agencies and securities exchanges as the Company may deem necessary or desirable; or

(c) During any period of time in which the Company deems that the exercisability of this option, the offer to sell the shares optioned hereunder, or the sale thereof, may violate a federal, state, local, or securities exchange rule, regulation, or law, or may cause the Company to be legally obligated to issue or sell more shares than the Company is legally entitled to issue or sell.

(d) Until you have paid or made suitable arrangements to pay (which may include payment through the surrender of Common Stock, unless prohibited by the Committee) (i) all federal, state, and local income tax withholding required to be withheld by the Company in connection with the option exercise and (ii) the employee's portion of other federal, state, and local payroll and other taxes due in connection with the option exercise.

(e) Until you have executed such shareholder agreements as shall be required by the Company. Such shareholder agreements may, at the Company's option, include (among other provisions) provisions requiring you to (i) enter into any "lock-up" agreements required by underwriters, (ii) vote trust agreements, (iii) grant to the Company or its nominees an option to repurchase the stock, (iv) not sell, pledge, or otherwise dispose of the stock without the consent of the Company, (v) maintain any Subchapter S elections made by the Company, (vi) grant rights of first refusal to the Company or its nominees with respect to the stock, and (vii) join in any sale of a majority or all of the outstanding stock of the Company

Even when the option vests and becomes exercisable, the option cannot be exercised unless certain conditions specified here are satisfied. Clause (a) contemplates the possibility that an option might be granted before shareholder approval is obtained and prevents the option from being exercised until such shareholder approval is obtained. Clauses (b) and (c) are designed to prevent the company from having to violate federal or state securities laws in permitting the exercise of the option or the rules of any securities exchange that requires the listing of the shares prior to exercise.

Clause (c) also prevents the company from having to issue more shares pursuant to the exercise of an option than the state charter (i.e., articles or certificate of incorporation) if the company permits.

Clause (d) is more important for non-ISOs that trigger a tax-withholding requirement and in states that might tax the exercise of ISOs.

Clause (e) is an important clause since it requires the employee to execute a shareholders' agreement before the employee may exercise the option. Some companies require the employee to execute the shareholders' agreement at the time of option grant, rather than at the time of exercise.

My preference is to have the employee execute the shareholders' agreement only at the time of option exercise for two reasons:

- The option forms are complicated enough for the employee to understand without having another complex shareholders' agreement added to the grant documents.
- The terms of the shareholders' agreement required by the company might change at the time of option exercise from what the company might have required at the time of option grant.

For example, at the time of exercise the company may not be a Subchapter S corporation and would not need the provisions of a shareholders' agreement that protected the Subchapter S election. By postponing the drafting and execution of the shareholders' agreement until option exercise, the company also gains some bargaining leverage if the optionee is threatening to quit and to take some customers or key employees along immediately after option exercise.

Option Forms

The stock option plans contained in appendixes 1 and 2 contain two forms of options for employees. The first form (called Appendix I of the plan) is an ISO. The second form (called Appendix II of the plan) is a non-ISO for employees. The only difference between the forms is that the non-ISO states that it is not intended to be an incentive stock option.

Each of the stock option plans also contains a form of option which can be granted to directors of the company and important nonemployee consultants. This form is designated at Appendix III of the stock option plans. Appendix III contains similar exit event vesting provisions to the other option forms.

A fourth appendix can be added in the event that options are to be granted also to suppliers or customers.

Option forms granted to employees vary in length from one page to the more lengthy option form that appears in appendixes 1 and 2. I prefer including all of the major option terms in the form actually signed by the employee, rather than including them in the plan that is not executed by the employee. This is particularly important in the event of litigation concerning the exact terms of the option granted to the employee. For example, if the option form requires the employee not to solicit customers or employees after he or she leaves the company, having that provision in the option form actually signed by the employee helps eliminate any argument that the employee was not aware of that restriction.

GENERAL ISSUES

Care must be taken in granting such options to both comply with securities law issues and to be sensitive to accounting concerns. For example, the SEC has recently taken the position that if the revenues of the company have been enhanced as a result of granting options to customers (i.e., they paid more for the products or services of the company because of the option grant), the company's revenues would have to be adjusted accordingly. Similarly, if suppliers have lowered the cost of goods to the company because of option grants, the cost of goods figure reported by the company should be adjusted to eliminate the option grant benefit.

Care should be taken in granting an option that is immediately exercisable, particularly options granted to directors. The Delaware courts have raised issues as to whether such option grants are proper. If the option is immediately exercisable, the director can exercise the option one day after appointment and then resign from the board of directors, with the company receiving no quid pro quo for the option grant.

CHAPTER 8

OTHER IMPORTANT OPTION PLAN PROVISIONS

A stock option is a contract with your employee, and a number of important provisions should be considered for inclusion in the stock option and the related option plan. A few of these provisions are discussed in this chapter. The exit event options in appendixes 1 and 2 have provisions that address the issues raised in this chapter and contain other important clauses.

PLAN ADMINISTRATION

Most option plans provide that the plan is to be administered by the board of directors of the company or by a committee of the board of directors. Depending on state law, the board could also delegate the function of issuing options to a committee including nondirectors of the company.

It is preferable in private companies to have only one or two directors responsible for the granting of options and not to include any nondirectors. The grant date of the option is sensitive to qualify for incentive stock option treatment, and the exercise price must equal or exceed the fair market value on the grant date. The more persons who must sign off on the grant decision, the greater will be the delay in granting the option. During the delay, the fair market value of the company can increase, thereby causing the option price to be lower than the fair market value.

The members of the board of directors or committee responsible for granting stock options should be protected from personal liability from that activity. The following provision is contained in appendixes 1 and 2 to accomplish that immunization:

No member of the Committee or the Board of Directors shall be liable for any act or omission (whether or not negligent) taken or omitted in good faith, or for the exercise of an authority or discretion granted in connection with the Plan to a Committee or the Board of Directors, or for the acts or omissions of any other members of a Committee or the Board of Directors.

The board of directors or committee granting stock options should also have the authority to construe the plan and the options issued under the plan into reconciled inconsistencies. Their decision should be final, binding, and conclusive on the optionees.

EXEMPTING THE OPTION FROM SECTION 162(M)

Section 162(m) of the Internal Revenue Code limits, in the case of a publicly held corporation, the tax deductions available to the company with respect to certain employee remuneration to the extent that the remuneration for a taxable year exceeds $1 million. This provision is applicable to the chief executive officer and the four highest-compensated officers other than the chief executive officer.

The profit obtained under a stock option can be exempted from Section 162(m) if there is a limit in the plan on the number of options that can be issued to any single person and this provision is approved by shareholders.

Private companies that are not certain whether there would be an IPO or sale exit should consider including such a limitation in their option plan. If the private company had an IPO subsequent to the issuance of the option and failed to include such a limitation in the original private company grant, the public company could be denied a tax deduction to the extent that the compensation exceeded the $1 million limitation of Section 162(m).

Section 3 of the option plan set forth in appendix 1 contains the following provision, designed to create this exemption from Section 162(m):

> No individual may receive options under this Plan for more than 80 percent of the total number of shares of the Company's Common Stock authorized for issuance under this Plan.

The 80 percent limitation is so high that it is unlikely that this figure will ever be exceeded for any individual. The appendix 2 exit event option for companies expecting only a sale exit contains a similar provision, even though it is probably superfluous.

NONCOMPETITION AND NONSOLICITATION OF CUSTOMER AND EMPLOYEE CLAUSES

Under the laws of many states, noncompetition agreements and nonsolicitation of customer agreements signed by employees are not legally enforceable unless a company buys some fresh consideration to the employee. It has therefore become typical to insert noncompetition and/or nonsolicitation of customer clauses in option grants.

The option grant provides evidence to the courts of fresh consideration to the employee and makes it much more likely that the clause will be legally enforceable.

A 1999 case in the United States Court of Appeals for the Ninth Circuit (which covers California and other western states) upheld IBM's suit against a former employee who exercised IBM's stock options and then went to work for a competitor. Dr. Bajorek, an IBM executive based in California, exercised stock options in March and April 1996. At the time the options were granted, Bajorek signed an agreement that if he went to work for a competitor within six months after his exercise, he would return any profits to IBM. At the time of each exercise, Dr. Bajorek signed a form certifying that he was in compliance with the noncompete terms and acknowledging that failure to comply would subject his profits to forfeiture. After exercising his options, Dr. Bajorek left IBM and immediately went to work for a competitor. IBM demanded that Dr. Bajorek return his option profits, which amounted to over $900,000. IBM lost in the U.S. District Court, which disregarded a provision in the option which made New York law govern. However, on appeal, IBM won in the U.S. Court of Appeals in the Ninth Circuit, which held that the dispute should be resolved in accordance with New York law and that the noncompetition agreement was enforceable under New York law.

In October 2000, IBM lost a similar option forfeiture suit in the United States District Court for the Southern District of New York when the court found that the former IBM executive did not leave IBM voluntarily but was forced into retirement.

NONCOMPETITION VERSUS NONSOLICITATION CLAUSES

A noncompetition clause generally provides that the option grantee will not, after he ceases to be your employee, provide services for a competitor for a specific time period The clause will also typically limit the geographic area in which competition is restricted.

Many employees object to a noncompetition clause, viewing it as unfair. The clause requires them to leave your industry after employment is terminated with your company. In addition, the use of this clause detracts from whatever psychological motivation has been given to them by the stock option.

A nonsolicitation of customers clause merely prevents the employee, after employment termination, from soliciting your existing customers. The clause does not prevent the employee from continuing to work in your industry and therefore is much more palatable to the employee.

An example of a nonsolicitation customer clause found in appendixes 1 and 2 of this book reads in part as follows:

> You covenant and agree that, in consideration of the grant to you of this stock option, you will not, for a period of two years after your employment with the Company ceases for any reason whatsoever (whether voluntary or not), except with the express prior written consent of the Company, directly or indirectly, whether as employee, owner, partner, member, consultant, agent, director, officer, shareholder, or in any other capacity, for your own account or for the benefit of any individual or entity, (i) solicit any customer of the Company for business which would result in such customer terminating their relationship with the Company; or

(ii) solicit or induce any individual or entity which is an employee of the Company to leave the Company or to otherwise terminate their relationship with the Company.

Nonsolicitation of Employees Clause

This clause prevents not only the solicitation by the option grantee of your customers but also the solicitation of your employees to leave your company.

NO REQUIREMENT TO CAUSE VESTING

The option plans in appendix 1 contains the following clause; a similar clause appears in the appendix 2 stock option:

Nothing herein shall modify your status as an at-will employee of the Company. Further, nothing herein guarantees you employment for any specified period of time. This means that either you or the Company may terminate your employment at any time for any reason, with or without cause, or for no reason. You recognize that, for instance, you may terminate your employment or the Company may terminate your employment prior to the date on which your option becomes vested or exercisable. You understand that the Company has no obligation to consider or effectuate a public offering of its stock or a Change of Control.

As noted in chapter 12, employees who are terminated on the eve of vesting will typically sue the company. This provision is designed to make it clear that the employee can be terminated without regard to this option and that the company is not obligated to cause the option to vest by having a public offering or a Change of Control.

DISPUTE RESOLUTION CLAUSES

In the relatively few circumstances in which a legal dispute occurs over a stock option, it is preferable to have the dispute resolved through binding and unappealable arbitration. Unlike court cases, which are public, arbitration can be conducted without publicity or other public awareness of the proceedings. Unlike juries, arbitrators almost never award punitive damages.

More important, lawsuits tend to be much more expensive than arbitration proceedings because of the extensive discovery permitted by the courts and the ability of the losing party to appeal. Although some limited discovery may be allowed by an arbitrator, it is typically less extensive and therefore less costly then pretrial discovery in a court proceedings.

The real advantage of arbitration in minimizing legal expenses lies in the ability to have the arbitrator's determination be final and unappealable. In contrast, a lawsuit in a court can go through endless appeals and, in certain cases, retrials of the case if significant errors were made by the judge.

The disadvantage of arbitration is the tendency of arbitrators to compromise, rather than finding wholly in favor of one party or the other. This disadvantage is more than offset by the greater efficiency and lower cost of the dispute resolution procedure provided by arbitration.

Appendixes 1 and 2 contain the following arbitration provision in the stock option form signed by the employee:

Any dispute or disagreement between you and the Company with respect to any portion of this option (excluding Attachment A hereto) or its validity, construction, meaning, performance, or your rights hereunder shall be settled by arbitration in accordance with the Commercial Arbitration Rules of the American Arbitration Association or its successor, as amended from time to time. However, prior to submission to arbitration you will attempt to resolve any disputes or disagreements with the Company over this option amicably and informally, in good faith, for a period not to exceed two weeks. Thereafter, the dispute or disagreement will be submitted to arbitration. At any time prior to a decision from the arbitrator(s) being rendered, you and the Company may resolve the dispute by settlement. You and the Company shall equally share the costs charged by the American Arbitration Association or its successor, but you and the Company shall otherwise be solely responsible for your own respective counsel fees and expenses. The decision of the arbitrator(s) shall be made in writing, setting forth the award, the reasons for the decision and award and shall be binding and conclusive on you and the Company. Further, neither you nor the Company shall appeal any such award. Judgment of a court of competent jurisdiction may be entered upon the award and may be enforced as such in accordance with the provisions of the award.

The exclusion from the arbitration provision for Attachment A permits the company to obtain an injunction from a court in the event the employee violates the nonsolicitation of customer or employee clauses of the stock option.

Choice of Law Clauses

The IBM case discussed earlier in this chapter makes it clear that the choice of law applicable to the option can make the difference between winning or losing the case. In general, states that are hostile to noncompetition clauses, such as California, should be avoided. However, the state whose laws are applicable to the interpretation of the option must have some reasonable relationship to the parties.

CHAPTER 9

EXPLAINING EXIT EVENT STOCK OPTIONS TO EXISTING EMPLOYEES AND NEW HIRES[1]

B efore establishing an exit event stock option plan, it is important to determine the best method of communicating the plan to your employees. Effective communication is extremely important to achieving your motivational goals.

If your options are given to a large group of employees, it is best to provide written communication to avoid misunderstandings. Written communication is also helpful when options are granted only to a few key employees, but is less crucial.

The difficulty with written communications is that the subject is inherently complex. Therefore, it is best to keep the communication simple, but add a lot of legal disclaimers. An attorney who specializes in this area can draft the disclosure for you.

1. The tax rates and tax concepts used in this book are based on the federal income tax law in effect in December 2000. Consult your tax adviser for the effect of changes enacted in 2001 or thereafter.

The following is an example of a written communication for a large group of employees of a private company who receive the exit event option contained in appendix 1.

ABC, Inc. Stock Option Plan
Questions and Answers

1. **Q. What is an employee stock option?**

   A. An employee stock option is a contractual right that is provided by a company to an employee to purchase, at the employee's option during the option term, one or more shares of the company's common stock at a fixed price, which is generally equal to the fair market value of the stock at the time of the option grant. Your option form contains an option price at which the stock may be purchased, a time frame (up to ten years) during which the option may be exercised, the conditions to exercise, and a vesting period. The option becomes valuable to the extent the fair market value of the stock in the company exceeds the option price per share as a result of the appreciation in the value of the stock during the option term.

2. **Q. What is the advantage to an employee of a stock option?**

   A. If the company's stock appreciates over time, the option holder can exercise the stock option at the lower fixed option price, thereby profiting from the excess of the fair market value of the stock over the option price.

3. **Q. If there is an IPO in which the company raises at least $15 million, when can I first exercise my option?**

   A. You may first exercise the option commencing one year after the IPO provided all of the conditions to exercisability are satisfied.

4. **Q. If there is a Change of Control, when can I first exercise my option?**

    A. One year after the date of the Change of Control.

5. **Q. If there is no IPO or Change of Control (as defined in the option), when can I first exercise my option?**

    A. Nine years and ten months after the grant date (provided all of the conditions to exercisability are satisfied). For example, if the grant date is January 1, 2001, and you have an option for 100 shares, you may exercise all 100 shares commencing October 2, 2010, and until the option terminates.

6. **Q. What is a "Change in Control"?**

    A. If John Doe (or in the event his death, a representative of his estate or his heirs) ceases being a director of the company or owns less than 10 percent of the company stock, that would be a "Change of Control." Or some other event may occur that the board of directors considers a "Change in Control."

7. **Q. When does my stock option terminate?**

    A. The scheduled termination date for your option is generally ten years after the grant date. Your option may terminate earlier if your employment terminates during the ten-year period.

8. **Q. If my employment terminates during the ten-year period, how long will I have to exercise my option?**

    A. You will have three months after the termination of your employment to exercise your option (one year in the case of death or certain disability terminations), and you may only exercise the option for the number of shares that you had a right to purchase on the date your employment terminated. If you fail to exercise the option within this time period, the option terminates and is of no force or effect. If your option is not exercisable on the date your employment terminates, you do not have the right to exercise the option after employment termination.

9. Q. **How can I exercise my stock option?**

A. You may exercise the option with cash or a check and, unless prohibited by the board of directors, with other stock of the company or some combination of cash, a check, or stock.

10. Q. **What is a "cashless exercise"?**

A. If the company's stock is publicly traded, the company may arrange for a broker to sell the stock to be acquired under your option and to use the net sale proceeds after broker's commission to pay the option price to the company and any additional tax withholding due as a result of your sale of the stock within one year after the exercise date. The company delivers the stock certificate to the broker, who remits the balance of the sale proceeds to you.

11. Q. **What are the federal income tax consequences of my option?**

A. The following is a simplified explanation of the federal income tax consequences of your stock option, and you should consult your personal tax adviser for further information. The company is granting options that are intended to be "incentive stock options" under the Internal Revenue Code. There is no regular federal income tax on either the grant date or on the exercise date of an incentive stock option in certain cases, but alternative minimum tax can be due on the option exercise. In general, if you sell stock acquired under the option more than one year after the exercise date and the sale date is more than two years after the grant date, the profit is treated as long-term capital gains (subject to certain exceptions). If you sell or otherwise make a disqualifying disposition of the stock you acquired under the option within one year after the exercise date or within two years from the grant date, the profit is treated as ordinary income and additional compensation to you from the company.

The following caveat should be inserted in any question and answer document provided to employees to explain their stock options:

The question and answers provided in this document and any accompanying memorandum are intended to be a simplified explanation of your stock option and are not intended to be either complete or exhaustive. Nothing contained in these documents shall be deemed to modify the terms and conditions contained in the company's stock option plan or the option form given to any individual employee. Employees are encouraged to seek information from their own personal advisers. Nothing contained in any stock option guarantees your employment for any specified time or obligates the company to effectuate an IPO or Change of Control.

If your company is not using exit event options, or if you wish a more detailed explanation, you can supplement or change these questions and answers by using the information contained in chapter 10, which is designed to be read by employee option holders.

OFFER LETTER TO NEW HIRES

As noted in chapter 6, any offer letter sent to potential new employees that references your stock option must contain one of the following:

- A copy of the actual stock option intended to be granted to the offeree together with a copy of the plan itself
- A reference to your specific option plan and an offer to provide a full copy to the offeree on request

An example of the second alternative would be language such as the following in your offer letter:

> Our company has adopted a stock option plan on _____ [insert the date the company's board of directors' adopted the plan], and you would be granted an option for _____ shares of the company's common stock on the first day of your employment with us. Your option exercise price would equal the fair market value of the company's common stock on the date the option is granted, as determined by the company. A copy of the complete stock option plan and your option form, and its nonsolicitation of customers and employee provisions, including its vesting provision, will be supplied to you on request so that you can read all of its terms and conditions prior to making your decision to join the company.

Although it is preferable to provide an exact copy of the stock option plan and option form with the offer letter you send to new hires, the language quoted in this example gives you reasonable protections against new hires who believe that they are vested on the first day of their employment with you.

If you do not have an option plan when you send out an offer letter to a new hire, it is preferable not to refer to any option plan. If you believe that you must refer to an option plan that you believe will be adopted in the future, use language such as the following:

> Our company is considering the adoption of a stock option plan. The final decision as to whether to adopt the plan will be made by our board of directors and shareholders. If a plan is adopted, it will contain certain vesting provisions, and these vesting provisions may require you to be employed for certain time periods and may also require certain events to have occurred, such as a sale or an initial public offering. The stock option plan will contain other terms and conditions, including a requirements that you not solicit customers or employees once you leave employment. If a stock option plan is adopted, we would expect that you would be eligible to receive an option under the plan.

I have seen offer letters to new hires that create problems on selling the company. The offer letter can create legal rights in new hires that were never intended. Therefore, all offer letters, whether containing an offer of an exit event option or otherwise, should be approved as to form by your company's attorney.

Chapter 10

What an Employee Should Know About His or Her Stock Options

T his chapter is designed to be read by employees who have been awarded a stock option.

1. **Q. What is an employee stock option?**

   A. An employee stock option is a contractual right that is provided by a company to an employee to purchase, at the employee's option during the option term, one or more shares of the company's common stock at a fixed price. The fixed price is generally equal to the fair market value of the stock at the time of the option grant. Your option form contains an option price at which the stock may be purchased, a time frame (typically up to ten years) during which the option may be exercised, the conditions to exercise, and a vesting period. The option becomes valuable to the extent the fair market value of the stock in the company exceeds the option price per share as a result of the appreciation in the value of the stock during the option term.

2. Q. What is the advantage to an employee of a stock option?

A. If the company's stock appreciates over time, the option holder can exercise the stock option at the lower fixed option price, thereby profiting from the excess of the fair market value of the stock over the option price.

3. Q. Are all stock options the same?

A. In general, no two stock options are identical. You must carefully read the terms of your stock option to understand its terms fully. If you can afford a lawyer to help you, use one who is familiar with stock options and their tax consequences. Tax lawyers at large corporate law firms can best help you. If you cannot afford a lawyer, request the company's lawyers to explain the terms of your stock options to you.

4. Q. What is the most important provision of your stock option?

A. The most important provision of your stock option is when it vests (i.e., when you may first exercise your option). Many options cannot be exercised immediately. The option may require you to continue to be employed by the company for a specified term of years before it can be exercised. For example, an option may be exercisable after one year with respect to one-third of the shares subject to the option, with an additional one-third being exercisable after each of the second and third years. Other options may require a certain event to occur, such as an initial public offering of the stock of the company or a Change of Control. Other options require you or the company to meet certain performance goals or profits (e.g., a 15 percent income in sales before the option becomes exercisable).

5. Q. How do I exercise my stock option once it becomes exercisable?

A. Once your option becomes exercisable, you may exercise it by paying cash (or a check) in the amount of the exercise price. Many options also permit you to pay all or a portion of the exercise price in other stock of the company. If your option permits you to use stock to pay the exercise price, the stock is typically valued at its fair market value at the time you surrender the stock certificates to pay the exercise price of the option.

6. Q. Are there any methods to exercise my option that do not require me to pay cash?

A. Yes. Two common methods are pyramiding and cashless exercises.

7. Q. What is pyramiding?

A. If you do not own any stock in your company, some options permit you to exercise your option for cash and then use that stock as the exercise price for additional stock acquired under your option. This is called *pyramiding*.

For example, suppose you have an option to purchase stock at an exercise price of $5 per share, and the fair market value of the stock has risen to $25 per share. If you paid $5, you could then acquire one share of stock. You could then surrender that one share of stock (worth $25) to the company in payment of the exercise price of five shares of stock. You could then surrender the five shares (worth $125) to the company in payment of the exercise price of twenty-five shares of stock. This could be repeated until your option is fully exercised.

The downside of pyramiding is that if you acquire stock under an incentive stock option and use that stock within one year as the exercise price for other stock to be acquired under your

ISO, you will have made a "disqualifying disposition" of the stock that you used as the exercise price and will recognize ordinary income with respect to the surrendered stock (discussed later).

8.   Q. Can I pyramid my stock options without actually surrendering stock certificates?

A. The IRS has issued a private letter ruling (reproduced in Appendix 7 of this book) that permits pyramiding without actually surrendering your stock certificates. The private letter ruling permits you to use a certification procedure instead of actually surrendering stock certificates. Under the private letter ruling, the shares you already own are called the *payment shares*. If the payment shares are held by a registered securities broker for you in "street name," you would provide the company with a notarized statement attesting to the number of shares owned that are intended to serve as payment shares. If you actually hold the certificates, you would provide the company with the certificate numbers. Upon receipt of the notarized statement for the payment shares from your broker, or upon confirmation of your ownership of the payment shares by the company's records, the company could treat the payment shares as being constructively exchanged and issue to you a new certificate for the net additional shares due to you (i.e., the number of shares subject to the option exercises less the number of payment shares).

Caution: A private letter ruling issued to another taxpayer need not be honored by the IRS for your option exercise. The certification procedure is only available if the company permits it. The basis and holding period for the plans you acquire is described later.

9. Q. Is there any reason why my company will not permit me to pyramid my option?

A. Many companies will not permit pyramiding under their option plans because they may suffer an accounting charge unless you have held the surrendered shares for at least six months.

10. Q. What is a cashless exercise?

A. Many public companies will permit a cashless exercise. However, a cashless exercise is typically not available for the exercise of stock options if the company is still private at the time of exercise.

A cashless exercise involves having a stockbroker referred to you by the company sell the stock you acquire under the option simultaneously with your exercise of the option. Your profit, which equals the excess of the sale price over the exercise price (less a brokerage commission), is then remitted to you by the broker, who also pays the option exercise price to the company.

Thus, whether or not pyramiding is permitted under your option, you may never have to pay the cash exercise price if your company is publicly traded and permits cashless exercises.

11. Q. Once my option becomes exercisable, when should I in fact exercise my option?

A. The decision as to when to exercise the option and whether to sell the stock you acquire under your option is an investment decision. Sometimes by being too greedy you can lose the stock appreciation that has already been realized. For an example of someone who may have been too greedy, read the *Wall Street Journal* article at the end of this chapter.

Your option allows you to profit from any appreciation in the stock for the full term of your option grant. Many employees who are entitled to exercise their stock options choose not to do so until close to the expiration date of their options in order to obtain the maximum benefit form their option. This permits them to have the benefit of the "free ride" on the stock for a longer term (i.e., you don't have to exercise the option to obtain the benefit of any appreciation in the value of the stock).

However, if you need cash and wait too long to exercise the option and sell the stock, there might not be enough time for the stock to recover from a temporary decline in value.

12. Q. Is the receipt of my stock option subject to any federal income tax?

A. No. The grant of an option to you will generally not result in the receipt of any federal income for federal income tax purposes. Although state and local income taxes generally do not apply to the grant of a stock option, you must check with your personal tax adviser to make certain that you are not in a state or local jurisdiction which taxes option grants.

13. Q. When my option vests and becomes exercisable, am I subject to any federal income tax?

A. No. The earliest time you would normally be subjected to tax is upon actual exercise of your option.

14. Q. What is an incentive stock option?

A. There are two types of options that you may have received:

- Incentive stock options (ISOs)
- Nonincentive stock options (non-ISOs; also called *nonqualified* or *nonstatutory stock options*)

The difference between ISOs and non-ISOs are in the federal income tax consequences to you. Both ISOs and non-ISOs may be identical in all other respects, including the duration of the option, the exercisability provisions, and the exercise price.

15. Q. How can I tell whether I have an ISO or a non-ISO?

A. The easy way is to ask your employer.

If your option states that it is not intended to be an incentive stock option, the Internal Revenue Code will honor that statement. If your option fails any of the tests for an ISO, it will be treated as a non-ISO regardless of what is stated in the option. For example, if your option has a term in excess of ten years or an option exercise price below the fair market value on the grant date (with a minor exception), it will be treated as a non-ISO. There are a number of other tests for an ISO, and flunking any of them will cause your option to be treated as a non-ISO.

16. Q. What are the federal income tax benefits of an ISO?

A. If you received an ISO, you will have no ordinary income tax at the time of exercise. However, the exercise may trigger alternative minimum tax for certain employees. Therefore, you must consult your tax adviser before exercising an incentive stock option. Even if you are subject to alternative minimum tax, you can avoid paying that tax if you sell or make another disqualifying disposition of the stock before the last day of the calendar year in which you exercise your stock option. However, if you do so, you will be taxed similarly to a non-ISO, as described later.

If you hold the stock acquired upon exercise of an ISO for at least one year from the exercise date, the appreciation above the exercise price when you do sell the stock will be considered long-term capital gains provided you satisfy two additional requirements:

- You do not sell or make another disqualifying disposition of the stock for two years after the option grant date.
- You were an employee on the grant date and continued to be an employee when you exercised the option or you exercised the option not more than three months after your employment terminated (one year in the case of death or certain kinds of disability).

17. Q. What is the federal income tax benefit to me of having long-term capital gains on the stock appreciation?

A. Ordinary compensation income can be taxed up to a maximum rate of 39.6 percent for federal income tax purposes. However, long-term capital gains is only taxed at a maximum rate of 20 percent.

18. Q. What happens if I exercise an incentive stock option but fail to hold the stock for one year after the exercise date and two years after the grant date?

A. If you have an incentive stock option but fail to hold it for at least one year after the exercise date and two years after the grant date, you will be treated on the sale or other "disqualifying disposition" as if you exercised a non-ISO, subject to one minor exception discussed later. The stock appreciation from the grant date will in general be taxed as ordinary compensation income.

19. Q. What is a disqualifying disposition?

A. A sale of stock acquired under an ISO within one year after exercise of the option or within two years after grant of the option is a disqualifying disposition and changes potential long-term capital gain into ordinary income.

However, other types of transfers may or may not be disqualifying dispositions:

- Death is not a disqualifying disposition.
- A transfer of ISO stock to your spouse—or to a former spouse in connection with a divorce—is not a disqualifying disposition.
- All gifts to nonspouses are disqualifying dispositions.
- A transfer of a stock certificate to a broker who will hold it in street name is not a disqualifying disposition.
- The IRS takes the position that a short sale of your company's stock while you hold ISO stock is a disqualifying disposition.
- Using ISO stock as collateral for a loan is not a disqualifying disposition.

20. Q. If I make a disqualifying disposition of stock I acquired under my ISO, what are the federal income tax consequences?

A. If you make a sale or other disqualifying disposition within one year after the exercise of an ISO or within two years after the grant of an ISO, you will be considered to have realized ordinary income on the date of the sale or other disqualifying disposition. The IRS does not require federal income tax withholding in connection with a sale or another disqualifying disposition, but you may have to file a declaration of estimated tax. Consult your personal tax adviser.

The amount of the income realized by you on the sale or other disqualifying disposition is computed as follows:

- If you sell the shares for an amount less than your exercise price (a catastrophe!), you do not report any compensation income for federal income tax purposes, and your loss is reported as a capital loss.
- If you sold the shares for an amount above your exercise price, but not higher than the fair market value of the shares on the date of exercise, you report your gain as compensation income.
- If you sell your shares at a price that is higher than the fair market value of your shares on the exercise date, you report two different items. The excess of the fair market value of your shares on the date of the ISO exercise over the exercise price is reported as ordinary compensation income. Any additional gain is reported as capital gain, which may be long- or short-term depending on how long you held the stock.

For example, suppose you exercise your ISO on January 1, 2002, at an exercise price of $5 per share, and at that time the fair market value of the stock was $25 per share. You then sell the stock on February 1, 2002, for $27 per share. You would recognize ordinary compensation income of $20 per share on February 1, 2002, and a short-term capital gain of $2 per share.

If you made a disqualifying disposition on February 1, 2002, other than a sale (e.g., a gift to your child) within one year after ISO exercise or within two years after ISO grant, you have to report $20 per share as ordinary compensation income on February 1, 2002. This is true even if the value of the stock had gone down after the date you exercised your ISO. If the disqualifying disposition involves a sale to a related person other than your spouse, any gain that exceeds the $20 figure would be treated as short-term capital gain.

21. Q. Is there any limit on the amount of long-term capital gains I can receive from my ISO?

A. Technically there is no limit. However, there is a $100,000 limit on the number of shares that will be treated as ISO shares each year in which your option is first exercisable. If your option exercise price multiplied by the number of shares subject to your option does not exceed $100,000, the limit is not applicable to you.

22. Q. If your stock option does exceed the $100,000 limit, how do you compute the maximum number of shares which will be treated as ISO shares?

A. The number of option shares that will be treated as ISO shares is computed by dividing into $100,000 the option price per share for the shares which first become exercisable in any calendar year. For example, suppose you have an option for shares at an exercise price of $20 per share that becomes first exercisable as follows: 5,000 shares in 2004; 8,000 shares in 2005. The 5,000 shares first exercisable in 2004 are all ISO shares since 5,000 × $20 does not exceed $100,000. However, of the 8,000 shares first exercisable in 2005, only 5,000 will qualify as ISO shares; the remaining 3,000 will not qualify since $100,000 ÷ $20 per share equals 5,000 shares.

If your rate of first exercisability never exceeds $100,000 in any calendar year, all of your shares will be treated as ISO shares. There is no limit on the amount of your long-term capital gain potential on ISO shares.

23. Q. Under what circumstances can I be subject to alternative minimum tax upon exercising an ISO?

A. The exercise of an ISO may trigger federal and state alternative minimum tax (AMT). Alternative minimum tax is a separate tax from regular income tax and was intended by Congress to close loopholes in the regular tax system for the wealthy. Unfortunately, the federal alternative minimum tax is affecting more people who are not wealthy and who are obtaining profits from ISOs. There is no easy method of determining whether you will or will not be liable for these taxes without consulting a tax adviser who will perform a computation for you.

A simple method of avoiding AMT is to project, with the help of a tax professional, your taxable income for both regular and AMT taxes for the tax year before exercising your ISO. Use Form 1040 (regular tax) and Form 6251 (alternative minimum tax) to perform this calculation. Determine your regular tax (assume $40,000) and your alternative minimum tax (assume $30,000). Subtract the difference ($10,000) and then divide the $10,000 by the AMT tax rate of 26 percent ($38,462) assuming 26 percent is your applicable AMT rate. Divide the $38,462 by the spread (assume $10), and you find that 3,846 shares may be exercised without triggering the AMT.

Regular tax (Form 1040):	$40,000
AMT (Form 6251):	$30,000

Difference:	$10,000
Divide by AMT rate (26 percent):	$36,462
Divide by spread per share:	$10
Maximum number of shares that may be exercised without AMT:	3,846

24. Q. If I am potentially subject to federal alternative minimum tax upon exercising an ISO, is there any way I can be certain that I will never have to pay the federal alternative minimum tax?

A. You can avoid paying any federal AMT by selling the ISO stock during the calendar year in which you exercised your ISO.

25. Q. What is the maximum federal alternative minimum tax rate, and how does it work?

A. The maximum rate for federal alternative minimum tax is 28 percent (26 percent on the first $175,000 for married couples, $87,800 for married couples filing separately). If your ISO profit is small, the chances are that you will not be subject to alternative minimum tax because of the AMT exemption: $45,000 for joint filers, $33,750 for singles, and $22,500 for married couples filing separately. However, this exemption is reduced by $0.25 for each dollar of AMT taxable income above $150,000 for couples ($112,000 for singles); filling out Form 6251 with the help of a tax professional is the only way to tell for certain. The payment of federal alternative minimum tax may permit you to obtain a credit in future years when you are not subject to this tax. Potentially, this credit is applicable to future federal income taxes may permit you eventually to recover all of the federal alternative minimum tax that you paid for the year in which you exercised your ISO. In addition, there are some benefits in computing your tax basis for the ISO stock for purposes of computing federal alternative minimum tax in the future.

The amount of your federal alternative minimum tax is also used in determining how much estimated federal income tax you have to declare and pay during the tax year.

26. Q. How are non-ISOs taxed?

A. If your option is not an incentive stock option, you will be deemed to have received taxable compensatory income on the date you exercise your option in an amount equal to the excess of the fair market value of the stock on that date over the option exercise price. For example, if your option has an exercise price of $5 per share and the fair market value of the stock on the date of exercise is $25 per share, you will, upon exercising your non-ISO, be deemed to have received $20 per share in compensation, taxable as ordinary income.

27. Q. Is federal income tax withholding required to be paid upon exercise of a non-ISO?

A. Yes. The ordinary income realized by you upon exercise of a non-ISO is subject to federal income tax withholding, typically in amounts up to 28 percent. In the previous example, you would be subject to federal tax withholding on the $20 per share compensation income of up to $5.60 per share (28 percent of $20). Therefore, in the previous example, you must be prepared to pay both the $5 exercise price and up to $5.60 in federal tax withholding. This is not a problem if you are permitted a "cashless" exercise, since the broker would pay the company both the $5 exercise price and the $5.60 withholding.

However, if your company is not public on the date of exercise or does not permit a cashless exercise price, you must be prepared to pay both the $5 exercise price plus the $5.60 tax withholding at the time of exercise.

28. Q. Can federal income withholding be paid by surrendering stock you own?

A. Some companies permit you to pay your exercise price and federal income tax withholding with other stock of the company, including stock you acquired on exercising your option. You must carefully check your option to see whether this is permitted. Any stock you use to pay your federal income tax withholding may be subject to tax. Consult your tax adviser for more information. If you use stock acquired under an ISO to pay for your federal income tax withholding upon exercise of your non-ISO, this use is considered a disposition of your ISO stock and may constitute a "disqualifying disposition."

29. Q. If I use stock to exercise my option, what are the federal income tax consequences?

A. If you use other company stock to exercise your non-ISO, you are treated as having made a tax-free exchange of old shares for an equal number of new shares (the "tax-free shares") and received additional shares (the "extra shares") for zero payment. The tax-free shares have the same basis and holding period as the shares you turned in. However, the fair market value of the extra shares are taxable as ordinary compensation income to you. They take a basis equal to the amount of income you realized, and your holding period begins on your exercise date. If you use shares you owned from the previous exercise of an ISO, the exchange will *not* be treated as a disqualifying disposition of the ISO stock, and the tax-free shares will continue to be ISO shares and must be held for the balance of the one year period after the exercise (or two years after grant).

Example: You have a non-ISO to purchase 1,000 shares at $5 per share (a total of $5,000). You exercise the option by turning in 300 shares having a fair market value of $20 per share on the exercise date. You would receive 300 tax-free shares having the same basis and holding period as the shares you surrendered, plus 700 shares with a basis of $20 per share and a holding period that begins when you exercised the non-ISO. You would recognize income of $14,000, the value of the extra shares. The same result would apply even if you surrendered as the exercise price shares that you originally acquired under an ISO and held for less than one year.

30. Q. Is there any state and local income tax on the exercise of a stock option?

   A. Before exercising your stock option, you must check applicable state and local taxes. Just because your exercise of an ISO is not subject to federal income tax does not mean that it is free of state or local income tax. For example, if you live in California, you can expect to pay a hefty amount of state alternative minimum tax on top of any federal alternative minimum tax when you exercise an ISO.

   If you are subject to both federal and state alternative minimum tax on the exercise of an ISO, proper timing of the payment of state taxes can reduce the amount of the federal AMT you pay or increase the amount of federal AMT that qualifies for a credit.

   You should consult a tax adviser before exercising your stock option.

31. Q. If I use stock to exercise my ISO, what are the federal income tax consequences?

A. An IRS private letter ruling reproduced in appendix 7 of this book spells out the consequences. IRS private letter rulings can be challenged by the IRS if you were not the recipient of the ruling. The federal income tax results depends on whether you used stock you acquired under an ISO and held less than the required holding period as the exercise price.

The IRS views the use of such ISO stock ("immature shares") as a disqualifying disposition of the ISO stock you used as the exercise price. The IRS does not reduce your reported income even though the old ISO stock has declined in value since the date of the prior ISO exercise. The shares you receive on exercise of the ISO are divided into two groups: a number of shares equal to the number of surrendered shares (the tax-free shares) and the additional shares (the extra shares). The tax-free shares have the same basis as the old ISO shares that had not satisfied their holding period that you surrendered, increased by the amount of income you reported because of the disqualifying disposition, but only for the purpose of determining whether any subsequent capital gain or loss or a sale is short- or long-term. For purposes of determining whether you satisfied the one year after exercise (or two years after grant) holding period for the tax-free shares, your holding period begins on the exercise date.

The extra shares have a basis equal to any cash you paid on exercise, and, if you paid no cash, your extra shares will probably have a zero basis. The extra shares are subject to the special holding periods applicable to ISO stock.

If you use old ISO stock that has satisfied the holding period (so-called "mature shares") or other shares, your federal income tax results are more favorable. No income is recognized in the exercise of the ISO for regular federal income tax purposes. The shares you receive are divided into two groups:

- the first group equals the number of shares you exchanged (the exchange shares).
- the second group equals all extra shares (the extra shares).

The exchange shares have the same federal income tax basis as the shares you turn in and the same holding period for purposes of determining whether a subsequent sale purchased long- or short-term capital gain or loss. However, your holding period for the exchange shares for purposes of determining subsequent disqualifying dispositions starts on the exercise date.

The extra shares have a basis equal to any share you used to exercise the ISO; therefore, your basis would probably be zero. The holding period for the extra shares starts on the exercise date for all purposes, including determining whether you made a disqualifying disposition.

This description is not intended to cover AMT consequences previously discussed.

32. Q. If I die, how long does my estate have to exercise my ISO and still obtain the federal income tax benefits of an ISO?

A. The Internal Revenue Code permits exercise of an ISO up to one year from the date of your death to obtain the federal income tax benefits of an ISO. Most options also permit a one-year period after death for the exercise to occur. However, you should carefully examine your own option form to make certain that the exercise period is not shorter than one year.

33. Q. If I am disabled and must leave employment, how long do I have to exercise my ISO and still obtain the federal income tax benefits of an ISO?

A. The Internal Revenue Code permits you to exercise your ISO up to one year after the date of your disability and still obtain the federal income tax benefits of an ISO, provided your disability meets the requirements of the Internal Revenue Code. To take advantage of the one-year period, the Internal Revenue Code requires that your disability be "permanent and total." An individual is considered permanently and totally disabled if he or she is unable to engage in any substantial gainful activity by reason of any medically determinable physical or mental impairment that can be expected to result in death or that has lasted or can be expected to last for a continuous period of not less than twelve months. Your option should be checked to make sure that your employer is allowing you the full one-year period permitted under the Internal Revenue Code.

34. Q. If I own ISO shares acquired on different dates, how can I be certain that I only sell the ISO shares that have satisfied the one-year holding period?

A. If you do not specify which shares you are selling, the tax law treats you as if you had sold the earliest shares you bought. This may not be in your interest because your earliest shares might have a lower option exercise price (and hence larger long-term capital gains potential) than ISO shares that you acquired at a later time that have also satisfied the one-year holding period.

To be certain that you are selling the ISO shares that will give you the best tax result, you must identify the specific certificates that you wish to sell, and if you do not have certificates, instruct your broker in writing as to the specific shares you wish to sell.

For example, suppose you purchased 100 ISO shares at $10 per share on January 1, 2001, purchased another 100 ISO shares at $12 per share on January 1, 2002, and wish to sell 100 shares in 2003. It may be in your best tax interest to sell the shares that were purchased on January 1, 2002. These shares have a higher tax basis— namely, $12 per share, than the shares purchased on January 1, 2001.

If you are using a broker to sell your shares, you should instruct him or her to sell the 100 shares that were acquired by you on January 1, 2002, and, if you possess the certificates, deliver the certificate representing those shares to the broker.

35. Q. Can I be required to declare and pay estimated federal and state income taxes in connection with my stock option?

A. Since the grant of a stock option to you does not normally subject you to any federal or state income tax, you do not have to be concerned about filing declarations or paying estimated tax on the grant date. However, if the exercise of your stock option or the subsequent sale or disqualifying disposition of the stock required under the option creates regular taxable income, capital gains, or alternative minimum tax, you may be obligated to make a declaration of estimated tax and to pay that tax under both federal and state income tax laws.

If you fail to make a declaration and pay estimated taxes when due, the IRS can assess interest and penalties. You can avoid interest and penalties by increasing the income tax withholding on your salary or wages from your employer in an amount sufficient to cover any estimated taxes due for the relevant calendar year.

If you qualify for certain safe harbors provided by the Internal Revenue Code, you can avoid interest and penalties for failure to make declarations and pay estimated taxes. These safe harbors include the following:

- If your federal income taxes due are less than $1,000.

- If your estimated income tax payments, when added to your income tax withholding and credits, equal 90 percent or more of your current year's tax liability.

- If your estimated income tax payments, when added to income tax withholding and credits, equals 100 percent of your prior year's income taxes. However, this safe harbor is not applicable if your adjusted gross income for the preceding taxable year exceeds $150,000, in which case the 100 percent rises to 112 percent if the preceding year was 2001 and goes down to 110 percent if the preceding year was 2002 or thereafter.

36. Q. If I am terminated by my employer without cause, can I still exercise my option?

A. Most option plans permit an employee who is terminated without cause to exercise their option for a period after the termination, typically three months. You must examine your specific option to determine whether it contains this right.

Some options also permit employees to exercise their option following termination of their employment for any reason, typically limited to three months after termination. Again you must examine your specific option.

Some options will not be exercisable after the date you are terminated for cause by your employer. This provision sometimes leads to a race between the employer and the employee. If the employee submits his or her exercise notice, together with appropriate payment, before the actual time of termination, the employee would generally win the race. This might happen, for example, if the employee hears rumors that he or she is about to be fired and decides to exercise his or her option in advance.

37. Q. Can I sell the stock I acquire under my stock option immediately after I exercise my option?

A. If the stock that you acquire under your option is publicly traded, and if the stock is either registered by your employer under the Securities Act of 1933 or exempt from such registration, you can sell your stock immediately after you exercise your option, provided there are no contractual restrictions on such resale contained in your stock option and there are no legal restrictions on your resale.

Many stock options contain contractual restrictions on its resale. For example, if your company is engaged in a public offering at the time of your option exercise, the underwriter might require all optionees to enter into "lockup agreements" that prevent the resale of the stock for a period of time, typically six months. You may be under a legal restriction on resale if, for example, your company is publicly traded and you have inside material information or you are a director or officer and have purchased stock within the last six months.

If the stock you acquire under your option is not publicly traded, there may be no one to repurchase the stock from you. Likewise, if your stock is not registered under the Securities Act of 1933 or is exempt from such registration, you will not be able to resell the stock except in a private placement, which might include a resale to the company or one of its principal shareholders.

38. Q. If my company's stock is not publicly traded at the time I exercise my stock option, how can I profit by exercising my stock option?

A. Many private companies will agree to repurchase some or all the shares acquired under stock options to provide liquidity to the employee. Sometimes the principal shareholders will do so.

You should not exercise your stock option if your company's stock is not publicly traded without first determining what resale rights you will have. Many times the resale rights will be contained in a shareholders' agreement that you are required to execute prior to exercising your stock option.

39. Q. If I am required to execute a shareholders' agreement to exercise my stock option, what are the typical provisions contained in the shareholders' agreement?

A. A typical shareholders' agreement will contain the following provisions:

- A provision preventing you from selling or otherwise transferring your stock without consent and subject to rights of first refusal

- A provision preventing you from pledging your stock without consent

- A provision for repurchasing your stock in the event of your death

- A provision for repurchasing your stock in the event your employment terminates

- A provision requiring you to execute lockup agreements with underwriters of public offerings of the company's stock

- A provision prohibiting you, after your employment terminates, from soliciting customers or employees of the company for a competitive business

There is no standard shareholders' agreement, and you must carefully review the exact terms of any shareholders' agreement that you are requested to execute as a condition of exercising your stock option.

40. Q. What is a transferable stock option?

A. Some employers will issue options that are transferable during the employee's lifetime. These options do not qualify as ISOs because they violate the requirement that ISOs can only be transferable by will or by the laws of descent and distribution after the employee's death.

The main reason that an employee would desire a transferable stock option is to use the stock option as a wealth transfer device to other family members, typically children or grandchildren, to reduce death taxes. If a stock option is transferred to a child to reduce death taxes and the child exercises the option, the option profit is still taxed to the employee who received the option. Therefore, unless you have significant wealth apart from the option with which to pay the federal and state income taxes resulting from the option exercised by your child, you will not want a transferable option.

AN ILLUSTRATIVE STORY FROM THE *WALL STREET JOURNAL*[1]

The following article, from July 10, 2000, illustrates the danger to employees who get too greedy with stock acquired under their ISOs and who ignore investment risk inherent in all stocks.

From Rags to Riches and Back: Web Craze Whipsaws a Consultant— Options Gave Jeffrey Seiff a Fortune He Had an Opportunity to Enjoy

At eight o'clock on a Friday night, Jeffrey Seiff is still at work. He works late many nights, now that he isn't a millionaire anymore.

He sits at his dining table, pounding at his notebook computer to finish a proposal for a prospective British client. He has credit-card bills, rent, and student loans to pay, too. But the late nights reflect his biggest worry—his tax bill, the government's reminder of what he once had.

"I'm feeling poor and pressured," Mr. Seiff says.

This isn't how it was supposed to be, back when Mr. Seiff was a wealthy dot-commer, way back four months ago. He set his own hours; he jetted off to Spain for vaca-

---

1. Republished with permission of the *Wall Street Journal*. Permission conveyed through Copyright Clearance Center, Inc.

tions; he crafted a plan to start his own company. Back then, his portfolio surpassed $1.2 million.

Then came the April plunge in tech stock. Minus all the taxes, the student loans, and an odd debt or two, he has about $200,000 of net worth left of a fortune built on tech-stock options. In less than 24 months, the 30-year-old has gone from penniless Stanford M.B.A. to millionaire Web start-up employee to owner of a small consultancy with huge bills to pay and shrunken means.

In his small dining room, Mr. Seiff sits surrounded by odd artifacts of good times interrupted. His dining table is part of a graceful set with yellow damask chairs he bought a year ago. Behind him in a glass fronted cabinet, 50 or so bottles of wine stand as mute witnesses to care-free buying sprees in Napa Valley. Now, he says, "I'm not buying anything anymore."

Getting on his feet, Mr. Seiff rifles through one of the piles of paper heaped on the table. He pulls out a stack of documents three inches thick: his taxes. He owes $86,000 in taxes, largely on shares he sold last year. "My whole life is mapping out differently," he says, compared with what he grew to expect during the hardworking but heady days of the Web boom. "When you give up your life for a protracted period of time—no dating, no hobbies—it seemed like the money was justified," he adds. "When it's all snatched away, you're suddenly wondering why you're doing this to begin with."

What's extraordinary about Mr. Seiff's wild ride is how ordinary it is in Silicon Valley. The free fall of many Internet stocks since April has forced thousands of employees at Web start-ups to abruptly scale down their lifestyles and expectations. While the lucky few at the top of company ladders are still millionaires or even billionaires—on paper, at least—a far larger number of Web-heads are living the tail end of the rags-to-riches-to-rags story.

The pain is perhaps sharpest among the younger Net set, a generation that had never experienced a market downturn in their professional lives. The sky was always the limit. Now, some are giving up on buying homes or postponing plans to have children. Big tax bills like Mr. Seiff's are increasingly common among those who exercised their stock options.

"It's very difficult to stay grounded on the value of your work," says Brett Atwood, a former manager at RealNetworks Inc. who has recently given up on his cherished dream of buying a house with cash. "When your stock doubles in a month, you develop unrealistic expectations that it could happen again."

"Ticker Shock"

In Silicon Valley, which coined the term "Webslaves" for the rank-and-file who sacrifice their personal lives for a shot at riches and glory, the pain is as personal as it is financial. At the San Francisco–based Money, Meaning and Choices Institute—established two years ago to help the suddenly rich handle their wealth—the founders have already coined a new term, "ticker shock," for the struggles of their suddenly-less-rich clientele.

Friends don't always share the pain, particularly those who don't join the dot-com gravy train. After all, Mr. Seiff, for one, still has work as a consultant for his own firm, called Intensivity, and his net worth is still more than when he started. One of his friends, Rob Coombs, works for an insurance company. He says he had to endure Mr. Seiff's boasts about his growing wealth last year and had little sympathy when Mr. Seiff began bemoaning his falling worth. "Maybe this means I'm a bad person," Mr. Coombs says, "but I thought: 'Good—none of you were worth this much money anyway.'"

Like many of the young dot-com workers who have flocked to Silicon Valley, Mr. Seiff didn't aspire to Internet wealth at first. The youngest child of a Long Island, New York, family, he was bored by his economics classes at Yale University. After graduation, he headed to Russia to teach at a small school. But once there, he found himself growing increasingly immersed in the business side of the school. Returning to the U.S., he joined a Boston consulting firm and later headed to Stanford Business School.

There, he caught Internet fever. In 1998, a friend told him about a new consulting start-up named Scient Corp. that focused on the Web. He quickly persuaded the firm's principals to hire him as a strategist, and in that year, he became Scient's 41st hire. The job paid roughly $100,000; Mr. Seiff declines to be specific, except to say he received options in the first year to purchase between 10,000 and 20,000 shares of Scient stock at $1.10 a share.

From his first day at work, Mr. Seiff was caught up in an amazing ride. The then-little-known firm was bagging top-drawer clients—names such as Chase Manhattan Corp, and eBay Inc. Scient was growing like crazy, doubling its ranks every quarter. Demand for its strategic-consulting services exploded, and Mr. Seiff began to work six days a week, traveling on a moment's notice.

As busy as it was, life at Scient was good. He attended sales meetings, celebrating as Scient repeatedly beat some of the biggest names in the technology-consulting business. He delighted in the way colleagues were teaching him the latest thinking on the Web. In December 1998, Scient threw a lavish Christmas bash, paying the air fare for Mr. Seiff's date to fly from New York to attend the festivities—an unaccustomed break from a work schedule that left little time for enjoying the money coming in.

In April 1999, a few weeks before Scient's initial public offering, Mr. Seiff took his first vacation from the firm, embarking on a whirlwind tour of Spain. When he graduated from Stanford, Mr. Seiff had no assets and owed $65,000 in student loans. But after he had worked for Scient less than a year, money was no object. For 10 days, he traveled first class through Barcelona and Ronda, snapping up a pricey plane ticket to Seville at the last minute. "I didn't plan anything," he says, estimating that the trip cost $10,000. "I didn't care about what I spent. I figured it cost a week's worth of options."

The day before he left for Spain, Mr. Seiff exercised all of his vested options. Like most other Internet companies, Scient prohibits employees from selling shares during a "lockup period" for several months after an IPO. But the company let employees exercise their options—buy shares at a previously set "strike price" ($1.10 in Mr. Seiff's case)—well ahead of when they can sell the stock. By exercising his options so close to the company's IPO, Mr. Seiff avoided the alternative minimum tax. That decision proved fateful, however, a year later.

Mr. Seiff's concern back then was that his success was costing him dearly in another area: his personal life. Frequent absences and long hours made it difficult to keep up with friends. And he was starting to sense that some of his friends resented his sudden wealth. "I'd talk about the Internet being so cool, my co-workers are so cool, I'm worth tons and tons of money," he recalls. "In retrospect, I can see why it gets trying."

His tales were particularly hard on friends who had chosen not to ride the Internet bandwagon. "He spoke with such bravado about how much his options were earning," says Mr. Coombs, a 33-year old manager at State Farm Insurance. "I work very hard, too, but that kind of windfall isn't coming to me. After a while, I didn't want to hear about it." Mr. Seiff's young roommates, who were working for far lower salaries, grew increasingly distant, a situation exacerbated by his long hours and heavy travel schedule.

Sleeping in a Basement

Things got so bad that by the time Scient went public, Mr. Seiff was effectively homeless. His options for that year alone were now worth nearly half a million dollars, but his roommates had disbanded while he was in Spain, and he didn't have time to find an apartment. For nearly two months, he bedded down in a friend's basement. When the friend needed the room for guests, Mr. Seiff was reduced to prowling around the cubicles of Scient at night, asking co-workers if he could stay with them.

"At some point, he was just working too hard," says Zerlina Chen Hayes, a Stanford classmate who works at start-up Productopia Inc. "He'd have dinner with me, then head straight back to work."

In early July, Mr. Seiff decided he was financially secure enough to light out on his own in consulting. He gave Scient notice, walking away from three years of unvested options. "I had no life, no hobbies, and I'd gained 20 pounds," he says. "I'd made more money than I ever thought I would. I could not work for six months and still survive."

He found a one-bedroom apartment. Owning almost no furniture, he headed to a sale at a Pacific Heights boutique and spent $11,000 on the spot on living-room and dining-room sets.

Mr. Seiff's Web boom continued. For the next five months, Scient's shares marched relentlessly northward—to $32, to $68.75 and then $90.25—sending his net worth up to the million-dollar mark. He set up Intensivity and snagged the Web-hosting and services provider Exodus Communications Inc. as his first big client.

Working from home, Mr. Seiff couldn't resist the temptation to check the progress of his portfolio all day. In the fall, his net worth was growing tens of thousands of dollars some days, a fact he pointed out in e-mails to friends.

"You were right, I made another $58,000 while I was sleeping!" he exulted in a Dec.10 e-mail to Hizam Haron. "Another dinner on me, I want to celebrate."

"Market apparently went crazy today; Scient is back at 90 from 85," he wrote in a Dec. 21 e-mail to Mr. Haron. "And everything else I've been buying went up by something like $25,000 altogether, too."

Mr. Seiff was making more in a few hours than many of his close friends earned in a year. He escorted a visiting teacher from Russia to Napa Valley, and then astounded her by dropping $2,000 on wine. He dined at the best restaurants and shocked friends with his impulse buying. "We were looking at floor cushions," recalls Mr. Haron, a San Francisco graphic designer. "I said I like them, but they were $230. He said, 'I'll take two.' . . . I couldn't believe it."

In December, Mr. Seiff landed consulting work for eBrainstorm Inc., a Miami Web-development firm focused on Latin America. The start-up's principals soon asked him to join as chief operating officer and transfer Silicon Valley operating practices to their environment. "It was a chance to take some of the things I'd learned and apply it at a much more senior level," Mr. Seiff says. The pay package didn't hurt, either: Salary in the mid-$100,000s, plus a generous expense account that included many trips back to San Francisco and housing in Miami.

Scient shares kept on rising. But Mr. Seiff's rocket ride began to worry his parents. As proud as they were of him they urged their youngest son to start selling stock. Operators of a small apparel manufacturer, Mr. Seiff's parents had personally experienced the perils of the stock market themselves, losing a bundle in the 1987 crash.

"Full of Surprises"

"We were being conservative," recalls Carolyn Seiff, who works as a commercial actress. "Those of us who have lived longer have already lived through downturns in the market, and we've also lived through sudden accident and death. We know that life is full of surprises."

But while Mr. Seiff was in Miami, Scient stock began to rocket upward at an even more explosive pace, reaching its peak at $130 a share on March 9. As a rich man, Mr. Seiff, already tired of the transcontinental commute, decided it was time to act on his idea of starting a company that would take advantage of the burgeoning interest in wireless Internet devices. His last day at eBrainstorm was April 1.

By this point, Mr. Seiff had grown convinced that Scient's shares had risen too quickly: He had already sold 10 percent of his stock last year at big gains to reinvest in other stocks, and decided to sell an additional 550 shares partly to prepare for the coming tax bite. But by studying models through carefully constructed spreadsheets in his notebook computer, Mr. Seiff realized that if he sold the bulk of his shares before April 13—a year and a day after he'd first exercised his options—he would have to pay the far higher tax rates for short-term capital gains. The would mean an additional $100,000 in taxes. Mr. Seiff would still be ahead so long as Scient's shares didn't fall far below $100 in the next two weeks. "I was gambling," he says. "wouldn't you wait two weeks for $100,000?"

Then Scient's shares went into a tailspin, skidding to the mid-60s. Mr. Seiff wasn't happy, but he had seen this before: Scient's shares had bounced down and up numerous times, often skidding 25 percent before soaring even higher. And now, numerous Internet companies that he held in high regard were also being pummeled: Sensing an opportunity, in later March Mr. Seiff had taken the money he had just gotten by selling Scient stock plus the savings he'd put away for his taxes and invested it in a variety of Internet stocks.

The result was disastrous. Instead of bouncing back, the market became even more vicious, punishing Scient and destroying his latest investments.

On April 17, the deadline to file his taxes, Mr. Seiff got out of bed and turned on his computer. Everything he had invested in had sunk to lows he didn't think possible: Scient, $130 a share just five weeks earlier, closed at $30.25. Shares of Art Technology Group Inc., an e-commerce software maker he had just invested in, slid from the $70s to $33.1875. His net worth had plummeted 78 percent, and he still owed more than $80,000 in income tax on the Scient options he had exercised.

Mr. Seiff tried to assess the damage. First he had to rebuild his spreadsheets, which hadn't been constructed to account for losses. "At the end of March, I was going home thinking I could do anything," he says. "A few weeks later, I don't have $25,000 in my bank account."

Almost overnight, his life had completely changed. For weeks, he'd been planning to get a dog, vowing to pay his landlord whatever it would take to get permission. Now, that seemed foolhardy. Plans for another European trip went out the window, too, as did brief thoughts of purchasing a home.

Moreover, executing his business idea, which he believed could take months of groundwork, would have to be put on hold. Unwilling to liquidate his holdings at their lows, Mr. Seiff told his accountant he would pay off his taxes gradually. He would have to return to his consulting business to raise the money.

It was about this time that Mr. Seiff discovered he couldn't expect solace from friends. "He was telling me that it doesn't make any sense, that everyone had gone crazy," says Geoffrey Benjamin, a recent University of San Francisco Business School graduate who worked at Mr. Seiff's consulting practice. "I paused and said that everyone was saying the same thing when the market was going up. . . . It's hard to be sympathetic because it was all fake money to begin with."

Half-Baked Home

Back home, Mr. Seiff makes mental notes of what he still needs to finish his one-bedroom apartment. The living room, its thickly painted walls illuminated mainly by an aging Victorian-style fixture, could use a wall hanging or two; the bedroom has two mattresses on the floor and little more. "This place doesn't feel like home," he says. "I never finished buying stuff."

Mr. Seiff spends many hours working there, the cords connecting his laptop computer snaking from the kitchen. The money is feast or famine—some weeks he sells $30,000 engagements, while others he spends waiting for clients' payment. Convinced the market correction was overdone, he has invested in a new set of stocks that are now rising.

Mr. Seiff's business is humming along nicely. He has completed engagements not only for big computers like Exodus and WineShopper.com, but also newer start-ups like ProductPOP, a venture that applies traditional marketing methods to online sales. He's in discussions with another consulting firm, Liquid Thinking, about joining forces on future projects.

A gradual recovery in Scient's stock and his other investments helped boost his assets recently. But then Scient's stock plummeted 20 percent on June 26 after two of its dot-com clients filed for bankruptcy. The stock has since risen slightly, to $43.75 in 4 P.M. Nasdaq Stock Market trading on Friday.

Mr. Seiff says he has learned at least one lesson: Internet workers often sacrifice too much for that ephemeral promise of getting rich quick. "When your job becomes your life, it also becomes your sense of self-worth," he writes in a recent e-mail, "and that has long-term consequences that we only think we can sidestep."

Crossing the street on a recent warm June day, Mr. Seiff recalls a thought he had while crossing a street on April 17—a thought he has had many days since—when he was dodging traffic to mail in the tax return that would help lay waste his fortune. "I felt," he says, "like God was telling me, 'I told you so.'"

Chapter 11

Developing an Ownership Culture

M ost entrepreneurs establish stock option plans for competitive reasons. Stock options are used to attract and retain key employees who might otherwise be lost to competitors or other businesses offering equity incentives.

However, some businesses also grant stock options to foster an ownership culture within the company. The idea is to get employees to think and act like owners. To achieve this objective, stock options are granted to all employees, not just to key employees.

If your objective is to establish an ownership culture within your business, granting stock options is only the first step. You must create a total environment that encourages employees to think and act like owners. Employees must believe that they have some say in management decisions. This participative management style is foreign to many entrepreneurs who view themselves as benevolent dictators.

For most entrepreneurs, creating an ownership culture is only a minor objective in creating a stock option plan. The primary objective is to stay competitive.

The following are descriptions of two companies that have allegedly created an ownership culture: Starbucks Coffee Company and Science Applications International.

EXAMPLE 1: STARBUCKS COFFEE COMPANY

In 1971, Jerry Baldwin, Zev Siegel, and Gordon Bowler founded the Starbucks Coffee Company. The original store sold whole coffee beans in Seattle's Pike Place Market—Seattle's legendary open-air farmer's market. In 1982, Howard Schultz joined the company as head of marketing. In 1983, Schultz traveled to Italy where he was impressed with the popularity of espresso bars and saw the potential to develop a similar culture in Seattle. In 1984, Schultz convinced the original founders of Starbucks to test the coffee bar concept in downtown Seattle. The coffee bar was overwhelmingly successful. In 1985, Schultz formed his own company and returned in 1987 to purchase Starbucks for $3.8 million.

In 1987, Schultz opened stores in Chicago and Vancouver, British Columbia. Schultz's vision was to open up coffee shops and retail stores all over the country, and in less than ten years, this vision has become a reality. From seventeen locations in 1987, Starbucks has grown to approximately 3,300 locations in 2000. Starbucks had an initial public offering in 1992, and its share price has exploded since that time.

From the beginning, Schultz believed that the most essential element to realizing his vision would be superior customer service, which he felt would only come from a motivated, educated, and committed staff, which Schultz referred to in *Inc.* magazine as "our only sustain-

able competitive advantage." To create a staff of this cal-
iber, he knew that employees would have to be treated
like business partners. Schultz's working-class roots rein-
forced this commitment to treating employees well. The
company has taken a variety of steps to implement this
vision.

All employees are called "partners," and all (including part-time) receive a significant benefits package. In
addition to stock ownership, this package includes
health, dental, and vision insurance, as well as career
counseling, paid vacation, and product discounts. While
many similar companies do not want to pay the extra
costs to provide benefits to part-time employees, Starbucks sees these costs as a worthwhile investment since
over two-thirds of its partners work part-time. Schultz
believes that the cost of providing part-time workers
with health benefits has more than paid for itself in pro-
ducing turnover rates that are a fraction of the industry
average.

Starbucks was the first privately held company to
offer stock options to part-time employees. The company
established a stock option plan in 1991 and a stock purchase plan in 1995. Approximately half of the employees
participate in one or both of these programs. Stock options
are available to any partner who is employed from April 1
to the end of the fiscal year, works at least 500 hours in
this period (twenty hours per week average), and is still
employed when options are distributed in January. Partners receive options based on a percentage of annual
wages. The target percentage is 10 percent, but consistently more in recent years, owing to the company's profitability. The grant price is that of the stock on the first
day of the fiscal year. There is a five-year vesting schedule
for stock options. Any partner can participate in the stock
purchase plan after working at least twenty hours per
week for ninety days. Partners can purchase stock at a 15
percent discount through a payroll deduction.

Training and Education

Starbucks has created an extensive training program that aims to cultivate the skills and knowledge of partners. Everyone hired to work in a retail capacity receives a minimum of twenty-five hours of training during their first two to four weeks with the company. These classes provide an orientation to the company and benefits plans, as well as a substantial foundation in customer service skills, coffee knowledge, and drink-making techniques. Partners who have been specially trained by the company teach the classes.

Starbucks has also developed a management training program to coach partners on leadership skills, advanced customer service, and diversity awareness, as well as succession planning and career development. Store managers are included in the management training program.

Meetings

Starbucks promotes its culture by allowing all partners to provide input and exchange ideas. Quarterly open forums, conducted by members of the senior management team, are held throughout the company. The purpose of these meetings is to update partners on developments in the company, go through the financials, and provide a chance for partners to ask questions and contribute their input on any issues.

Retail meetings occur on an ad hoc basis to discuss any concerns pertinent to all or some stores within a particular region. Again, all partners receive an open invitation to attend.

Starbucks also holds educational meetings to allow "nonretail" partners to learn about developments within the company, and partner connection groups try to get people together with similar interests and hobbies outside work. Nonretail partners are also actively encouraged to spend a few days each quarter working in either a store or roasting plant.

Other Efforts

Starbucks has also developed a process called Mission Review that allows partners and customers to voice their concerns to the company by filling out a standard card that can be found in any Starbucks location. A group of partners at the corporate offices, who are specially selected and trained for this role, responds to each issue, question, or problem. A few of the major issues are discussed at the open forums, including a description of the issues, how the company responded, what action was taken, and the results.

Starbucks has an employee newsletter that is distributed to all partners and discusses developments within the company, as well as issues relating to benefits and ownership programs.

EXAMPLE 2: SCIENCE APPLICATIONS INTERNATIONAL

Science Applications International Corporation (SAIC) is the fourth largest majority employee-owned company in the United States. SAIC was founded in 1969 as an employee-owned company by Dr. Robert Beyster. Because the management group at the large defense contractor where he previously worked was driven more by the financial interests of outside shareholders than by the important research he and other scientists were doing, Dr. Beyster decided that the ownership of his newly founded company would be placed primarily in the hands of its employees.

He began by allowing employees to purchase an amount of stock that reflected their contribution to building the company and providing quality services to their customers. Since then, the ownership system has been expanded and refined to include an array of equity compensation methods, involving most of the company's 41,000 employees. Only employees, directors, and consultants may purchase stock or receive stock bonuses or option awards. People who leave the company must offer to sell their stock back to SAIC, to assure that the company remains employee owned. SAIC now ranks as the largest employee-owned high-tech firm in the nation.

SAIC stock does not trade on any national exchange. The company's board of directors determines the fair market value of the stock with the assistance of a nationally recognized independent appraisal firm. The board uses a formula that takes into account net income, stockholders' equity, number of shares outstanding, and a market factor that is adjusted by the board to reflect the condition of the market for publicly traded securities of comparable companies. This valuation is then judged for accuracy by an independent appraiser.

Stock Ownership Plans

Whereas in most companies a few at the top get most of the rewards, at SAIC its top thirty elected officers and directors and their families hold only 3 percent of the direct ownership. This includes the stock owned by SAIC's founder and largest shareholder, Dr. Robert Beyster, who owns 1.3 percent of the company. Approximately 76 percent of the company is held by current employees through direct ownership and retirement plans. Another 20 percent is held predominately by former employees. To keep the company employee owned, SAIC's stock and retirement plans currently require employees to divest their SAIC stock upon termination in most situations.

Over 75 percent of the staff is technical, including professional engineers, computer scientists, and physical scientists. Employees own approximately 90 percent of SAIC through a stock program that incorporates various employee ownership mechanisms. Ownership is largely dispersed. While SAIC's stock program provides a minimum amount of ownership to all employees, it gives employees the opportunity to acquire significant amounts of additional stock through powerful merit and performance-based incentives. To encourage employees to accept the responsibilities and rewards of ownership, the company has established several stock acquisition methods. Employees may:

- purchase stock directly
- be awarded stock through bonuses and stock options as recognition of outstanding performance
- purchase stock through SAIC's Employee Stock Purchase Plan (ESPP) at a 10 percent discount through after-tax payroll deductions
- receive and buy shares through SAIC's qualified retirement plans (ESRP and the optional Cash or Deferred Arrangement [CODA], SAIC's 401[k] plan)

To provide liquidity for its stock while remaining privately held, SAIC has developed its own internal stock market, Bull Inc., which is a wholly owned broker-dealer subsidiary. Four times a year, Bull Inc. matches buyers and sellers of SAIC stock, enabling any shareholder to trade through this internal market. Anyone who wishes to purchase stock must receive approval from the company. Employees own the majority of the stock, and all other shareholders have a direct and significant connection to the company: directors, key consultants, immediate family members of employees, the company's retirement plans, and some former employees. Employees must sell their stock back to the company when they leave (this applies to all stock acquired by employees after October 1, 1981).

Employee Participation

SAIC encourages employees to become deeply involved in their jobs and the company, to seek information, provide and solicit input, and take responsibility and act ethically to make the company profitable. This philosophy has been firmly embedded in SAIC's culture from the very beginning. The company makes every effort to place decision making and responsibility at the lowest possible level. Realizing that not all employees can be involved in every decision, SAIC has developed a "loose/tight" management style to address this situation. The "loose" element encourages a broader cross section of employees to become involved in consensus decision making where it is feasible and practical on issues that directly affect all employees.

Formal participation occurs through approximately twenty different committees, which deal with a wide range of corporate issues. Committees with board members deal with issues such as company ethics, stock policy, and technological advances. Other committees are predominantly management oriented and promote discussion, communication, and consensus on issues such as business development, the outcome of particular projects, operational issues, financial incentives for employees, capital expenditures, technological issues, marketing strategies, and potential risk areas for the company.

A variety of committees are open to a large number of employees. The most important of these committees is the Technical Environment Committee (TEC), which monitors issues relating to the work environment and employee morale and motivation. The TEC is composed of thirty-five staff-level employees from a broad cross section of the company. Line managers in different divisions nominate employees to serve on the committee. Division managers are given the freedom to develop their own ways to choose nominees. Some divisions go through a formal, democratic process of nominating people, while in other divisions, the process is more informal. The TEC chairperson attends board of directors meetings to offer input from the committee and reports back on what is discussed and decided at board meetings. The TEC has been actively involved in the past with career development, fringe benefits, and dispute resolution procedures, among other issues.

Training and Education

SAIC conducts on-site seminars about the stock system and distributes literature explaining technical issues relating to the plans, how employees can participate in and benefit from stock ownership, as well as the corporate philosophy behind employee ownership. Throughout the year, employees receive literature that keeps them abreast of new developments, accomplishments, financials, and the activities of the committees. SAIC utilizes an intranet to permit employees to access information about the company.

CHAPTER 12

VESTING OPTIONS

O ptions should vest (i.e., become exercisable) in a manner that satisfies your business objectives. If your business objectives are to drive toward an IPO or sale, then vesting should ideally not happen prior to the IPO or sale. Even an IPO or sale should arguably not immediately vest the options.

After an IPO, you will need motivated key employees to satisfy your post-IPO projections to increase your post-IPO market price. Therefore, vesting should not begin before one year after your IPO. Since there is typically a six-month lockup period after the IPO, a one-year restriction merely extends the lockup for an additional six months.

Some companies begin partial vesting one year after the IPO but do not fully vest one year after the IPO. Some vest at the rate of 20 percent per year after the IPO and some at 50 percent per year or other rates. This is an individual decision that should be tailored to your company's culture and peculiarities.

SALE VESTING

If you sell your company for all cash, one may argue you have no reason to delay vesting beyond the sale closing dates. However, that is shortsighted. A buyer will typically want your key employees to remain after the sale, at a minimum for a reasonable transition period. That could be accomplished by having the buyer enter into employment contracts with your key employees. However, if your key employees want to leave on the sale date because their options vest, there is little that you or the buyer can do.

Therefore, the wiser course is to vest options at least three to six months (and possibly one year) after the sale closing date. This strategy provides your optionees with incentive to provide transition services for the buyer. By giving your key employees incentives to stay for this transition period, you remove a key negative factor to the sale process.

VESTING SURVEYS

The following surveys of vesting conditions were provided by the National Center for Employee Ownership. The four most common types of vesting include the following:

- *Cliff vesting*: all of an employee's options become exercisable at one time, on one date (e.g., two years from the date of grant).
- *Straight vesting*: an employee's options become exercisable at the same percentage each year (e.g., four-year vesting with 25 percent becoming vested each year at the anniversary date of the grant).

- *Step vesting*: the percentage of options exercisable each year (period) varies according to some individual formula (e.g., four-year vesting in which 40 percent vests in year 1 and 20 percent vests in each of years 2, 3, and 4).

- *Performance vesting*: an employee's options become fully exercisable when a particular corporate goal is reached (e.g., a share price target, a revenue goal, or another measurable determinant).

See tables 12.1 and 12.2 for summaries of the types of vesting and the number of years in the vesting schedule.

LEGAL ISSUES

A number of cases have involved employees whose employment was terminated shortly before their options vested. If you terminate a poorly performing employee shortly before his or her option has fully vested, you will likely be sued if the unvested option is of value. Therefore, it is recommended that you not give options to poorly performing employees.

The following is a summary of a few of these cases[1]:

Fleming v. Parametric Tech. Corp. (U.S. District Court for the Central District of California, 1977).

The defendant company Parametric, a software company headquartered in Massachusetts, claimed it fired Fleming, a California resident, for poor performance and that, in any event, it had the right to terminate the at-will employment relationship at

---

1. Reprinted with permission from the NASPP's 1999 annual conference materials.

TABLE 12.1
TYPE OF VESTING

	Management	Nonmanagement (ongoing grants)	Nonmanagement (one-time grants)	Nonmanagement (new-hire grants)
Cliff	3%	9%	47%	4%
Straight	76%	68%	21%	68%
Step	11%	13%	6%	15%
Performance	—	13%	16%	15%
Other	10%	10%	11%	11%
Total	100%	100%	100%	100%

n = 92

TABLE 12.2
NUMBER OF YEARS IN THE VESTING SCHEDULE

	Management	Nonmanagement (ongoing grants)	Nonmanagement (one-time grants)	Nonmanagement (new-hire grants)
1 year	1%	1%	19%	—
2 years	3%	3%	13%	2%
3 years	18%	12%	31%	5%
4 years	52%	59%	25%	72%
5 years	22%	22%	6%	19%
7 years	1%	1%	—	—
Average	4.08 years	4.10 years	3.19 years	4.19 years

n = 87

any time. Fleming argued that he was fired primarily because the vesting date for his in-the-money stock options was approaching and that Parametric breached its obligation to deal in good faith by depriving him of unvested stock options that had been "earned" and were nothing more than a deferred payment for past efforts. The parties agreed that Fleming's employment was at-will and governed by Massachusetts law.

Fleming received five stock option grants during his three years of employment: when he joined the company and, thereafter, when achieving quotas and major account targets. The options vested in four equal annual installments beginning one year after the date of grant. The last grant was made seven months before Parametric asked Fleming for his resignation because of poor performance. At Fleming's request, Parametric extended his termination date by over one month to permit vesting of two increments of his options. Fleming exercised all his vested stock options (about half the options granted) before his employment was terminated. The unvested portions of Fleming's options would not have been completely vested until almost $3^{1}/_{2}$ years after his termination date.

The option plan provided that "in the event that an Optionee's employment is terminated for any reason (voluntary or involuntary), each option . . . shall expire to the extent not previously exercised ten (10) days after such Optionee's employment termination." Parametric Brief on Appeal at 11. The option plan recited that its purpose was to provide "additional incentive to promote the growth, development, and financial success of the Company's business," and each option letter agreement, signed by both parties, provided that

Parametric desired "to provide Employee with an incentive to promote the business of the Company . . . and to encourage the Employee to continue employment with the Company." *Id.* The option plan recited that its operation did not confer any rights of continued employment or interfere in any way with the right of Parametric to terminate the employment of any employee.

A jury in Los Angeles awarded Fleming $1.6 million in damages, equal to his estimation of the value of the unvested options. The Ninth Circuit affirmed.

Fleming had relied on *Fortune v. National Cash Register Co.,* 373 Mass. 96, 364 N.E.2d 1251 (1977). The *"Fortune* doctrine" imposes an implied covenant of good faith and fair dealing on at-will employers that prevents an employer from depriving an employee of compensation earned for past services.

On appeal, Parametric argued unsuccessfully that a First Circuit case applying Massachusetts law, which was published after the conclusion of the trial in this matter, required reversal of the district court's judgment. In *Sargent v. Tenaska, Inc.,* 108 F.3d 5 (1st Cir. 1997), the First Circuit found that unvested future ownership interests are not recoverable as a matter of law, noting that under the *Fortune* doctrine, the Massachusetts Supreme Judicial court "has confirmed [a terminated at-will employee's] recovery to 'identifiable, future benefit[s] . . . reflective of past services.'" *Id.* at 8 (citation omitted). In its grant of summary judgment in favor of the defendant employer, the *Sargent* court reasoned that "ordinarily, a colorable *periodic* vesting schedule crudely delineates the line between past and future services." *Id.* at 9.

Knox v. Microsoft Corp.
(Washington Appellate Court, 1998)

In this case, Knox, a management employee terminated by Microsoft after nine years' employment, held stock options which provided that, if he was terminated for any reason, any unvested options would be canceled and any vested options had to be exercised within 90 days or three months. After he was terminated, Knox exercised his stock options within the required time period and Microsoft canceled his unvested options. Knox then sued Microsoft for breach of an implied employment contract arising from Microsoft's handbooks, policies and practices.

A jury in Washington rejected Microsoft's contention that Knox was an at-will employee and awarded Knox $650,000 in damages for lost earnings and benefits because of the wrongful termination. The trial court, however, had previously granted Microsoft summary judgment precluding the jury from awarding any damages for both the unvested stock options that were canceled and the forced "early exercise" of the vested options. The appellate court reversed the summary judgment and remanded the case for trial on these elements of damages. The Washington Supreme Court denied review, and the case has been remanded for a trial on the remaining damage claims.

Knox had eight separate option agreements granted at different times under Microsoft's 1981 stock option plan and 1991 stock option plan. Each agreement provided as follows:

> No Employment Right. Nothing in this option or the Plan shall confer upon Optionee any right with respect to continuation of employment with the Company, nor shall it interfere

in any way with Optionee's right or the Company's right to terminate the employment relationship at any time, with or without cause.

All but the first few option grants under the 1991 plan also contained a provision stating:

Value of Unvested Options. In consideration of the grant of this option, Optionee agrees that upon and following termination of Optionee's Continuous Status as an Employee for any reason, any unvested portion of this option shall be deemed to have a value of zero dollars.

Knox received cover letters with each stock option agreement cautioning him to read the agreements carefully:

Enclosed are copies of the [stock option plan] and the Information Statement for the Company's [stock option plan], together with two copies of the Non-Qualified Option Agreement. You should read each of these documents carefully to accept the option, sign the original copy of the Stock Option Agreement and return it.

Knox executed the agreements, all of which contained the following acknowledgment:

Acknowledgment. By Optionee's signature below, Optionee acknowledges receipt of copies of this Agreement and the Plan, and understands and agrees that this option is subject to all the terms, conditions, and restrictions stated in both this Agreement and in the Plan.

Thompson v. Sundance Publ'g.
(Massachusetts Superior Court, 1977)

Thompson was first hired as a consultant, then negotiated an employment agreement pursuant to which he would earn up to a 1.5 percent equity interest in the company over a five-year period. Thompson was fired less than one month before the first annual installment of the equity interest would have vested. He was advised that he was being terminated for economic reasons and that he could continue working as a consultant.

The lower court denied Thompson's claim that the letter of employment setting forth the five-year equity participation schedule constituted an enforceable five-year employment contract, since the letter did not set forth other essential terms of the employment agreement, specifically the length of employment.

Thompson had argued that, even if he was an at-will employee, Sundance breached the covenant of good faith and fair dealing by terminating him for the sole purpose of denying vesting of his equity participation interest.

On appeal, Thompson prevailed. The Massachusetts Superior Court applied the *"Fortune* doctrine" in finding that Thompson had stated a claim that would withstand summary judgment, since he had placed in dispute the true motivation of Sundance in terminating his employment. The court noted that, in *Fortune v. National Cash Register Co.*, 373 Mass. 96, 105, 364 N.E.2d 1251, 1257 (1997), the Massachusetts Supreme Judicial Court implied a covenant of good faith and fair dealing "to prevent overreaching by employers and the forfeiture by employees of benefits almost earned by the rendering of substantial services."

Chapter 13

Option Duration and Exercising Options

I ncentive stock options cannot have a term of more than ten years. If you own or are deemed to own (see chapter 3) more than 5 percent of the stock of your company, your incentive stock option cannot have a term of more than five years, and the option price must be at least 110 percent of the fair market value in the grant date.

The longer the term of the option, the more valuable the option. An option with a ten-year term provides a longer opportunity for the grantee to realize appreciation in the value of the stock above the option exercise price.

An incentive stock option typically terminates three months after the date employment terminates, but not later than the scheduled expiration date. If an incentive stock option permits exercise more than three months after employment termination, and if the employee in fact exercises more than three months after employment termination, the employee loses any opportunity for long-term capital gains. The option is treated as the exercise of a nonincentive stock option.

In the event of the employee's death or disability (as defined in the Internal Revenue Code), an incentive stock option typically permits the employee (or his or her estate) to exercise the option during a one-year period after the date of death or disability. Again, if the incentive stock option permits exercise more than one year after such death or disability, and the employee (or his or her estate) in fact exercises more than one year after death or disability, the benefits of an incentive stock option are lost.

Table 13.1 reflects the most recent survey from the National Association of Employee Ownership on option expiration periods for management and nonmanagement personnel.

Table 13.2 reflects the most recent survey from the National Center for Employee Ownership on option expiration periods in the event of death, disability, retirement, voluntary termination, and involuntary termination.

LEGAL CASES ON DURATION

Most stock options terminate upon termination of the employment of the optionee or within three months thereafter. The following case illustrates some of the problems in interpreting the termination of employment clauses in stock option grants.[1]

Boustany v. Monsanto Co. No. 01-97-01142-W, 1999 Tex. App. LEXIS 6146 (Tex. Ct. App. Aug 19, 1999).

This case was brought by 110 management employees of Fisher Controls International, Inc., which had

---

1. Reprinted with permission from the NASPP's 1999 annual conference materials.

Table 13.1
Expiration Periods (Time After Grant)

	Management	Nonmanagement (ongoing grants)	Nonmanagement (one-time grants)	Nonmanagement (new-hire grants)
1 year	2%	1%	11%	2%
2 years	—	—	—	—
3 years	3%	4%	16%	2%
5 years	3%	4%	16%	2%
7 years	—	—	—	—
10 years	91%	90%	68%	94%
Other	3%	5%	—	2%
Total	100%	100%	100%	100%
	$n = 90$	$n = 77$	$n = 19$	$n = 46$

TABLE 13.2
EXPIRATION PERIODS WITH SPECIAL CONSIDERATIONS: MANAGEMENT

	Death	Disability	Retirement	Voluntary Termination	Involuntary Termination
1–3 months	12%	15%	48%	68%	59%
3–6 months	20%	19%	14%	9%	11%
1 year	48%	43%	16%	2%	3%
2 years	5%	1%	1%	—	—
3 years	3%	2%	1%	—	1%
5 years	3%	2%	2%	—	—
Original term[1]	7%	15%	14%	1%	2%
Forfeit	—	—	—	16%	17%
Other	2%	2%	4%	3%	6%
Total	100%	100%	100%	100%	100%

n = 86

1. The expiration period continues according to the original term of the options.

been a wholly owned subsidiary of Monsanto. On October 1, 1992, Monsanto sold Fisher to Emerson Electric. Fisher continued as a separate corporation wholly owned by Emerson Electric. The plaintiff employees continued employment in their same positions with Fisher.

Monsanto had granted plaintiffs stock options under its stock option plans, which provided that the options were exercisable for ten years, except that, if the optionee's employment by Monsanto or its subsidiaries was terminated for any reason, unvested options were cancelled and vested options were exercisable for only three months. The options had exercise prices ranging from $44 to $57. At the time Fisher was sold in October 1992, Monsanto's stock price was $54. By August 1993, the stock was trading at $66. In June 1996, the stock was trading at $157, and thereafter was split.

Monsanto argued that its sale of Fisher had resulted in a termination of employment under the terms of its stock option plans which resulted in the cancellation of unvested options and the acceleration of the exercise deadline for vested options.

Plaintiffs argued that their rights under their stock options were unaffected by the change in ownership of Fisher, because they were still employed by Fisher, in the same management positions performing the same job tasks, and the fact that Fisher was not owned by a different group of shareholders did not alter their contractual rights as continuing employees of Fisher.

The Texas Court of Appeals, applying Delaware law, reversed the trial court's grant of summary judgment in favor of Monsanto. As a preface to reaching its decision, the court noted that, in construing the Monsanto stock option plan and letter agreements, it must "consider each part with every other part so that the effect can be determined." *Id.* at *7. The court then noted the purpose clause of the plans, which stated the plans were designed to attract and retain personnel of exceptional ability "for the Company and its Subsidiaries" and to motivate such personnel "to make a maximum contribution to Company objectives." *Id.* at *8.

Despite the references in the plan to subsidiaries of Monsanto, the court found that no "termination of employment" had occurred, even though Fisher was no longer a subsidiary of Monsanto, because the employees still remained employees of the same corporation. The court stated that "[m]indful of our duty to give words their plain meaning, we conclude no 'termination of employment' occurred here. Monsanto could have included a change-in-control-of-subsidiary provision in the documents, but it did not." *Id.* at *12. The court noted that the stock option letter agreements provided for acceleration of vesting in the event of a change in control of Monsanto and interpreted this clause to mean that the options become immediately exercisable upon a change of control and remained exercisable for their ten-year term.

It should be noted that the stock option plans contained in appendixes 1 and 2 of this book explicitly provide that if an employee is employed by a subsidiary, his or her employment is deemed terminated when the company is no longer a subsidiary.

The following case illustrates that even sophisticated public companies such as American International Group, the insurance giant, can get into trouble with oral promises of stock options.

Collins v. American International Group, Inc. No. 14365, 1998 Del. Ch. LEXIS 67 (Del Ch. Apr. 28, 1998), aff'd without op., 719 A.2d 947 (Del. 1998), reported in full, 1998 Del. LEXIS 375 (Del. Oct. 15, 1998).

In this case, Collins, an executive of American International Group, Inc. ("AIG"), had received numerous stock option grants during his 26 years of service with AIG. Collins typically waited until immediately prior to the end of an option term to exercise his options with already owned stock, so that he could use fewer appreciated shares to pay the purchase price.

The AIG stock option plan and Collins' Stock option letter agreements provided that the options would expire if not exercised within 90 days after termination of employment because of early retirement. In July 1992, Collins agreed to take early retirement at AIG's request. At that time, Collins held both vested and unvested options. One month prior to the expiration of the options' ten-year term and over one year after his termination of employment, Collins attempted to exercise all his options.

Collins presented evidence that AIG senior executives orally agreed to permit his options to vest and be exercisable through the terms of the options and that AIG had permitted other early retirees to exercise their stock options more than 90 days after their termination dates. Collins also argued that AIG knew of his past practice of delaying exercise until just before the end of an option term. Based on the credibility of the parties, the trial court found that AIG's agents had made a promise to Collins that his options would continue to vest and remain exercisable through the expiration date of the options, but that the promise was not enforceable as a contract because of a lack of consideration, since Collins had agreed to take early retirement before negotiating the terms of the options' expiration. However, relying on the equitable doctrine of promissory estoppel, the court found that justice required that Collins be allowed to exercise his options, but only to the extent the options were vested at the end of 90 days after his retirement date.

The court's finding was based on the oral promise AIG's agents made to Collins, and Collins' reliance on those promises to his detriment. The court displayed its sympathy for Collins, noting his long years of service to the company, including service in Iran at the time the Shah was deposed. The court also noted that AIG had a policy of notifying current employees of expiring options, but that it did not provide similar notification to employees who had taken early retirement. The court noted the stock plan administrator's unfortunate response to the following question posed by Collins' counsel: "once [an employee has] left AIG, you are not concerned anymore about the employee or former employee, is that correct?" The response: "Yes." *Id.* at *10.

EXERCISING STOCK OPTIONS

All option plans universally permit options to be exercised with cash (e.g., a check). Many option plans also permit options to be exercised with other stock of the company owned by the employee valued at its fair market value on the date of exercise. To avoid an accounting charge, options plans typically restrict the use of stock acquired under the same option within the past six months from being used as the exercise consideration. Options plans that permit the use of stock as the exercise consideration will also typically permit the exercise with part cash, part stock.

Most employees do not exercise their stock option until they absolutely have to. Typically, employees do not want to have their cash tied up in an investment. Therefore, most employees will want to exercise their stock options and immediately sell the option stock.

There are two common cashless methods of exercising options:

- Cashless brokerage transaction (only available to public companies)
- Using company stock as the exercise consideration, including other stock acquired under the same option (so-called "pyramiding")

In a cashless brokerage transaction, the employee sells the stock to be acquired upon option exercise before the option is actually exercised. The broker commits to the company to deliver the portion of the sale proceeds representing the option exercise price to the company on the settlement date and the company delivers the stock certificate to the broker to permit the completion of the settlement. The broker pays the company the option exercise price out of the sale proceeds and pays the balance to the employee (less a brokerage commission, of course, if the broker acted as agent).

The second cashless method of exercising options is to pay the exercise consideration with other stock of the company, including stock acquired under the same option. This method is only available if the option form specifically permits the use of stock as the exercise price.

For example, suppose the employee held an option for 1,000 shares of your stock at an exercise price of $10 per share, and the fair market value at the time of exercise was $30 per share. The employee could pay $10 to acquire one share that was worth $30. The employee could then use that one share as the exercise consideration to purchase three shares ($30 in share value acquires three shares at $10 per share). The employee could then surrender the three shares to acquire nine shares. He could then surrender nine shares to acquire twenty-seven shares. He could then surrender twenty-seven shares to acquire eighty-one shares, and so on, until the option is entirely exercised. The option "profit" in this example is $20,000 (1,000 shares multiplied by $20 spread per share). At the end of the pyramid, the employee should wind up with approximately 666 shares, each of which is worth $30.

The pyramiding method of exercise requires the employee to acquire and then surrender stock certificates repetitively. This approach involves a lot of paperwork. The IRS has provided a mechanism to avoid this paperwork, provided the employee has shares outside the option. The IRS permits the employee to attest to other shares that he or she owns outside the option as the option exercise price and then receive just the extra shares that equal the "profit" in the option.

In the foregoing example, an IRS ruling would permit the employee to attest to other shares he or she owns as the exercise price of $10,000 (333 shares at $30 per share). The company would then issue an additional 666 shares representing the option profit and not require the employee ever to deliver the designated shares to the company.

The IRS ruling assumes that there are other shares (outside the option to be exercised) that the employee owns that can be used as the exercise consideration. If not, the IRS ruling cannot be used. Instead, a cashless brokerage transaction, if available, may be more effective.

If shares used in the pyramid have not been held by the employee for more than six months, an accounting charge will be made for the pyramid. Therefore, an option form permitting the use of stock as well as cash as the exercise consideration should give the company the right to limit this form of exercise in order to prevent excessive accounting charges.

RESTRICTIONS ON OPTION EXERCISABILITY

Even if options otherwise become vested (i.e., exercisable), it is wise to insert other restrictions on option exercisability, such as the following:

- If the company is still privately held at the time of option exercise, the company should condition option exercise on the employee entering into a shareholder agreement, such as the one contained in appendix 3.

- The company should condition option exercise on shareholder approval of the option plan (if such shareholder approval was not previously obtained) or the effective date of charter amendments needed to increase the authorized shares sufficiently to permit the exercise of the option.

- The company should prevent an exercise that violates federal or state securities laws or listing requirements of stock markets in which the stock trades.

- The company should require the employee to pay any tax withholding due as a condition of exercising.

TAX EXERCISE USING CASH AS THE EXERCISE PRICE

The following are two examples of the federal income tax consequences of using cash as the exercise price of an ISO:

Example 1: One June 30, 2002, you received an ISO giving you the right to purchase 100 shares of employer stock for $10 a share. You exercised on June 2003, when the market price was $16. Your per-share basis is $10 (exercise price). You sell on

August 2, 2004, for $25 a share. The sale date is more than two years after the June 30, 2002, grant date and more than twelve months after the June 2, 2003, exercise date. Therefore, your entire $1,500 profit is treated as a long-term capital gain qualifying for the 20 percent rate.

Example 2: The facts are the same as the previous example. For 2003 AMT purposes, you reported a $600 positive adjustment (the spread on the exercise date) on Form 6251 (Alternative Minimum Tax—Individuals). Your per-share basis for AMT purposes is $16 (market value on the exercise date). When you prepare your 2004 return, you should complete IRS form 8801 (Credit for Prior Year Minimum Tax) to see whether you qualify for an AMT credit. On your 2004 Form 6251, you will report a $600 negative adjustment to account for the difference between regular tax and AMT basis in your shares, so your AMT gain will be only $900. If you have any AMT credit, you will probably be able to use it to reduce your 2004 tax. Any leftover credit gets carried over to 2005.

If the employees exercise their incentive stock options and immediately sell the stock, they have made a disqualifying disposition of their stock since they did not satisfy their one year holding period. They immediately recognized ordinary income equal to the excess of the sale price over the exercise price. However, if the sale price of the stock is greater than the fair market value on the stock on the date of exercise, the ordinary income realized is limited to spread at exercise, and the excess of the sale price over the fair market value at exercise is treated as short-term capital gain.

For example, assume that the employee in the previous example exercises her ISO on July 1, 2004, at an exercise price of $10 per share when the fair market value was $30 per share. She then sold the stock on July 2, 2004, at the price of $31 per share. The employee would be deemed to realize $20 per share as ordinary income and $1 as short-term capital gain.

However, suppose the employee sold the shares at $29 per share on July 2, 2004. The employee would only realize $19 per share in ordinary income (rather than $20 per share with a $1 per-share short-term capital loss).

TAXATION OF STOCK-FOR-STOCK EXERCISES

The following is a discussion of the federal income tax consequences of using company stock to exercise stock options:

Exercise of Non-ISOs

When shares are delivered to pay the exercise price of a non-ISO (either by physical delivery or by attestation), the "disposition" of the shares is generally not a taxable event. Instead, it is treated by the IRS as a like-kind exchange, with the shares delivered to exercise the option (or the shares constructively delivered through attestation) retaining their original cost basis and holding period. The new shares representing the spread would have a basis equal to the market price at exercise (because the executive has been taxed based on that price). The holding period of the new shares for capital gain purposes begins on the option exercise date.

Exercise of ISOs

The delivery of shares to pay the exercise price of an ISO is also generally treated as a like-kind exchange (with the old shares retaining their cost basis and capital gain holding period, and the new shares having a zero basis and a new holding period), unless the shares delivered are "immature ISO shares" (i.e., shares previously received upon exercise of an ISO that have not satisfied the ISO holding periods).

Watch Out for Disqualifying Dispositions When Using ISO Stock to Exercise ISOs

Where immature ISO shares are delivered to exercise an ISO, there would be a disqualifying disposition of the delivered shares. However, there would be no disqualifying disposition where immature ISO shares are delivered to exercise a non-ISO. (Note that, whether ISO or non-ISO shares are used to exercise an ISO, all shares received upon exercise are new ISO shares for ISO holding period purposes.)

To illustrate the foregoing point, consider these examples:

1. Non-ISO Exercise Using Immature ISO Stock. On June 1, 2001, an executive exercises an ISO to purchase 100 shares of company stock. On December 31, 2001, the executive delivers (by actual delivery or certification) the 100 immature ISO shares to exercise an non-ISO for 150 shares. There is no disqualifying disposition, but 100 of the 150 shares now owned by the executive retain the status of the immature ISO shares purchased June 1, 2001 (old basis, old holding period).

2. ISO Exercise Using Immature ISO Stock. If, instead, the executive uses the 100 June 1, 2001, immature ISO shares to exercise an ISO for 150 shares on December 31, 2001, there is a disqualifying disposition of the 100 ISO shares, and all

150 shares received on December 31, 2001 (even where attestation is used), are new ISO shares with a new ISO holding period beginning on December 31, 2001).

3. ISO Exercise Using Mature ISO Stock. If the employee exercises the 150-share ISO on December 3, 2001, using 100 mature ISO shares (or shares purchased in the open market or non-ISO shares), no income is recognized on the delivery of the previously owned 100 shares (because there is no disqualifying disposition), and no capital gain is recognized; the old 100 shares retain their old basis and capital gain holding period, but all 150 shares take on a new ISO holding period beginning December 31, 2001.

The federal income tax basis and holding periods for the acquired shares are more fully discussed in question 31 of chapter 10.

Chapter 14

Transferable Stock Options and Underwater Stock Options[1]

O ptions that are transferable during your lifetime are a useful device to transfer wealth and minimize federal death taxes, which can be as high as 55 to 60 percent. However, option transfers should be considered only if you have more than sufficient wealth for yourself and your spouse apart from the options. If that is not the case, skip this section.

Since ISOs must by law be nontransferable during your lifetime, an option that is transferable during your lifetime would be a non-ISO. Thus, upon exercise by your transferee (e.g., your child), the exercise will result in ordinary income in the amount of the excess of the fair market value of stock over the option exercise price. This taxable income must be recognized by the donor, namely you.

1. Coauthored with Robert Broder, Philadelphia Office, Blank Rome Comisky & McCauley LLP.

If you transfer a transferable option, you will have to pay federal income taxes on the option exercise by your transferee. Since the amount of these taxes are not determinable at the time of the transfer, only at the time of exercise, you had better be certain that you have sufficient wealth so that even after paying a large amount of income tax, you have sufficient wealth left for yourself and your spouse for your lifetime.

Consequently, transferable options should only be considered by very wealthy business owners and very wealthy key employees. However, if you do qualify, recent private letter rulings by the IRS and recent SEC amendments to registration Form S-8 have facilitated the transfer of options if permitted by the option plan.

Tax Advantages and Consequences

The transfer of nonqualified stock options to family members (or trusts benefiting them) can achieve three significant tax advantages:

- Option appreciation in value is transferred to the donees for federal death tax purposes (but not for federal income tax purposes).
- Gift taxes on the transfers are minimized because of the valuation of the option.
- The family member or trusts further benefit when the transferor pays the income tax resulting from the exercise of the option.

Let's take a closer look at each of the fundamental tax consequences that result from the transfers of an option:

- *No income tax consequences upon making options transferable or actual transfer.* The IRS has determined that making non-ISOs transferable to family members (or trusts benefiting them) does not make the options transferable for purposes of determining whether they have a "readily ascertainable fair market value" on which income tax should be paid. In addition, there is no income taxable event at the time of a actual transfer.

- *Income recognized by optionee at exercise.* When the family member or trust ultimately exercises the option, the amount by which the fair market value of the shares on the date of exercise exceeds the option exercise price (i.e., the "spread") will generally be taxable to the transferor as compensation income. It is generally accepted that the payment of the income tax by the transferor is not a gift to the family member or trust.

- *Basis of stock for transferee.* Upon exercise, the family member or trust obtains a tax basis for the stock equal to the exercise price paid plus the amount taxed as ordinary income to the transferor. In effect, the tax basis for computing gain or loss equals the fair market value of the stock on the donee's date of exercise.

- *Valuation of the gift.* Although there are no federal income tax consequences upon transfer to a family member or trust, the transfer will constitute a "gift" for federal gift tax purposes. *Caution:* If options are transferred before they vest, the gift tax consequences of making the transfer will be unknown by the transferor, and could result in a significant gift if the stock price undergoes substantial appreciation before the date of full vesting.

Assuming that (1) the options are exercisable (i.e., vested) at the time of transfer, (2) the donee may subsequently exercise the option at his or her discretion, and (3) the transferor retains no interest or reversion in the options or the underlying stock, neither the options nor the underlying shares should be included in the estate of the transferor.

The income recognized by the transferor as compensation will generally be deductible for federal income tax purposes by the employer, subject to the limitations of Section 162 of the Internal Revenue Code, and this deduction is not affected by the option transfer.

Registration of Transferable Options Under the Securities Act of 1933

Most companies register their stock-based plans under the Securities Act of 1933 on Form S-8. In the hands of most people (other than control persons or other "affiliates" of the issuer), shares that were acquired from the company pursuant to an effective registration statement may be freely resold. Absent such registration, however, the shares acquired upon exercise of the options would be subject to certain limitations on resale under the federal securities laws (see the discussion of SEC Rule 701 in chapter 17).

Effective April 7, 1999, the SEC amended Form S-8 to make it available for the exercise of employee benefit plan options by an employee's family member who acquired the options from the employee through a gift or domestic relations order. The two essential criteria to preserve Form S-8 registration of the issuance of shares upon exercise of the options are:

- The transfer is to a "family member."
- Such transfer is made through a gift or domestic relations order.

The term *family member* is defined to include "any child, stepchild, grandchild, parent, stepparent, grandparent, spouse, former spouse, sibling, niece, nephew, mother-in-law, father-in-law, son-in-law, daughter-in-law, brother-in-law, or sister-in-law, including adoptive relationships, any person sharing the employee's household (other than a tenant or employee), a trust in which these persons have more than 50 percent beneficial interest, a foundation in which these persons (or the employee) control the management of the assets, and any other entity in which these persons (or the employee) own more than 50 percent of the voting interest."

Form S-8 requires an issuer to deliver to each plan participant a plan prospectus containing "material information regarding the plan and its operations that will enable participants to make an informed decision regarding investment in the plan." The SEC has expressed its view that such "material information" should include a discussion of the material estate and gift tax consequences to the employee/transferor of an option transfer, if the Form S-8 relates to an employee benefit plan that permits the transfer of options granted thereunder.

The company is required to deliver an updated plan prospectus to the family member or trust at or before their exercise of the option, as well as all shareholder communications and other reports furnished to shareholders on a continuing basis that the family member or trust does not otherwise receive. This places an administrative burden on the company that is entirely dependent on the transferor's reporting the actual transfer to the issuer. Accordingly, the company should require employees to promptly report any transfer of their options by including such a reporting requirement in the stock option.

UNDERWATER STOCK OPTIONS

Underwater stock options refers to options containing an exercise price that is substantially higher than the current fair market value of the stock. This is a typical problem for public companies whose stock prices are more volatile than the fair market value of the stock of private companies. However, even private companies can suffer from underwater options if they suffer from reverses in revenues, profits, or industry prospects.

The volatility of the stock price of public companies has been increased as a result of three phenomena:

- Momentum investing, typically as a result of day traders, and the reverse process when the momentum disappears
- The tendency of the markets to punish companies who miss earnings targets
- Fads and fashions (e.g., the euphoria over Internet stocks selling to consumers, followed by the unreasonably negative views of this same industry)

When options go underwater, whatever exhilarating emotion the employee enjoyed on receiving the stock is converted into a depression. This is particularly true if a significant portion of the employee's total compensation is composed of options.

Employees are particularly disturbed when the company is doing well financially, but the financial performance is not reflected in the stock price. This may be due to a stock market phenomenon beyond the employee's control, such as a change in price earnings multiples for the entire industry.

When options are underwater and the depressed market price is expected to last indefinitely, key employees may start sending out résumés. Companies may be forced to develop alternative cash incentive plans or other incentives not tied to the stock price.

Many companies would prefer not to develop alternative cash incentive plans for two reasons:

- Any cash incentive plan will reduce accounting earnings, versus a properly structured option plan that does not affect accounting earnings.

- Cash incentives may use up cash that is needed to operate and grow the business.

Accordingly, companies with underwater options tend to favor repricing their existing stock options. However, FASB Interpretation 44 has made it clear that repricing underwater options will cause a charge to earnings.

In addition, any repricing of underwater options will incur the wrath of shareholders. Shareholders believe that if their stock valuations are depressed, the key employees of the company should suffer along with them. Misery loves company.

Enlightened shareholders should recognize the depressed market prices may not be the result of poor company performance. In addition, it is not in the shareholders' interest to have the company lose important executives because of underwater options.

According to an article on repricing stock options in the July 2000 issue of *Treasury and Risk Management,* "the earnings pain is worth the employee retention gain." Companies that have repriced underwater options include Netscape Communications, Oracle, 3Com, Barnesandnoble.com, Seagate Technology, and many others. According to the National Center for Employee Ownership, 36 percent of public companies with broad-based stock option plans lowered option exercise prices between 1994 and 1997.

Methods of Repricing Options

There is no single method for handling underwater options. Some of the methods used to deal with underwater options are as follows:

- If the company makes annual option grants, accelerate the grant date for the new options (with the lower option prices) and/or increase the size of the new grant.

- Exchange underwater options for new options containing a longer vesting schedule than the underwater options or other provisions more favorable to the company.

- Exchange underwater ISOs for non-ISOs, to give the company a guaranteed tax deduction upon exercise.

- If underwater options are about to expire, extend the option term for an additional period (e.g., ten years), but keep the same or higher option price as the underwater options.

- Exchange underwater options for a smaller number of lower-priced options.

- Have the executive forego a cash bonus in consideration of a lower-priced option.

- Grant new options in tandem with underwater options, with exercise of the new options canceling a proportionate number of shares of the underwater options.

- Grant new options in exchange for underwater options, and insert golden handcuff provisions in the new options, such as anticompetitive and trade secret forfeiture provisions.

Iomega Corp., a manufacturer of computer zip drives, suffering from underwater options, developed a plan in 2000 to exchange underwater options for new option grants with a lower option price. The exchange included a tiered approach so the employees had to turn in from 1.5 to 2.5 of their old options for one of the repriced options. Iomega also sought shareholder approval for the exchange. However, they were unsuccessful in avoiding an accounting charge under FASB Interpretation 44 as a result of the exchange.

Under Section 424(h) of the Internal Revenue Code, reducing the price of an ISO is deemed to be the granting of a new option. Since the new option has a reduced option exercise price below the fair market value of the stock on the original grant date, the option is thereafter considered to be a non-ISO.

Accelerating the exercisability of an ISO will *not* disqualify the option from ISO treatment for tax purposes.

The SEC staff may view an option exchange offer as a tender offer subject to complex tender offer rules, particularly if the option exchange offer is made to a sizeable group of optionees.

CHAPTER 15

LIMITED LIABILITY COMPANIES AND LIMITED PARTNERSHIPS[1]

Many businesses are organized as limited partnerships or, more recently, limited liability companies (LLCs). These noncorporate entities are treated as partnerships for federal income tax purposes; therefore, the income or losses of the entities flow through to the owners and are not subject to income tax at the entity level. Flow-through entities that are taxed as partnerships provide greater flexibility to the entrepreneur than either Subchapter S or Subchapter C corporations. However, flow-through entities taxed as partnerships have two major tax disadvantages:

- Only a corporation can establish an incentive stock option (ISO) plan; therefore, entities taxed as partnerships do not qualify for ISOs.

- Only a corporation can engage in a tax-free merger or similar tax-free reorganization with another cor-

---

1. Coauthored with Harry Lamb, Philadelphia Office, Blank Rome Comisky & McCauley LLP.

poration; therefore, entities taxed as a partnership cannot be acquired by a corporation in a tax-free reorganization.

There are additional differences between corporations and entities taxed as partnerships when it comes to using equity interests in the entity to compensate service providers. Since LLCs are becoming increasingly common as the preferred form of noncorporate business entity (except where the entity operates in a state that imposes entity-level taxes on LLCs), the balance of this discussion will focus on the equity compensation rules applicable to LLCs and the comparable rules applicable to corporations. However, keep in mind that the federal income tax rules applicable to LLCs apply equally to general and limited partnerships.

A share of stock of a corporation represents two distinct economic interests: a share of the capital (i.e., assets) and a share of the profits of the business. Generally, it is not possible to separate the capital and profits interests inherent in each share of stock. That is, a share of stock carries a proportionate share of both the capital and profits in the corporation. In contrast, an interest in an LLC can carry either both a share of the capital and profits or just a share of the profits.

Although an LLC cannot establish an ISO, it can provide a so-called "profits interest" to service providers. A profits interest gives the owner of the interest a percentage share of the profits of the business, including a share in the appreciation in the value of the business that is considered part of the "profits" when the business is sold, but does not give the owner an immediate interest in the capital of the business. Rather, the entrepreneur or other owners of the LLC hold all of the interests in the capital of the business, plus all of the profits except for the profits interest that is awarded to the service providers.

The IRS has conceded that it will not treat the receipt of a profits interest in an LLC as a currently taxable event to the recipient or the company. In contrast, the receipt of stock of a corporation in exchange for services pursuant to a stock bonus plan or exercise of a non-ISO results in the recognition of taxable ordinary compensation income to the recipient equal to the fair market value of the stock in excess of the amount paid for the stock by the recipient. If the stock is "vested" when received, the taxable income is recognized immediately. If the stock is not vested and the recipient does not make a timely election under Section 83(b) of the Internal Revenue Code to treat the stock as vested for tax purposes, the tax on the stock is deferred until the stock vests. However, when the stock does vest, the amount included as taxable ordinary compensation income is based on the fair market value of the stock at that time (which is presumably higher than the value when the stock was transferred).

One technique to avoid the ordinary income problem is the incentive stock option plan discussed previously in this book. Since an ISO must have an exercise price equal to at least the fair market value of the stock on the date the option is granted, the ISO essentially represents a right to participate in future appreciation in value, but to do so generally at long-term capital gain rates. As discussed later, this is similar to the effect of receiving a profits interest in an LLC. Unfortunately, ISOs have certain disadvantages compared to profits interests in LLCs. For example, upon exercise of an ISO, the employee may have to pay alternative minimum tax. In addition, Section 422(d) of the Internal Revenue Code may limit the number of option shares with respect to which long-term capital gains are achievable under an ISO (i.e., $100,000 per year of exercise price, based on the date the options can first be exercised). See chapter 3.

Neither of these disadvantages are present when an individual receives an interest in an LLC for services. Generally, if the owner of the interest holds the interest for more than one year, gain on the sale of the interest is taxed as long-term capital gain, except with respect to ordinary income attributable to certain "hot assets" under complex tax rules. If the LLC sells the business, presumably a substantial portion of the gain on the sale will be long-term capital gain (or, more accurately, "Section 1231 gain," which is essentially the same thing), and the holder of the interest will be taxed at long-term capital gain rates on his or her share of that gain.

As noted earlier, the receipt of a profits interest in an LLC has an additional tax advantage because there is no current income recognition from receipt of the interest. However, the receipt of a capital interest in an LLC for services is taxable to the extent of the fair market value of the interest at the time it vests, much like the treatment of corporate stock described earlier. As might be expected, there are economic as well as tax differences between the receipt of a profits or capital interest. Therefore, it is essential to understand these differences and compare the tax advantages of a profits interest to the economic cost of taking a profit rather than a capital interest.

For example, assume A and B are the current equal owners of AB, LLC. The assets of AB, LLC were purchased for $100,000, and now have a fair market value of $500,000. AB, LLC has no liabilities. A and B want to give C a 5 percent interest in AB, LLC for services that C provided to AB, LLC. But do they mean a 5 percent capital interest or a 5 percent profits interest? The key to distinguishing between the two is to do a hypothetical liquidation analysis: who would get what if, immediately after the grant of the interest to C, the AB, LLC sold all of its assets for their fair market value and distributed the net proceeds in liquidation? If A and B would receive the entire $500,000 proceeds, then C has only a profits interest—that is, the right to receive 5 percent of only future income and appreciation in the value of the assets. C would not have to pay any tax on receipt of the profits interest. However, if C would receive $25,000 (i.e., 5 percent of the $500,000 value), and A and B would receive $237,500 each, C has a capital interest and would have to pay tax on the fair market value of that interest.

There are two points to keep in mind when comparing these two alternatives. The most obvious is that the favorable tax treatment from receipt of a profits interest came at the cost of giving up a share of the current value of the assets of AB, LLC. Of course, that may be precisely what was intended by A and B; the $400,000 of appreciation in the assets represents "profit" to A and B, but is not a "profits interest" as to C, and A and B may have had no desire to give C a share of that appreciation.

Second, the fair market value of the assets is essential to the determination of whether the interest is a profits or capital interest. If the IRS subsequently determined that the assets had a fair market value of $800,000 at the time of the award of the 5 percent interest to C, the amount that C would receive on a hypothetical immediate liquidation of AB, LLC would be $15,000 (5 percent of the $300,000 appreciation above the $500,000 that would be distributed entirely to A and B). Such a redetermination of value would indicate that C had in fact received a capital interest subject to immediate tax at its fair market value. However, the amount subject to tax would not necessarily be the $15,000 liquidation value. The liquidation analysis is done only to determine whether the interest is a capital or profits interest. Once the liquidation analysis establishes that the interest is a capital interest, the amount subject to tax is the fair market value of the interest, which is the price a willing, informed buyer would pay a willing, informed seller to purchase the interest. Thus, the fair market value of C's interest could be more or less than the liquidation value, taking into account factors such as whether the interest is marketable or carries an ability to control the LLC.

Certain other requirements must be satisfied for the IRS to treat an interest as a profits interest; for example, the IRS requires the interest be held for at least two years to be treated as a profits interest. Also, careful drafting of the LLC agreement is essential to assure that both the economic and tax objectives of the parties are achieved.

Other factors are often overlooked when awarding a profits interest. For example, an owner of an interest in an LLC is not an "employee" of the LLC for tax purposes and therefore is not entitled to certain tax-free fringe benefits. Furthermore, the owner's share of income of the LLC, including fixed payments that may have been salary prior to the receipt of the interest in the LLC, is now self-employment income, subject to self-employment tax and estimated tax payments rather than the withholding requirements applicable to salary and wages. Many individuals who are economically sophisticated nevertheless may not be aware of all of the economic, tax, and administrative implications of owning an interest in an LLC. The subject is extremely complex and requires the assistance of an experienced tax lawyer.

An example of an LLC operating agreement that awards profits interests is contained in appendix 3. The B, C, and D units referred to in appendix 3 were awarded to different classes of employees and other service providers, with each having a different profits percentage. The value of these units depends on the return on invested capital to the holders of the Class A units, who were the original investors. If the holders of the B, C, or D units terminated their services for the LLC, the LLC obtains repurchase rights, with the repurchase price increasing the longer the service was provided.

CHAPTER 16

ACCOUNTING FOR STOCK OPTIONS

Stock options and tax-qualified stock purchase plans are the only forms of compensation that are capable of avoiding an accounting charge. To avoid an accounting charge, stock options must satisfy the requirements of Accounting Principles Board Opinion No. 25 for a fixed plan on the grant date and FASB Interpretation 44, which are discussed later in this chapter.

If you have no great interest in either the accounting for stock options or securities law issues, skip this chapter and chapter 17 and start with chapter 18, which deals with stock bonus plans.

ACCOUNTING BACKGROUND

Generally accepted accounting principles for stock-based awards to employees are contained in two primary accounting standards: APB 25 and Statement of Financial Accounting Standards No. 123, *Accounting for Stock-Based Compensation* (Statement 123). In addition, numerous interpretations, technical bulletins, and Emerging Issues Task Force (EITF) consensuses address the accounting for specific stock compensation transactions or particular provisions that may exist in certain stock-based awards (e.g., settlement methods, reload options). FASB Interpretation 44, effective July 1, 2000, is discussed later in this chapter and supersedes many of these interpretations.

Corporations have a choice of measuring expense for stock-based awards using either APB 25 (i.e., the "intrinsic value" method) or Statement 123 (i.e., the fair value method). Most corporations continue to follow the APB 25 accounting rules for recognition purposes and provide pro forma financial statement footnote disclosures of what net income and earnings per share would have been had Statement 123's fair value method been used. Alternatively, Statement 123 encourages, but does not require, corporations to recognize expense for stock-based awards based on their "fair value" on the date of grant. This chapter primarily discusses the general concepts associated with APB 25 and provides only an overview of Statement 123.

Table 16.1 gives an overview of selected major differences between Statement 123 and APB 25.

APB 25

When applying APB 25, compensation expense is measured by the "intrinsic value" method. Under this method, compensation expense is determined on the measurement date—that is, the first date on which both the number of shares the employee is entitled to receive and the

TABLE 16.1
OVERVIEW OF SELECTED MAJOR DIFFERENCES BETWEEN SFAS 123 AND APB OPINION 25[1]

	SFAS 123	APB Opinion 25
Fixed stock options		
Measurement date	At date of grant	At date of grant
Compensation cost	Fair value at grant date using option pricing model	Any excess of market price over exercise price
Performance-based stock options		
Measurement date	At date of grant	When the number of shares issuable and exercise price are known
Compensation cost	Fair value at grant date using option pricing model	Any excess of market price over exercise price at measurement date
Employee stock purchase plans (broad-based plans)		
Measurement date	At date of grant	At date of grant
Compensation cost	Discount from market price, unless discount is reasonable (usually 5 percent)	Discount from market price, unless discount is 15 percent or less

Under SFAS 128, basic earnings per share does not include option dilution. Option dilution is included in computing diluted earnings per share.

---

1. Reprinted with permission of BDO Seidman LLP.

exercise price, if any, are known. Compensation expense, if any, is measured based on the award's intrinsic value (i.e., the excess of the market price of the stock over the exercise price on the measurement date).

When the measurement date occurs on the date of grant or award date, the plan is a *fixed* plan because the compensation expense, if any, is determinable on that date (i.e., "fixed") and not subsequently adjusted. Often, the compensation expense associated with fixed stock option awards is zero because the exercise price is set equal to the market price of the underlying stock (i.e., intrinsic value is zero). By contrast, the measurement date for plans with *variable* terms does not occur until sometime after the grant date. Under variable plans, either the number of shares the employee is entitled to receive or the exercise price is unknown at the grant date. Frequently, variable plans contain performance targets or contingencies that affect the terms of the award. For example, the number of options that the employee ultimately receives may depend on the attainment of financial measures, such as earnings per share or sales. Compensation expense related to variable awards is measured using the stock price on the date the number of shares and the exercise price are known.

Accruing Compensation for Services

Compensation expense in stock options, purchase, and award plan should be recognized as expense in one or more periods in which an employee performs services (past or future). The basic principle is that stock awards are being made in exchange for employee services. Therefore, the compensation expense associated with the award should be recorded as services are rendered. The award may specify the period or periods of employee service, or the period or periods may be inferred from the terms or from the past pattern of awards. Any portion of measured compensation that applies to services yet to be performed should be recognized in future periods. Normally, the period to recognize compensation expense should not exceed the vesting period or other period in which restrictions are imposed. When there is no evidence to support whether the award is for the current or future services, it should be presumed that the award is for service in the period granted or in prior periods.

Fixed Plans

The defining characteristic of a fixed plan is that the terms (i.e., number of shares and exercise price) are fixed. Said another way, at the date of grant or award, both the number of shares of stock that may be acquired by or awarded to an employee and the cash, if any, to be paid by the employee are known. The measurement date is the grant date for fixed plans because the number of shares and price per share are known and "fixed" at that date. Compensation expense is measured by the difference between the quoted market price of the stock at the grant date and the price, if any, to be paid by an employee. When a fixed option is granted at an exercise price equal to the quoted market price of the stock on the grant date, no compensation is recognized. For example, assume a public corporation grants options to employees to purchase 900,000 shares for $10 a share. The market price of the corporation's stock on the date of the grant is $10. If the option in this example is fixed, no compensation expense is recognized because the intrinsic value is zero.

In some cases, the exercise price of stock options is set at a discount from fair market value, which results in compensation expense under APB 25 for the aggregate discount, amortized over the vesting period. The amortization of compensation expense over the service period should be recognized on a straight-line basis or some other systematic or rational basis over the service period.

The following example illustrates the computation of compensation expense for the grant of a fixed-discount stock option.

Background Information

Date of grant: January 1, 2000

Expiration date: December 31, 2009

Number of options granted: 50,000

Exercise price: $5 per share

Quoted market price at date of grant: $8 per share

The options become exercisable five years from the date of grant based solely on the employee's continued employment. If the employment terminates prior to the end of 2004, the entire stock option award is canceled.

Measurement Date on the Grant Date

Market price	$ 8
Exercise price	5
Compensation expense per option	$ 3
Number of options granted	50,000
Compensation expense	$150,000

The measurement date for this arrangement is the grant date because both the number of options and the price per option are known at that date. The "fixed" compensation expense of $150,000 is recognized in a systematic and rational manner over the five-year service period. In this example, a straight-line expense allocation of $30,000 per year is a common method used to record the expense.

Variable Plans

When the number of shares of stock that may be acquired by or awarded to an employee or the price to be paid by the employee, or both, are not determinable until after the grant date, the arrangement is referred to as a *variable plan*. A common variable award is a stock appreciation right. A stock appreciation right entitles an employee to receive cash, stock, or a combination of cash and stock in an amount equivalent to any excess of the market value of a specific number of shares of the corporation's stock over a stated price. The indeterminate factors usually depend on events that are not specified or determinable at the grant date. When variable plan awards are granted, compensation is measured as the amount by which the quoted market price of the corporation's stock exceeds the amount, if any, to be paid by an employee at the measurement date. However, with a variable plan, the measurement date is not the grant date. Therefore, changes (either increases or decreases) in the quoted market price of the stock between the grant date and the measurement date result in a change in the measure of compensation for the right or award. With a variable plan, estimates of compensation expense are recorded before the measurement date based on the quoted market price of the stock at intervening dates. The estimated compensation may fluctuate because of changes in the quoted market price of the stock. Therefore, the accounting for a variable plan requires the recomputation of estimated compensation expense until the measurement date. FASB Interpretation No. 28, *Accounting for Stock Appreciation Rights and Other Variable Stock Option or Award Plans* (FIN 28), discusses how to account for and measure compensation associated with variable plan awards. Compensation is recognized as expense over the period the employee performs related services.

The following example illustrates the annual computation of compensation expense for a stock appreciation right (i.e., a variable award) that vests 100 percent at the end of year 4.

Background Information

Date of grant: January 1, 2000

Expiration date: December 31, 2009

Vesting date: 100 percent of grant at the end of 2003

Number of shares: 1,000

Exercise price: $25 per share

Quoted market price at date of grant: $25 per share

Market price per share assumptions (at December 31 of subsequent years):

- 2000—$26
- 2001—$27
- 2002—$30
- 2003—$29

Date	Market Price	Intrinsic Value Per Share	Aggregate Compensation
12/31/00	$26	$1	$1,000
12/31/01	$27	$2	$2,000
12/31/02	$30	$5	$5,000
12/31/03	$29	$4	$4,000

Date	Percentage Accrued	Compensation Accrued to Date	Compensation Expense
12/31/00	25%	$ 250	$ 250
12/31/01	50%	$1,000	$ 750
12/31/02	75%	$3,750	$2,750
12/31/03	100%	$4,000	$ 250

On December 31, 2003, the employee exercises the right to receive share appreciation for the 1,000 shares. Because of the effect of market price changes, a corporation possibly could have negative compensation expense (i.e., income) in reporting periods other than the first reporting period. However, a corporation is never allowed to report a cumulative amount of compensation as a negative amount.

Accruing compensation expense may require estimates, and adjustments of those estimates in later periods may be necessary in accordance with APB Opinion No. 20, *Accounting Changes*.

Factors Affecting the Determination of the Measurement Date

A careful analysis of the specific terms of a stock compensation plan and each individual grant is necessary under APB 25 to determine whether it should be accounted for as variable or fixed. However, as a general rule, any features of a plan that could result in the exercise price or number of shares changing, either directly or indirectly, are indicators that the plan is variable. Following are some of the more common provisions that can lead to the ultimate measurement date occurring subsequent to the grant date:

- An exercise price that changes based on time or performance-related criteria
- A variable number of shares being issued upon option exercise, such as a greater number of shares if performance goals are met
- Dividend equivalents that convert to extra shares upon option exercise
- Stock price targets whereby the award vests only if the stock price reaches certain levels
- Stock option plans having a cash bonus feature to reimburse employees for the tax payable on the

taxable income resulting from the exercise of a nonqualified option

- The repurchase of stock acquired by an employee under a stock compensation award. In practice, a repurchase of shares within six months of an employee's exercise of a stock option would result in a new measurement date
- Exercise of a stock option by exchanging shares not held long enough to satisfy the six-month accounting holding period requirement, rather than cash for the exercise price
- Certain nonrecourse employer stock loans
- Extension of the length of the option period beyond that included in the original plan agreement, such as upon retirement or termination
- Grants that are subject to stockholder approval, but stockholder approval is uncertain
- Accelerating vesting provisions to give an employee an award he or she otherwise would have lost

Because of the complex and subjective judgments often required in accounting for stock compensation arrangements and the negative consequences of unintentionally establishing a variable plan, new plans or amendments to existing plans (including provisions that affect stock option arrangements that are included in employment agreements) should be considered carefully prior to their implementation.

Accounting for Income Tax Benefits

The tax effects of stock-based awards are generally recognized for financial reporting purposes only if such awards are structured to result in deductions on the corporation's income tax return. For example, a corporation generally receives a tax deduction for a non-ISO in an amount equal to the excess of the market price of the stock on the date of exercise over the exercise price (i.e., the intrinsic value). For tax-deductible stock-based awards, compensation expense (if any) is recognized in the financial statements in different amounts and in different periods than when the actual tax deduction is taken. Therefore, if stock compensation expense is recognized in a tax return in a period different from the one in which stock compensation expense is recognized for financial statement purposes, deferred tax assets are also recognized.

However, when a deduction is taken in the tax return for stock compensation, but stock compensation expense has not been and will never be recorded for financial statement purposes (or the compensation expense recognized is a lesser amount than the ultimate tax deduction), the excess deduction should be reflected as an increase to additional paid-in capital and not as reduction of income tax expense. If the tax deduction is less than total stock compensation expense for financial statement purposes, the corporation may deduct the difference from additional paid-in capital to the extent that tax reductions under the same or similar stock compensation plans have been included in additional paid-in capital.

STATEMENT 123 OVERVIEW

Statement 123 was intended to address what the FASB considered to be inconsistencies and inaccuracies embodied in the existing accounting literature (i.e., APB 25 and related interpretations), particularly for stock options. To determine how to account for a stock-based award, Statement 123 requires corporations to distinguish between awards of equity instruments and those under which the corporation incurs a liability to the employee in an amount based on the price of the company's stock. Equity instruments include awards such as outright grants of shares, nonvested stock, stock options, and stock appreciation rights payable in shares. Awards treated as liabilities include those that the corporation is obligated to settle in cash, such as stock appreciation rights payable in cash.

Corporations that decide to adopt the fair value method for accounting purposes will recognize compensation expense for virtually all options based on their fair value on the date of grant. The fair value of options granted by public corporations is estimated using complex option-pricing models (e.g., the Black-Scholes or binomial model). Nonpublic corporations are permitted to use a simpler method known as the "minimum value" method. Corporations that elect to remain under APB 25 are, in effect, required to maintain two sets of accounting records—one following APB 25's intrinsic value method for recognition purposes, and another following Statement 123's fair value method for footnote disclosure purposes.

Table 16.2 illustrates the compensation costs computation under Statement 123.

TABLE 16.2
ILLUSTRATION OF COMPENSATION COST COMPUTATION[1]

Assume the following facts:

Fixed options granted: 10,000

Vesting: 100 percent at the end of 3 years

Stock price: $25

Exercise price: $25

Expected life of options: 6 years

Using the last three items as inputs as well as the risk-free interest rate, expected volatility and expected dividend yield, assume the Black-Scholes option-pricing model produces a fair value of $8.50 each option.

---

1. Reprinted with permission of BDO Seidman LLP.

TABLE 16.2 *(continued)*

Based on historical employee turnover rates and expectations about the future, forfeitures are expected to be about 3 percent per year. Based on that estimate, total compensation cost (or total award value) over the three-year vesting period is $77,577 (10,000 × [0.97 × 0.97 × 0.97] × $8.50), and the annual expense is $25,859 ($77,577 ÷ 3 [the vesting period]).

Assume that in year 2 management now concludes that the rate of forfeiture is likely to average 6 percent per year over the three-year vesting period. The total compensation cost that should be recognized during the three-year period and the related annual expense would change as follows:

Revised total award value: $70,600 (10,000 × [0.94 × 0.94 × 0.94] × $8.50)

Revised annual expense: $23,533 ($70,600 ÷ 3)

The expense for years 2 and 3 would be computed as follows:

Year 2

Cumulative expense for years 1 and 2	$47,066 ($23,533 × 2)
Expense recognized in year 1	$25,859
Total year 2 expense	$21,207

Year 3

Cumulative expense for 3-year period	$70,600
Expense recognized in years 1 and 2	$47,066
Total year 3 expense	$23,534
Total	$70,600

The following table summarizes the pretax compensation expense that would be recorded during the three-year period:

Year	Total Award Value	Pretax Cost for Year	Cumulative Pretax Cost
1	$77,577	$25,859	$25,859
2	$70,600	$21,207	$47,066
3	$70,600	$23,534	$70,600

OPTION-PRICING MODELS

The most commonly used methodologies for valuing publicly traded options include the Black-Scholes model and the Cox-Ross-Rubinstein binomial pricing models. Private companies are permitted to use the minimum value method, which does not incorporate a stock volatility element. Basically, the minimum value method is a present value methodology.

Black-Scholes Option-Pricing Model

The Black-Scholes model, developed in the early 1970s, is more widely used to value stock options than any other model. It uses complex mathematical formulas based on probabilities of possible stock price appreciation. The model was originally developed for traded "European" options, exercisable only on the last day of the option term, and for nondividend-paying stock. The original model has been modified to account for dividend-paying stocks and for "American" options, exercisable at any point during the option term.

The Black-Scholes model incorporates several other important assumptions, some of which may limit its usefulness in valuing nontraded options such as employee stock options. Those assumptions are as follows:

- There are no margin requirements, taxes, or transaction costs such as commissions.
- The risk-free interest rate is constant over time.
- The dividend yield is constant over time.
- The stock price can change only by very small amounts during short periods of time.
- Options are short-lived.
- The volatility of the stock is constant over time.

Because of the significance of volatility on expected returns in Black-Scholes, this model generally produces high values for options of companies with high stock volatility and low dividends, and low values for options of companies with low stock volatility and high dividend yields.

The Black-Scholes option formula for a call option is as follows:

$$c = Se^{-q(T-t)}N(d_1) - Xe^{-r(T-t)}N(d_2)$$

where

c	= value of the call option
S	= current stock price
X	= strike price of the option
q	= expected dividend yield
$T-t$	= time to expiration
r	= expected risk-free rate
$N(dx)$	= probability that a random draw from a standard normal distribution is less than dx.

Observation
Some critics of the Black-Scholes model question its usefulness in predicting an option's value because it contains no *explicit* assumption for the expected future stock appreciation. However, Black-Scholes reflects the risk-free return and the stock's expected volatility, thereby implicitly incorporating a potential level of future stock appreciation.

Cox-Ross-Rubinstein (Binomial) Model

The Cox-Ross-Rubinstein model, also called the *binomial model,* is based on the same general theory as the Black-Scholes model and considers an iterative series of valuation curves with factors differing over time. As such, the Cox-Ross-Rubinstein model provides a greater degree of flexibility and sophistication in valuing options as assumptions can be varied over the option term. Because it assigns value to the possibility of early exercise (i.e., exercise on any day other than the last day of the option term), the binomial model through this iterative process more appropriately values the effect of dividends. As a result, the Black-Scholes and binomial models will produce different option values, depending on the significance of changes in the dividend yield.

In addition to dividend inputs, the binomial model allows the use of different interest rates. Depending on the future interest rate assumptions used, this model will generate different option values. For companies with no expected dividends, or with a constant dividend yield, the binomial model generally produces a value similar to Black-Scholes. Accordingly, while the binomial model is far more flexible than the Black-Scholes model because it permits a variety of assumptions, the result may be approximately the same.

Minimum Value Method

Statement 123 indicates that a private company may estimate the value of its options without consideration of the expected volatility of its stock. This method of estimating an option's value is referred to as the *minimum value method,* which is a present value concept.

A simple illustration of the minimum value method is as follows:

Company X, a nonpublic entity, grants 100 stock options on its stock to each of its 100 employees. The options cliff-vest after three years. The fair value of the stock and the exercise price of the options is $5, the expected life of the options is eight years, and the risk-free interest rate is 7.5 percent per annum. Company X calculates a *minimum value* for each option. The so-called minimum value does not take into account the expected volatility of the underlying stock.

Fair value of stock	$5.00
Present value of exercise price (compounded daily at a discount rate of 7.5 percent per annum)	– 2.74
Minimum value of each option	$2.26

FASB INTERPRETATION 44

Effective July 1, 2000, the Financial Accounting Standards Board ("FASB") issued interpretation 44 which, among other things, provided some of the following major interpretations of APB 25:

- The common law definition of employee should be used for purposes of applying APB 25. Therefore, options granted to independent contractors would not qualify.

- An option granted to a nonemployee member of the board of directors for services provided as a director would qualify under APB 25 if the director (1) was elected by the shareholders or (2) was appointed to a position on the board that will be filled by a shareholder election when the existing term for that position expires.

- APB 25 would still be applicable for option shares repurchased by the company at fair market value to meet the employer's minimum statutory tax-withholding obligation (e.g., resulting from exercising a non-ISO), but not in excess of that minimum.

Under FASB Interpretation 44, if a modification of a stock option has any of the following effects, it will cause unfavorable accounting consequences:

- Renews or extends the award's life (e.g., acceleration of vesting) or provides for a renewal or extension if a specified future separation from employment (e.g., death or disability) occurs
- Reduces the award's exercise price (commonly called *repricing*)
- Increases the number of shares to be issued under an award, including the addition of a feature that provides for a new award to be granted automatically when an existing award is exercised if specified conditions are met (commonly called a *reload feature*)

Under FASB Interpretation 44, if a stock option plan is subject to shareholder approval, an option granted under that plan is not deemed granted until the approval is obtained, unless the approval is essentially a formality (e.g., if management and the members of the board of directors control enough votes to approve the plan). If management and the board do not control sufficient votes to approve the plan, a stock option grant that is subject to shareholder approval will cause an accounting charge if, on the date of the actual shareholder approval, the fair market value of the stock exceeds the exercise price.

For private companies, FASB Interpretation 44 provides an ability for the company to require employees who have exercised stock options to resell their shares to the company without requiring variable accounting, provided certain requirements are satisfied. Among these requirements are that the repurchase not be expected to occur within six months after the option exercise. In the case of an option where the fair value is deemed to be the book value of the stock, and therefore the exercise price was based on book value, the repurchase price could be based on the book value at the time of the repurchase, rather than the actual fair value. Accordingly, a provision permitting the company to "call" (i.e., repurchase) the shares more than six months after exercise at their then fair value (or book value in the case of a book value option) would not foreclose APB 25 treatment.

FASB Interpretation 44 was effective July 1, 2000, and is to be applied prospectively to new option grants and related transactions that occur after that date, subject to several exceptions. FASB Interpretation 44 is complex and beyond the scope of this book. A discussion of FASB Interpretation 44 is provided by the accounting firm of BDO Seidman, LLP, and is reproduced in appendix 8. The complexity of the subject suggests that you would be wise to consult your accountant on every aspect of establishing stock option and other equity incentive plans.

ACCOUNTING ISSUES OF EXIT EVENT OPTIONS

If you could ignore accounting issues, ideally stock options would never vest unless there was an IPO or sale. If an IPO or sale never occurred prior to the ten-year maximum term of the incentive stock option, the option would never become exercisable and would expire unexercisable and unexercised ten years after the grant date.

While such a provision may be ideal from the viewpoint of the shareholders, it is certainly not ideal from the viewpoint of key employees. Such key employees realize nothing from their stock options.

Arguably, key employees should not benefit if their efforts have not resulted in an IPO or sale. However, they may have produced the conditions required for an IPO or sale, and the shareholders may have decided not to take the exit for personal reasons or because the IPO or sale valuations were not sufficiently higher. Shareholders can reasonably argue that key employees should not benefit if an exit is not in fact achieved by the shareholders.

Regardless of the merits of these arguments, it is not possible today to avoid a charge against accounting income if the options cannot vest unless there is a sale or IPO. APB 25 would dictate that the measurement date was the date of the sale or IPO and not the grant date; accordingly, there would be an accounting charge to earnings on the sale or IPO date.

If you wish to avoid a charge against your accounting income for the value of the stock options, the stock options must vest at some point during their ten-year term, assuming the employee is still employed by you. For example, a vesting nine years and ten years after the grant date would satisfy the accounting requirements, assuming that it is more likely than not that employees will remain for this period. The "more likely than not" test is an interpretation by the Securities and Exchange Commission (SEC) and might not be applied to private companies.

Therefore, if a company is concerned about its accounting income, it is typical to permit the option to vest at some point (assuming the employee continues to be employed) and then have the option vesting accelerated if there is an earlier IPO or sale.

The SEC keeps tightening the rules in an attempt to narrow the accounting loophole for stock options. Therefore, accounting considerations are important, and an accounting firm with SEC expertise should review the option plan for compliance with current SEC interpretations.

Accounting considerations may not be as important as in the past. Many Internet companies and technology companies have enjoyed IPOs with little revenues, let alone earnings. However, the IPO market for Internet companies has changed.

Accounting earnings are clearly important to "old economy" companies wishing to have IPOs and to certain consumer-oriented Internet companies as well. Even if your company is an old economy company, a single charge against your accounting earnings in the quarter in which your IPO occurs would probably not affect your post-IPO valuation.

The major problem with an accounting charge for options occurs if the charge will reduce your post-IPO earnings for any significant period of time. This could hurt both your pre- and post-IPO valuation. You will need the help of an accounting firm with SEC expertise make the determination.

SPECIAL ACCOUNTING ISSUES ON SALE EXITS

If your option plan produces an accounting charge to your accounting income, it could reduce the value of your company if the buyer's postsale closing accounting income were adversely affected. This is an unusual situation. The most typical situation is that the buyer's postsale closing income is not affected by option accounting charges of the seller. The proposed elimination of pooling accounting will mean that in the future all acquisitions will be accounted for using purchase accounting. The seller's preclosing income is irrelevant to a buyer in an acquisition accounted for by the purchase method of accounting.

Under FASB Interpretation 44 discussed earlier, the buyer's postclosing income may be adversely affected if the buyer assumes the seller's unvested options. Therefore, it may be preferable to accelerate option vesting if there is a change of control and to have the buyer issue new options to your employees.

If options are reducing your preclosing accounting income, it is very important when selling your business to reflect your accounting income on a pro forma basis without the option accounting charge. This is because certain buyers value businesses based on a multiplier of accounting charges resulting from stock options and could reduce your valuation unless they are clearly separately reflected in your pro forma financial statements. Most buyers, seeing such separate pro forma financial statements, would not lower the valuation of your business for option accounting charges that did not adversely affect cash flow.

CHAPTER 17

STOCK OPTION SECURITIES LAW ISSUES

You cannot grant stock options without complying with federal and state securities laws. An option is an offer to sell stock in your company. If the option is not currently exercisable, the option will be deemed an offer to sell when the option does become exercisable.

The SEC has adopted Rule 701, which is designed to provide a safe harbor for private companies from the registration requirements of the Securities Act of 1933. (called here the "1933 Act"). If you strictly comply with Rule 701 in your option grants, you need not worry about registering your stock under the 1933 Act.

Even if you do strictly comply with Rule 701, your option grants may still be exempt from the registration requirements of the 1933 Act if, for example, your offering complies with Regulation D of the 1933 Act, the "private placement" exemption under Section 4(2) of the 1933 Act, the exemption for intrastate offerings (Section 3[a][11] of the 1933 Act and Rule 147 thereunder), the exemption for all accredited investor offerings (Section 4[6] of the 1933 Act), or other applicable registration exemptions (e.g., Regulation A).

Even if you comply with Rule 701, you should check state securities laws before adopting an option plan to make certain that the option grants are exempt from registration or qualification under applicable state laws. In most states, some form of exemption exists for option grants to employees.

RULE 701

Rule 701 is only applicable to private companies (i.e., nonreporting companies). Public companies can generally register their stock under the 1933 Act on a Form S-8 Registration Statement and are not entitled to the benefits of Rule 701. Rule 701 does not exempt sales by control persons or other affiliates of the issuer, such as sales by entrepreneurs.

If your company qualifies under Rule 701, it can sell an unlimited number of securities (but limited for any given twelve-month period) to its employees and employees of its parent, its majority-owned subsidiaries, and majority-owned subsidiaries of your company's parent pursuant to a written compensatory benefit plan or written compensation contract. A compensatory benefit plan includes (among others) an option plan, a stock bonus plan, stock appreciation plan, and other similar plans. These securities may be sold to employees, directors, general partners, trustees (if the company is organized as a business trust), officers, consultants and advisers, and their family members who acquire such securities from such persons through gifts or domestic relations orders. Rule 701 exempts offers of sales to former employees, directors, and so forth, only if such persons were employed by or provided services to the company at the time the securities were offered. The term *employee* also includes insurance agents who are exclusive agents of the issuer, its subsidiaries, or parents or derived more than 50 percent of their annual income from these entities.

Rule 701 is available to consultants and advisers only if they meet all of the following requirements:

- They are natural persons.
- They provide bona fide services to the issuer, its parents, its majority-owned subsidiaries, or majority-owned subsidiaries of the issuer's parents.
- The services are not in connection with the offer of sale of securities in a capital-raising transaction, and they do not directly or indirectly promote or maintain a market for the issuer's securities.

The amount of securities sold under Rule 701 (including sales during the prior twelve months in reliance on Rule 701) may not exceed the greater of

- $1 million, *or*
- 15 percent of your company's total assets measured at its most recent balance sheet date, *or*
- 15 percent of your company's outstanding securities of the class being issued (including securities issuable under currently exercisable or convertible warrants, options, rights or other securities not originally issued pursuant to Rule 701) at its most recent balance sheet date.

For purposes of calculating whether your company's Rule 701 sales are within this maximum amount, options are treated as securities sold by your company on the date of grant and at the exercise price, without regard to whether the option is then vested or exercisable. This is an important provision since the financial tests are based on the option exercise price at the time of grant and not the fair market value of the stock at the time the option is exercised. For example, you can grant options for one million shares exercisable at $0.01 per share (which equals $10,000 under the test set forth earlier), even though when the options are exercised your shares have appreciated to $100 per share and the total fair market value of the stock issued is then $100 million.

Rule 701 contains no limitation on the type of distribution in which your company may engage, the number of offerees or purchasers, or the sophistication of the offerees or purchasers. However, each purchaser must be an employee, director, officer, consultant, or adviser, or, in certain cases such as an option exercise, a person who formerly held such a position when the option was granted or a family member of such a person.

There are no specific disclosure requirements (i.e., no formal private offering memorandum is required). However, the offering (like all sales of securities) is nevertheless subject to the general antifraud provisions of the federal securities laws requiring that all "material" information be made available to purchasers and that any offering materials neither misstate a material fact nor omit a material fact necessary to prevent the offering materials or any other statements from being misleading. In addition, if your company sells more than $5 million of securities in reliance on this exemption in any twelve-month period, your company must deliver to purchasers a written disclosure of the risks associated with an investment in your company's securities, a summary of material terms of the compensatory plan, and certain company financial statements. For an option, such disclosure is required for a reasonable period before option exercise.

Securities received in a Rule 701 offering are "restricted securities" that cannot be resold without 1933 Act registration or an exemption. However, ninety days after your company becomes a 1934 Act reporting company (typically ninety days after your IPO becomes effective), securities issued by your company under Rule 701 to noncontrol persons will be free of the requirements of SEC Rule 144 and can be freely resold. Securities acquired by you and other control persons under Rule 701 can be sold pursuant to Rule 144, except that there are no holding periods. This means that you and other control persons can sell up to 1 percent of the outstanding stock every three months or, if higher, one week's average trading volume, subject, of course, to any lockup agreement you entered into in connection with your IPO. Your Rule 144 sales must also conform to the public information manner of sale and notice requirements of Rule 144.

If your company is not a 1934 Act reporting company at the time the options are exercised, the restricted securities cannot be resold by you or your employees without an exemption from the registration provisions of federal and state securities laws. In general, a private placement resale exemption (Section 4[1] of the 1933 Act) will be the most likely exemption available. Any shares certificates that issue upon the exercise of stock options should be appropriately legended.

A Rule 701 offering is not exempt from state laws, and not all states have conformed their blue sky laws to SEC's Rule 701.

RULE 16B-3

If your company's stock is publicly traded, your public stock is probably registered under Section 12 of the Securities Exchange Act of 1934 (called here the 1934 Act) and is subject to the short-swing profit rules of Section 16 of that law. Section 16(b) of the 1934 Act permits the company (with certain exceptions) to recover any profit realized by a director, officer, or more than 10 percent

beneficial owner from any sale and repurchase, or purchase and sale, of any equity security (whether or not registered under the 1934 Act) of the company within a
period of less than six months' (short-swing) profits. A
grant of an option is considered a "purchase" of the underlying stock for purposes of Section 16(b) unless your company complies with Rule 16b-3.

Why worry about complying with Rule 16b-3? A
short-swing profit is deemed to have been realized if,
within a period of less than six months, there is either (1)
a purchase and subsequent sale of the equity security at
a higher price or (2) a sale and subsequent purchase of
the equity security at a lower price. An action to recover
short-swing profits may be instituted by the company or
by the owner of any security of the company if the company refuses to bring suit within sixty days after request
or fails to prosecute the action diligently. If you do not
comply with Rule 16b-3, any sale of your stock within six
months before or after the option grant could be matched
with the "purchase" resulting from the option grant and
create liability for the optionee under Section 16.

To comply with Rule 16b-3 in connection with an
option grant, you must comply with one of the three following requirements:

- The option grant must be approved by the board of
  directors or a committee of the board of directors
  that is composed solely of two or more Nonemployee Directors (defined below); *or*

- the option grant must be approved or ratified by
  either (1) the affirmative votes of the holders of a
  majority of the securities of the company present,
  or represented, and entitled to vote in a meeting
  held in accordance with state law and the SEC
  proxy rules or (2) the written consents of the holders of the majority of the securities of the company
  entitled to vote which consents are obtained in

compliance with the SEC proxy rules, provided such ratification occurs not later than the date of the next annual meeting of shareholders; *or*

- the securities subject to the option grant are held by the officer or director for a period of six months following the date of the option grant.

The first alternative is the one normally used by publicly held companies. If it is not practical for the board of directors to ratify every option grant, it is best to have a committee of the board of directors composed solely of two or more Nonemployee Directors. A Nonemployee Director means a director who meets the following four requirements:

- Is not currently an officer of the company or a parent or subsidiary or otherwise currently employed by any of those entities
- Does not receive compensation, directly or indirectly, from the company or a parent or subsidiary for services as a consultant or in any capacity other than as a director, except for compensation not exceeding a $60,000 threshold
- Does not possess a material interest in any material transaction with the company or its parent or subsidiary that would require proxy disclosure under the SEC rules
- Is not engaged in a business relationship that would require proxy disclosure under the SEC rules

ANTIFRAUD RULES

Even if your stock option plan complies with the registration provisions of federal and state securities laws, you still have to be concerned about the antifraud provisions of these laws. When an employee exercises an option, your company is selling stock to the employee, which is a security subject to these laws. This is true even though your company is completely private and has only you as its sole shareholder.

Rule 10b-5 of the 1934 Act generally makes it unlawful for any person—directly or indirectly, by the use of any means or instrumentality of interstate commerce, the mails, or any facilities of any national securities exchange—to employ any manipulative or deceptive device in connection with the purchase or sale of securities. Rule 10b-5 applies to both private as well as public purchases and sales of securities. A violation of Rule 10b-5 requires proof of "scienter," which means that the plaintiff must prove an intentional or at least a reckless act.

If you make any material misstatement (or omit to state material information necessary to make your statement not misleading) to an employee who then exercises a stock option in reliance on your misstatement or omission, both the company and you could have personal liability to the employee. Likewise, if your company or you repurchase stock from an employee that was previously acquired upon option exercise and make a material misstatement or omission in connection with the repurchase, both the company and you could have personal liability to the employee. A number of cases have been brought by employees who sold their stock back to the company shortly before the sale of the company or its IPO that would have yielded them a much higher price.

The courts have viewed as "material" any information that could be considered important by the average prudent investor. Care must be taken in connection with the grant of stock options, the exercise of stock options, and the repurchase of stock acquired under options to avoid violating Rule 10b-5 and similar provisions of state securities laws.

Chapter 18

Stock Bonus Plans[1]

A lthough stock bonus grants may be simpler to effectuate, they have significant disadvantages compared to incentive stock options. As previously noted, these disadvantages are as follows:

- The stock bonus is taxable to the employee on the grant date unless there are vesting conditions (versus stock options, which are not taxable on the grant date unless there is an established trading market for the options).

- The employee receiving a stock bonus becomes a shareholder immediately and is entitled to the rights and privileges of a shareholder.

- Stock bonuses may reward employees who have not contributed to the past growth of the company (e.g., new employees); in contrast, incentive stock

---

1. Coauthored with Joseph Gulant, New York City Office, Blank Rome Comisky & McCauley LLP.

options only reward employees for stock appreciation that occurs *after* the option grant date.

- The grant of the stock bonus increases issued and
outstanding stock and reduces basic earnings per
share, which is an important figure for publicly
held companies (versus unexercised stock options
that are only reflected in diluted earnings per
share, which is less important to securities analysts of publicly held companies).

- Applicable income tax withholding requirements
may require a significant cash outlay by the company notwithstanding that compensation is paid in
stock.

Some companies avoid the first and last disadvantage by creating a partial stock–partial cash bonus
award, with the cash portion equal to the federal and
state income taxes payable by the employee on the total
bonus. Since your company is entitled to an immediate
tax deduction equal to the total value of the bonus, the
tax benefit to your company partially offsets the cash cost
of the award. The cash portion of the payment can also be
used to satisfy the company's tax withholding requirements in connection with the stock issuance.

Alternatively, some companies loan to the employee
an amount sufficient to pay his or her taxes, as discussed
later.

The following sections describe three examples of the
problems with stock bonuses and some of the solutions.

EXAMPLE 1

On January 1, 2001, Employee A receives 1,000 shares of
Corporation X as a bonus on a date, and the Corporation
X stock has a fair market value of $10 per share.

Employee A is treated as having received taxable compensation equal to $10,000 (i.e., 1,000 shares at $10 per share), and Corporation X will be entitled to deduct this compensatory payment as if it paid cash in an equivalent amount. The initial tax basis (or cost) of the stock to the employee will be its fair market value on the date of issuance, or $10 per share. Assuming that Employee A's effective tax rate for federal, state, and local income tax purposes is 42 percent, Employee A will owe income tax from the stock grant equal to approximately $4,200.

- *Potential "phantom income" problem.* If Employee A is unable to sell a portion of his shares to pay this tax due to transferability restrictions inherent in the stock or a lack of a public or private market or securities laws restrictions (as the case may be), he will be required to pay this tax liability with other funds. A stock bonus may therefore create "phantom income"—that is, a current tax liability to the employee without any corresponding cash payment. As noted earlier, this problem may be mitigated to the extent that a portion of the bonus is paid in cash.

- *Employer tax withholding issue.* As the amount paid to the employee is treated as wage compensation for federal income tax purposes, the employer has an obligation to withhold upon the amount of the payment and to pay applicable employment taxes (i.e., social security, federal unemployment, and Medicare/Medicaid taxes; income tax withholding; etc.), notwithstanding that the payment is made in kind rather than in cash. Failure to withhold will potentially make the employer corporation secondarily liable for all or a portion of the income tax liability of an employee who subsequently fails to pay the income tax due in connection with the transaction. The employer could potentially obviate this problem by withholding a larger percentage of the cash compensation otherwise paid to the employee as regular compensation and/or making a portion of the payment in cash (as described previously).

Assume further that Employee A holds the stock for two years after issuance and then sells all of his stock for $200 per share. As Employee A will have held the stock for more than one year prior to the time of sale, he will recognize long-term capital gain for federal income tax purposes based on the excess of the amount realized upon the sale ($200,000) over his tax basis (or cost) of the shares ($10,000), or $190,000. Assuming that Employee A's effective federal, state, and local income tax rate on long-term capital gains is 23 percent, A would pay approximately $43,700 in taxes as a result of the sale. Consequently, A would net on an after-tax basis $152,100 as a result of stock grant—that is, gross proceeds ($200,000) less the sum of (1) the amount of tax paid as compensation income at issuance ($4,200) and (2) the capital gains tax paid upon the disposition of the shares ($43,700).

Most companies would not want the employee to obtain a fully vested interest in the stock bonus. Therefore, they may place vesting conditions on the stock bonus, such as a requirement to remain an employee a certain number of years in order to become fully vested and/or certain performance requirements (e.g., a certain increase in revenues or profits). Vesting restrictions may take many different forms, including *cliff vesting,* in which all of the stock issued to an employee will vest on a certain defined date; or *stepped vesting,* pursuant to which the stock issued partially vests at certain intervals over a defined period.

These vesting conditions prevent the employee from realizing any taxable income until the stock vests. Although this may seem to be an advantage to the employee, it may actually be a disadvantage since when the stock vests, it becomes taxable as compensation on each vesting date, and the employee must pay tax based on the fair market value of the stock on the vesting date. If the stock has appreciated from the grant date to the vesting date, the employee pays income taxes at ordinary income tax rates (rather than the generally lower capital gains tax rates) on the appreciated value of the stock on the vesting date. In that case, the employee may not have enough cash to pay the taxes he owes, even if the original award included a cash portion.

Example 2

Same facts as example 1, except that the stock is issued subject to forfeiture to the extent that Employee A fails to continue to be employed by Corporation X for a two-year period following issuance. Employee A satisfies the vesting requirement on January 1, 2003, at which time the stock is trading at $200 per share.

Employee A will recognize compensation income at the time of vesting (i.e., two years after issuance) equal to the excess of the fair market value of the Corporation X stock on that date ($200) over the amount paid for the stock ($0), or $200,000 in the aggregate. Assuming an effective federal and state income tax rate of 42 percent on the compensation income, Employee A will owe income tax of $84,000, and will receive property having a net value equal to $116,000 in connection with the transaction. A's holding period with respect to the stock will start on the date that the stock vested.

As can be seen from the foregoing example, the appreciation in value after issuance but prior to vesting of restricted shares causes an employee to recognize significantly more compensation income than would otherwise have been the case had the employee received unrestricted shares, and the timing of the compensatory payment is different (i.e., the employee is subject to tax when the restrictions on the stock lapse rather than when the stock was transferred to the employee). If an employee anticipates that the stock received will increase significantly in value after its issuance but prior to vesting, he may make an election under Section 83(b) of the Internal Revenue Code of 1986, as amended, to be taxed on the receipt of the stock without regard to any vesting restrictions other than those that will not lapse (e.g., transferability restrictions in a shareholders' agreement).

Employees must make a "Section 83(b)" election within thirty days after the stock grant. A copy of the IRS form that must be filed to make the Section 83(b) election and the related instructions appear in appendix 10. A Section 83(b) election has the advantage of permitting the employee to be taxed at long-term capital gains rates on the stock appreciation after the grant date, assuming the long-term capital gains holding period is satisfied (similar to the tax treatment of a grant of unrestricted stock).

However, the major disadvantages of the Section 83(b) election are as follows:

- The employee must pay federal income tax for the year in which the stock bonus is received, even though the stock may never vest (e.g., if employment is terminated before the stock fully vests).

- If the restricted stock does not appreciate in the period after issuance but prior to exercise, the employee would accelerate tax liability unnecessarily by making the Section 83(b) election.

- If the stock does not ultimately vest, the employee will not be entitled to any tax deductions or capital losses equal to the income previously recognized by the employee as a result of the Section 83(b) election.

As noted earlier, many companies provide a portion of the bonus in cash sufficient to pay employee's income taxes due in the year in which the stock bonus is received in order to mitigate these problems. The cash can either be a bonus or a loan that must be repaid. Typically, the repayment date is tied to the vesting of the stock bonus. Thus, if the employee must be employed for five years for the stock to vest, the loan repayment is triggered in five years.

If a note is used with the principal repayment tied to the vesting schedule, interest will have to be paid each year by the employee on the principal. If the note provides for interest to accrue and not be payable until the principal is due, interest will be imputed, and the company will have to recognize annual imputed interest income with the employee obtaining an annual imputed interest expense.

Example 3

Assume the same facts as example 2, except that Employee A makes a Section 83(b) election shortly after the restricted stock is transferred to him. The stock had a fair market value of $10 per share at the time of its issuance (disregarding the vesting restrictions for these purposes). Employee A then holds the stock for more than two years and sells it for $200 per share after the stock has vested shares.

As a result of the Section 83(b) election, Employee A will recognize $10,000 of compensation income (i.e., the excess of the fair market value of the stock received over the amount paid for the stock) in the tax year in which the stock is issued to him, notwithstanding the vesting requirements inherent in the stock that could ultimately cause him to forfeit his shares. Assuming a 42 percent effective federal and state income tax rate on compensation income, Employee A will pay $4,200 in taxes in the year in which the stock was issued. Corporation X will be entitled to a corresponding income tax deduction in the amount of $4,200. Employee A's holding period with respect to the stock begins on the date that the stock was transferred to him. As noted before, Corporation X may fund Employee A's income tax liability through either a cash bonus or a loan. As a result of the Section 83(b) election, no further compensation income will be recognized by Employee A when the stock vests (i.e., the continuing employment criteria is satisfied), and Employee A will recognize no further gain or loss with respect to the stock until the stock is sold. At that time, he will recognize capital gain or loss equal to the excess of the amount realized on the sale over his tax basis in the shares.

Assuming Employee A sells all of the stock at a time when it is worth $200 per share, he will recognize long-term capital gain equal to the excess of the amount realized $200,000 over his tax basis in the stock of $10,000, or $190,000. Assuming a 23 percent effective federal, state, and local capital gains tax rate, Employee A will pay $43,700 in capital gains taxes. As a result, he will receive net proceeds of $152,100—that is, $200,000 gross proceeds less the sum of (1) the $4,200 of tax paid on compensation upon the making of the Section 83(b) election and (2) the $43,700 paid upon the sale of the stock. Hence, by making a Section 83(b) election, Employee A would be placed in a similar tax position as in the case of the unrestricted stock issuance described in example 1.

UNVESTED STOCK OF START-UPS

Finally, in many start-up business situations (including e-commerce ventures), employers may issue restricted stock to employees with a nominal value in exchange for a payment equal to the then fair market value of the stock (e.g., $0.01 per share). The restriction typically contains vesting conditions that require the employee to forfeit the stock or to resell it to the corporation for a nominal price if employment is terminated within certain periods.

Although this result may be counterintuitive, *the employee may still generate significant compensation income with respect to his receipt of the stock notwithstanding that he paid an amount equal to the fair market value of the stock at the time of transfer.* Specifically, in the absence of a Section 83(b) election, the compensation element with respect to the stock issuance would not be determined until the stock vests (i.e., when the restrictions lapse), at which time the stock may be worth significantly more than the employee's exercise price.

An employee can protect against this problem by making a Section 83(b) election at the time she receives the restricted stock. In that case, no income tax would be payable at the time of issuance as the employee has paid full and fair value for the stock, and the risk of tax on compensation at ordinary income rates with respect to stock appreciation prior to vesting would be eliminated.

The rules described above arguably may not apply to stock that is issued to an employee at its fair market value at the time of issuance and is not then subject to any vesting requirements, such as unrestricted stock issued to founders. Even though a venture capitalist may subsequently require the employee to agree to vesting restrictions on this stock as a quid pro quo for an investment in the company, it is arguable that the shares are not subject to Section 83(b) because they were not issued originally as compensation for services.

If the employer sells the stock to an employee at its fair market value and the stock is not restricted by vesting conditions, there is no taxable transaction. However, the employee is free to terminate his of her employment and still retain the stock.

CHAPTER 19

PHANTOM STOCK PLANS

A phantom stock plan is a cash bonus plan in which the amount of the cash bonus is dependent on the increase in the value of the stock in your company. The value of the stock of publicly held companies is easily determined. However, the value of the stock of a privately held company that is used to measure the amount of the cash bonus is not subject to precise determination.

Many methods of valuing the stock of a privately held company are available. The major methods include a multiplier of EBITDA, a discounted cash flow valuation, an industry-specific formula valuation, and, if all else fails, liquidation value. Some companies adopt plans that allow the board of directors the discretion to determine the valuation from time to time in their good-faith judgment.

Appendix 5 of this book contains a phantom stock plan for a private company that is designed to motivate the key employees to help achieve the highest possible sale price for the company. The principals of the private company developed the plan to align the interest of their key employees with their own interest in obtaining the highest price for the company. The plan was also designed to reward employees with a higher cash bonus if the sale occurred at an earlier date than at a later date.

The plan contemplates that the company will ultimately be sold for approximately six times EBITDA, less long-term debt, within the next five years. The plan rewards the key employees for growth in the EBITDA from the year prior to the plan adoption to the date an agreement of sale is signed in the next five years. The key employees' reward is a percentage of the EBITDA growth multiplied by 5, instead of 6, to provide a safety margin in case the business is ultimately sold at a lower multiplier than 6.

It is possible to increase the EBITDA of any company by borrowing large amounts of funds and hiring additional salespeople and engaging in other marketing activities. The plan punishes the key employees for increases in debt that are not offset by greater increases in the valuation of the company.

The key employees are motivated not to increase the amount of the long-term debt of the company unless the projected EBITDA growth, when multiplied by the applicable multiplier for the company exceeds the long-term debt. In a sale of the company, it is typical for the buyer to reduce the purchase price by the amount of the long-term debt that must be assumed or, alternatively, to require the seller to pay such long-term debt out of the proceeds of the sale.

The key employees are also motivated not to decrease the working capital of the company, since any potential buyer would expect a minimum amount of working capital and would reduce the purchase price if such minimum amount were not part of the transaction.

If the owners of the company take lesser compensation during the five-year period, this is treated as if the company had borrowed funds from them in the amount of the compensation reduction. Likewise, an increase in the owners' compensation during the five-year period is treated as a reduction of indebtedness and is rewarded.

Many types of phantom stock plans exist; the one in appendix 5 is only one example. However, many of the plans are poorly designed to achieve the exit objectives of the business's owners. Examples of such plans include plans in which incentives peak too early, resulting in higher income in years before the sale year and lower income in the sale year. This results in a reduction in the ultimate purchase price of the business. Adopting such a plan is like shooting yourself in the foot!

Other plans reward employees for down years followed by up years. For example, before the plan is adopted, assume that the company has a $1 million EBITDA. In year 1 after the plan is adopted, the EBITDA is reduced to $800,000. In year 2 after the plan is adopted, the EBITDA rises back to $1 million. Some plans actually reward the employees for the $200,000 increase in EBITDA, even though the business has made no progress whatsoever in its growth. To avoid these kinds of mistakes, it is important that you consult with knowledgeable professionals in establishing the plan. If your ultimate objective is a high sale price for your company, these professionals should include an expert on sale valuations as well as a compensation expert.

ANALYSIS OF THE PHANTOM STOCK PLAN

The following are key provisions of the phantom stock plan and an analysis of the provisions:

> The total number of units, or fractions of a unit, of Phantom Stock Appreciation Rights which may be

awarded to participants pursuant to the Plan shall not exceed one hundred thousand (100,000) full units in the aggregate. More than 100,000 full units may be issued under the Plan if authorized by the Company's Board of Directors or Committee and a majority of the holders of outstanding units or fractions of a unit.

The figure 100,000 units is arbitrary. It is intended to permit a sufficiently large number of units to be granted to each key employee so that the employee believes that they have a significant phantom stock interest.

It is much more impressive to an employee to have 10,000 phantom stock appreciation rights than to have 100 phantom stock appreciation rights, even though their economic interest may be exactly the same.

Each phantom stock appreciation right will have a value dependent on the formula used in the plan. An example of the valuation of each unit is contained as an exhibit to the plan in appendix 9.

Not all of the 100,000 units should be immediately issued to key employees since the company may need some units for possible new hires.

The term "Change in Control" shall mean either one of the following events: (A) the closing date for the merger or consolidation of the Company with another corporation if one or more of the holders of voting shares of the Company immediately prior to the merger or consolidation do not beneficially own, immediately after the merger or consolidation, shares of the corporation issuing cash or securities in the merger or consolidation (or its parent corporation) entitling one or more of such holders to 51 percent or more of all voting shares of the entity issuing cash or securities in the merger or consolidation, or (B) the closing date for the sale of all or substantially all the assets or stock of the Company if one or more shareholders of the Company do not own 51 percent or more of the voting shares of the acquiring entity (or its parent corporation).

The phantom stock appreciation rights under this plan have no value unless there is a Change of Control as defined. A Change of Control does not occur until there is an actual closing date of an agreement for sale or a merger or consolidation. In addition, as noted later, the employee will not fully vest unless he or she continues with the buyer for a period of time.

Some financial buyers will insist that the entrepreneur continue to hold a small percentage of the controlling entity in the purchase, typically 5 to 15 percent, to permit the financial buyer to use recapitalization accounting for the acquisition. Therefore, a Change of Control does not require 100 percent of the stock to be sold, but only 51 percent. This is an optional provision, and some companies may prefer that the trigger be 100 percent change of ownership.

Each outstanding unit (or fractions thereof) of Phantom Stock Appreciation Rights shall be redeemed within 30 days after the expiration of one year subsequent to the date of a Change of Control for the valuation set forth in Section 2.3, provided that the grantee has continued to be a full-time employee of the Company or its successor for a period of one year subsequent to the date of a Change of Control (or such shorter period as the Company or its successor shall determine in

> writing) at a compensation level (excluding this
> Plan) at least equal to what such grantee was paid
> immediately prior to the date of the Change of
> Control and within 30 miles of such grantee's pri-
> mary work location prior to the date of the Change
> of Control.

This provision helps ensure that key employees will remain with the buyer for a reasonable period of time after the Change of Control. The buyer may wish to require certain key employees to enter into employment contracts, and this provision helps motivate them to do so.

The buyer may not wish to retain all of the key employees. In that case, the one-year provision can be waived by the company and immediate payment made of the value of the phantom stock appreciation rights.

> (a) Determine the Adjusted EBITDA (as hereafter
> defined) of the Company for the Calculation
> Period (as hereafter defined). The term
> "Adjusted EBITDA" refers to the income of the
> Company as determined in accordance with
> generally accepted principles consistently
> applied after such figure has been adjusted to
> eliminate the effect of any income taxes, inter-
> est, depreciation, amortization, any salaries
> and fringe benefits paid to Owner 1 or Owner 2,
> and any payments to Owner 3. The term "Cal-
> culation Period" shall refer to the 12 consecu-
> tive calendar months ending at the end of the
> calendar month immediately prior to the date
> of the written agreement which, if consum-
> mated, would result in the Change of Control.
> (b) Determine the Adjusted EBITDA of the Com-
> pany for calendar year 2000, which shall be
> deemed to equal $4,000,000.

(c) Subtract the result of Clause (b) from the result of Clause (a). If the result of Clause (b) is greater than the result of Clause (a), no value shall be ascribed to the Phantom Stock Appreciation Rights.

(d) If the subtraction of the result of Clause (a) from the result of Clause (b) is a positive figure, multiply such figure by 5.

This formula was designed to reward key employees for increases in the earnings before interest, taxes, and depreciation/amortization (as adjusted for certain items, adjusted EBITDA) from the year 2000 adjusted EBITDA of $4 million. The concept was to motivate employees to increase the adjusted EBITDA above $4 million.

The entrepreneur determined that the company would most likely be sold for a multiple of six times EBITDA, less long-term debt. The employees were rewarded for adjusted EBITDA increases based on a multiple of 5. The entrepreneur therefore benefited from each dollar of increase in the Adjusted EBITDA into two ways:

- Only a small proportion (25 percent) of the total incremental value of the company was given to the employees who received phantom stock appreciation rights, with 75 percent redounding to the owners' benefit.

- Each dollar of incremental EBITDA assigned to the employees was valued at less than the actual projected market value to the entrepreneur of such dollar incremental EBITDA (a multiple of 5 versus an actual projected multiplier of 6).

The adjustments to EBITDA were designed to eliminate excessive salaries and fringe benefits that were paid to the owners which would not be continued by any proposed buyer.

The "Calculation Period" for the valuation of the phantom stock appreciation rights was designed to be the same period of time that a buyer would use in valuing the company. Obviously, trying to project a buyer's valuation methodology is always risky, and there is no guarantee that they would use either the EBITDA method of valuation or the same calculation period as is used in this plan. However, my experience has been that most purchase-sale transactions tend to have an EBITDA component to the valuation, and that component usually includes the twelve-month period that ends during the calendar month prior to the date of the agreement of sale.

If any significant time will elapse between the date of the agreement of sale and the actual closing, consideration should be given to changing the calculation period so that it ends in the calendar month immediately prior to the actual closing.

> (e) Adjust the result of Clause (d) by the following:
>   (i) subtract any capital contribution made by the Company's shareholders to the Company after December 31, 2000, and on or prior to the close of business on the date of the Change of Control, except to the extent that such capital contribution is equal to any capital withdrawal by the shareholder from the Company after December 31, 2000 (other than withdrawals for tax purposes in amounts determined by the independent public accountants for the Company). Any decrease in the annual compensation of Owner 1 or Owner 2 from the annual compensation rate in effect on the date of this Plan shall be deemed a capital contribution by the shareholders of the Company.

(ii) compare the long-term indebtedness of the Company at the close of business on the date of the Change of Control to the long-term indebtedness of the Company at the close of business on December 31, 2000. Any increase in the indebtedness on the date on the Change of Control over the indebtedness at the close of business on December 31, 2000, shall be subtracted from the result of Clause (d). Any decrease in the long-term indebtedness on the date on the Change of Control over the long-term indebtedness on December 31, 2000, shall be added to the result of Clause (d). In computing "long-term indebtedness", any increase in the balance sheet account for split-dollar insurance premium payments for insurance on the lives of either Owner 1 and Owner 2 between December 31, 2000, and the date of the Change of Control shall be subtracted from long-term indebtedness on the date of the Change of Control and any decrease in such balance sheet account between December 31, 2000, and the date of the Change of Control shall be added to the long-term indebtedness on the date of the Change of Control.

(iii) compare the working capital at the close of business on the date of the Change of Control to the working capital at the close of business on December 31, 2000. Any increase in the working capital at the close of business on the date of the Change of Control over the working capital at the close of business on December 31, 2000, shall be added to the result of Clause (d).

> Any decrease in the working capital at the close of business on the date of the Change of Control over the working capital at the close of business on December 31, 2000, shall be subtracted from the result of Clause (d).
>
> (iv) the terms "long-term indebtedness" and "working capital," as used herein, shall be interpreted consistently with the definition of similar terms, if any, which are used in the agreement which resulted in the Change of Control.
>
> (f) Determine whichever is the lower figure: (i) the result of Clause (d) without the adjustments by the provisions of Clause (e); or (ii) the result of Clause (d) as adjusted by the provisions of Clause (e). Multiply the lower figure by 25 percent.
>
> (g) Divide the result of Clause (f) by the number of outstanding units (or fractions thereof) of Phantom Stock Appreciation Rights on the date of the Change of Control.

The purpose of these adjustments is to better align the interest of the management group receiving the phantom stock appreciation rights with the owner's interests. For example, if the owner is required to contribute more capital to the company to increase the EBITDA, the amount the owner receives from the ultimate sale of the company is decreased because of his increased investment. This provision punishes the employee one dollar for each one dollar of the amount required to be contributed by the owner to the capital.

It is possible to grow the EBITDA of many companies by increasing your expenditures for marketing your products or services. That expenditure comes at a price if you do not have sufficient internally generated funds to finance these marketing expenditures and are required to contribute additional capital to finance them. If the employees were not penalized for this additional capital, they would have incentive to increase marketing expenses without regard to the effect on the owners. This provision makes the key employee think twice before requiring you to inject additional capital into your company.

Likewise, key employees are penalized for increasing your long-term indebtedness. The amount of your long-term indebtedness reduces the ultimate sale price that you realized from the company. Again, this provision makes the key employee think twice before borrowing long-term funds to increase EBITDA.

Many buyers require a minimum amount of net working capital to be in your company at the time of the closing of the sale. (*Net working capital* is the amount of your current assets less your current liabilities.)

Since key employees can increase EBITDA with short-term bank loans that may decrease your net working capital, this provision punishes them for decreases in your net working capital from the base year.

Employees are rewarded under this provision for withdrawals of equity by the owners, decreases in long-term indebtedness, and increases in net working capital.

Clause (f) in the sample provides that the participants in the plan will receive 25 percent of the increase in the Adjusted EBITDA after it has been multiplied by 5. Clause (g) then takes the total pot and divides it by the number of phantom stock appreciation rights units that are outstanding.

All units (or fractions thereof) of Phantom Stock Appreciation Rights shall automatically be forfeited upon termination of the grantee's employment for

any reason (including disability or death),
whether voluntarily or involuntarily, except that
termination by the Company of the grantee's
employment without cause within 6 months prior
to the date of a Change of Control shall not result
in a termination or forfeiture. Forfeited units (or
fractions thereof) shall no longer be considered
outstanding units (or fractions thereof) and may
be reissued by the Company under this Plan. The
Company's Board of Directors may, in its sole
judgment, allocate forfeited units (or fractions
thereof) to the remaining grantees of Phantom
Stock Appreciation Rights if the Company's Board
of Directors determines that the remaining
grantees can operate as effectively without the
grantee whose units (or fractions thereof) were
forfeited.

If employment terminates, the grantee of the phantom stock appreciation rights forfeit their rights. The only
exception is if the employment is terminated without
cause by the company within six months prior to the date
of the Change of Control. This was designed to protect
employees from arbitrary dismissals in contemplation of
the sale of the company.

CHAPTER 20

EMPLOYEE STOCK PURCHASE PLANS

An employee stock purchase plan (ESPP) permits an employer to grant options to a broad-based group of employees to purchase the employer's stock, usually through a payroll deduction mechanism. These plans will often permit the employees to purchase stock at a discount of up to 15 percent of the fair market value of the stock, and often the purchase price will be based on the lower of the fair market value at the date of grant or the fair market value at the date of exercise. As long as the plan meets the requirements of Section 423 of the Internal Revenue Code for a "qualified" ESPP, the employees will enjoy generally favorable income tax treatment.

Section 423 of the Internal Revenue Code (see appendix 6) contains the following requirements for a tax-qualified ESPP:

- The plan provides that options are to be granted only to employees of the employer corporation or of its parent of subsidiary corporation to purchase stock in any such corporation.

- The plan is approved by the shareholders of the granting corporation within twelve months before or after the date the plan is adopted.

- Under the terms of the plan, no employee can be granted an option if such employee owns or is deemed to own stock possessing or deemed to possess more than 5 percent of the total combined voting power or value of all classes of stock of the employer corporation or of its parent or subsidiary.

- Under the plan terms, options are to be granted to all employees of any corporation whose employees are granted any such options, except that designated classes of employees may (but need not be) excluded (e.g., employees with less than two years of employment, who are customarily employed twenty hours or less per week or less than five months in any calendar year; and certain highly compensated employees).

- Under the plan terms, all employees granted such options have the same rights and privileges, except that the amount of stock that may be purchased may bear a uniform relationship to total compensation or the basic or regular rate of compensation, and the plan may provide that no employee may purchase more than the maximum amount of stock fixed in the plan.

- Under the plan terms, the option price is not less than the smaller of (1) 85 percent of fair market value at the time of grant or (2) 85 percent of fair market value at the time of exercise.

- Under the plan terms, the option cannot be exercised after twenty-seven months, except that if the option price is not less than 85 percent of fair market value *at the time of exercise,* the twenty-seven months can be extended to five years.

- Under the plan terms, no employee can be granted options that permit his or her rights to purchase stock under all such plans to accrue at a rate exceeding $25,000 of the fair market value of such stock (determined on grant date) for each calendar year for which the option is outstanding. (The term *accrue* in general refers to when the option or any portion first becomes exercisable.)
- Under the plan terms, the option is not transferable by the individual other than by will or the laws of descent or distribution, and it is exercisable, during the individual's life time, only by that individual.

Just like an ISO, there are special holding periods for stock acquired under an ESPP. These holding periods are identical to the ISO holding periods (no disposition for two years after grant and one year after exercise). There is also an employment requirement with Section 423 plans that is identical to the employment requirement necessary to obtain long-term capital gains treatment for ISOs. There is a special rule requiring employees to recognize ordinary income to the extent that the option price was below 100 percent of the fair market value of the stock on the option granting, subject to certain exceptions.

DISADVANTAGES AND ADVANTAGES

A tax-qualified ESPP compared to an ordinary stock option plan has the following disadvantages:

- The options cannot be limited only to key employees but in general must be given to all full-time employees subject to certain exceptions.
- The option term is limited to twenty-seven months from the grant date (versus ten years for an ISO),

except that the term can be as long as five years if the option price is 85 percent or more of the fair market value of the stock at the time of exercise.

- Holders of more than 5 percent of the voting stock cannot receive options under this plan.

These disadvantages are serious and cause many companies not to adopt the tax-qualified ESPP. However, a tax-qualified ESPP has a few advantages over an ISO, such as the following:

- The option price can be lower than 85 percent of fair market value on the grant date (versus 100 percent for an ISO) or 85 percent of the fair market value on the exercise date.
- Alternative minimum tax does not apply on the exercise of an option granted under ESPP.
- A tax-qualified ESPP will not cause an accounting charge under FASB Interpretation 44.

For example, assume that on the grant date, the fair market value of the stock is $30 and on the exercise date the fair market value of the stock if $20. Assume that the tax-qualified ESPP permits the employee an option for twenty-seven months to purchase the stock at the lesser of 85 percent of the fair market value on the grant date or the exercise date. The employee would pay only $17 for the stock. Thus, the option price can never be underwater (i.e., more than the fair market value of the stock). In contrast, an ISO can have an exercise price that is significantly higher than the current fair market of the stock, since the ISO exercise price must be established at the date of the grant.

From the company's viewpoint, the employee's ability to purchase stock at less than 85 percent of the fair market value on the grant date or exercise date is a mixed blessing. It is true that the option can never be underwater. However, should the employees be rewarded for poor performance if their performance reduced the fair market value of the stock from the grant date to the exercise date?

The fair market value of the stock could have dropped after the grant date without any fault by the employees. For example, if the stock market as a whole dropped or the industry price to earnings multiples decreased, the employees should arguably not be punished. The company may have grown significantly after the grant date, but that growth may not be reflected in the stock price.

EMPLOYEE STATUS

The ESPP document must specifically limit participation to employees of the sponsoring employer corporation, its parent, or subsidiary corporations. The IRS has ruled that only employees of a "corporation" may participate in a qualified ESPP under Section 423. For example, Internal Revenue Service states that employees of a partnership or other unincorporated entity may not participate in a qualified ESPP even if the partnership or unincorporated entity may be related to, or even a subsidiary of, the corporation sponsoring the plan. The rules of Section 423 do, however, prohibit participation in qualified ESPP of employees who own or are deemed to own 5 percent or more of the voting power or value of the stock in the sponsoring corporation. This means that any employee owning stock cannot be granted options if, immediately after the options are granted, that employee owns 5 percent or more of the voting power or value of the stock.

The sponsoring corporation may exclude certain employees from participating in a qualified ESPP. The permitted exclusions include certain part-time employees (defined as employees customarily employed less than twenty hours a week or for not more than five months in a calendar year), employees who have been employed for less than two years, and highly compensated employees as defined in Section 414(q) for tax-qualified plan purposes. There is no exclusion permitted for employees merely because they are collectively bargained employees.

STOCK AS OPTION PROPERTY

As with ISOs, upon exercise of the option granted under a qualified ESPP, the employee must receive stock of the employer corporation or the stock of the parent or subsidiary corporation of the employer. Employer stock for this purpose can be any class of stock, including voting or nonvoting common or preferred stock.

ALL EMPLOYEES MUST HAVE THE SAME RIGHTS AND PRIVILEGES

All employees participating in the plan must have the same rights and privileges. Notwithstanding this requirement, the plan may provide certain limitations on employee participation. Although the determination of the option price, option payment provisions, and all other provisions must be uniform for all employees, the plan may place limits on the maximum number of options that can be exercised under the plan. It also may limit the number of options that employees may be granted to a specified percentage of compensation. The percentage of compensation limit cannot be used, however, to exclude employees from participation such as restricting participation only to those employees whose compensation is above a certain level. There is no specific definition of compensation under Section 423.

LIMITATION ON YEARLY GRANTS

A tax-qualified ESPP cannot permit an employee to accrue the right to purchase stock under the plan at a rate the exceeds $25,000 of the fair market value of the stock (determined when the option is granted) for each calendar year for which the option is outstanding. If the plan options are limited in duration to twenty-seven months, this means that up to $75,000 in fair market value of stock (determined on grant date) can be subject to options. However, this does not limit the total option profit upon exercise. See the similar discussion of Section 422(d) in chapter 3.

For example, suppose options limited in duration to twenty-seven months are granted under a tax-qualified ESPP on November 1, 2001, expiring January 31, 2003, at an exercise price of $8.50 per share when the fair market value of the stock is $10 per share. Options for up to 2,500 shares (25,000 divided by $10) can become exercisable in 2001 and in 2002, and additional 2,500 shares can become exercisable on January 1, 2003. If the fair market value of the 2,500 shares on January 31, 2003, was $108.50 per share, the employee would have an overall profit of $750,000 if all of the 7,500 shares were purchased and sold on January 31, 2003.

EXERCISE PRICE

The exercise price of an option granted under a qualified ESPP must not be less than either (1) 85 percent of the fair market value of the sponsoring corporation's stock at the time of grant or (2) 85 percent of the stock's fair market value at the time the option is exercised, whichever is less. If the terms of an offering under a stock purchase plan do not meet these requirements, all options granted under that offering will be treated as not having been granted under a tax-qualified ESPP. The option price may be stated as a dollar amount or as a percentage of fair market value of the corporation's stock; but if the option price is stated as a dollar amount, this amount must at least equal 85 percent of the fair market value of the corporation stock at the time the option is granted.

   Example: On January 1, 2000, Joe, an employee of C Corporation, is granted an option under C's ESPP to purchase 1,000 shares of C's Common Stock on December 31, 2000. Under C's plan, the purchase price is 90 percent of the fair market value of C's stock on the grant date or the exercise date, whichever produces the lower price. The fair market value of C's stock is $10 per share on January 1, 2000 (the grant date), and $20 per share on December 31, 2000 (the exercise date). Joe may exercise his option on December 31, 2000, by paying $9,000, receive stock with a value of $20,000, and still have the favorable tax treatment afforded by Section 423.

DURATION OF OPTION

If the exercise price of the option is at least 85 percent of the fair market value of the corporation's stock at the time the option is exercised, the maximum allowable option exercise period is five years from the date of grant. If the option exercise is determined in any other manner, such as a flat dollar amount, the option must be exercised within twenty-seven months from the date of grant of the option. The plan must specifically provide for these option exercise periods; if it fails to do so, none of the options granted under the plan will be considered as made under a tax-qualified ESPP. If the option exercise price is the lesser of 85 percent of the fair market value of the stock at exercise, but not more than some other fixed amount, the option period must be no more than twenty-seven months from the date of grant.

RESTRICTIONS ON TRANSFER

A tax-qualified ESPP must prohibit the transfer of options issued under the plan, except for transfers by will or the laws of descent or distribution, and the option must be exercisable during the employee's lifetime only by the employee. These transfer restrictions are the same as for ISOs.

OTHER PERMITTED PLAN PROVISIONS

Like an ISO plan, a tax-qualified ESPP can contain additional terms so long as those terms do not conflict with any of the Section 423 requirements for a qualified ESPP. Typical additional terms include provisions concerning when options will be granted, the method of paying the option exercise price, and limitations on when options can be exercised.

TAX TREATMENT OF EMPLOYEE

The tax treatment of an employee, including the holding period requirements for tax-qualified ESPP shares, is similar to that of an ISO. If an employee is granted an option under a tax-qualified ESPP, the employee does not recognize taxable income upon exercise of the option. On the other hand, if the option is not issued under a tax-qualified ESPP, or if the option or the option holder fails to meet the requirements of Section 423, the employee will generally recognize compensation income at the time of exercise of the option in an amount equal to the excess of the fair market value of the stock over the option exercise price. The basis for determining gain or loss upon the employee's subsequent disposition of stock acquired under a tax-qualified ESPP is the option exercise price, adjusted, as discussed later, for any compensation income recognized upon the disposition of the shares.

The holding period for stock acquired through a tax-qualified ESPP is the later of two years after the date of grant of the option or one year from the date of transfer of the stock pursuant to the option. If the employee disposes of the stock acquired by exercising an option under a tax-qualified ESPP before the expiration of this statutory holding period, a "disqualifying disposition" occurs, and the employee will recognize as compensation income in the year of the disqualifying disposition the amount by which the fair market value of the stock at that time exceeds the option exercise price. On the other hand, if the sale of the stock occurs after the holding period expires, the employee recognizes a long-term capital gain at the time of the sale in an amount equal to the excess of the proceeds of the sale over the exercise price plus the amount of any discount taxable as compensation income.

If an option issued under a tax-qualified ESPP was issued with a discount of not more than 15 percent, the holder must include in taxable income at the time of the sale or other disposition of the stock, or upon the employee's death while holding the stock, the amount by which either the fair market value of the stock (1) at the time of grant or (2) at the time of disposition or death, whichever is less, exceeds the exercise price. The employee's basis for determining capital gain or loss on the disposition of the option stock is increased by the amount of the compensation income so recognized.

Example 1: On January 1, 2000, all employees of M Corporation are granted options under an Section 423 ESPP to purchase M Corporation stock on December 31, 2000, at 85 percent of the fair market value of M's stock on the grant date or the exercise date, whichever is lower.

The fair market value of M's stock on January 1, 2000, is $20 per share, and the fair market value on December 31, 2000, is $40 per share. Susan, an employee of M Corporation, exercises options to buy 1,000 shares of M stock on December 31, 2000, paying $17,000 for the shares (85 percent × $20 per share × 1,000 shares).

On June 1, 2002, Susan sells the 1,000 shares of M Stock for $50 per share. She will have compensation income of $3,000 (15 percent × $20 per share × 1,000 shares) and a long-term capital gain of $30,000 ($50,000 amount realized on sale, minus $20,000 basis in the shares).

Example 2: Assume the same facts as in the prior example, except that Susan sells the stock for $35 per share on June 1, 2001. She will have compensation income of $18,000 (amount realized of $35,000, minus purchase price of $17,000) and no capital gain since the sale was a disqualifying disposition.

Example 3: Assume the same facts as before, except that Susan sells the stock for $35 per share on January 2, 2002. She will have $3,000 of compensation income and $15,000 of long-term capital gains.

TAX TREATMENT OF EMPLOYER

The deductions permitted to the employer under an ESPP are also similar to an ISO. The employer may not deduct the difference between the fair market value of the option stock and the option exercise price if the option is issued under a tax-qualified ESPP. If, however, the option is treated as not being granted under a tax-qualified ESPP, just as with non-ISOs, the employer is entitled to a compensation deduction equal to the amount the employee includes in income in the employer's taxable year corresponding to the year in which the employee is required to include the amount as income. This will normally occur as a result of the employee's disqualifying disposition of the shares. The employer may be required to withhold income and other payroll taxes in such a case.

Currently, there is no FICA withholding on the ESPP purchase date based on an IRS revenue ruling issued in 1971. However, this issue is currently under reconsideration by the IRS.

SAMPLE TAX-QUALIFIED ESPP

Appendix 11 contains a tax-qualified ESPP with the longest option period permitted under Section 423. The employee is given five years to exercise the option. If the option is in fact exercised within twenty-seven months of the grant date, the option price is the lesser of 85 percent of the fair market value of the stock on the grant date or exercise date. However, if the option is in fact exercised after twenty-seven months, the option price becomes 85 percent of the fair market value of the stock on the exercise date.

This provision encourages employees to exercise the option within the twenty-seven month period but allows the employee up to five years to exercise the option if he or she is willing to pay what would probably be a higher exercise price.

Most tax-qualified ESPP are not as generous to employees. Many only allow a short period to exercise the option (e.g., six months) and may set an exercise price of 90 or 95 percent of fair market value on the grant date or exercise date, whichever is smaller.

Some plans set a minimum dollar figure on the option exercise price to prevent an employee from profiting from depressed market prices for the stock.

CONCLUSION

A tax-qualified ESPP provides a broad-based stock option with no accounting charge. Employees can be given up to a 15 percent discount to encourage stock ownership. If you believe the Rutgers study (see chapter 1) that broad-based stock option plans produce productivity gains exceeding their equity dilution, you should seriously consider this alternative to the traditional key employee option plan.

An ESPP is most suited to a publicly traded company that has a liquid marketplace for resales of ESPP stock. A private company should only consider an ESPP if it is willing to provide a similar marketplace for resale of ESPP stock. This can only be accomplished by private companies with sufficient cash resources to fund such a private market.

Appendix 1

Private Company
[Sale or IPO Exit]
ABC, Inc.
2001 Stock Option Plan

1. **Purpose of Plan**

   The purpose of this 2001 Stock Option Plan (the "Plan") is to provide additional incentive to officers, other key employees, and directors of, and important consultants to, ABC, Inc., a Pennsylvania corporation (the "Company"), and each present or future parent or subsidiary corporation, by encouraging them to invest in shares of the Company's common stock, no par value ("Common Stock"), and thereby acquire a proprietary interest in the Company and an increased personal interest in the Company's continued success and progress.

2. **Aggregate Number of Shares**

   200,000 shares of the Company's Common Stock shall be the aggregate number of shares which may be issued under this Plan. Notwithstanding the foregoing, in the event of any change in the outstanding shares of the Common Stock of the Company by reason of a stock dividend, stock split, combination of shares, recapitalization, merger, consolidation, transfer of assets, reorganization, conversion or what the Committee (defined in Section 4[a]), deems in its sole discretion to be similar circumstances, the aggregate number and kind of shares which may be issued under this Plan shall be appropriately adjusted in a manner determined in the sole discretion of the Committee. Reacquired shares of the Company's Common Stock, as well as unissued shares, may be used for the purpose of this Plan. Common Stock of the Company subject to options which have terminated unexercised, either in whole or in part, shall be available for future options granted under this Plan.

3. **Class of Persons Eligible to Receive Options**

   All officers and key employees of the Company and of any present or future Company parent or subsidiary corporation are eligible to receive an option or options under this Plan. All directors of, and important consultants to, the Company and of any present or future Company parent or subsidiary corporation are also eligible to receive an option or options under this Plan. The individuals who shall, in fact, receive an option or options shall be selected by the Committee, in its sole discretion, except as otherwise specified in Section 4 hereof. No individual may receive options under this Plan for more than 80 percent of the total number of shares of the Company's Common Stock authorized for issuance under this Plan.

4. **Administration of Plan**

   (a) Prior to the registration of the Company's Common Stock under Section 12 of the Securities Exchange Act of 1934, this Plan shall be administered by the Company's Board of Directors and, after such registration, by an Option Committee ("Committee") appointed by the Company's Board of Directors. The Committee shall consist of a minimum of two and a maximum of five members of the Board of Directors, each of whom shall be a "Nonemployee Director" within the meaning of Rule 16(b)(3) under the Securities Exchange Act of 1934, as amended, or any future corresponding rule, except that the failure of the Committee for any reason to be composed solely of Nonemployee Directors shall not prevent an option from being considered granted under this Plan. The Committee shall, in addition to its other authority and subject to the provisions of this Plan, determine which individuals shall in fact be granted an option or options, whether the option shall be an Incentive Stock Option or a Nonqualified Stock Option (as such terms are defined in Section 5[a]), the number of shares to be subject to each of the options, the time or times at which the options shall be granted, the rate of option exercisability, and, subject to Section 5 hereof, the price at which each of the options is exercisable and the duration of the option. The term "Committee," as used in this Plan and the options granted hereunder, refers to the Board of Directors prior to the registration of the Company's Common Stock under Section 12 of the Securities Exchange Act of 1934 and, after such registration, to the Committee; prior to such registration, the Board of Directors may consist of only one director.

(b) The Committee shall adopt such rules for the conduct of its business and administration of this Plan as it considers desirable. A majority of the members of the Committee shall constitute a quorum for all purposes. The vote or written consent of a majority of the members of the Committee on a particular matter shall constitute the act of the Committee on such matter. The Committee shall have the right to construe the Plan and the options issued pursuant to it, to correct defects and omissions and to reconcile inconsistencies to the extent necessary to effectuate the Plan and the options issued pursuant to it, and such action shall be final, binding and conclusive upon all parties concerned. No member of the Committee or the Board of Directors shall be liable for any act or omission (whether or not negligent) taken or omitted in good faith, or for the exercise of an authority or discretion granted in connection with the Plan to a Committee or the Board of Directors, or for the acts or omissions of any other members of a Committee or the Board of Directors. Subject to the numerical limitations on Committee membership set forth in Section 4(a) hereof, the Board of Directors may at any time appoint additional members of the Committee and may at any time remove any member of the Committee with or without cause. Vacancies in the Committee, however caused, may be filled by the Board of Directors, if it so desires.

5. Incentive Stock Options and Nonqualified Stock Options

(a) Options issued pursuant to this Plan may be either Incentive Stock Options granted pursuant to Section 5(b) hereof or Nonqualified Stock Options granted pursuant to Section 5(c) hereof, as determined by the Committee. An "Incentive Stock Option" is an option which satisfies all of the requirements of Section 422(b) of the Internal Revenue Code of 1986, as amended (the "Code") and the regulations thereunder, and a "Nonqualified Stock Option" is an option which either does not satisfy all of those requirements or the terms of the option provide that it will not be treated as an Incentive Stock Option. The Committee may grant both an Incentive Stock Option and a Nonqualified Stock Option to the same person, or more than one of each type of option to the same person. The option price for options issued under this Plan shall be equal at least to the fair market value (as defined below) of the Company's Common Stock on the date of the grant of the option. The fair market value of the Company's Common Stock on any particular date shall mean the last reported sale price of a share of the Company's Common Stock on any stock exchange on which such stock is then listed or admitted to trading, or on the NASDAQ National Market System or Small Cap NASDAQ, on such date, or if no sale took place on such day, the last such date on which a sale took place, or if the Common Stock is not then quoted on the NASDAQ National Market System or Small Cap NASDAQ, or listed or admitted to trading on any stock exchange, the average of the bid and asked prices in the over-the-counter market on such date, or if none of the foregoing, a price determined in good faith by the Committee to equal the fair market value per share of the Common Stock.

(b) Subject to the authority of the Committee set forth in Section 4(a) hereof, Incentive Stock Options issued pursuant to this Plan shall be issued substantially in the form set forth in Appendix I hereof, which form is hereby incorporated by reference and made a part hereof, and shall contain substantially the terms and conditions set forth therein. Incentive Stock Options shall not be exercisable after the expiration of ten years from the date such options are granted, unless terminated earlier under the terms of the option, except that options granted to individuals described in Section 422(b)(6) of the Code shall conform to the provisions of Section 422(c)(5) of the Code. At the time of the grant of an Incentive Stock Option hereunder, the Committee may, in its discretion, amend or supplement any of the option terms contained in Appendix I for any particular optionee, provided that the option as amended or supplemented satisfies the requirements of Section 422(b) of the Code and the regulations thereunder. Each of the options granted pursuant to this Section 5(b) is intended, if possible, to be an "Incentive Stock Option" as that term is defined in Section 422(b) of the Code and the regulations thereunder. In the event this Plan or any option granted pursuant to this Section 5(b) is in any way inconsistent with the applicable legal requirements of the Code or the regulations thereunder for an Incentive Stock Option, this Plan and such option shall be deemed automatically amended as of the date hereof to conform to such legal requirements, if such conformity may be achieved by amendment.

(c) Subject to the authority of the Committee set forth in Section 4(a) hereof, Nonqualified Stock Options issued to officers and other key employees pursuant to this Plan shall be issued substantially in the form set forth in Appendix II hereof, which form is hereby incorporated by reference and made a part hereof, and shall contain substantially the terms and conditions set forth therein. Subject to the authority of the Committee set forth in Section 4(a) hereof, Nonqualified Stock Options issued to directors and important consultants pursuant to this Plan shall be issued substantially in the form set forth in Appendix III hereof, which form is hereby incorporated by reference and made a part hereof, and shall contain substantially the terms and conditions set forth therein. Nonqualified Stock Options shall expire ten years after the date they are granted, unless terminated earlier under the option terms. At the time of granting a Nonqualified Stock Option hereunder, the Committee may, in its discretion, amend or supplement any of the option terms contained in Appendix II or Appendix III for any particular optionee.

(d) Neither the Company nor any of its current or future parent, subsidiaries or affiliates, nor their officers, directors, shareholders, stock option plan committees, employees or agents shall have any liability to any optionee in the event (i) an option granted pursuant to Section 5(b) hereof does not qualify as an "Incentive Stock Option" as that term is used in Section 422(b) of the Code and the regulations thereunder; (ii) any optionee does not obtain the tax treatment pertaining to an Incentive Stock Option; or (iii) any option granted pursuant to Section 5(c) hereof is an "Incentive Stock Option."

6. Amendment, Supplement, Suspension, and Termination

Options shall not be granted pursuant to this Plan after the expiration of ten years from the date the Plan is adopted by the Board of Directors of the Company. The Board of Directors reserves the right at any time, and from time to time, to amend or supplement this Plan in any way, or to suspend or terminate it, effective as of such date, which date may be either before or after the taking of such action, as may be specified by the Board of Directors; provided, however, that such action shall not, without the consent of the optionee, affect options granted under the Plan prior to the actual date on which such action occurred. If an amendment or supplement of this Plan is required by the Code or the regulations thereunder to be approved by the shareholders of the Company in order to permit the granting of "Incentive Stock Options" (as that term is defined in Section 422(b) of the Code and regulations thereunder) pursuant to the amended or supplemented Plan, such amendment or supplement shall also be approved by the shareholders of the Company in such manner as is prescribed by the Code and the regulations thereunder. If the Board of Directors voluntarily submits a proposed amendment, supplement, suspension or termination for shareholder approval, such submission shall not require any future amendments, supplements, suspensions or terminations (whether or not relating to the same provision or subject matter) to be similarly submitted for shareholder approval.

7. Effectiveness of Plan

This Plan shall become effective on the date of its adoption by the Company's Board of Directors, subject however to approval by the holders of the Company's Common Stock in the manner as prescribed in the Code and the regulations thereunder. Options may be granted under this Plan prior to obtaining shareholder approval, provided such options shall not be exercisable until shareholder approval is obtained.

8. General Conditions

(a) Nothing contained in this Plan or any option granted pursuant to this Plan shall confer upon any employee the right to continue in the employ of the Company or any affiliated or subsidiary corporation or interfere in any way with the rights of the Company or any affiliated or subsidiary corporation to terminate his employment in any way.

(b) Nothing contained in this Plan or any option granted pursuant to this Plan shall confer upon any director or consultant the right to continue as a director of, or consultant to, the Company or any affiliated or subsidiary corporation or interfere in any way with the rights of the Company or any affiliated or subsidiary corporation, or their respective shareholders, to terminate the directorship of any such director or the consultancy relationship of any such consultant.

(c) Corporate action constituting an offer of stock for sale to any person under the terms of the options to be granted hereunder shall be deemed complete as of the date when the Committee authorizes the grant of the option to such person, regardless of when the option is actually delivered to such person or acknowledged or agreed to by him.

(d) The terms "parent corporation" and "subsidiary corporation" as used throughout this Plan, and the options granted pursuant to this Plan, shall (except as otherwise provided in the option form) have the meaning that is ascribed to that term when contained in Section 422(b) of the Code and the regulations thereunder, and the Company shall be deemed to be the grantor corporation for purposes of applying such meaning.

(e) References in this Plan to the Code shall be deemed to also refer to the corresponding provisions of any future United States revenue law.

(f) The use of the masculine pronoun shall include the feminine gender whenever appropriate.

APPENDIX I

INCENTIVE STOCK OPTION

To: _____
          Name

         _____
          Address

Date of Grant: _____

You are hereby granted an option, effective as of the date hereof, to purchase _____ shares of common stock, no par value ("Common Stock"), of ABC, Inc., a Pennsylvania corporation (the "Company"), at a price of $____ per share pursuant to the Company's Stock Option Plan (the "Plan").

This option shall terminate and is not exercisable after ten years from the date of its grant (the "Scheduled Termination Date"), except if terminated earlier as hereafter provided.

Your option may first be exercised on and after nine years and ten months from the date of grant, but not before that time, unless there is an Acceleration Event (as hereafter defined), in which case this option shall become immediately exercisable, except as hereafter provided. An "Acceleration Event" refers to a date which is one year after the earlier of the following: (a) the first closing date for the initial public offering ("IPO") of the Common Stock of the Company (or of a parent corporation) in which the Company (or such parent corporation) raises at least $15 million, or (b) the date of a "Change of Control" (as defined below). A "Change of Control" shall be deemed to have occurred upon the happening of any of the following events:

1. If John Doe (or in the event of his death, a representative of his estate or his heirs) ceases to be a director of the Company or a successor to the Company by merger or other form of acquisition;

2. If John Doe (or in the event of his death, a representative of his estate or his heirs) ceases to own at least 10 percent of the stock of the Company or a successor to the Company by merger or other form of acquisition; or

3. Any other event deemed to constitute a "Change of Control" by the Committee.

Notwithstanding the foregoing, if on the date of an Acceleration Event, you have not been employed by the Company for a total of at least three (3) years, this option will not be exercisable in full on the date of an Acceleration Event, but instead shall be exercisable as follows: (a) if on the date of an Acceleration Event you have been employed by the Company for a total of two (2) or more years, this option will be exercisable for two-thirds of the total number of shares then subject to this option, and the remaining one-third of the total number of shares then subject to this option will become exercisable after you have been employed by the Company for a total of three (3) years; (b) if on the date of an Acceleration Event you have been employed by the Company for a total of one (1) year or more and less than two (2) years, this option will be exercisable for one-third of the total number of shares then subject to this option and an additional one-third each of the total number of shares then subject to this option shall become exercisable when you have been employed by the Company for two (2) years and three (3) years, respectively; (c) if on the date of an Acceleration Event you have been employed by the Company for a total of less than one (1) year, this option will not be exercisable until you have been employed by the Company for a total of one (1) year, at which time this option will be exercisable for one-third of the total number of shares then subject to this option and an additional one-third each of the total number of shares then subject to this option shall become exercisable when you have been employed by the Company for two (2) years and three (3) years, respectively.

In the event of an IPO of the Common Stock of a parent corporation of the Company, and provided such parent corporation assumes the obligations of the Company under this Plan, this option shall thereupon pertain solely to the Common Stock of such parent corporation and the Company shall have no obligation whatsoever hereunder. In the event of an IPO in which the Company or its parent corporation has two classes of Common Stock, only one of which is issued to the public in the IPO, this option shall pertain solely to the class of Common Stock issued to the public in the IPO.

You may exercise your option by giving written notice to the Secretary of the Company on forms supplied by the Company at its then principal executive office, accompanied by payment of the option price for the total number of shares you specify that you wish to purchase. The payment may be in any of the following forms: (a) cash, which may be evidenced by a check and includes cash received from a stock brokerage firm in a so-called "cashless exercise"; (b) (unless prohibited by the Committee) certificates representing shares of Common Stock of the Company, which will be valued by the Secretary of the Company at the fair market value per share of the Company's Common Stock (as determined in accordance with the Plan) on the date of delivery of such certificates to the Company, accompanied by an assignment of the stock to the Company; or (c) (unless prohibited by the Committee) any combination of cash and Common Stock of the Company valued as provided in clause (b). The use of the so-called "attestation procedure" to exercise a stock option may be permitted by the Committee. Any assignment of stock shall be in a form and substance satisfactory to the Secretary of the Company, including guarantees of signature(s) and payment of all transfer taxes if the Secretary deems such guarantees necessary or desirable.

Your option will, to the extent not previously exercised by you, terminate three months after the date on which your employment by the Company or a Company subsidiary corporation is terminated (whether such termination be voluntary or involuntary) other than by reason of disability as defined in Section 22(e)(3) of the Internal Revenue Code of 1986, as amended (the "Code"), and the regulations thereunder, or death, in which case your option will terminate one year from the date of termination of employment due to disability or death (but in no event later than the Scheduled Termination Date). After the date your employment is terminated, as aforesaid, you may exercise this option only for the number of shares which you had a right to purchase and did not purchase on the date your employment terminated. If you are employed by a Company subsidiary corporation, your employment shall be deemed to have terminated on the date your employer ceases to be a Company subsidiary corporation, unless you are on that date transferred to the Company or another Company subsidiary corporation. Your employment shall not be deemed to have terminated if you are transferred from the Company to a Company subsidiary corporation, or vice versa, or from one Company subsidiary corporation to another Company subsidiary corporation.

If you die while employed by the Company or a Company subsidiary corporation, your executor or administrator, as the case may be, may, at any time within one year after the date of your death (but in no event later than the Scheduled Termination Date), exercise the option as to any shares which you had a right to purchase and did not purchase during your lifetime. If your employment with the Company or a Company parent or subsidiary corporation is terminated by reason of your becoming disabled (within the meaning of Section 22(e)(3) of the Code and the regulations thereunder), you or your legal guardian or custodian may at any time within one year after the date of such termination (but in no event later than the Scheduled Termination Date), exercise the option as to any shares which you had a right to purchase and did not purchase prior to such termination. Your executor, administrator, guardian, or custodian must present proof of his authority satisfactory to the Company prior to being allowed to exercise this option.

In the event of any change in the outstanding shares of the Common Stock of the Company by reason of a stock dividend, stock split, combination of shares, recapitalization, merger, consolidation, transfer of assets, reorganization, conversion, or what the Committee deems in its sole discretion to be similar circumstances, the number and kind of shares subject to this option and the option price of such shares shall be appropriately adjusted in a manner to be determined in the sole discretion of the Committee.

In the event of a liquidation or proposed liquidation of the Company, including (but not limited to) a transfer of assets followed by a liquidation of the Company, or in the event of a Change of Control (as previously defined) or proposed Change of Control, the Committee shall have the right to require you to exercise this option upon thirty (30) days prior written notice to you. If at the time such written notice is given this option is not otherwise exercisable, the written notice will set forth your right to exercise this option even though it is not otherwise exercisable. In the event this option is not exercised by you within the thirty (30) day period set forth in such written notice, this option shall terminate on the last day of such thirty (30) day period, notwithstanding anything to the contrary contained in this option.

This option is not transferable otherwise than by will or the laws of descent and distribution, and is exercisable during your lifetime only by you, including, for this purpose, your legal guardian or custodian in the event of disability. Until the option price has been paid in full pursuant to due exercise of this option and the purchased shares are delivered to you, you do not have any rights as a shareholder of the Company. The Company reserves the right not to deliver to you the shares purchased by virtue of the exercise of this option during any period of time in which the Company deems, in its sole discretion, that such delivery would violate a federal, state, local, or securities exchange rule, regulation, or law.

Notwithstanding anything to the contrary contained herein, this option is not exercisable until all the following events occur and during the following periods of time:

(a) Until the Plan pursuant to which this option is granted is approved by the shareholders of the Company in the manner prescribed by the Code and the regulations thereunder;

(b) Until this option and the optioned shares are approved and/or registered with such federal, state, and local regulatory bodies or agencies and securities exchanges as the Company may deem necessary or desirable; or

(c) During any period of time in which the Company deems that the exercisability of this option, the offer to sell the shares optioned hereunder, or the sale thereof, may violate a federal, state, local, or securities exchange rule, regulation, or law, or may cause the Company to be legally obligated to issue or sell more shares than the Company is legally entitled to issue or sell.

(d) Until you have paid or made suitable arrangements to pay (which may include payment through the surrender of Common Stock, unless prohibited by the Committee) (i) all federal, state, and local income tax withholding required to be withheld by the Company in connection with the option exercise and (ii) the employee's portion of other federal, state, and local payroll and other taxes due in connection with the option exercise.

(e) Until you have executed such shareholder agreements as shall be required by the Company. Such shareholder agreements may, at the Company's option, include (among other provisions) provisions requiring you to (i) enter into any "lock-up" agreements required by underwriters, (ii) vote on trust agreements, (iii) grant to the Company or its nominees an option to repurchase the stock, (iv) not sell, pledge or otherwise dispose of the stock without the consent of the Company, (v) maintain any Subchapter S elections made by the Company, (vi) grant rights of first refusal to the Company or its nominees with respect to the stock, and (vii) join in any sale of a majority or all of the outstanding stock of the Company.

The following two paragraphs shall be applicable if, on the date of exercise of this option, the Common Stock to be purchased pursuant to such exercise has not been registered under the Securities Act of 1933, as amended, and under applicable state securities laws, and shall continue to be applicable for so long as such registration has not occurred:

(a) The optionee hereby agrees, warrants and represents that he will acquire the Common Stock to be issued hereunder for his own account for investment purposes only, and not with a view to, or in connection with, any resale or other distribution of any of such shares, except as hereafter permitted. The optionee further agrees that he will not at any time make any offer, sale, transfer, pledge, or other disposition of such Common Stock to be issued hereunder without an effective registration statement under the Securities Act of 1933, as amended, and under any applicable state securities laws or an opinion of counsel acceptable to the Company to the effect that the proposed transaction will be exempt from such registration. The optionee shall execute such instruments, representations, acknowledgments, and agreements as the Company may, in its sole discretion, deem advisable to avoid any violation of federal, state, local, or securities exchange rule, regulation, or law.

(b) The certificates for Common Stock to be issued to the optionee hereunder shall bear the following legend:

> "The shares represented by this certificate have not been registered under the Securities Act of 1933, as amended, or under applicable state securities laws. The shares have been acquired for investment and may not be offered, sold, transferred, pledged, or otherwise disposed of without an effective registration statement under the Securities Act of 1933, as amended, and under any applicable state securities laws or an opinion of counsel acceptable to the Company that the proposed transaction will be exempt from such registration."

The foregoing legend shall be removed upon registration, of the legended shares under the Securities Act of 1933, as amended, and under any applicable state laws or upon receipt of any opinion of counsel acceptable to the Company that said registration is no longer required.

The sole purpose of the agreements, warranties, representations, and legend set forth in the two immediately preceding paragraphs is to prevent violations of the Securities Act of 1933, as amended, and any applicable state securities laws.

It is the intention of the Company and you that this option shall, if possible, be an "Incentive Stock Option" as that term is used in Section 422(b) of the Code and the regulations thereunder. In the event this option is in any way inconsistent with the legal requirements of the Code or the regulations thereunder for an "Incentive Stock Option," this option shall be deemed automatically amended as of the date hereof to conform to such legal requirements, if such conformity may be achieved by amendment. To the extent that the number of shares subject to this option which are exercisable for the first time exceed the $100,000 limitation contained in Section 422(d) of the Code, this option will not be considered an Incentive Stock Option.

Nothing herein shall modify your status as an at-will employee of the Company. Further, nothing herein guarantees you employment for any specified period of time. This means that either you or the Company may terminate your employment at any time for any reason, with or without cause, or for no reason. You recognize that, for instance, you may terminate your employment or the Company may terminate your employment prior to the date on which your option becomes vested or exercisable. You understand that the Company has no obligation to consider or effectuate a public offering of its stock or a Change of Control.

Any dispute or disagreement between you and the Company with respect to any portion of this option (excluding Attachment A hereto) or its validity, construction, meaning, performance, or your rights hereunder shall be settled by arbitration in accordance with the Commercial Arbitration Rules of the American Arbitration Association or its successor, as amended from time to time. However, prior to submission to arbitration you will attempt to resolve any disputes or disagreements with the Company over this option amicably and informally, in good faith, for a period not to exceed two weeks. Thereafter, the dispute or disagreement will be submitted to arbitration. At any time prior to a decision from the arbitrator(s) being rendered, you and the Company may resolve the dispute by settlement. You and the Company shall equally share the costs charged by the American Arbitration Association or its successor, but you and the Company shall otherwise be solely responsible for your own respective counsel fees and expenses. The decision of the arbitrator(s) shall be made in writing, setting forth the award, the reasons for the decision and award and shall be binding and conclusive on you and the Company. Further, neither you nor the Company shall appeal any such award. Judgment of a court of competent jurisdiction may be entered upon the award and may be enforced as such in accordance with the provisions of the award.

This option shall be subject to the terms of the Plan in effect on the date this option is granted, which terms are hereby incorporated herein by reference and made a part hereof. In the event of any conflict between the terms of this option and the terms of the Plan in effect on the date of this option, the terms of the Plan shall govern. This option constitutes the entire understanding between the Company and you with respect to the subject matter hereof and no amendment, supplement, or waiver of this option, in whole or in part, shall be binding upon the Company unless in writing and signed by the President of the Company. This option and the performances of the parties hereunder shall be construed in accordance with and governed by the laws of the State of Pennsylvania.

In consideration of the grant to you of this option, you hereby agree to the confidentiality and noninterference provisions set forth in Attachment A hereto.

Please sign the copy of this option and return it to the Company's Secretary, thereby indicating your understanding of and agreement with its terms and conditions, **including Attachment A hereto.**

ABC, Inc.

By: _____

I hereby acknowledge receipt of a copy of the foregoing stock option and the Plan, and having read them hereby signify my understanding of, and my agreement with, their terms and conditions, **including Attachment A hereto.** I accept this option in full satisfaction of any previous written or verbal promises made to me by the Company with respect to option grants.

_____   _____

(Signature)   (Date)

Attachment A to Stock Option

Confidentiality and Noninterference

(a) You covenant and agree that, in consideration of the grant to you of this stock option, you will not, during your employment with the Company or at any time thereafter, except with the express prior written consent of the Company or pursuant to the lawful order of any judicial or administrative agency of government, directly or indirectly, disclose, communicate or divulge to any individual or entity, or use for the benefit of any individual or entity, any knowledge or information with respect to the conduct or details of the Company's business which you, acting reasonably, believe or should believe to be of a confidential nature and the disclosure of which not to be in the Company's interest.

(b) You covenant and agree that, in consideration of the grant to you of this stock option, you will not, during your employment with the Company and for a period of two years thereafter, except with the express prior written consent of the Company, directly or indirectly, whether as employee, owner, partner, consultant, agent, director, officer, shareholder or in any other capacity, engage in or assist any individual or entity to engage in any act or action which you, acting reasonably, believe or should believe would be harmful or inimical to the interests of the Company.

(c) You covenant and agree that, in consideration of the grant to you of this stock option, you will not, for a period of two years after your employment with the Company ceases for any reason whatsoever (whether voluntary or not), except with the express prior written consent of the Company, directly or indirectly, whether as employee, owner, partner, consultant, agent, director, officer, shareholder or in any other capacity, for your own account or for the benefit of any individual or entity, (i) solicit any customer of the Company for business which would result in such customer terminating their relationship with the Company; or (ii) solicit or induce any individual or entity which is an employee of the Company to leave the Company or to otherwise terminate their relationship with the Company.

(d) The parties agree that any breach by you of any of the covenants or agreements contained in this Attachment A will result in irreparable injury to the Company for which money damages could not adequately compensate the Company and therefore, in the event of any such breach, the Company shall be entitled (in addition to any other rights and remedies which it may have at law or in equity) to have an injunction issued by any competent court enjoining and restraining you and/or any other individual or entity involved therein from continuing such breach. The existence of any claim or cause of action which you may have against the Company or any other individual or entity shall not constitute a defense or bar to the enforcement of such covenants. If the Company is obliged to resort to the courts for the enforcement of any of the covenants or agreements contained in this Attachment A, or if such covenants or agreements are otherwise the subject of litigation between the parties, and the Company prevails in such enforcement or litigation, then the term of such covenants and agreements shall be extended for a period of time equal to the period of such breach, which extension shall commence on the later of (a) the date on which the original (unextended) term of such covenants and agreements is scheduled to terminate or (b) the date of the final court order (without further right of appeal) enforcing such covenant or agreement.

(e) If any portion of the covenants or agreements contained in this Attachment A, or the application hereof, is construed to be invalid or unenforceable, the other portions of such covenant(s) or agreement(s) or the application thereof shall not be affected and shall be given full force and effect without regard to the invalid or enforceable portions to the fullest extent possible. If any covenant or agreement in this Attachment A is held unenforceable because of the area covered, the duration thereof, or the scope thereof, then the court making such determination shall have the power to reduce the area and/or duration and/or limit the scope thereof, and the covenant or agreement shall then be enforceable in its reduced form.

(f) For purposes of this Attachment A, the term "the Company" shall include the Company, any successor to the Company and all present and future direct and indirect subsidiaries and affiliates of the Company.

APPENDIX II

NONQUALIFIED STOCK OPTION FOR
OFFICERS AND OTHER KEY EMPLOYEES

To: _____
        Name

_____
        Address

Date of Grant: _____

You are hereby granted an option, effective as of the date hereof, to purchase _____ shares of common stock, no par value ("Common Stock"), of ABC, Inc., a Pennsylvania corporation (the "Company"), at a price of $____ per share pursuant to the Company's Stock Option Plan (the "Plan").

This option shall terminate and is not exercisable after ten years from the date of its grant (the "Scheduled Termination Date"), except if terminated earlier as hereafter provided.

Your option may first be exercised on and after nine years and ten months from the date of grant, but not before that time, unless there is an Acceleration Event (as hereafter defined), in which case this option shall become immediately exercisable, except as hereafter provided. An "Acceleration Event" refers to a date which is one year after the earlier of the following: (a) the first closing date for the initial public offering ("IPO") of the Common Stock of the Company (or of a parent corporation) in which the Company (or such parent corporation) raises at least $15 million, or (b) the date of a "Change of Control" (as defined below). A "Change of Control" shall be deemed to have occurred upon the happening of any of the following events:

1. If John Doe (or in the event of his death, a representative of his estate or his heirs) ceases to be a director of the Company or a successor to the Company by merger or other form of acquisition;

2. If John Doe (or in the event of his death, a representative of his estate or his heirs) ceases to own at least 10 percent of the stock of the Company or a successor to the Company by merger or other form of acquisition; or

3. Any other event deemed to constitute a "Change of Control" by the Committee.

Notwithstanding the foregoing, if on the date of an Acceleration Event, you have not been employed by the Company for a total of at least three (3) years, this option will not be exercisable in full on the date of an Acceleration Event, but instead shall be exercisable as follows: (a) if on the date of an Acceleration Event you have been employed by the Company for a total of two (2) or more years, this option will be exercisable for two-thirds of the total number of shares then subject to this option, and the remaining one-third of the total number of shares then subject to this option will become exercisable after you have been employed by the Company for a total of three (3) years; (b) if on the date of an Acceleration Event you have been employed by the Company for a total of one (1) year or more and less than two (2) years, this option will be exercisable for one-third of the total number of shares then subject to this option and an additional one-third each of the total number of shares then subject to this option shall become exercisable when you have been employed by the Company for two (2) years and three (3) years, respectively; (c) if on the date of an Acceleration Event you have been employed by the Company for a total of less than one (1) year, this option will not be exercisable until you have been employed by the Company for a total of one (1) year, at which time this option will be exercisable for one-third of the total number of shares then subject to this option and an additional one-third each of the total number of shares then subject to this option shall become exercisable when you have been employed by the Company for two (2) years and three (3) years, respectively.

In the event of an IPO of the Common Stock of a parent corporation of the Company, and provided such parent corporation assumes the obligations of the Company under this Plan, this option shall thereupon pertain solely to the Common Stock of such parent corporation and the Company shall have no obligation whatsoever hereunder. In the event of an IPO in which the Company or its parent corporation has two classes of Common Stock, only one of which is issued to the public in the IPO, this option shall pertain solely to the class of Common Stock issued to the public in the IPO.

You may exercise your option by giving written notice to the Secretary of the Company on forms supplied by the Company at its then principal executive office, accompanied by payment of the option price for the total number of shares you specify that you wish to purchase. The payment may be in any of the following forms: (a) cash, which may be evidenced by a check and includes cash received from a stock brokerage firm in a so-called "cashless exercise"; (b) (unless prohibited by the Committee) certificates representing shares of Common Stock of the Company, which will be valued by the Secretary of the Company at the fair market value per share of the Company's Common Stock (as determined in accordance with the Plan) on the date of delivery of such certificates to the Company, accompanied by an assignment of the stock to the Company; or (c) (unless prohibited by the Committee) any combination of cash and Common Stock of the Company valued as provided in clause (b). The use of the so-called "attestation procedure" to exercise a stock option may be permitted by the Committee. Any assignment of stock shall be in a form and substance satisfactory to the Secretary of the Company, including guarantees of signature(s) and payment of all transfer taxes if the Secretary deems such guarantees necessary or desirable.

Your option will, to the extent not previously exercised by you, terminate three months after the date on which your employment by the Company or a Company subsidiary corporation is terminated (whether such termination be voluntary or involuntary) other than by reason of disability as defined in Section 22(e)(3) of the Internal Revenue Code of 1986, as amended (the "Code"), and the regulations thereunder, or death, in which case your option will terminate one year from the date of termination of employment due to disability or death (but in no event later than the Scheduled Termination Date). After the date your employment is terminated, as aforesaid, you may exercise this option only for the number of shares which you had a right to purchase and did not purchase on the date your employment terminated. If you are employed by a Company subsidiary corporation, your employment shall be deemed to have terminated on the date your employer ceases to be a Company subsidiary corporation, unless you are on that date transferred to the Company or another Company subsidiary corporation. Your employment shall not be deemed to have terminated if you are transferred from the Company to a Company subsidiary corporation, or vice versa, or from one Company subsidiary corporation to another Company subsidiary corporation.

If you die while employed by the Company or a Company subsidiary corporation, your executor or administrator, as the case may be, may, at any time within one year after the date of your death (but in no event later than the Scheduled Termination Date), exercise the option as to any shares which you had a right to purchase and did not purchase during your lifetime. If your employment with the Company or a Company parent or subsidiary corporation is terminated by reason of your becoming disabled (within the meaning of Section 22(e)(3) of the Code and the regulations thereunder), you or your legal guardian or custodian may at any time within one year after the date of such termination (but in no event later than the Scheduled Termination Date), exercise the option as to any shares which you had a right to purchase and did not purchase prior to such termination. Your executor, administrator, guardian, or custodian must present proof of his authority satisfactory to the Company prior to being allowed to exercise this option.

In the event of any change in the outstanding shares of the Common Stock of the Company by reason of a stock dividend, stock split, combination of shares, recapitalization, merger, consolidation, transfer of assets, reorganization, conversion, or what the Committee deems in its sole discretion to be similar circumstances, the number and kind of shares subject to this option and the option price of such shares shall be appropriately adjusted in a manner to be determined in the sole discretion of the Committee.

In the event of a liquidation or proposed liquidation of the Company, including (but not limited to) a transfer of assets followed by a liquidation of the Company, or in the event of a Change of Control (as previously defined) or proposed Change of Control, the Committee shall have the right to require you to exercise this option upon thirty (30) days prior written notice to you. If at the time such written notice is given this option is not otherwise exercisable, the written notice will set forth your right to exercise this option even though it is not otherwise exercisable. In the event this option is not exercised by you within the thirty (30) day period set forth in such written notice, this option shall terminate on the last day of such thirty (30) day period, notwithstanding anything to the contrary contained in this option.

This option is not transferable otherwise than by will or the laws of descent and distribution, and is exercisable during your lifetime only by you, including, for this purpose, your legal guardian or custodian in the event of disability. Until the option price has been paid in full pursuant to due exercise of this option and the purchased shares are delivered to you, you do not have any rights as a shareholder of the Company. The Company reserves the right not to deliver to you the shares purchased by virtue of the exercise of this option during any period of time in which the Company deems, in its sole discretion, that such delivery would violate a federal, state, local, or securities exchange rule, regulation, or law.

Notwithstanding anything to the contrary contained herein, this option is not exercisable until all the following events occur and during the following periods of time:

(a) Until the Plan pursuant to which this option is granted is approved by the shareholders of the Company in the manner prescribed by the Code and the regulations thereunder;

(b) Until this option and the optioned shares are approved and/or registered with such federal, state, and local regulatory bodies or agencies and securities exchanges as the Company may deem necessary or desirable; or

(c) During any period of time in which the Company deems that the exercisability of this option, the offer to sell the shares optioned hereunder, or the sale thereof, may violate a federal, state, local, or securities exchange rule, regulation, or law, or may cause the Company to be legally obligated to issue or sell more shares than the Company is legally entitled to issue or sell.

(d) Until you have paid or made suitable arrangements to pay (which may include payment through the surrender of Common Stock, unless prohibited by the Committee) (i) all federal, state, and local, income tax withholding required to be withheld by the Company in connection with the option exercise and (ii) the employee's portion of other federal, state, and local payroll and other taxes due in connection with the option exercise.

(e) Until you have executed such shareholder agreements as shall be required by the Company. Such shareholder agreements may, at the Company's option, include (among other provisions) provisions requiring you to (i) enter into any "lock-up" agreements required by underwriters, (ii) vote on trust agreements, (iii) grant to the Company or its nominees an option to repurchase the stock, (iv) not sell, pledge or otherwise dispose of the stock without the consent of the Company, (v) maintain any Subchapter S elections made by the Company, (vi) grant rights of first refusal to the Company or its nominees with respect to the stock, and (vii) join in any sale of a majority or all of the outstanding stock of the Company.

The following two paragraphs shall be applicable if, on the date of exercise of this option, the Common Stock to be purchased pursuant to such exercise has not been registered under the Securities Act of 1933, as amended, and under applicable state securities laws, and shall continue to be applicable for so long as such registration has not occurred:

(a) The optionee hereby agrees, warrants, and represents that he will acquire the Common Stock to be issued hereunder for his own account for investment purposes only, and not with a view to, or in connection with, any resale or other distribution of any of such shares, except as hereafter permitted. The optionee further agrees that he will not at any time make any offer, sale, transfer, pledge, or other disposition of such Common Stock to be issued hereunder without an effective registration statement under the Securities Act of 1933, as amended, and under any applicable state securities laws or an opinion of counsel acceptable to the Company to the effect that the proposed transaction will be exempt from such registration. The optionee shall execute such instruments, representations, acknowledgements, and agreements as the Company may, in its sole discretion, deem advisable to avoid any violation of federal, state, local, or securities exchange rule, regulation, or law.

(b) The certificates for Common Stock to be issued to the optionee hereunder shall bear the following legend:

> "The shares represented by this certificate have not been registered under the Securities Act of 1933, as amended, or under applicable state securities laws. The shares have been acquired for investment and may not be offered, sold, transferred, pledged, or otherwise disposed of without an effective registration statement under the Securities Act of 1933, as amended, and under any applicable state securities laws or an opinion of counsel acceptable to the Company that the proposed transaction will be exempt from such registration."

The foregoing legend shall be removed upon registration of the legended shares under the Securities Act of 1933, as amended, and under any applicable state laws or upon receipt of any opinion of counsel acceptable to the Company that said registration is no longer required.

The sole purpose of the agreements, warranties, representations, and legend set forth in the two immediately preceding paragraphs is to prevent violations of the Securities Act of 1933, as amended, and any applicable state securities laws.

It is the intention of the Company and you that this option shall not be an "Incentive Stock Option" as that term is used in Section 422(b) of the Code and the regulations thereunder.

Nothing herein shall modify your status as an at-will employee of the Company. Further, nothing herein guarantees you employment for any specified period of time. This means that either you or the Company may terminate your employment at any time for any reason, with or without cause, or for no reason. You recognize that, for instance, you may terminate your employment or the Company may terminate your employment prior to the date on which your option becomes vested or exercisable. You understand that the Company has no obligation to consider or effectuate a public offering of its stock or a Change of Control.

Any dispute or disagreement between you and the Company with respect to any portion of this option (excluding Attachment A hereto) or its validity, construction, meaning, performance, or your rights hereunder shall be settled by arbitration in accordance with the Commercial Arbitration Rules of the American Arbitration Association or its successor, as amended from time to time. However, prior to submission to arbitration you will attempt to resolve any disputes or disagreements with the Company over this option amicably and informally, in good faith, for a period not to exceed two weeks. Thereafter, the dispute or disagreement will be submitted to arbitration. At any time prior to a decision from the arbitrator(s) being rendered, you and the Company may resolve the dispute by settlement. You and the Company shall equally share the costs charged by the American Arbitration Association or its successor, but you and the Company shall otherwise be solely responsible for your own respective counsel fees and expenses. The decision of the arbitrator(s) shall be made in writing, setting forth the award, the reasons for the decision and award, and shall be binding and conclusive on you and the Company. Further, neither you nor the Company shall appeal any such award. Judgment of a court of competent jurisdiction may be entered upon the award and may be enforced as such in accordance with the provisions of the award.

This option shall be subject to the terms of the Plan in effect on the date this option is granted, which terms are hereby incorporated herein by reference and made a part hereof. In the event of any conflict between the terms of this option and the terms of the Plan in effect on the date of this option, the terms of the Plan shall govern. This option constitutes the entire understanding between the Company and you with respect to the subject matter hereof and no amendment, supplement, or waiver of this option, in whole or in part, shall be binding upon the Company unless in writing and signed by the President of the Company. This option and the performances of the parties hereunder shall be construed in accordance with and governed by the laws of the State of Pennsylvania.

In consideration of the grant to you of this option, you hereby agree to the confidentiality and noninterference provisions set forth in Attachment A hereto.

Please sign the copy of this option and return it to the Company's Secretary, thereby indicating your understanding of and agreement with its terms and conditions, **including Attachment A hereto.**

ABC, Inc.

By:_____

I hereby acknowledge receipt of a copy of the foregoing stock option and, having read it, hereby signify my understanding of, and my agreement with, its terms and conditions, **including Attachment A hereto.**

_____   _____
(Signature)   (Date)

Attachment A to Stock Option

Confidentiality and Noninterference

(a) You covenant and agree that, in consideration of the grant to you of this stock option, you will not, during your employment with the Company or at any time thereafter, except with the express prior written consent of the Company or pursuant to the lawful order of any judicial or administrative agency of government, directly or indirectly, disclose, communicate or divulge to any individual or entity, or use for the benefit of any individual or entity, any knowledge or information with respect to the conduct or details of the Company's business which you, acting reasonably, believe or should believe to be of a confidential nature and the disclosure of which not to be in the Company's interest.

(b) You covenant and agree that, in consideration of the grant to you of this stock option, you will not, during your employment with the Company and for a period of two years thereafter, except with the express prior written consent of the Company, directly or indirectly, whether as employee, owner, partner, consultant, agent, director, officer, shareholder or in any other capacity, engage in or assist any individual or entity to engage in any act or action which you, acting reasonably, believe or should believe would be harmful or inimical to the interests of the Company.

(c) You covenant and agree that, in consideration of the grant to you of this stock option, you will not, for a period of two years after your employment with the Company ceases for any reason whatsoever (whether voluntary or not), except with the express prior written consent of the Company, directly or indirectly, whether as employee, owner, partner, consultant, agent, director, officer, shareholder or in any other capacity, for your own account or for the benefit of any individual or entity, (i) solicit any customer of the Company for business which would result in such customer terminating their relationship with the Company; or (ii) solicit or induce any individual or entity which is an employee of the Company to leave the Company or to otherwise terminate their relationship with the Company.

(d) The parties agree that any breach by you of any of the covenants or agreements contained in this Attachment A will result in irreparable injury to the Company for which money damages could not adequately compensate the Company and therefore, in the event of any such breach, the Company shall be entitled (in addition to any other rights and remedies which it may have at law or in equity) to have an injunction issued by any competent court enjoining and restraining you and/or any other individual or entity involved therein from continuing such breach. The existence of any claim or cause of action which you may have against the Company or any other individual or entity shall not constitute a defense or bar to the enforcement of such covenants. If the Company is obliged to resort to the courts for the enforcement of any of the covenants or agreements contained in this Attachment A, or if such covenants or agreements are otherwise the subject of litigation between the parties, and the Company prevails in such enforcement or litigation, then the term of such covenants and agreements shall be extended for a period of time equal to the period of such breach, which extension shall commence on the later of (a) the date on which the original (unextended) term of such covenants and agreements is scheduled to terminate or (b) the date of the final court order (without further right of appeal) enforcing such covenant or agreement.

(e) If any portion of the covenants or agreements contained in this Attachment A, or the application hereof, is construed to be invalid or unenforceable, the other portions of such covenant(s) or agreement(s) or the application thereof shall not be affected and shall be given full force and effect without regard to the invalid or enforceable portions to the fullest extent possible. If any covenant or agreement in this Attachment A is held unenforceable because of the area covered, the duration thereof, or the scope thereof, then the court making such determination shall have the power to reduce the area and/or duration and/or limit the scope thereof, and the covenant or agreement shall then be enforceable in its reduced form.

(f) For purposes of this Attachment A, the term "the Company" shall include the Company, any successor to the Company and all present and future direct and indirect subsidiaries and affiliates of the Company.

APPENDIX III

**NONQUALIFIED STOCK OPTION FOR DIRECTORS
AND IMPORTANT CONSULTANTS**

To: _____
                  Name

_____
                  Address

Date of Grant: _____

You are hereby granted an option, effective as of the date hereof, to purchase _____ shares of common stock, no par value ("Common Stock"), of ABC, Inc., a Pennsylvania corporation (the "Company"), at a price of $____ per share pursuant to the Company's Stock Option Plan (the "Plan").

This option shall terminate and is not exercisable after ten years from the date of its grant (the "Scheduled Termination Date"), except if terminated earlier as hereafter provided.

Your option may first be exercised on and after nine years and ten months from the date of grant, but not before that time, unless there is an Acceleration Event (as hereafter defined), in which case this option shall become immediately exercisable, except as hereafter provided. An "Acceleration Event" refers to a date which is one year after the earlier of the following: (a) the first closing date for the initial public offering ("IPO") of the Common Stock of the Company (or of a parent corporation) in which the Company (or such parent corporation) raises at least $15 million, or (b) the date of a "Change of Control" (as defined below). A "Change of Control" shall be deemed to have occurred upon the happening of any of the following events:

1. If John Doe (or in the event of his death, a representative of his estate or his heirs) ceases to be a director of the Company or a successor to the Company by merger or other form of acquisition;

2. If John Doe (or in the event of his death, a representative of his estate or his heirs) ceases to own at least 10 percent of the stock of the Company or a successor to the Company by merger or other form of acquisition; or

3. Any other event deemed to constitute a "Change of Control" by the Committee.

Notwithstanding the foregoing, if on the date of an Acceleration Event, you have not been a director of, or consultant to, the Company or any of its subsidiaries or affiliates for a combined total of at least three (3) years, this option will not be exercisable in full on the date of an Acceleration Event, but instead shall be exercisable as follows: (a) if on the date of an Acceleration Event you have been a director of, or consultant to, the Company or any of its subsidiaries or affiliates for a combined total of two (2) or more years, this option will be exercisable for two-thirds of the total number of shares then subject to this option, and the remaining one-third of the total number of shares then subject to this option will become exercisable after you have been a director of, or consultant to, the Company or any of its subsidiaries or affiliates for a combined total of three (3) years; (b) if on the date of an Acceleration Event you have been a director of, or consultant to, the Company or any of its subsidiaries or affiliates for a combined total of more than one (1) year and less than two (2) years, this option will be exercisable for one-third of the total number of shares then subject to this option and an additional one-third each of the total number of shares then subject to this option shall become exercisable when you have been a director of, or consultant to, the Company or any of its subsidiaries or affiliates for two (2) years and three (3) years, respectively; (c) if on the date of an Acceleration Event you have been a director of, or consultant to, the Company or any of its subsidiaries or affiliates for a combined total of less than one (1) year, this option will not be exercisable until you have been a director of, or consultant to, the Company and any of its subsidiaries or affiliates for a combined total of one (1) year, at which time this option will be exercisable for one-third of the total number of shares then subject to this option and an additional one-third each of the total number of shares then subject to this option shall become exercisable when you have been a director of, or consultant to, the Company or any of its subsidiaries or affiliates for two (2) years and three (3) years, respectively.

In the event of an IPO of the Common Stock of a parent corporation of the Company, and provided such parent corporation assumes the obligations of the Company under this Plan, this option shall thereupon pertain solely to the Common Stock of such parent corporation and the Company shall have no obligation whatsoever hereunder. In the event of an IPO in which the Company or its parent corporation has two classes of Common Stock, only one of which is issued to the public in the IPO, this option shall pertain solely to the class of Common Stock issued to the public in the IPO.

You may exercise your option by giving written notice to the Secretary of the Company on forms supplied by the Company at its then principal executive office, accompanied by payment of the option price for the total number of shares you specify that you wish to purchase. The payment may be in any of the following forms: (a) cash, which may be evidenced by a check and includes cash received from a stock brokerage firm in a so-called "cashless exercise"; (b) (unless prohibited by the Committee) certificates representing shares of Common Stock of the Company, which will be valued by the Secretary of the Company at the fair market value per share of the Company's Common Stock (as determined in accordance with the Plan) on the date of delivery of such certificates to the Company, accompanied by an assignment of the stock to the Company; or (c) (unless prohibited by the Committee) any combination of cash and Common Stock of the Company valued as provided in clause (b). The use of the so-called "attestation procedure" to exercise a stock option may be permitted by the Committee. Any assignment of stock shall be in a form and substance satisfactory to the Secretary of the Company, including guarantees of signature(s) and payment of all transfer taxes if the Secretary deems such guarantees necessary or desirable.

Your option will, to the extent not previously exercised by you, terminate three months after the date on which you cease for any reason to be a director of, or consultant to, the Company or a subsidiary corporation (whether by death, disability, resignation, removal, failure to be reappointed, reelected or otherwise, or the expiration of any consulting arrangement, and regardless of whether the failure to continue as a director or consultant was for cause or without cause or otherwise), but in no event later than ten years from the date this option is granted. After the date you cease to be a director or consultant, you may exercise this option only for the number of shares which you had a right to purchase and did not purchase on the date you ceased to be a director or consultant. If you are a director of, or consultant to, a subsidiary corporation, your directorship or consultancy shall be deemed to have terminated on the date such company ceases to be a subsidiary corporation, unless you are also a director of, or consultant to, the Company or another subsidiary corporation, or on that date became a director of, or consultant to, the Company or another subsidiary corporation. Your directorship or consultancy shall not be deemed to have terminated if you cease being a director of, or consultant to, the Company or a subsidiary corporation but are or concurrently therewith become a director of, or consultant to, the Company or another subsidiary corporation.

In the event of any change in the outstanding shares of the Common Stock of the Company by reason of a stock dividend, stock split, combination of shares, recapitalization, merger, consolidation, transfer of assets, reorganization, conversion or what the Committee deems in its sole discretion to be similar circumstances, the number and kind of shares subject to this option and the option price of such shares shall be appropriately adjusted in a manner to be determined in the sole discretion of the Committee.

In the event of a liquidation or proposed liquidation of the Company, including (but not limited to) a transfer of assets followed by a liquidation of the Company, or in the event of a Change of Control (as previously defined) or proposed Change of Control, the Committee shall have the right to require you to exercise this option upon thirty (30) days prior written notice to you. If at the

time such written notice is given this option is not otherwise exercisable, the written notice will set forth your right to exercise this option even though it is not otherwise exercisable. In the event this option is not exercised by you within the thirty (30) day period set forth in such written notice, this option shall terminate on the last day of such thirty (30) day period, notwithstanding anything to the contrary contained in this option.

This option is not transferable otherwise than by will or the laws of descent and distribution, and is exercisable during your lifetime only by you, including, for this purpose, your legal guardian or custodian in the event of disability. Until the option price has been paid in full pursuant to due exercise of this option and the purchased shares are delivered to you, you do not have any rights as a shareholder of the Company. The Company reserves the right not to deliver to you the shares purchased by virtue of the exercise of this option during any period of time in which the Company deems, in its sole discretion, that such delivery would violate a federal, state, local, or securities exchange rule, regulation, or law.

Notwithstanding anything to the contrary contained herein, this option is not exercisable until all the following events occur and during the following periods of time:

(a) Until the Plan pursuant to which this option is granted is approved by the shareholders of the Company in the manner prescribed by the Code and the regulations thereunder;

(b) Until this option and the optioned shares are approved and/or registered with such federal, state, and local regulatory bodies or agencies and securities exchanges as the Company may deem necessary or desirable; or

(c) During any period of time in which the Company deems that the exercisability of this option, the offer to sell the shares optioned hereunder, or the sale thereof, may violate a federal, state, local, or securities exchange rule, regulation, or law, or may cause the Company to be legally obligated to issue or sell more shares than the Company is legally entitled to issue or sell.

(d) Until you have paid or made suitable arrangements to pay (which may include payment through the surrender of Common Stock, unless prohibited by the Committee) (i) all federal, state, and local income tax withholding required to be withheld by the Company in connection with the option exercise and (ii) the employee's portion of other federal, state, and local payroll and other taxes due in connection with the option exercise.

(e) Until you have executed such shareholder agreements as shall be required by the Company. Such shareholder agreements may, at the Company's option, include (among other provisions) provisions requiring you to (i) enter into any "lock-up" agreements required by underwriters, (ii) vote on trust agreements, (iii) grant to the Company or its nominees an option to repurchase the stock, (iv) not sell, pledge or otherwise dispose of the stock without the consent of the Company, (v) maintain any Subchapter S elections made by the Company, (vi) grant rights of first refusal to the Company or its nominees with respect to the stock, and (vii) join in any sale of a majority or all of the outstanding stock of the Company.

The following two paragraphs shall be applicable if, on the date of exercise of this option, the Common Stock to be purchased pursuant to such exercise has not been registered under the Securities Act of 1933, as amended, and under applicable state securities laws, and shall continue to be applicable for so long as such registration has not occurred:

(a) The optionee hereby agrees, warrants and represents that he will acquire the Common Stock to be issued hereunder for his own account for investment purposes only, and not with a view to, or in connection with, any resale or other distribution of any of such shares, except as hereafter permitted. The optionee further agrees that he will not at any time make any offer, sale, transfer, pledge, or other disposition of such Common Stock to be issued hereunder without an effective registration statement under the Securities Act of 1933, as amended, and under any applicable state securities laws or an opinion of counsel acceptable to the Company to the effect that the proposed transaction will be exempt from such registration. The optionee shall execute such instruments, representations, acknowledgments, and agreements as the Company may, in its sole discretion, deem advisable to avoid any violation of federal, state, local, or securities exchange rule, regulation, or law.

(b) The certificates for Common Stock to be issued to the optionee hereunder shall bear the following legend:

> "The shares represented by this certificate have not been registered under the Securities Act of 1933, as amended, or under applicable state securities laws. The shares have been acquired for investment and may not be offered, sold, transferred, pledged, or otherwise disposed of without an effective registration statement under the Securities Act of 1933, as amended, and under any applicable state securities laws or an opinion of counsel acceptable to the Company that the proposed transaction will be exempt from such registration."

The foregoing legend shall be removed upon registration of the legended shares under the Securities Act of 1933, as amended, and under any applicable state laws or upon receipt of any opinion of counsel acceptable to the Company that said registration is no longer required.

The sole purpose of the agreements, warranties, representations, and legend set forth in the two immediately preceding paragraphs is to prevent violations of the Securities Act of 1933, as amended, and any applicable state securities laws.

It is the intention of the Company and you that this option shall not be an "Incentive Stock Option" as that term is used in Section 422(b) of the Code and the regulations thereunder.

Nothing herein guarantees your term as a director of, or consultant to, the Company for any specified period of time. This means that either you or the Company may terminate your relationship with the Company at any time for any reason, with or without cause, or for no reason. You recognize that, for instance, the Company may terminate your relationship with the Company prior to the date on which your option becomes vested or exercisable. You understand that the Company has no obligation to consider or effectuate a public offering of its stock or a Change of Control.

Any dispute or disagreement between you and the Company with respect to any portion of this option (excluding Attachment A hereto) or its validity, construction, meaning, performance, or your rights hereunder shall be settled by arbitration in accordance with the Commercial Arbitration Rules of the American Arbitration Association or its successor, as amended from time to time. However, prior to submission to arbitration you will attempt to resolve any disputes or disagreements with the Company over this option amicably and informally, in good faith, for a period not to exceed two weeks. Thereafter, the dispute or disagreement will be submitted to arbitration. At any time prior to a decision from the arbitrator(s) being rendered, you and the Company may resolve the dispute by settlement. You and the Company shall equally share the costs charged by the American Arbitration Association or its successor, but you and the Company shall otherwise be solely responsible for your own respective counsel fees and expenses. The decision of the arbitrator(s) shall be made in writing, setting forth the award, the reasons for the decision and award, and shall be binding and conclusive on you and the Company. Further, neither you nor the Company shall appeal any such award. Judgment of a court of competent jurisdiction may be entered upon the award and may be enforced as such in accordance with the provisions of the award.

This option shall be subject to the terms of the Plan in effect on the date this option is granted, which terms are hereby incorporated herein by reference and made a part hereof. In the event of any conflict between the terms of this option and the terms of the Plan in effect on the date of this option, the terms of the Plan shall govern. This option constitutes the entire understanding between the Company and you with respect to the subject matter hereof and no amendment, supplement, or waiver of this option, in whole or in part, shall be binding upon the Company unless in writing and signed by the President of the Company. This option and the performances of the parties hereunder shall be construed in accordance with and governed by the laws of the State of Pennsylvania.

In consideration of the grant to you of this option, you hereby agree to the confidentiality and noninterference provisions set forth in Attachment A hereto.

Please sign the copy of this option and return it to the Company's Secretary, thereby indicating your understanding of and agreement with its terms and conditions, **including Attachment A hereto.**

ABC, Inc.

By: _____

I hereby acknowledge receipt of a copy of the foregoing stock option and, having read it, hereby signify my understanding of, and my agreement with, its terms and conditions, **including Attachment A hereto.**

_____   _____

(Signature)   (Date)

Attachment A to Stock Option

Confidentiality and Noninterference

(a) You covenant and agree that, in consideration of the grant to you of this stock option, you will not, during your term as a director of, or a consultant to, the Company or at any time thereafter, except with the express prior written consent of the Company or pursuant to the lawful order of any judicial or administrative agency of government, directly or indirectly, disclose, communicate or divulge to any individual or entity, or use for the benefit of any individual or entity, any knowledge or information with respect to the conduct or details of the Company's business which you, acting reasonably, believe or should believe to be of a confidential nature and the disclosure of which not to be in the Company's interest.

(b) You covenant and agree that, in consideration of the grant to you of this stock option, you will not, during your term as a director of, or a consultant to, the Company and for a period of two years thereafter, except with the express prior written consent of the Company, directly or indirectly, whether as employee, owner, partner, consultant, agent, director, officer, shareholder or in any other capacity, engage in or assist any individual or entity to engage in any act or action which you, acting reasonably, believe or should believe would be harmful or inimical to the interests of the Company.

(c) You covenant and agree that, in consideration of the grant to you of this stock option, you will not, for a period of two years after your term as a director of, or a consultant to, the Company ceases for any reason whatsoever (whether voluntary or not), except with the express prior written consent of the Company, directly or indirectly, whether as employee, owner, partner, consultant, agent, director, officer, shareholder or in any other capacity, for your own account or for the benefit of any individual or entity, (i) solicit any customer of the Company for business which would result in such customer terminating their relationship with the Company; or (ii) solicit or induce any individual or entity which is an employee of the Company to leave the Company or to otherwise terminate their relationship with the Company.

(d) The parties agree that any breach by you of any of the covenants or agreements contained in this Attachment A will result in irreparable injury to the Company for which money damages could not adequately compensate the Company and therefore, in the event of any such breach, the Company shall be entitled (in addition to any other rights and remedies which it may have at law or in equity) to have an injunction issued by any competent court enjoining and restraining you and/or any other individual or entity involved therein from continuing such breach. The existence of any claim or cause of action which you may have against the Company or any other individual or entity shall not constitute a defense or bar to the enforcement of such covenants. If the Company is obliged to resort to the courts for the enforcement of any of the covenants or agreements contained in this Attachment A, or if such covenants or agreements are otherwise the subject of litigation between the parties, and the Company prevails in such enforcement or litigation, then the term of such covenants and agreements shall be extended for a period of time equal to the period of such breach, which extension shall commence on the later of (a) the date on which the original (unextended) term of such covenants and agreements is scheduled to terminate or (b) the date of the final court order (without further right of appeal) enforcing such covenant or agreement.

(e) If any portion of the covenants or agreements contained in this Attachment A, or the application hereof, is construed to be invalid or unenforceable, the other portions of such covenant(s) or agreement(s) or the application thereof shall not be affected and shall be given full force and effect without regard to the invalid or enforceable portions to the fullest extent possible. If any covenant or agreement in this Attachment A is held unenforceable because of the area covered, the duration thereof, or the scope thereof, then the court making such determination shall have the power to reduce the area and/or duration and/or limit the scope thereof, and the covenant or agreement shall then be enforceable in its reduced form.

(f) For purposes of this Attachment A, the term "the Company" shall include the Company, any successor to the Company and all present and future direct and indirect subsidiaries and affiliates of the Company.

PRIVATE COMPANY
[SALE ONLY EXIT]
XYZ, INC.
2001 STOCK OPTION PLAN

1. Purpose of Plan

The purpose of this 2001 Stock Option Plan (the "Plan") is to provide additional incentive to officers, other key employees, and directors of, and important consultants to, XYZ, Inc., a Pennsylvania corporation (the "Company"), and each present or future parent or subsidiary corporation, by encouraging them to invest in shares of the Company's common stock, no par value ("Common Stock"), and thereby acquire a proprietary interest in the Company and an increased personal interest in the Company's continued success and progress.

2. Aggregate Number of Shares

200,000 shares of the Company's Common Stock shall be the aggregate number of shares which may be issued under this Plan. Notwithstanding the foregoing, in the event of any change in the outstanding shares of the Common Stock of the Company by reason of a stock dividend, stock split, combination of shares, recapitalization, merger, consolidation, transfer of assets, reorganization, conversion or what the Committee (defined in Section 4[a]), deems in its sole discretion to be similar circumstances, the aggregate number and kind of shares which may be issued under this Plan shall be appropriately adjusted in a manner determined in the sole discretion of the Committee. Reacquired shares of the Company's Common Stock, as well as unissued shares, may be used for the purpose of this Plan. Common Stock of the Company subject to options which have terminated unexercised, either in whole or in part, shall be available for future options granted under this Plan.

3. Class of Persons Eligible to Receive Options

All officers and key employees of the Company and of any present or future Company parent or subsidiary corporation are eligible to receive an option or options under this Plan. All directors of, and important consultants to, the Company and of any present or future Company parent or subsidiary corporation are also eligible to receive an option or options under this Plan. The individuals who shall, in fact, receive an option or options shall be selected by the Committee, in its sole discretion, except as otherwise specified in Section 4 hereof. No individual may receive options under this Plan for more than 80 percent of the total number of shares of the Company's Common Stock authorized for issuance under this Plan.

4. Administration of Plan

(a) This Plan shall be administered by the Company's Board of Directors or by an Option Committee ("Committee") appointed by the Company's Board of Directors. The Committee shall consist of a minimum of two and a maximum of five members of the Board of Directors. The Committee shall, in addition to its other authority and subject to the provisions of this Plan, determine which individuals shall in fact be granted an option or options, whether the option shall be an Incentive Stock Option or a Non-Qualified Stock Option (as such terms are defined in Section 5[a]), the number of shares to be subject to each of the options, the time or times at which the options shall be granted, the rate of option exercisability, and, subject to Section 5 hereof, the price at which each of the options is exercisable and the duration of the option. The term "Committee", as used in this Plan and the options granted hereunder, refers to the Board of Directors or the Committee, as applicable.

(b) The Committee shall adopt such rules for the conduct of its business and administration of this Plan as it considers desirable. A majority of the members of the Committee shall constitute a quorum for all purposes. The vote or written consent of a majority of the members of the Committee on a particular matter shall constitute the act of the Committee on such matter. The Committee shall have the right to construe the Plan and the options issued pursuant to it, to correct defects and omissions and to reconcile inconsistencies to the extent necessary to effectuate the Plan and the options issued pursuant to it, and such action shall be final, binding and conclusive upon all parties concerned. No member of the

Committee or the Board of Directors shall be liable for any act or omission (whether or not negligent) taken or omitted in good faith, or for the exercise of an authority or discretion granted in connection with the Plan to a Committee or the Board of Directors, or for the acts or omissions of any other members of a Committee or the Board of Directors. Subject to the numerical limitations on Committee membership set forth in Section 4(a) hereof, the Board of Directors may at any time appoint additional members of the Committee and may at any time remove any member of the Committee with or without cause. Vacancies in the Committee, however caused, may be filled by the Board of Directors, if it so desires.

5. Incentive Stock Options and Non-Qualified Stock Options

(a) Options issued pursuant to this Plan may be either Incentive Stock Options granted pursuant to Section 5(b) hereof or Non-Qualified Stock Options granted pursuant to Section 5(c) hereof, as determined by the Committee. An "Incentive Stock Option" is an option which satisfies all of the requirements of Section 422(b) of the Internal Revenue Code of 1986, as amended (the "Code") and the regulations thereunder, and a "Non-Qualified Stock Option" is an option which either does not satisfy all of those requirements or the terms of the option provide that it will not be treated as an Incentive Stock Option. The Committee may grant both an Incentive Stock Option and a Non-Qualified Stock Option to the same person, or more than one of each type of option to the same person. The option price for options issued under this Plan shall be equal at least to the fair market value (as defined below) of the Company's Common Stock on the date of the grant of the option. The fair market value of the Company's Common Stock on any particular date shall mean the last reported sale price of a share of the Company's Common Stock on any stock exchange on which such stock is then listed or admitted to trading, or on the NASDAQ National Market System or Small Cap NASDAQ, on such date, or if no sale took place on such day, the last such date on which a sale took place, or if the Common Stock is not then quoted on the NASDAQ National Market System or Small Cap NASDAQ, or listed or admitted to trading on any stock exchange, the average of the bid and asked prices in the over-the-counter market on such date, or if none of the foregoing, a price determined in good faith by the Committee to equal the fair market value per share of the Common Stock.

(b) Subject to the authority of the Committee set forth in Section 4(a) hereof, Incentive Stock Options issued pursuant to this Plan shall be issued substantially in the form set forth in Appendix I hereof, which form is hereby incorporated by reference and made a part hereof, and shall contain substantially the terms and conditions set forth therein. Incentive Stock Options shall not be exercisable after the expiration of ten years from the date such options are granted, unless terminated earlier under the terms of the option, except that options granted to individuals described in Section 422(b)(6) of the Code shall conform to the provisions of Section 422(c)(5) of the Code. At the time of the grant of an Incentive Stock Option hereunder, the Committee may, in its discretion, amend or supplement any of the option terms contained in Appendix I for any particular optionee, provided that the option as amended or supplemented satisfies the requirements of Section 422(b) of the Code and the regulations thereunder. Each of the options granted pursuant to this Section 5(b) is intended, if possible, to be an "Incentive Stock Option" as that term is defined in Section 422(b) of the Code and the regulations thereunder. In the event this Plan or any option granted pursuant to this Section 5(b) is in any way inconsistent with the applicable legal requirements of the Code or the regulations thereunder for an Incentive Stock Option, this Plan and such option shall be deemed automatically amended as of the date hereof to conform to such legal requirements, if such conformity may be achieved by amendment.

(c) Subject to the authority of the Committee set forth in Section 4(a) hereof, Non-Qualified Stock Options issued to officers and other key employees pursuant to this Plan shall be issued substantially in the form set forth in Appendix II hereof, which form is hereby incorporated by reference and made a part hereof, and shall contain substantially the terms and conditions set forth therein. Subject to the authority of the Committee set forth in Section 4(a) hereof, Non-Qualified Stock Options issued to directors and important consultants pursuant to this Plan shall be issued substantially in the form set forth in Appendix III hereof, which form is hereby incorporated by reference and made a part hereof, and shall contain substantially the terms and conditions set forth therein. Non-Qualified Stock Options shall expire ten years after the date they are granted, unless terminated earlier under the option terms. At the time of granting a Non-Qualified Stock Option hereunder, the Committee may, in its discretion, amend or supplement any of the option terms contained in Appendix II or Appendix III for any particular optionee.

(d) Neither the Company nor any of its current or future parent, subsidiaries or affiliates, nor their officers, directors, shareholders, stock option plan committees, employees or agents shall have any liability to any optionee in the event (i) an option granted pursuant to Section 5(b) hereof does not qualify as an "Incentive Stock Option" as that term is used in Section 422(b) of the Code and the regulations thereunder; (ii) any optionee does not obtain the tax treatment pertaining to an Incentive Stock Option; or (iii) any option granted pursuant to Section 5(c) hereof is an "Incentive Stock Option."

6. Amendment, Supplement, Suspension, and Termination

Options shall not be granted pursuant to this Plan after the expiration of ten years from the date the Plan is adopted by the Board of Directors of the Company. The Board of Directors reserves the right at any time, and from time to time, to amend or supplement this Plan in any way, or to suspend or terminate it, effective as of such date, which date may be either before or after the taking of such action, as may be specified by the Board of Directors; provided, however, that such action shall not, without the consent of the optionee, affect options granted under the Plan prior to the actual date on which such action occurred. If an amendment or supplement of this Plan is required by the Code or the regulations thereunder to be approved by the shareholders of the Company in order to permit the granting of "Incentive Stock Options" (as that term is defined in Section 422[b] of the Code and regulations thereunder) pursuant to the amended or supplemented Plan, such amendment or supplement shall also be approved by the shareholders of the Company in such manner as is prescribed by the Code and the regulations thereunder. If the Board of Directors voluntarily submits a proposed amendment, supplement, suspension or termination for shareholder approval, such submission shall not require any future amendments, supplements, suspensions or terminations (whether or not relating to the same provision or subject matter) to be similarly submitted for shareholder approval.

7. Effectiveness of Plan

This Plan shall become effective on the date of its adoption by the Company's Board of Directors, subject however to approval by the holders of the Company's Common Stock in the manner as prescribed in the Code and the regulations thereunder. Options may be granted under this Plan prior to obtaining shareholder approval, provided such options shall not be exercisable until shareholder approval is obtained.

8. General Conditions

(a) Nothing contained in this Plan or any option granted pursuant to this Plan shall confer upon any employee the right to continue in the employ of the Company or any affiliated or subsidiary corporation or interfere in any way with the rights of the Company or any affiliated or subsidiary corporation to terminate his employment in any way.

(b) Nothing contained in this Plan or any option granted pursuant to this Plan shall confer upon any director or consultant the right to continue as a director of, or consultant to, the Company or any affiliated or subsidiary corporation or interfere in any way with the rights of the Company or any affiliated or subsidiary corporation, or their respective shareholders, to terminate the directorship of any such director or the consultancy relationship of any such consultant.

(c) Corporate action constituting an offer of stock for sale to any person under the terms of the options to be granted hereunder shall be deemed complete as of the date when the Committee authorizes the grant of the option to such person, regardless of when the option is actually delivered to such person or acknowledged or agreed to by him.

(d) The terms "parent corporation" and "subsidiary corporation" as used throughout this Plan, and the options granted pursuant to this Plan, shall (except as otherwise provided in the option form) have the meaning that is ascribed to that term when contained in Section 422(b) of the Code and the regulations thereunder, and the Company shall be deemed to be the grantor corporation for purposes of applying such meaning.

(e) References in this Plan to the Code shall be deemed to also refer to the corresponding provisions of any future United States revenue law.

(f) The use of the masculine pronoun shall include the feminine gender whenever appropriate.

APPENDIX I

INCENTIVE STOCK OPTION

To: _____
              Name

       _____
              Address

Date of Grant: _____

You are hereby granted an option, effective as of the date hereof, to purchase _____ shares of common stock, no par value ("Common Stock"), of XYZ, Inc., a Pennsylvania corporation (the "Company"), at a price of $____ per share pursuant to the Company's Stock Option Plan (the "Plan").

This option shall terminate and is not exercisable after ten years from the date of its grant (the "Scheduled Termination Date"), except if terminated earlier as hereafter provided.

Your option may first be exercised if and only if there is a Change of Control (as hereafter defined) prior to the Scheduled Termination Date, but shall not otherwise be exercisable. A "Change of Control" shall be deemed to have occurred upon the happening of any of the following events:

1. If John Doe (or in the event of his death, a representative of his estate or his heirs) ceases to be a director of the Company or a successor to the Company by merger or other form of acquisition;

2. If John Doe (or in the event of his death, a representative of his estate or his heirs) ceases to own at least 10 percent of the stock of the Company or a successor to the Company by merger or other form of acquisition; or

3. Any other event deemed to constitute a "Change of Control" by the Committee.

You may exercise your option by giving written notice to the Secretary of the Company on forms supplied by the Company at its then principal executive office, accompanied by payment of the option price for the total number of shares you specify that you wish to purchase. The payment may be in any of the following forms: (a) cash, which may be evidenced by a check and includes cash received from a stock brokerage firm in a so-called "cashless exercise"; (b) (unless prohibited by the Committee) certificates representing shares of Common Stock of the Company, which will be valued by the Secretary of the Company at the fair market value per share of the Company's Common Stock (as determined in accordance with the Plan) on the date of delivery of such certificates to the Company, accompanied by an assignment of the stock to the Company; or (c) (unless prohibited by the Committee) any combination of cash and Common Stock of the Company valued as provided in clause (b). The use of the so-called "attestation procedure" to exercise a stock option may be permitted by the Committee. Any assignment of stock shall be in a form and substance satisfactory to the Secretary of the Company, including guarantees of signature(s) and payment of all transfer taxes if the Secretary deems such guarantees necessary or desirable.

Your option will, to the extent not previously exercised by you, terminate three months after the date on which your employment by the Company or a Company subsidiary corporation is terminated (whether such termination be voluntary or involuntary) other than by reason of disability as defined in Section 22(e)(3) of the Internal Revenue Code of 1986, as amended (the "Code"), and the regulations thereunder, or death, in which case your option will terminate one year from the date of termination of employment due to disability or death (but in no event later than the Scheduled Termination Date). After the date your employment is terminated, as aforesaid, you may exercise this option only for the number of shares which you had a right to purchase and did not purchase on the date your employment terminated. If you are employed by a Company subsidiary corporation, your employment shall be deemed to have terminated on the date your employer ceases to be a Company subsidiary corporation, unless you are on that date transferred to the Company or another Company subsidiary corporation. Your employment shall not be deemed to have terminated if you are transferred from the Company to a Company subsidiary corporation, or vice versa, or from one Company subsidiary corporation to another Company subsidiary corporation.

If you die while employed by the Company or a Company subsidiary corporation, your executor or administrator, as the case may be, may, at any time within one year after the date of your death (but in no event later than the Scheduled Termination Date), exercise the option as to any shares which you had a right to purchase and did not purchase during your lifetime. If your employment with the Company or a Company parent or subsidiary corporation is terminated by reason of your becoming disabled (within the meaning of Section 22[e][3] of the Code and the regulations thereunder), you or your legal guardian or custodian may at any time within one year after the date of such termination (but in no event later than the Scheduled Termination Date), exercise the option as to any shares which you had a right to purchase and did not purchase prior to such termination. Your executor, administrator, guardian, or custodian must present proof of his authority satisfactory to the Company prior to being allowed to exercise this option.

In the event of any change in the outstanding shares of the Common Stock of the Company by reason of a stock dividend, stock split, combination of shares, recapitalization, merger, consolidation, transfer of assets, reorganization, conversion, or what the Committee deems in its sole discretion to be similar circumstances, the number and kind of shares subject to this option and the option price of such shares shall be appropriately adjusted in a manner to be determined in the sole discretion of the Committee.

In the event of a liquidation or proposed liquidation of the Company, including (but not limited to) a transfer of assets followed by a liquidation of the Company, or in the event of a Change of Control (as previously defined) or proposed Change of Control, the Committee shall have the right to require you to exercise this option upon thirty (30) days prior written notice to you. If at the time such written notice is given this option is not otherwise exercisable, the written notice will set forth your right to exercise this option even though it is not otherwise exercisable. In the event this option is not exercised by you within the thirty (30) day period set forth in such written notice, this option shall terminate on the last day of such thirty (30) day period, notwithstanding anything to the contrary contained in this option.

This option is not transferable otherwise than by will or the laws of descent and distribution, and is exercisable during your lifetime only by you, including, for this purpose, your legal guardian or custodian in the event of disability. Until the option price has been paid in full pursuant to due exercise of this option and the purchased shares are delivered to you, you do not have any rights as a shareholder of the Company. The Company reserves the right not to deliver to you the shares purchased by virtue of the exercise of this option during any period of time in which the Company deems, in its sole discretion, that such delivery would violate a federal, state, local, or securities exchange rule, regulation, or law.

Notwithstanding anything to the contrary contained herein, this option is not exercisable until all the following events occur and during the following periods of time:

(a) Until the Plan pursuant to which this option is granted is approved by the shareholders of the Company in the manner prescribed by the Code and the regulations thereunder;

(b) Until this option and the optioned shares are approved and/or registered with such federal, state, and local regulatory bodies or agencies and securities exchanges as the Company may deem necessary or desirable; or

(c) During any period of time in which the Company deems that the exercisability of this option, the offer to sell the shares optioned hereunder, or the sale thereof, may violate a federal, state, local, or securities exchange rule, regulation, or law, or may cause the Company to be legally obligated to issue or sell more shares than the Company is legally entitled to issue or sell.

(d) Until you have paid or made suitable arrangements to pay (which may include payment through the surrender of Common Stock, unless prohibited by the Committee) (i) all federal, state, and local income tax withholding required to be withheld by the Company in connection with the option exercise and (ii) the employee's portion of other federal, state, and local payroll and other taxes due in connection with the option exercise.

(e) Until you have executed such shareholder agreements as shall be required by the Company. Such shareholder agreements may, at the Company's option, include (among other provisions) provisions requiring you to (i) vote on trust agreements, (ii) grant to the Company or its nominees an option to repurchase the stock, (iii) not sell, pledge or otherwise dispose of the stock without the consent of the Company, (iv) maintain any Subchapter S elections made by the Company, (v) grant rights of first refusal to the Company or its nominees with respect to the stock, and (vi) join in any sale of a majority or all of the outstanding stock of the Company.

The following two paragraphs shall be applicable if, on the date of exercise of this option, the Common Stock to be purchased pursuant to such exercise has not been registered under the Securities Act of 1933, as amended, and under applicable state securities laws, and shall continue to be applicable for so long as such registration has not occurred:

(a) The optionee hereby agrees, warrants and represents that he will acquire the Common Stock to be issued hereunder for his own account for investment purposes only, and not with a view to, or in connection with, any resale or other distribution of any of such shares, except as hereafter permitted. The optionee further agrees that he will not at any time make any offer, sale, transfer, pledge, or other disposition of such Common Stock to be issued hereunder without an effective registration statement under the Securities Act of 1933, as amended, and under any applicable state securities laws or an opinion of counsel acceptable to the Company to the effect that the proposed transaction will be exempt from such registration. The optionee shall execute such instruments, representations, acknowledgments, and agreements as the Company may, in its sole discretion, deem advisable to avoid any violation of federal, state, local, or securities exchange rule, regulation, or law.

(b) The certificates for Common Stock to be issued to the optionee hereunder shall bear the following legend:

> "The shares represented by this certificate have not been registered under the Securities Act of 1933, as amended, or under applicable state securities laws. The shares have been acquired for investment and may not be offered, sold, transferred, pledged, or otherwise disposed of without an effective registration statement under the Securities Act of 1933, as amended, and under any applicable state securities laws or an opinion of counsel acceptable to the Company that the proposed transaction will be exempt from such registration."

The foregoing legend shall be removed upon registration of the legended shares under the Securities Act of 1933, as amended, and under any applicable state laws or upon receipt of any opinion of counsel acceptable to the Company that said registration is no longer required.

The sole purpose of the agreements, warranties, representations, and legend set forth in the two immediately preceding paragraphs is to prevent violations of the Securities Act of 1933, as amended, and any applicable state securities laws.

It is the intention of the Company and you that this option shall, if possible, be an "Incentive Stock Option" as that term is used in Section 422(b) of the Code and the regulations thereunder. In the event this option is in any way inconsistent with the legal requirements of the Code or the regulations thereunder for an "Incentive Stock Option," this option shall be deemed automatically amended as of the date hereof to conform to such legal requirements, if such conformity may be achieved by amendment. To the extent that the number of shares subject to this option which are exercisable for the first time exceed the $100,000 limitation contained in Section 422(d) of the Code, this option will not be considered an Incentive Stock Option.

Nothing herein shall modify your status as an at-will employee of the Company. Further, nothing herein guarantees you employment for any specified period of time. This means that either you or the Company may terminate your employment at any time for any reason, with or without cause, or for no reason. You recognize that, for instance, you may terminate your employment or the Company may terminate your employment prior to the date on which your option becomes vested or exercisable. You understand that the Company has no obligation to consider or effectuate a Change of Control and therefore this option may never become exercisable.

Any dispute or disagreement between you and the Company with respect to any portion of this option (excluding Attachment A hereto) or its validity, construction, meaning, performance, or your rights hereunder shall be settled by arbitration in accordance with the Commercial Arbitration Rules of the American Arbitration Association or its successor, as amended from time to time. However, prior to submission to arbitration you will attempt to resolve any disputes or disagreements with the Company over this option amicably and informally, in good faith, for a period not to exceed two weeks. Thereafter, the dispute or disagreement will be submitted to arbitration. At any time prior to a decision from the arbitrator(s) being rendered, you and the Company may resolve the dispute by settlement. You and the Company shall equally share the costs charged by the American Arbitration Association or its successor, but you and the Company shall otherwise be solely responsible for your own respective counsel fees and expenses. The decision of the arbitrator(s) shall be made in writing, setting forth the award, the reasons for the decision and award and shall be binding and conclusive on you and the Company. Further, neither you nor the Company shall appeal any such award. Judgment of a court of competent jurisdiction may be entered upon the award and may be enforced as such in accordance with the provisions of the award.

This option shall be subject to the terms of the Plan in effect on the date this option is granted, which terms are hereby incorporated herein by reference and made a part hereof. In the event of any conflict between the terms of this option and the terms of the Plan in effect on the date of this option, the terms of the Plan shall govern. This option constitutes the entire understanding between the Company and you with respect to the subject matter hereof and no amendment, supplement, or waiver of this option, in whole or in part, shall be binding upon the Company unless in writing and signed by the President of the Company. This option and the performances of the parties hereunder shall be construed in accordance with and governed by the laws of the State of Pennsylvania.

In consideration of the grant to you of this option, you hereby agree to the confidentiality and noninterference provisions set forth in Attachment A hereto.

Please sign the copy of this option and return it to the Company's Secretary, thereby indicating your understanding of and agreement with its terms and conditions, **including Attachment A hereto.**

XYZ, Inc.

By: _____

I hereby acknowledge receipt of a copy of the foregoing stock option and the Plan, and having read them hereby signify my understanding of, and my agreement with, their terms and conditions, **including Attachment A hereto.** I accept this option in full satisfaction of any previous written or verbal promises made to me by the Company with respect to option grants.

_____   _____

(Signature)   (Date)

Attachment A to Stock Option

Confidentiality and Noninterference

(a) You covenant and agree that, in consideration of the grant to you of this stock option, you will not, during your employment with the Company or at any time thereafter, except with the express prior written consent of the Company or pursuant to the lawful order of any judicial or administrative agency of government, directly or indirectly, disclose, communicate or divulge to any individual or entity, or use for the benefit of any individual or entity, any knowledge or information with respect to the conduct or details of the Company's business which you, acting reasonably, believe or should believe to be of a confidential nature and the disclosure of which not to be in the Company's interest.

(b) You covenant and agree that, in consideration of the grant to you of this stock option, you will not, during your employment with the Company and for a period of two years thereafter, except with the express prior written consent of the Company, directly or indirectly, whether as employee, owner, partner, consultant, agent, director, officer, shareholder or in any other capacity, engage in or assist any individual or entity to engage in any act or action which you, acting reasonably, believe or should believe would be harmful or inimical to the interests of the Company.

(c) You covenant and agree that, in consideration of the grant to you of this stock option, you will not, for a period of two years after your employment with the Company ceases for any reason whatsoever (whether voluntary or not), except with the express prior written consent of the Company, directly or indirectly, whether as employee, owner, partner, consultant, agent, director, officer, shareholder or in any other capacity, for your own account or for the benefit of any individual or entity, (i) solicit any customer of the Company for business which would result in such customer terminating their relationship with the Company; or (ii) solicit or induce any individual or entity which is an employee of the Company to leave the Company or to otherwise terminate their relationship with the Company.

(d) The parties agree that any breach by you of any of the covenants or agreements contained in this Attachment A will result in irreparable injury to the Company for which money damages could not adequately compensate the Company and therefore, in the event of any such breach, the Company shall be entitled (in addition to any other rights and remedies which it may have at law or in equity) to have an injunction issued by any competent court enjoining and restraining you and/or any other individual or entity involved therein from continuing such breach. The existence of any claim or cause of action which you may have against the Company or any other individual or entity shall not constitute a defense or bar to the enforcement of such covenants. If the Company is obliged to resort to the courts for the enforcement of any of the covenants or agreements contained in this Attachment A, or if such covenants or agreements are otherwise the subject of litigation between the parties, and the Company prevails in such enforcement or litigation, then the term of such covenants and agreements shall be extended for a period of time equal to the period of such breach, which extension shall commence on the later of (a) the date on which the original (unextended) term of such covenants and agreements is scheduled to terminate or (b) the date of the final court order (without further right of appeal) enforcing such covenant or agreement.

(e) If any portion of the covenants or agreements contained in this Attachment A, or the application hereof, is construed to be invalid or unenforceable, the other portions of such covenant(s) or agreement(s) or the application thereof shall not be affected and shall be given full force and effect without regard to the invalid or enforceable portions to the fullest extent possible. If any covenant or agreement in this Attachment A is held unenforceable because of the area covered, the duration thereof, or the scope thereof, then the court making such determination shall have the power to reduce the area and/or duration and/or limit the scope thereof, and the covenant or agreement shall then be enforceable in its reduced form.

(f) For purposes of this Attachment A, the term "the Company" shall include the Company, any successor to the Company and all present and future direct and indirect subsidiaries and affiliates of the Company.

APPENDIX II

**NON-QUALIFIED STOCK OPTION FOR
OFFICERS AND OTHER KEY EMPLOYEES**

To: _____
                    Name

        _____
                    Address

Date of Grant: _____

You are hereby granted an option, effective as of the date hereof, to purchase _____ shares of common stock, no par value ("Common Stock"), of XYZ, Inc., a Pennsylvania corporation (the "Company"), at a price of $____ per share pursuant to the Company's Stock Option Plan (the "Plan").

This option shall terminate and is not exercisable after ten years from the date of its grant (the "Scheduled Termination Date"), except if terminated earlier as hereafter provided.

Your option may first be exercised if and only if there is a Change of Control (as hereafter defined) prior to the Scheduled Termination Date, but shall not otherwise be exercisable. A "Change of Control" shall be deemed to have occurred upon the happening of any of the following events:

1. If John Doe (or in the event of his death, a representative of his estate or his heirs) ceases to be a director of the Company or a successor to the Company by merger or other form of acquisition;

2. If John Doe (or in the event of his death, a representative of his estate or his heirs) ceases to own at least 10 percent of the stock of the Company or a successor to the Company by merger or other form of acquisition; or

3. Any other event deemed to constitute a "Change of Control" by the Committee.

You may exercise your option by giving written notice to the Secretary of the Company on forms supplied by the Company at its then principal executive office, accompanied by payment of the option price for the total number of shares you specify that you wish to purchase. The payment may be in any of the following forms: (a) cash, which may be evidenced by a check and includes cash received from a stock brokerage firm in a so-called "cashless exercise"; (b) (unless prohibited by the Committee) certificates representing shares of Common Stock of the Company, which will be valued by the Secretary of the Company at the fair market value per share of the Company's Common Stock (as determined in accordance with the Plan) on the date of delivery of such certificates to the Company, accompanied by an assignment of the stock to the Company; or (c) (unless prohibited by the Committee) any combination of cash and Common Stock of the Company valued as provided in clause (b). The use of the so-called "attestation procedure" to exercise a stock option may be permitted by the Committee. Any assignment of stock shall be in a form and substance satisfactory to the Secretary of the Company, including guarantees of signature(s) and payment of all transfer taxes if the Secretary deems such guarantees necessary or desirable.

Your option will, to the extent not previously exercised by you, terminate three months after the date on which your employment by the Company or a Company subsidiary corporation is terminated (whether such termination be voluntary or involuntary) other than by reason of disability as defined in Section 22(e)(3) of the Internal Revenue Code of 1986, as amended (the "Code"), and the regulations thereunder, or death, in which case your option will terminate one year from the date of termination of employment due to disability or death (but in no event later than the Scheduled Termination Date). After the date your employment is terminated, as aforesaid, you may exercise this option only for the number of shares which you had a right to purchase and did not purchase on the date your employment terminated. If you are employed by a Company subsidiary corporation, your employment shall be deemed to have terminated on the date your employer ceases to be a Company subsidiary corporation, unless you are on that date transferred to the Company or another Company subsidiary corporation. Your employment shall not be deemed to have terminated if you are transferred from the Company to a Company subsidiary corporation, or vice versa, or from one Company subsidiary corporation to another Company subsidiary corporation.

If you die while employed by the Company or a Company subsidiary corporation, your executor or administrator, as the case may be, may, at any time within one year after the date of your death (but in no event later than the Scheduled Termination Date), exercise the option as to any shares which you had a right to purchase and did not purchase during your lifetime. If your employment with the Company or a Company parent or subsidiary corporation is terminated by reason of your becoming disabled (within the meaning of Section 22[e][3] of the Code and the regulations thereunder), you or your legal guardian or custodian may at any time within one year after the date of such termination (but in no event later than the Scheduled Termination Date), exercise the option as to any shares which you had a right to purchase and did not purchase prior to such termination. Your executor, administrator, guardian, or custodian must present proof of his authority satisfactory to the Company prior to being allowed to exercise this option.

In the event of any change in the outstanding shares of the Common Stock of the Company by reason of a stock dividend, stock split, combination of shares, recapitalization, merger, consolidation, transfer of assets, reorganization, conversion, or what the Committee deems in its sole discretion to be similar circumstances, the number and kind of shares subject to this option and the option price of such shares shall be appropriately adjusted in a manner to be determined in the sole discretion of the Committee.

In the event of a liquidation or proposed liquidation of the Company, including (but not limited to) a transfer of assets followed by a liquidation of the Company, or in the event of a Change of Control (as previously defined) or proposed Change of Control, the Committee shall have the right to require you to exercise this option upon thirty (30) days prior written notice to you. If at the time such written notice is given this option is not otherwise exercisable, the written notice will set forth your right to exercise this option even though it is not otherwise exercisable. In the event this option is not exercised by you within the thirty (30) day period set forth in such written notice, this option shall terminate on the last day of such thirty (30) day period, notwithstanding anything to the contrary contained in this option.

This option is not transferable otherwise than by will or the laws of descent and distribution, and is exercisable during your lifetime only by you, including, for this purpose, your legal guardian or custodian in the event of disability. Until the option price has been paid in full pursuant to due exercise of this option and the purchased shares are delivered to you, you do not have any rights as a shareholder of the Company. The Company reserves the right not to deliver to you the shares purchased by virtue of the exercise of this option during any period of time in which the Company deems, in its sole discretion, that such delivery would violate a federal, state, local, or securities exchange rule, regulation, or law.

Notwithstanding anything to the contrary contained herein, this option is not exercisable until all the following events occur and during the following periods of time:

(a) Until the Plan pursuant to which this option is granted is approved by the shareholders of the Company in the manner prescribed by the Code and the regulations thereunder;

(b) Until this option and the optioned shares are approved and/or registered with such federal, state, and local regulatory bodies or agencies and securities exchanges as the Company may deem necessary or desirable; or

(c) During any period of time in which the Company deems that the exercisability of this option, the offer to sell the shares optioned hereunder, or the sale thereof, may violate a federal, state, local, or securities exchange rule, regulation, or law, or may cause the Company to be legally obligated to issue or sell more shares than the Company is legally entitled to issue or sell.

(d) Until you have paid or made suitable arrangements to pay (which may include payment through the surrender of Common Stock, unless prohibited by the Committee) (i) all federal, state, and local income tax withholding required to be withheld by the Company in connection with the option exercise and (ii) the employee's portion of other federal, state, and local payroll and other taxes due in connection with the option exercise.

(e) Until you have executed such shareholder agreements as shall be required by the Company. Such shareholder agreements may, at the Company's option, include (among other provisions) provisions requiring you to (i) vote on trust agreements, (ii) grant to the Company or its nominees an option to repurchase the stock, (iii) not sell, pledge or otherwise dispose of the stock without the consent of the Company, (iv) maintain any Subchapter S elections made by the Company, (v) grant rights of first refusal to the Company or its nominees with respect to the stock, and (vi) join in any sale of a majority or all of the outstanding stock of the Company.

The following two paragraphs shall be applicable if, on the date of exercise of this option, the Common Stock to be purchased pursuant to such exercise has not been registered under the Securities Act of 1933, as amended, and under applicable state securities laws, and shall continue to be applicable for so long as such registration has not occurred:

(a) The optionee hereby agrees, warrants and represents that he will acquire the Common Stock to be issued hereunder for his own account for investment purposes only, and not with a view to, or in connection with, any resale or other distribution of any of such shares, except as hereafter permitted. The optionee further agrees that he will not at any time make any offer, sale, transfer, pledge, or other disposition of such Common Stock to be issued hereunder without an effective registration statement under the Securities Act of 1933, as amended, and under any applicable state securities laws or an opinion of counsel acceptable to the Company to the effect that the proposed transaction will be exempt from such registration. The optionee shall execute such instruments, representations, acknowledgements, and agreements as the Company may, in its sole discretion, deem advisable to avoid any violation of federal, state, local, or securities exchange rule, regulation, or law.

(b) The certificates for Common Stock to be issued to the optionee hereunder shall bear the following legend:

> "The shares represented by this certificate have not been registered under the Securities Act of 1933, as amended, or under applicable state securities laws. The shares have been acquired for investment and may not be offered, sold, transferred, pledged, or otherwise disposed of without an effective registration statement under the Securities Act of 1933, as amended, and under any applicable state securities laws or an opinion of counsel acceptable to the Company that the proposed transaction will be exempt from such registration."

The foregoing legend shall be removed upon registration of the legended shares under the Securities Act of 1933, as amended, and under any applicable state laws or upon receipt of any opinion of counsel acceptable to the Company that said registration is no longer required.

The sole purpose of the agreements, warranties, representations, and legend set forth in the two immediately preceding paragraphs is to prevent violations of the Securities Act of 1933, as amended, and any applicable state securities laws.

It is the intention of the Company and you that this option shall not be an "Incentive Stock Option" as that term is used in Section 422(b) of the Code and the regulations thereunder.

Nothing herein shall modify your status as an at-will employee of the Company. Further, nothing herein guarantees you employment for any specified period of time. This means that either you or the Company may terminate your employment at any time for any reason, with or without cause, or for no reason. You recognize that, for instance, you may terminate your employment or the Company may terminate your employment prior to the date on which your option becomes vested or exercisable. You understand that the Company has no obligation to consider or effectuate a Change of Control and therefore this option may never become exercisable.

Any dispute or disagreement between you and the Company with respect to any portion of this option (excluding Attachment A hereto) or its validity, construction, meaning, performance, or your rights hereunder shall be settled by arbitration in accordance with the Commercial Arbitration Rules of the American Arbitration Association or its successor, as amended from time to time. However, prior to submission to arbitration you will attempt to resolve any disputes or disagreements with the Company over this option amicably and informally, in good faith, for a period not to exceed two weeks. Thereafter, the dispute or disagreement will be submitted to arbitration. At any time prior to a decision from the arbitrator(s) being rendered, you and the Company may resolve the dispute by settlement. You and the Company shall equally share the costs charged by the American Arbitration Association or its successor, but you and the Company shall otherwise be solely responsible for your own respective counsel fees and expenses. The decision of the arbitrator(s) shall be made in writing, setting forth the award, the reasons for the decision and award and shall be binding and conclusive on you and the Company. Further, neither you nor the Company shall appeal any such award. Judgment of a court of competent jurisdiction may be entered upon the award and may be enforced as such in accordance with the provisions of the award.

This option shall be subject to the terms of the Plan in effect on the date this option is granted, which terms are hereby incorporated herein by reference and made a part hereof. In the event of any conflict between the terms of this option and the terms of the Plan in effect on the date of this option, the terms of the Plan shall govern. This option constitutes the entire understanding between the Company and you with respect to the subject matter hereof and no amendment, supplement, or waiver of this option, in whole or in part, shall be binding upon the Company unless in writing and signed by the President of the Company. This option and the performances of the parties hereunder shall be construed in accordance with and governed by the laws of the State of Pennsylvania.

In consideration of the grant to you of this option, you hereby agree to the confidentiality and noninterference provisions set forth in Attachment A hereto.

Please sign the copy of this option and return it to the Company's Secretary, thereby indicating your understanding of and agreement with its terms and conditions, **including Attachment A hereto.**

XYZ, Inc.

By:_____

I hereby acknowledge receipt of a copy of the foregoing stock option and, having read it, hereby signify my understanding of, and my agreement with, its terms and conditions, **including Attachment A hereto.**

_____   _____

(Signature)   (Date)

Attachment A to Stock Option

Confidentiality and Noninterference

(a) You covenant and agree that, in consideration of the grant to you of this stock option, you will not, during your employment with the Company or at any time thereafter, except with the express prior written consent of the Company or pursuant to the lawful order of any judicial or administrative agency of government, directly or indirectly, disclose, communicate or divulge to any individual or entity, or use for the benefit of any individual or entity, any knowledge or information with respect to the conduct or details of the Company's business which you, acting reasonably, believe or should believe to be of a confidential nature and the disclosure of which not to be in the Company's interest.

(b) You covenant and agree that, in consideration of the grant to you of this stock option, you will not, during your employment with the Company and for a period of two years thereafter, except with the express prior written consent of the Company, directly or indirectly, whether as employee, owner, partner, consultant, agent, director, officer, shareholder or in any other capacity, engage in or assist any individual or entity to engage in any act or action which you, acting reasonably, believe or should believe would be harmful or inimical to the interests of the Company.

(c) You covenant and agree that, in consideration of the grant to you of this stock option, you will not, for a period of two years after your employment with the Company ceases for any reason whatsoever (whether voluntary or not), except with the express prior written consent of the Company, directly or indirectly, whether as employee, owner, partner, consultant, agent, director, officer, shareholder or in any other capacity, for your own account or for the benefit of any individual or entity, (i) solicit any customer of the Company for business which would result in such customer terminating their relationship with the Company; or (ii) solicit or induce any individual or entity which is an employee of the Company to leave the Company or to otherwise terminate their relationship with the Company.

(d) The parties agree that any breach by you of any of the covenants or agreements contained in this Attachment A will result in irreparable injury to the Company for which money damages could not adequately compensate the Company and therefore, in the event of any such breach, the Company shall be entitled (in addition to any other rights and remedies which it may have at law or in equity) to have an injunction issued by any competent court enjoining and restraining you and/or any other individual or entity involved therein from continuing such breach. The existence of any claim or cause of action which you may have against the Company or any other individual or entity shall not constitute a defense or bar to the enforcement of such covenants. If the Company is obliged to resort to the courts for the enforcement of any of the covenants or agreements contained in this Attachment A, or if such covenants or agreements are otherwise the subject of litigation between the parties, and the Company prevails in such enforcement or litigation, then the term of such covenants and agreements shall be extended for a period of time equal to the period of such breach, which extension shall commence on the later of (a) the date on which the original (unextended) term of such covenants and agreements is scheduled to terminate or (b) the date of the final court order (without further right of appeal) enforcing such covenant or agreement.

(e) If any portion of the covenants or agreements contained in this Attachment A, or the application hereof, is construed to be invalid or unenforceable, the other portions of such covenant(s) or agreement(s) or the application thereof shall not be affected and shall be given full force and effect without regard to the invalid or enforceable portions to the fullest extent possible. If any covenant or agreement in this Attachment A is held unenforceable because of the area covered, the duration thereof, or the scope thereof, then the court making such determination shall have the power to reduce the area and/or duration and/or limit the scope thereof, and the covenant or agreement shall then be enforceable in its reduced form.

(f) For purposes of this Attachment A, the term "the Company" shall include the Company, any successor to the Company and all present and future direct and indirect subsidiaries and affiliates of the Company.

APPENDIX III

**NON-QUALIFIED STOCK OPTION FOR DIRECTORS
AND IMPORTANT CONSULTANTS**

To: _____
              Name

        _____
              Address

Date of Grant: _____

You are hereby granted an option, effective as of the date hereof, to purchase _____ shares of common stock, no par value ("Common Stock"), of XYZ, Inc., a Pennsylvania corporation (the "Company"), at a price of $____ per share pursuant to the Company's Stock Option Plan (the "Plan").

This option shall terminate and is not exercisable after ten years from the date of its grant (the "Scheduled Termination Date"), except if terminated earlier as hereafter provided.

Your option may first be exercised if and only if there is a Change of Control (as hereafter defined) prior to the Scheduled Termination Date, but shall not otherwise be exercisable. A "Change of Control" shall be deemed to have occurred upon the happening of any of the following events:

1. If John Doe (or in the event of his death, a representative of his estate or his heirs) ceases to be a director of the Company or a successor to the Company by merger or other form of acquisition;

2. If John Doe (or in the event of his death, a representative of his estate or his heirs) ceases to own at least 10 percent of the stock of the Company or a successor to the Company by merger or other form of acquisition; or

3. Any other event deemed to constitute a "Change of Control" by the Committee.

You may exercise your option by giving written notice to the Secretary of the Company on forms supplied by the Company at its then principal executive office, accompanied by payment of the option price for the total number of shares you specify that you wish to purchase. The payment may be in any of the following forms: (a) cash, which may be evidenced by a check and includes cash received from a stock brokerage firm in a so-called "cashless exercise"; (b) (unless prohibited by the Committee) certificates representing shares of Common Stock of the Company, which will be valued by the Secretary of the Company at the fair market value per share of the Company's Common Stock (as determined in accordance with the Plan) on the date of delivery of such certificates to the Company, accompanied by an assignment of the stock to the Company; or (c) (unless prohibited by the Committee) any combination of cash and Common Stock of the Company valued as provided in clause (b). The use of the so-called "attestation procedure" to exercise a stock option may be permitted by the Committee. Any assignment of stock shall be in a form and substance satisfactory to the Secretary of the Company, including guarantees of signature(s) and payment of all transfer taxes if the Secretary deems such guarantees necessary or desirable.

Your option will, to the extent not previously exercised by you, terminate three months after the date on which you cease for any reason to be a director of, or consultant to, the Company or a subsidiary corporation (whether by death, disability, resignation, removal, failure to be reappointed, reelected or otherwise, or the expiration of any consulting arrangement, and regardless of whether the failure to continue as a director or consultant was for cause or without cause or otherwise), but in no event later than ten years from the date this option is granted. After the date you cease to be a director or consultant, you may exercise this option only for the number of shares which you had a right to purchase and did not purchase on the date you ceased to be a director or consultant. If you are a director of, or consultant to, a subsidiary corporation, your directorship or consultancy shall be deemed to have terminated on the date such company ceases to be a subsidiary corporation, unless you are also a director of, or consultant to, the Company or another subsidiary corporation, or on that date became a director of, or consultant to, the Company or another subsidiary corporation. Your directorship or consultancy shall not be deemed to have terminated if you cease being a director of, or consultant to, the Company or a subsidiary corporation but are or concurrently therewith become a director of, or consultant to, the Company or another subsidiary corporation.

In the event of any change in the outstanding shares of the Common Stock of the Company by reason of a stock dividend, stock split, combination of shares, recapitalization, merger, consolidation, transfer of assets, reorganization, conversion or what the Committee deems in its sole discretion to be similar circumstances, the number and kind of shares subject to this option and the option price of such shares shall be appropriately adjusted in a manner to be determined in the sole discretion of the Committee.

In the event of a liquidation or proposed liquidation of the Company, including (but not limited to) a transfer of assets followed by a liquidation of the Company, or in the event of a Change of Control (as previously defined) or proposed Change of Control, the Committee shall have the right to require you to exercise this option upon thirty (30) days prior written notice to you. If at the time such written notice is given this option is not otherwise exercisable, the written notice will set forth your right to exercise this option even though it is not otherwise exercisable. In the event this option is not exercised by you within the thirty (30) day period set forth in such written notice, this option shall terminate on the last day of such thirty (30) day period, notwithstanding anything to the contrary contained in this option.

This option is not transferable otherwise than by will or the laws of descent and distribution, and is exercisable during your lifetime only by you, including, for this purpose, your legal guardian or custodian in the event of disability. Until the option price has been paid in full pursuant to due exercise of this option and the purchased shares are delivered to you, you do not have any rights as a shareholder of the Company. The Company reserves the right not to deliver to you the shares purchased by virtue of the exercise of this option during any period of time in which the Company deems, in its sole discretion, that such delivery would violate a federal, state, local, or securities exchange rule, regulation, or law.

Notwithstanding anything to the contrary contained herein, this option is not exercisable until all the following events occur and during the following periods of time:

(a) Until the Plan pursuant to which this option is granted is approved by the shareholders of the Company in the manner prescribed by the Code and the regulations thereunder;

(b) Until this option and the optioned shares are approved and/or registered with such federal, state, and local regulatory bodies or agencies and securities exchanges as the Company may deem necessary or desirable; or

(c) During any period of time in which the Company deems that the exercisability of this option, the offer to sell the shares optioned hereunder, or the sale thereof, may violate a federal, state, local, or securities exchange rule, regulation, or law, or may cause the Company to be legally obligated to issue or sell more shares than the Company is legally entitled to issue or sell.

(d) Until you have paid or made suitable arrangements to pay (which may include payment through the surrender of Common Stock, unless prohibited by the Committee) (i) all federal, state, and local income tax withholding required to be withheld by the Company in connection with the option exercise and (ii) the employee's portion of other federal, state, and local payroll and other taxes due in connection with the option exercise.

(e) Until you have executed such shareholder agreements as shall be required by the Company. Such shareholder agreements may, at the Company's option, include (among other provisions) provisions requiring you to (i) vote on trust agreements, (ii) grant to the Company or its nominees an option to repurchase the stock, (iii) not sell, pledge or otherwise dispose of the stock without the consent of the Company, (iv) maintain any Subchapter Selections made by the Company, (v) grant rights of first refusal to the Company or its nominees with respect to the stock, and (vi) join in any sale of a majority or all of the outstanding stock of the Company.

The following two paragraphs shall be applicable if, on the date of exercise of this option, the Common Stock to be purchased pursuant to such exercise has not been registered under the Securities Act of 1933, as amended, and under applicable state securities laws, and shall continue to be applicable for so long as such registration has not occurred:

(a) The optionee hereby agrees, warrants and represents that he will acquire the Common Stock to be issued hereunder for his own account for investment purposes only, and not with a view to, or in connection with, any resale or other distribution of any of such shares, except as hereafter permitted. The optionee further agrees that he will not at any time make any offer, sale, transfer, pledge, or other disposition of such Common Stock to be issued hereunder without an effective registration statement under the Securities Act of 1933, as amended, and under any applicable state securities laws or an opinion of counsel acceptable to the Company to the effect that the proposed transaction will be exempt from such registration. The optionee shall execute such instruments, representations, acknowledgments, and agreements as the Company may, in its sole discretion, deem advisable to avoid any violation of federal, state, local, or securities exchange rule, regulation, or law.

(b) The certificates for Common Stock to be issued to the optionee hereunder shall bear the following legend:

>"The shares represented by this certificate have not been registered under the Securities Act of 1933, as amended, or under applicable state securities laws. The shares have been acquired for investment and may not be offered, sold, transferred, pledged, or otherwise disposed of without an effective registration statement under the Securities Act of 1933, as amended, and under any applicable state securities laws or an opinion of counsel acceptable to the Company that the proposed transaction will be exempt from such registration."

The foregoing legend shall be removed upon registration of the legended shares under the Securities Act of 1933, as amended, and under any applicable state laws or upon receipt of any opinion of counsel acceptable to the Company that said registration is no longer required.

The sole purpose of the agreements, warranties, representations, and legend set forth in the two immediately preceding paragraphs is to prevent violations of the Securities Act of 1933, as amended, and any applicable state securities laws.

It is the intention of the Company and you that this option shall not be an "Incentive Stock Option" as that term is used in Section 422(b) of the Code and the regulations thereunder.

Nothing herein guarantees your term as a director of, or consultant to, the Company for any specified period of time. This means that either you or the Company may terminate your relationship with the Company at any time for any reason, with or without cause, or for no reason. You recognize that, for instance, the Company may terminate your relationship with the Company prior to the date on which your option becomes vested or exercisable. You understand that the Company has no obligation to consider or effectuate a Change of Control and therefore this option may never become exercisable.

Any dispute or disagreement between you and the Company with respect to any portion of this option (excluding Attachment A hereto) or its validity, construction, meaning, performance, or your rights hereunder shall be settled by arbitration in accordance with the Commercial Arbitration Rules of the American Arbitration Association or its successor, as amended from time to time. However, prior to submission to arbitration you will attempt to resolve any disputes or disagreements with the Company over this option amicably and informally, in good faith, for a period not to exceed two weeks. Thereafter, the dispute or disagreement will be submitted to arbitration. At any time prior to a decision from the arbitrator(s) being rendered, you and the Company may resolve the dispute by settlement. You and the Company shall equally share the costs charged by the American Arbitration Association or its successor, but you and the Company shall otherwise be solely responsible for your own respective counsel fees and expenses. The decision of the arbitrator(s) shall be made in writing, setting forth the award, the reasons for the decision and award and shall be binding and conclusive on you and the Company. Further, neither you nor the Company shall appeal any such award. Judgment of a court of competent jurisdiction may be entered upon the award and may be enforced as such in accordance with the provisions of the award.

This option shall be subject to the terms of the Plan in effect on the date this option is granted, which terms are hereby incorporated herein by reference and made a part hereof. In the event of any conflict between the terms of this option and the terms of the Plan in effect on the date of this option, the terms of the Plan shall govern. This option constitutes the entire understanding between the Company and you with respect to the subject matter hereof and no amendment, supplement, or waiver of this option, in whole or in part, shall be binding upon the Company unless in writing and signed by the President of the Company. This option and the performances of the parties hereunder shall be construed in accordance with and governed by the laws of the State of Pennsylvania.

In consideration of the grant to you of this option, you hereby agree to the confidentiality and noninterference provisions set forth in Attachment A hereto.

Please sign the copy of this option and return it to the Company's Secretary, thereby indicating your understanding of and agreement with its terms and conditions, **including Attachment A hereto.**

XYZ, Inc.

By: _____

I hereby acknowledge receipt of a copy of the foregoing stock option and, having read it, hereby signify my understanding of, and my agreement with, its terms and conditions, **including Attachment A hereto.**

_____   _____

(Signature)   (Date)

Attachment A to Stock Option

Confidentiality and Noninterference

(a) You covenant and agree that, in consideration of the grant to you of this stock option, you will not, during your term as a director of, or a consultant to, the Company or at any time thereafter, except with the express prior written consent of the Company or pursuant to the lawful order of any judicial or administrative agency of government, directly or indirectly, disclose, communicate or divulge to any individual or entity, or use for the benefit of any individual or entity, any knowledge or information with respect to the conduct or details of the Company's business which you, acting reasonably, believe or should believe to be of a confidential nature and the disclosure of which not to be in the Company's interest.

(b) You covenant and agree that, in consideration of the grant to you of this stock option, you will not, during your term as a director of, or a consultant to, the Company and for a period of two years thereafter, except with the express prior written consent of the Company, directly or indirectly, whether as employee, owner, partner, consultant, agent, director, officer, shareholder or in any other capacity, engage in or assist any individual or entity to engage in any act or action which you, acting reasonably, believe or should believe would be harmful or inimical to the interests of the Company.

(c) You covenant and agree that, in consideration of the grant to you of this stock option, you will not, for a period of two years after your term as a director of, or a consultant to, the Company ceases for any reason whatsoever (whether voluntary or not), except with the express prior written consent of the Company, directly or indirectly, whether as employee, owner, partner, consultant, agent, director, officer, shareholder or in any other capacity, for your own account or for the benefit of any individual or entity, (i) solicit any customer of the Company for business which would result in such customer terminating their relationship with the Company; or (ii) solicit or induce any individual or entity which is an employee of the Company to leave the Company or to otherwise terminate their relationship with the Company.

(d) The parties agree that any breach by you of any of the covenants or agreements contained in this Attachment A will result in irreparable injury to the Company for which money damages could not adequately compensate the Company and therefore, in the event of any such breach, the Company shall be entitled (in addition to any other rights and remedies which it may have at law or in equity) to have an injunction issued by any competent court enjoining and restraining you and/or any other individual or entity involved therein from continuing such breach. The existence of any claim or cause of action which you may have against the Company or any other individual or entity shall not constitute a defense or bar to the enforcement of such covenants. If the Company is obliged to resort to the courts for the enforcement of any of the covenants or agreements contained in this Attachment A, or if such covenants or agreements are otherwise the subject of litigation between the parties, and the Company prevails in such enforcement or litigation, then the term of such covenants and agreements shall be extended for a period of time equal to the period of such breach, which extension shall commence on the later of (a) the date on which the original (unextended) term of such covenants and agreements is scheduled to terminate or (b) the date of the final court order (without further right of appeal) enforcing such covenant or agreement.

(e) If any portion of the covenants or agreements contained in this Attachment A, or the application hereof, is construed to be invalid or unenforceable, the other portions of such covenant(s) or agreement(s) or the application thereof shall not be affected and shall be given full force and effect without regard to the invalid or enforceable portions to the fullest extent possible. If any covenant or agreement in this Attachment A is held unenforceable because of the area covered, the duration thereof, or the scope thereof, then the court making such determination shall have the power to reduce the area and/or duration and/or limit the scope thereof, and the covenant or agreement shall then be enforceable in its reduced form.

(f) For purposes of this Attachment A, the term "the Company" shall include the Company, any successor to the Company and all present and future direct and indirect subsidiaries and affiliates of the Company.

APPENDIX 3

SHAREHOLDERS' AGREEMENT

Agreement dated as of the __ day of _____ by and between JOE SMITH, residing at _____ (herein called "Executive") and ABC, INC., a Pennsylvania corporation (herein called the "Company").

BACKGROUND

The Executive holds at option to purchase shares of the Company's common stock and wishes to exercise the option. The option requires the Executive to execute a shareholders' agreement with the Company prior to and as a condition of exercising the option. The purpose of this Agreement is to serve as the Shareholders' Agreement.

NOW, THEREFORE, in consideration of the mutual covenants set forth herein, and intending to be legally bound hereby, the parties hereto agree as follows:

1. Transfer Restrictions

1.1 General Transfer Restrictions. The Executive shall not Transfer, and the Company shall not recognize any purported Transfer (as defined herein) of, all or any part of his Shares (as defined herein), except as provided pursuant to this Agreement, and any such Transfer shall be null and void and of no force or effect. For purposes of this Agreement, the term "Shares" refers to all shares of the stock of the Company or any successor to the Company (including any holding company owning directly or indirectly all or substantially all of the outstanding stock of the Company), now owned by the Executive or hereafter acquired by the Executive in any manner whatsoever (including but not limited to, option exercise, stock dividend, gift, transfer or otherwise). For purposes of this Agreement, the term "Transfer" refers to the disposing of all or a portion of, or any interest in, the Shares (legal or equitable), by any means, direct or indirect, absolute or conditional, voluntary or involuntary, including, but not limited to, by sale, assignment, pledge, hypothecation, encumbrance, court order, operation of law, equitable or other distribution after divorce or separation, settlement, exchange, abandonment, waiver, gift, bequest, alienation, or other disposal. For purposes of this Agreement, the term "Person" refers to a natural person, corporation, partnership, limited liability company, trust, estate, joint venture, sole proprietorship, government (and any branch or subdivision thereof), governmental agency, association, cooperative or other entity.

There shall be legibly endorsed upon each of the stock certificates representing the Shares a legend substantially as follows:

"THIS CERTIFICATE IS TRANSFERABLE ONLY UPON COMPLIANCE WITH THE PROVISIONS OF A CERTAIN STOCKHOLDERS' AGREEMENT DATED AS OF _____, A COPY OF WHICH IS NOW ON FILE AT THE OFFICE OF THE SECRETARY OF THE COMPANY. THE SECURITIES REPRESENTED BY THIS CERTIFICATE HAVE NOT BEEN REGISTERED UNDER FEDERAL SECURITIES LAWS OR APPLICABLE STATE SECURITIES LAWS AND MAY NOT BE SOLD, PLEDGED, OR OTHERWISE TRANSFERRED OR DISPOSED OF WITHOUT AN OPINION OF COUNSEL FOR THE COMPANY THAT SUCH SALE, PLEDGE, TRANSFER OR OTHER DISPOSITION DOES NOT VIOLATE SUCH FEDERAL OR STATE SECURITIES LAWS."

1.2 Lockup Agreements. In the event of a public offering registered under the Securities Act of 1933 of the Company stock or the stock of a holding company owning all or substantially all of the Company stock, Executive shall agree with the managing underwriter or placement agent, if any, to the same restrictions on the transfer of the Shares as are agreed to by holders of more than 50 percent of the outstanding common stock of the Company or such holding company. Executive hereby irrevocably appoints the President of the Company as Executive's agent and attorney-in-fact, to execute all "lock-up" and similar transfer restriction agreements on behalf of Executive as are required by such underwriter or placement agent.

1.3 <u>Provisions Relating to Subchapter "S" Corporation.</u> The following provisions shall apply during any period of time that the Company has a Subchapter "S" election in effect pursuant to Section 1361 et seq. of the Internal Revenue Code of 1986, as amended (hereafter called the "Code").

1.3.1 <u>Additional Transfer Restrictions.</u> If for any reason the Executive is permitted to Transfer any of the Shares pursuant to any other provision of this Agreement or otherwise, and notwithstanding anything to the contrary contained herein, Executive shall not Transfer any of the Shares to any Person if such Transfer would cause, directly or indirectly, the Company's Subchapter "S" election to terminate. Transfers prohibited under this Section include, without limitation, Transfers (a) to any Person which would cause the Company to have more shareholders than the number of shareholders permitted under Section 1361 of the Code, (b) to any nonresident alien, (c) to any Person who is not permitted to be a shareholder of Subchapter "S" corporations under the Code, or (d) to any Person which would in any other way cause a termination of the Company's Subchapter "S" election. No Transfer permitted by this Agreement shall be effective to vest any right, title or ownership of the Shares unless: (i) Executive delivers to the Company an opinion of counsel, satisfactory to the Company in its sole discretion, indicating that such Transfer shall not: (a) cause, directly or indirectly, a termination of the Company's Subchapter "S" election or (b) violate any applicable federal or state securities laws; (ii) the transferee delivers to the Company documents and agreements as the Company's legal counsel may reasonably request, including, but not limited to, a shareholders' agreement in form and substance satisfactory to the Company; and (iii) the Company approves the Transfer after receiving written notice of the prospective transferee.

1.3.2 <u>Representations.</u> Executive represents and warrants to the Company and agrees as follows: (a) Executive is a legal resident of the United States; (b) Executive has not made, or caused to be made, a Transfer of any Shares, or an interest therein; and (c) Executive shall, if requested by the Company, consent to the elections under Section 1362(e)(3)(A) of the Code (in the event of termination of the Company's Subchapter "S" election), Section 1377(a)(2) of the Code (in the event of termination of a stockholder's interest) and any similar election under state law or the corresponding provisions of any subsequent internal revenue law.

1.3.3 <u>Indemnification for Breach.</u> If the Executive's breach of any provision of this Agreement causes the Company's Subchapter "S" election to terminate, then the Executive shall indemnify the other stockholders of the Company (the "Indemnitees") for the following: any loss of any federal, state and local income tax benefits during the period in which the Company is ineligible to make a "S" election, and during any additional period for which the Company and/or the Indemnitees are subject to tax under Sections 1374, 1375, 1363(d), or 1368(c)(2) of the Code, which result from the termination. For the purposes of this Section, "federal, state and local income tax benefits" means the excess of (a) Indemnitees' share of federal, state and local income taxes imposed on the Company as a "C" corporation (as described in the Code) or under Sections 1374 or 1375 of the Code as a result of the termination, plus the Indemnitees' share of the federal, state and local income taxes on the Company's actual or constructive dividend distributions, assuming such distributions are made by the Company, over (b) each Indemnitees' share of federal, state, and local income taxes that would have been imposed on the Company if the Subchapter "S" election had not terminated and if the Company had the same items of income, loss, deduction, and credit (hereafter called "Tax Items") that the Company had throughout the term of this indemnification, plus the amount of federal, state, and local income taxes that the Indemnitees would have paid on the Tax Items which would have been passed through to the Indemnitees had the Company been an "S" corporation.

1.3.4 Effect of Prohibited Actions. Any Transfer or other action, direct or indirect, taken by a Person that would cause a termination or revocation of the Company's Subchapter "S" election shall be null and void and of no force or effect, notwithstanding anything to the contrary contained herein.

1.3.5 Dividend Payments. The Company shall declare dividends from time to time in order to enable Executive to pay all federal, state and local taxes on Executive's share of the Company's taxable income. Such dividends shall be declared in amounts sufficient to enable Executive to pay such taxes as if Executive were subject to tax at the highest marginal income tax rates then in effect.

2. Call Rights; Required Sale Obligations; Voting; Holding Company

2.1 Call Rights. The Executive agrees that the Company or its nominee shall have the right to repurchase the Shares at any time after one year from the date of exercise by the Executive of Executive's stock option, such repurchase to be on the terms and conditions set forth in Sections 5 and 6 of this Agreement. Such repurchase rights shall be in addition to the repurchase rights set forth in Sections 3 and 4 hereof.

2.2 Required Sale Obligations. If stockholders of the Company (herein called the "Selling Stockholders") intend to sell more than 50% of the outstanding common stock of the Company to an unrelated third party in a bona fide transaction, or intend to engage in a transaction which the Company's board of directors determines in good faith to result in a change of control of the Company, the Company shall give Executive written notice of such intent. If so requested by the Company in such written notice, Executive agrees to sell or exchange all Shares to such unrelated third party upon the same terms and conditions as are being offered to the Selling Stockholders. Executive hereby irrevocably appoints the Company as Executive's agent and attorney-in-fact to execute and deliver on behalf of Executive such stock powers, endorsements, and assignments as are necessary to complete such a sale or exchange of the Shares.

2.3 Voting Agreement. In the event of any dispute between or among the shareholders of the Company, the Executive shall vote the Shares as directed by the board of directors of the Company. The Executive hereby irrevocably grants to the President of the Company a proxy to vote the Shares as provided in this Section 2.3 and such proxy shall be deemed coupled with an interest.

2.4 Holding Company. In the event that the holders of more than 50 percent of the outstanding common stock of the Company transfer their stock to a holding company, in exchange for the same proportionate share of the common stock of the holding company, the Executive shall, on request by the Company, transfer the Shares to the holding company in exchange for the same proportionate share of the common stock of the holding company.

3. Voluntary Transfer

3.1 To the fullest extent permitted by law, the Executive shall be prohibited from any voluntary Transfer of all or any part of the Shares, except as specifically provided in this Agreement. If and to the extent Executive is required by law to be permitted to voluntarily Transfer all or any part of the Shares, and if Executive desires to voluntarily Transfer all or any part of the Shares during Executive's lifetime in a bona fide transaction with an unrelated third party, the Executive shall give the Company and the non-selling stockholders of the Company written notice of such desire. Such notice shall contain the identity of the proposed purchaser and the price and terms of the proposed transaction. The Company or its nominee shall then have the option to purchase all Shares within sixty (60) days after receipt of such notice. If the Company or its nominee fails to exercise such option, then any of the non-selling stockholders of the Company shall have a similar option to purchase all of such Shares pro rata, based on their respective ownership of Company's common stock, expiring thirty (30) days after expiration of the Company's option.

3.2 If the Company or its nominee and the non-selling stockholders of the Company each fail to exercise such options as to all of the Shares, Executive may thereafter dispose of the Shares free of the restrictions of this Agreement (but subject to the provisions of Section 1.3 hereof), to the proposed purchaser and on the price and terms described in the original notice, but only to the extent such Transfer is required to be permitted by law and provided the proposed purchaser enters into a stockholders' agreement in form and substance satisfactory to the Company. Notwithstanding anything contained herein to the contrary, however, if the Company and such non-selling stockholders fail to exercise their options hereunder as to the Share, and if Executive does not, in fact, dispose the Shares to the proposed purchaser and on the price and terms described in the original notice within sixty (60) days after the options to the Company or its nominee and the non-selling stockholders expire, the Executive may not dispose of the Shares at a subsequent date without first providing the written notice required in this Section and again offering the Shares to the Company or its nominee and such non-selling stockholders pursuant to the terms of this Section.

3.3 The purchase price of any Shares sold by the Executive to the Company or its nominee or any of the non-selling stockholders of the Company pursuant to the provisions of this Section 3.1 shall be determined in accordance with the provisions of Sections 5 and 6 of this Agreement or at the price and terms contained in such offer, whichever (whether price or terms or both) is more favorable to the purchasers, as determined by the purchasers.

4. **Executive's Employment Termination, including Death and Disability.** If the Executive's employment with the Company is terminated for any reason whatsoever, whether voluntarily or involuntarily and including termination which results from the Executive's death or disability, then the Company or its nominee may, in its sole discretion, elect to purchase, and in the event of such election Executive (and, in the event of Executive's death, Executive's estate) shall sell, Executive's (and such estate's) Shares at any time after such termination. The purchase price and the terms for the sale shall be determined in accordance with the provisions of Section 5 and 6 of this Agreement.

5. **Determination of Executive's Purchase Price**

5.1 In the event of the sale of the Shares hereunder by Executive or Executive's estate pursuant to Section 4 hereof, or in the event of a sale pursuant to Section 3.1 hereof to which this Section 5 is applicable because the price is more favorable to the purchasers, the purchase price of all of the Shares owned by Executive or his estate shall be equal to the higher of:

   (a) The proceeds, if any, actually received by the Company under any insurance policies insuring Executive's life; or

   (b) An amount equal to the Formula Value (as defined in Section 5.2 below), multiplied by a fraction the numerator of which is the number of shares of the Company common stock held by Executive as of the date of the purchase and the denominator of which is the total number of shares of the Company common stock issued and outstanding as of the date of the purchase.

5.2 The Formula Value is an amount equal to the fair value of the stock of the Company as determined in good faith by the board of directors of the Company.

5.3 In the event of any dispute concerning the Formula Value, the dispute shall be settled by the outside independent accountants for the Company, whose decision shall be final, binding and conclusive.

6. **Payment of Purchase Price.** In the event of the sale of the Shares hereunder by Executive or Executive's estate pursuant to Section 4 hereof, or in the event of a sale pursuant to Section 3.1 hereof to which this Section 6 is applicable because the terms of the sale are more favorable to the purchasers, the entire purchase price of Shares being purchased pursuant hereto shall be paid in forty-eight (48) equal consecutive monthly installments. The first monthly installment shall be due sixty (60) days

after the date of the exercise of the right to purchase pursuant to Section 3.1 or the date of the termination of Executive's employment pursuant to Section 4 or, if later, sixty (60) days after the date Executive's estate representative is qualified, if applicable. Any amounts owed by Executive to the purchaser or the Company or to any of the other stockholders of the Company shall be deducted from the aggregate purchase price to be paid to Executive pursuant to Section 5 and 6 hereof. If Executive is entitled to severance pay from the Company, the first monthly installment shall be postponed until the calendar month following the last month in which Executive receives severance pay. The aggregate purchase price less any indebtedness owed by Executive (and in the event of Executive's death, less any insurance proceeds required to be paid to Executive under this Section 6) shall be evidenced by a non-negotiable promissory note made by the Company (or its assignee as purchaser), or by the non-selling stockholders of the Company who exercise their option pursuant to Section 3.1 or Section 4 hereof, as applicable, and shall bear interest on the unpaid balance at the prime rate as established from time to time by the Company's principal banker, which interest shall accrue on the date of the exercise of the option to purchase under Section 3.1 or, if Section 4 is applicable, sixty (60) days after termination of employment pursuant to Section 4 hereof. Such note shall provide for the acceleration of the due date of all unpaid installments upon a default in the payment of any installment of such note that continues for a period of sixty (60) days after notice of such default is given to the maker. Such note shall give the maker the option of prepayment without notice or penalty, in whole or in part at any time. Should Executive be deceased, then any insurance proceeds received by the Company shall be payable on account of the obligation due, and the balance, if any, payable in forty-eight equal monthly installments. The non-selling stockholders of the Company shall have no liability for payment of the purchase price except for non-selling stockholders who exercise their option or election pursuant to Section 3.1 or Section 4 hereof, as applicable.

7. **Life Insurance**

     7.1   The Company may apply for and own life insurance on the life of Executive in order to fully or partially fund the Company's obligations hereunder, and shall be the sole beneficiary under any such policies. The Company agrees to pay the premiums as they become due on such insurance policies owned by it and to maintain such policies in force during the term of this Agreement. Any dividends on the policies prior to maturity or death of the insured shall be disposed of as the Company or the then policy owner may direct.

     7.2   Upon a purchase of Executive's Shares pursuant to the terms of this Agreement, except on the death of Executive, Executive shall have the right to purchase from the Company such portion of the life insurance policies on his own life then owed by the Company. The purchase price of such policies shall be the appropriate portion of the then cash surrender value of any such policy, plus the unearned portion of any premiums which shall have been paid, less any indebtedness thereon.

8. **Termination.** This Agreement shall terminate on the written agreement of Executive and the Company. In the event of a sale of the Shares, the Executive's consent to the termination of this Agreement shall no longer be required. The Company may, at its option, terminate this Agreement at any time after a public offering registered under the Securities Act of 1933 of the stock of the Company or of a holding company. The termination of this Agreement shall not affect the enforceability of any lock-up agreement executed pursuant to Section 1.2 hereof, and any such lock-up agreement shall continue in full force and effect after termination of this Agreement.

9. **Arbitration.** If any dispute, controversy or claim arising out of this Agreement cannot be agreeably settled by the parties, such dispute, controversy or claim shall be settled by arbitration by a single arbitrator in Philadelphia, Pennsylvania in accordance with the then current rules of the American Arbitration Association and a judgment upon the arbitration award may be entered in any court having jurisdic-

tion thereof. Any award rendered by the arbitrator shall be final and binding, and not subject to appeal or other judicial review, and judgment thereon may be entered in any court of competent jurisdiction. Nothing contained herein shall restrict the Company from seeking equitable remedies in a court of competent jurisdiction for any alleged violations by the Executive of the provisions hereof. Notwithstanding the foregoing, the provisions of this section shall not apply to any dispute, controversy or claim related to Section 5.2 hereof, which dispute, controversy, or claim shall be settled as set forth in Section 5.3 hereof.

10. **Equitable Relief; Exclusive Jurisdiction.** The Company shall be entitled to specifically enforce the obligations of the Executive hereunder, it being agreed that damages would not be an adequate remedy for the breach by the Executive of his obligations hereunder. In the event that a dispute, controversy, or claim arises in connection with this Agreement in which the Company seeks equitable relief from a court, the parties hereto irrevocably consent to the exclusive jurisdiction of the Court of Common Pleas of Philadelphia County, Pennsylvania, and/or United States District Court for the Eastern District of Pennsylvania in any action or proceeding between the parties hereto and both of the parties agree to service of process by hand delivery or by certified mail, to the addresses for each party which appear on the records of the Company.

11. **Entire Agreement.** This Agreement, together with all other documents, instruments, certificates, and agreements executed in connection herewith, sets forth the entire understanding between and among the parties with respect to the subject matter hereof and supersedes all prior and contemporaneous, written, oral, expressed or implied, communications, agreements, and understandings with respect to the subject matter hereof.

12. **Amendment, Supplement, or Termination.** This Agreement shall not be amended, supplemented or terminated (other than as provided in Section 8), without the written consent of all parties; in the event of a sale of the Shares pursuant to Section 4 hereof, or the exercise of the option pursuant to Section 3.1 hereof, Executive's consent to the amendment, supplement, or termination of this Agreement shall no longer be required. No action taken by the Company hereunder, including without limitation any waiver, consent, or approval, shall be effective unless approved by a majority of the Company's Board of Directors.

13. **Successors and Assigns.** This Agreement shall be binding upon the parties, their heirs, executors, legal representatives, successors, and assigns. The Company may freely assign its right to acquire the Shares under the various circumstances specified herein.

14. **Notices.** All notices, requests, demands, consents or other communications required or permitted to be given under this Agreement shall be in writing and shall be deemed to have been duly given if and when (a) delivered personally, (b) mailed by first class certified mail, return receipt requested, postdated prepaid, or (c) sent by a nationally recognized express courier service, postage, or delivery charges prepaid, to the parties at their respective addresses stated below or to such other addresses of which the parties may give notice in accordance with this Section.

If to the Company, to:	ABC, Inc.
	(Address)
With a copy to:	Blank Rome Comisky & McCauley LLP
	One Logan Square
	Philadelphia, PA 19103
	Attn: Frederick D. Lipman, Esquire
If to the Executive, to:	Joe Smith
	(Address)

15. Severability. If any provision of this Agreement is construed to be invalid, illegal or unenforceable, then the remaining provisions hereof shall not be affected thereby and shall be enforceable without regard thereto.

16. References. All words used in this Agreement shall be construed to be of such number and gender as the context requires or permits.

17. Controlling Law. This Agreement is made under, and shall be governed by, construed and enforced in accordance with, the substantive laws of the Commonwealth of Pennsylvania applicable to agreements made and to be performed entirely therein. The rule of construction that ambiguities are construed against the draftsperson shall not be applicable to this Agreement.

18. Waivers and Further Agreements. Neither the failure nor delay on the part of either party to exercise any right, remedy, power or privilege under this Agreement shall operate as a waiver thereof, nor shall the single or partial exercise of any right, remedy, power, or privilege preclude any other or further exercise of the same or any other right, remedy, power, or privilege. No waiver shall be effective unless it is in writing and is signed by the party asserted to have granted such waiver.

19. Expenses. Each party shall pay such party's own expenses incident to the performance or enforcement of this Agreement, including all fees and expenses of counsel for all activities of such counsel undertaken pursuant to this Agreement, except as otherwise herein specifically provided.

20. Section Headings. The headings of the sections of this Agreement are for convenience of reference only and shall not affect the interpretation of this Agreement.

IN WITNESS WHEREOF, the parties hereto have executed this Agreement as of the date first above mentioned.

ABC, INC.

By: _____

Title:_____

_____
Signature of Executive

SPOUSAL CONSENT TO SHAREHOLDERS' AGREEMENT

I, _____, am the spouse of _____, the Executive named in the foregoing Shareholders' Agreement. I have read the agreement and know of its contents and provisions. I am aware that my spouse, as a party to the Shareholders' Agreement, has agreed to sell all of my spouse's shares in the Company, including any interest I may have now or in the future in such shares, including, but not limited to, any community property interest I may have, upon the occurrence of certain events set forth in the Shareholders' Agreement and subject to its terms and conditions. I hereby consent to the terms, conditions and provisions of the Shareholders' Agreement, and agree that my interest, if any, in the shares shall be subject to the Shareholders' Agreement. By this consent, I do not waive any rights I have under law to receive the proceeds of such shares.

_____
Spouse of Executive

APPENDIX 4

QRX, INC.
STOCK OPTION PLAN

ARTICLE I
INTRODUCTION

1.1 **Establishment.** QRX, Inc., a Nevada corporation, hereby establishes the QRX, Inc. Stock Option Plan for certain key employees of the Company and certain directors and consultants to the Company. The Plan permits the grant of incentive stock options within the meaning of Code 422 and non-qualified stock options to certain key employees of the Company and to certain directors and consultants to the Company.

1.2 **Purposes.** The purposes of the Plan are to provide those who are selected for participation in the Plan with added incentives to continue in the long-term service of the Company and to create in such persons a more direct interest in the future success of the operations of the Company by relating incentive compensation to increases in shareholder value, so that the income of those participating in the Plan is more closely aligned with the income of the Company's shareholders. The Plan is also designed to provide a financial incentive that will help the Company attract, retain and motivate the most qualified employees, directors, and consultants.

ARTICLE II
DEFINITIONS

2.1 **"Affiliated Corporation"** means any corporation or other entity that is affiliated with the Plan Sponsor through stock ownership or otherwise and is designated as an "Affiliated Corporation" by the Board, provided, however, that for purposes of Incentive Options granted pursuant to the Plan, an "Affiliated Corporation" means any parent or subsidiary of the Plan Sponsor as defined in Code 424.

2.2 **"Award"** means an Option issued under the Plan.

2.3 **"Board"** means the Board of Directors of the Plan Sponsor.

2.4 **"Code"** means the Internal Revenue Code of 1986, as it may be amended from time to time.

2.5 **"Committee"** means a committee established under Article V of the Plan which is empowered to take actions with respect to the administration of the Plan.

2.6 **"Company"** means the Plan Sponsor and the affiliated Corporations.

2.7 **"Disabled"** or **"Disability"** shall have the meaning given to such terms in Code 22(e)(3).

2.8 **"Effective Date"** means the effective date of the Plan which is November 4, 1997; however, the adoption of those provisions of the Plan by the Board of Directors which relate to the grant of Incentive Options is subject to approval and ratification by the shareholders of the Plan Sponsor within twelve months of the effective date. Incentive Options granted under the Plan prior to the approval of the Plan by the shareholders of the Plan Sponsor shall be subject to approval of the Plan by the shareholders of the Plan Sponsor.

2.9 **"Eligible Employees"** means those key employees (including, without limitation, officers and directors who are also employees) of the Company, upon whose judgment, initiative and efforts the Company is, or will become, largely dependent for the successful conduct of its business. For purposes of the Plan, an employee is an individual whose wages are subject to the withholding of federal income tax under Code 3401.

2.10 **"Eligible Individuals"** means those consultants to the Company and directors of the Company who are determined by the Committee to be individuals whose services are important to the Company.

2.11 *"Fair Market Value"* means the average of the mean between the bid and the asked prices of the Stock or the closing price, as applicable, on the principal stock exchange or automated quotation system market on which the Stock is traded, over the five consecutive trading days ending on a particular date or by such other method as the Committee may specify at the time an Award is granted. If the price of the Stock is not reported on any securities exchange or national market system, the Fair Market Value of the Stock on a particular date shall be as determined by the Committee in good faith by applying any reasonable valuation method. If, upon exercise of an Option, the exercise price is paid by a broker's transaction, Fair Market Value, for purposes of the exercise, shall be the price at which the Stock is sold by the broker.

2.12 *"Incentive Option"* means an Option designated as an incentive stock option and granted in accordance with Code 422.

2.13 *"Initial Public Offering"* means the consummation of an underwritten public offering of shares of common stock of the Plan Sponsor pursuant to the Securities Act of 1933, as amended.

2.14 *"1934 Act"* means the Securities Exchange Act of 1934, as it may be amended from time to time.

2.15 *"Non-Qualified Option"* means any Option other than an Incentive Option.

2.16 *"Option"* means a right to purchase Stock at a stated or formula price for a specified period of time. Options granted under the Plan shall be either Incentive Options or Non-Qualified Options.

2.17 *"Option Agreement"* shall have the meaning given to it in Section 4.3.

2.18 *"Option Holder"* means a Participant who has been granted one or more Options under the Plan.

2.19 *"Option Price"* means the price at which each share of Stock subject to an Option may be purchased, determined in accordance with Subsection 4.3(b).

2.20 *"Participant"* means an Eligible Employee or Eligible Individual designated by the Committee during the term of the Plan to receive one or more Options under the Plan.

2.21 *"Plan"* means the QRX, Inc. Stock Option Plan.

2.22 *"Plan Sponsor"* means QRX, Inc. and any successor thereto.

2.23 *"Section"* or *"Subsection"* means a reference to a section or subsection of the Plan, unless another reference specifically applies.

2.24 *"Share"* means a share of Stock.

2.25 *"Stock"* means the common stock of the Plan Sponsor.

ARTICLE III
PARTICIPATION

3.1 Participants in the Plan shall be those Eligible Employees who, in the judgment of the Committee, are performing, or during the term of their incentive arrangement will perform, vital services in the management, operation and development of the Company, and significantly contribute, or are expected to significantly contribute, to the achievement of long-term corporate economic objectives. Eligible Individuals shall be selected from those non-employee consultants to the Company and directors of the Company who are performing services important to the operation and growth of the Company. Participants may be granted from time to time one or more Awards.

ARTICLE IV
OPTIONS

4.1 *Grant of Options.* A Participant may be granted one or more Options. Options shall be granted as of the date specified in the Option Agreement. The Committee in its sole discretion shall designate whether an Option is an Incentive Option or a Non-Qualified Option. Only Non-Qualified Options may be granted to Eligible Individuals. The Committee may grant both an Incentive Option and a Non-Qualified Option to an Eligible Employee at the same time or at different times. Incentive Options and Non-Qualified Options, whether granted at the same time or at different times, shall be deemed to have been awarded in separate grants and shall be clearly identified. In no event shall the exercise of one Option affect the right to exercise any other Option or affect the number of shares for which any other Option may be exercised. The grant to each Option shall be separately approved by the Committee, and the receipt of one Option shall not result in automatic receipt of any other Option. Upon determination by the Committee to grant an Option to a Participant, the Committee shall enter into a Option Agreement with the Participant.

4.2 *Restrictions on Incentive Options.* Incentive Options granted to an Option Holder who is the holder of record of 10 percent or more of the outstanding Stock of the Plan Sponsor shall have an Option Price equal to 10 percent of the Fair Market Value of the Shares on the date of grant of the Option and the Option Period for any such Option shall not exceed five years.

4.3 *Stock Option Agreements.* Each Option granted under the Plan shall be evidenced by a written stock option certificate or agreement (an "Option Agreement"). An Option Agreement shall be issued by the Plan Sponsor in the name of the Participant to whom the Option is granted (the "Option Holder") and in such form as may be approved by the Committee. The Option Agreement shall incorporate and conform to the conditions in the Plan as well as any other terms and conditions that are not inconsistent as the Committee may consider appropriate. In the event of any inconsistency between the provisions of the Plan and any Option Agreement, the provisions of the Plan shall govern.

(a) *Number of Shares.* Each Option Agreement shall state that it covers a specified number of shares of Stock, as determined by the Committee.

(b) *Price.* The price at which each share of Stock covered by an Option may be purchased shall be determined in each case by the Committee and set forth in the Option Agreement. The price of an Incentive Option shall not be less than 100 percent of the Fair Market Value of the Stock on the date the Incentive Option is granted.

(c) *Duration of Options.* Each Option Agreement shall state the period of time, determined by the Committee, within which the Option may be exercised by the Option Holder (the "Option Period"). The Option Period must end not more than ten years from the date the Option is granted.

(d) *Restrictions on Exercise.* The Option Agreement shall also set forth any restrictions on Option exercise during the Option Period, if any, as may be determined by the Committee. Each Option shall become exercisable (vest) over such period of time, if any, or upon such events, as determined by the Committee.

(e) *Termination of Services, Death, or Disability.* The Committee may specify the period, if any, after which an Option may be exercised following termination of the Option Holder's services in the Option Agreement. If the Option Agreement does not specify the period of time following termination of service during which Options may be exercised, the time periods in this Subsection shall apply.

(i) **Termination for Cause.** If the services of the Option Holder are terminated within the Option Period for "cause," as determined by the Company, the Option shall thereafter be void for all purposes. "Cause" shall have the meaning assigned to it by the Option Holder's employment agreement, if the Company has entered into an employment agreement with the Option Holder; otherwise termination for "cause" shall mean termination of employment as a result of a violation of any Company policy, procedure or guideline, or engaging in any of the following forms of misconduct: conviction of any felony or of any misdemeanor involving dishonesty or moral turpitude; theft or misuse of the Company's property or time; use of alcohol or controlled substances on the Company's premises or appearing on such premises while intoxicated or under the influence of drugs not prescribed by a physician, or after having abused prescribed medications; illegal use of any controlled substance; illegal gambling on the Company's premises; discriminatory or harassing behavior, whether or not illegal under federal, state or local law; willful misconduct; or falsifying any document or making any false or misleading statement relating to employment by the Company; or injures the economic or ethical welfare of the Company by misconduct or inattention to duties and responsibilities, or fails to meet the Company's performance expectations, as determined by the Company in its sole discretion.

(ii) **Disability.** If the Option Holder becomes Disabled, the Option may be exercised by the Option Holder within six months following the Option Holder's termination of services on account of Disability (provided that such exercise must occur within the Option Period), but not thereafter. The Option may be exercised only with respect to the shares which had become exercisable on or before the date of the Option Holder's termination of services because of Disability.

(iii) **Death.** If the Option Holder dies during the Option Period while still performing services for the Company or within the six month period referred to in (ii) above or the three-month period referred to in (iv) below, the Option may be exercised by those entitled to do so under the Option Holder's will or by the laws of descent and distribution within six months following the Option Holder's death, (provided that such exercise must occur within the Option Period), but not thereafter. The Option may be exercised only with respect to the shares as to which the Option had become exercisable on or before the date of the Option Holder's death.

(iv) **Termination for Reasons Other than Cause, Disability, or Death.** If the Option Holder is no longer employed by the Company or performing services for the Company for any reason other than Cause, Disability or the Option Holder's death, the Option may be exercised by the Option Holder within three months following the date of termination (provided that the exercise must occur within the Option Period), but not thereafter. The Option may be exercised only as to the shares with respect to which the Option had become exercisable on or before the date of termination of services.

4.4 *Transferability.* Each Option shall not be transferable by the Option Holder except by will or pursuant to the laws of descent and distribution. Each Option is exercisable during the Option Holder's lifetime only by him or her, or in the event of Disability or incapacity, by his or her guardian or legal representative. The Committee may, however, provide at the time of grant or thereafter that the Option Holder may transfer a Non-Qualified Option to a member of the Option Holder's immediate family, a trust of which members of the Option Holder's immediate family are the only beneficiaries, or a partnership of which members of the Option Holder's immediate family or trusts for the sole benefit of the Option Holder's immediate family are the only partners. Immediate family means the Option Holder's spouse, issue (by birth or adoption), parents, grandparents, and siblings (including half brothers and sisters and adopted siblings). During the Option Holder's lifetime the Option Holder may not transfer an Incentive Option under any circumstances.

4.5 **Manner of Exercise.** The method for exercising each Option granted hereunder shall be by delivery to the Plan Sponsor of (1) written notice specifying the number of Shares with respect to which such Option is exercised, (2) payment in full of the exercise price and any liability the Company may have for withholding of federal, state, or local income or other taxes incurred by reason of the exercise of the Option, (3) representation meeting the requirements of Section 7.1 if requested by the Plan Sponsor, and (4) a shareholders' agreement meeting the requirements of Section 7.4 if requested by the Plan Sponsor. The purchase of such Shares shall take place at the principal offices of the Plan Sponsor within thirty days following delivery of such notice, at which time the Option Price of the Shares shall be paid in full. If the Option Price is paid by means of a broker's loan transaction, in whole or in part, the closing of the purchase of the Stock under the Option shall take place (and the Option shall be treated as exercised) on the date on which, and only if, the sale of Stock upon which the broker's loan was based has been closed and settled, unless the Option Holder makes an irrevocable written election, at the time of exercise of the Option, to have the exercise treated as fully effective for all purposes upon receipt of the Option Price by the Plan Sponsor regardless of whether or not the sale of the Stock by the broker is closed and settled. A properly executed certificate or certificates representing the Shares shall be delivered to the Option Holder upon payment. If Options on less than all shares evidenced by an Option Agreement are exercised, the Plan Sponsor shall deliver a new Option Agreement evidencing the Option on the remaining shares upon delivery of the Option Agreement for the Option being exercised.

4.6 **Payment of the Exercise Price.** The exercise price shall be paid by any of the following methods or any combination of the following methods at the election of the Option Holder, or by any other method approved by the Committee upon the request of the Option Holder:

(a) in cash.

(b) by certified check, cashier's check or other check acceptable to the Plan Sponsor, payable to the order of the Plan Sponsor.

(c) by delivery to the Plan Sponsor of certificates representing the number of shares then owned by the Option Holder, the Fair Market Value of which equals the purchase price of the Stock purchased pursuant to the Option, properly endorsed for transfer to the Plan Sponsor. No Option may be exercised by delivery to the Plan Sponsor of certificates representing Stock, unless such Stock has been held by the Option Holder for more than six months. The Fair Market Value of any shares of Stock delivered in payment of the purchase price upon exercise of the Option under the Plan shall be the Fair Market Value as of the exercise date. The exercise date shall be the day of delivery of the certificates for the Stock used as payment of the Option Price.

(d) by delivery to the Plan Sponsor of a properly executed notice of exercise together with irrevocable instructions to a broker to deliver to the Plan Sponsor promptly the amount of the proceeds of the sale of all or a portion of the Stock or of a loan from the broker to the Option Holder required to pay the Option Price.

4.7 **Withholding Requirement.** The Plan Sponsor's obligations to deliver shares of Stock upon the exercise of any Option shall be subject to the Participant's satisfaction of all applicable federal, state and local income and other tax withholding requirements.

(a) **Non-Qualified Options.** Upon exercise of an Option, the Option Holder shall make appropriate arrangements with the Company to provide for the amount of additional withholding required by Code 3102 and 3402 and applicable state income tax laws, including payment of such taxes through delivery of shares of Stock or by withholding Stock to be issued under the Option.

(b) **Incentive Options.** If an Option Holder makes a disposition (as defined in Code 424[c]) of any Stock acquired pursuant to the exercise of an Incentive Option prior to the expiration of two years from the date on which the Incentive Option was granted or prior to the expiration of one year from the date on which the Option was exercised, the Option Holder shall send written notice to the Company at the Company's principal place of business of the date of such disposition, the number of shares disposed of, the amount of proceeds received from such disposition and any other information relating to such disposition as the Company may reasonably request. The Option Holder shall, in the event of such a disposition, make appropriate arrangements with the Company to provide for the amount of additional withholding, if any, required by Code 3102 and 3402 and applicable state income tax laws.

4.8 **Withholding With Stock.** The Committee may, In its sole discretion, grant the Participant an election to pay all such amounts of tax withholding, or any part thereof, by electing to transfer to the Plan Sponsor, or to have the Plan Sponsor withhold from shares otherwise issuable to the Participant, shares of Stock having a value equal to the amount required to be withheld or such lesser amount as may be elected by the Participant. All elections shall be subject to the approval or disapproval of the Committee. The value of shares of Stock to be withheld shall be based on the Fair Market Value of the Stock on the date that the amount of tax to be withheld is to be determined (the "Tax Date"). Any such elections by Participants to have shares of Stock withheld for this purpose will be subject to the following restrictions:

(a) All elections must be made prior to the Tax Date.

(b) All elections shall be irrevocable.

(c) If the Participant is an officer or director of the Plan Sponsor within the meaning of Section 16 of the 1934 Act ("Section 16"), the Participant must satisfy the requirements of such Section 16 and any applicable Rules thereunder with respect to the use of Stock to satisfy such tax withholding obligation.

4.9 **Shareholder Privileges.** No Option Holder shall have any rights as a shareholder with respect to any shares of Stock covered by an Option until the Option Holder becomes the holder of record of such Stock, and no adjustments shall be made for dividends or other distributions or other rights as to which there is a record date preceding the date such Option Holder becomes the holder of record of such Stock, except as provided in the Plan.

ARTICLE V
PLAN ADMINISTRATION

5.1 **Committee.** The Plan shall be administered by a Committee appointed by and serving at the pleasure of the Board of Directors, consisting of not less than two Directors (the "Committee"). The Board of Directors may from time to time remove members from or add members to the Committee, and vacancies on the Committee, howsoever caused, shall be filled by the Board of Directors. After the stock is registered under Section 12 of the 1934 Act, the Committee shall be so constituted at all times as to permit the Plan to comply with Rule 16b-3 or any successor rule promulgated under the 1934 Act. Members of the Committee and any subcommittee or special committee shall be appointed from time to time by the Board, shall serve at the pleasure of the Board and may resign at any time upon written notice to the Board.

5.2 **Committee Meetings and Actions.** The Committee shall hold meetings at such times and places as it may determine. A majority of the members of the Committee shall constitute a quorum, and the acts of the majority of the members present at a meeting or a consent in writing signed by all members of the Committee shall be the acts of the Committee and shall be final, binding and conclusive upon all persons, including the Company, its shareholders, and all persons having any interest in Options which may be or have been granted pursuant to the Plan.

5.3 **Powers of Committee.** In accordance with the provisions of the Plan, the Committee shall, in its sole discretion, select the Participants from among the Eligible Employees and Eligible Individuals, determine the Awards to be made pursuant to the Plan, and the time at which such Awards are to be made, fix the Option Price, period and manner in which an Option becomes exercisable, and establish such other terms under the Plan as the Committee may deem necessary or desirable and consistent with the terms of the Plan. The Committee shall determine the form or forms of the agreements with Participants that shall evidence the particular provisions, terms, conditions, rights, and duties of the Plan Sponsor and the Participants with respect to Awards granted pursuant to the Plan, which provisions need not be identical except as may be provided herein. The Committee shall have the full and exclusive right to grant and determine terms and conditions of all Options granted under the Plan. In granting Options, the Committee shall take into consideration the contribution the Option Holder has made or may make to the success of the Company or its subsidiaries and such other factors as the Committee shall determine. The Committee may from time to time adopt such rules and regulations for carrying out the purposes of the Plan as it may deem proper and in the best interests of the Company. The Committee may correct any defect, supply any omission, or reconcile any inconsistency in the Plan or in any agreement entered into hereunder in the manner and to the extent it shall deem expedient and it shall be the sole and final judge of such expediency. No member of the Committee shall be liable for any action or determination made in good faith. The determinations, interpretations, and other actions of the Committee pursuant to the provisions of the Plan shall be binding and conclusive for all purposes and on all persons.

5.4 **Interpretation of Plan.** The determination of the Committee as to any disputed question arising under the Plan, including questions of construction and interpretation, shall be final, binding and conclusive upon all persons, including the Company, its shareholders, and all persons having any interest in Options that may be or have been granted pursuant to the Plan.

5.5 **Indemnification.** Each person who is or shall have been a member of the Committee or of the Board of Directors shall be indemnified and held harmless by the Plan Sponsor against and from any loss, cost, liability, or expense that may be imposed upon or reasonably incurred in connection with or resulting from any claim, action, suit or proceeding to which such person may be a party or in which such person may be involved by reason of any action taken or failure to act under the Plan and against and from any and all amounts paid in settlement thereof, with the Company's approval, or paid in satisfaction of a judgment in any such action, suit or proceeding against him, provided such person shall give the Company an opportunity, at its own expense, to handle and defend the same before undertaking to handle and defend it on such person's own behalf. The foregoing right of indemnification shall not be exclusive of, and is in addition to, any other rights of indemnification to which any person may be entitled under the Plan Sponsor's Articles of Incorporation or Bylaws, as a matter of law, or otherwise, or any power that the Company may have to indemnify them or hold them harmless.

ARTICLE VI
STOCK SUBJECT TO THE PLAN

6.1 **Number of Shares.** The number of Shares that are authorized for issuance under the Plan in accordance with the provisions of the Plan and subject to such restrictions or other provisions as the Committee may from time to time deem necessary shall not exceed 200,000, subject to the provisions regarding changes in capital. The Shares may be either authorized and unissued Shares or previously issued Shares acquired by the Plan Sponsor. This authorization may be increased from time to time by approval of the Board and by the stockholders of the Plan Sponsor if, in the opinion of counsel for the Plan Sponsor, stockholder approval is required. Shares of Stock that may be issued upon exercise of Options under the Plan shall be applied to reduce the maximum number of Shares remaining available for use under the Plan. The Plan Sponsor shall at all times during the term of the Plan and while any Options are outstanding retain as authorized and unissued Stock at least the number of Shares from time to time required under the provisions of the Plan, or otherwise assure itself of its ability to perform its obligations hereunder.

6.2 *Unused Stock.* Any shares of Stock that are subject to an Option that expires or for any reason is terminated unexercised and any shares of Stock withheld for the payment of taxes or received by the Plan Sponsor as payment of the exercise price of an Option shall automatically become available for use under the Plan; however, no more than 200,000 shares of Stock may be awarded pursuant to Incentive Options.

6.3 *Adjustments for Stock Splits and Stock Dividends.* If the Plan Sponsor shall at any time increase or decrease the number of its outstanding Shares or change in any way the rights and privileges of such Shares by means of the payment of a stock dividend or any other distribution upon such shares payable in Stock, or through a stock split, subdivision, consolidation, combination, reclassification or recapitalization involving the Stock, then in relation to the Stock that is affected by one or more of the above events, the numbers, rights and privileges of the following shall be increased, decreased or changed in like manner as if they had been issued and outstanding, fully paid and nonassessable at the time of such occurrence: (i) the Shares as to which Awards may be granted under the Plan and (ii) the Shares then included in each outstanding Award granted hereunder.

6.4 *Other Distributions and Changes in the Stock.* If the Plan Sponsor distributes assets or securities of persons other than the Plan Sponsor (excluding cash or distributions referred to in Section 6.3) with respect to the Stock, or if the Plan Sponsor grants rights to subscribe pro rata for additional Shares or for any other securities of the Plan Sponsor to the holders of its Stock, or if there is any other change (except as described in Section 6.3) in the number or kind of outstanding Shares or of any stock or other securities into which the Stock will be changed or for which it has been exchanged, and if the Committee in its discretion determines that the event equitably requires an adjustment in the number or kind of Shares subject to an Option, an adjustment in the Option Price or the taking of any other action by the Committee, including without limitation, the setting aside of any property for delivery to the Participant upon the exercise of an Option or the full testing of an Option, then such adjustments shall be made, or other action shall be taken by the Committee and shall be effective for all purposes of the Plan and on each outstanding Option.

6.5 *General Adjustment Rules.* No adjustment or substitution provided for in this Article shall require the Plan Sponsor to sell a fractional share of Stock under any Option, or otherwise issue a fractional share of Stock, and the total substitution or adjustment with respect to each Option and other Award shall be limited by deleting any fractional share. In the case of any such substitution or adjustment, the aggregate Option Price for the total number of shares of Stock then subject to an Option shall remain unchanged but the Option Price per share under each such Option shall be equitably adjusted by the Committee to reflect the greater or lesser number of shares of Stock or other securities into which the Stock subject to the Option may have been changed, and appropriate adjustments shall be made to other Awards to reflect any such substitution or adjustment.

6.6 *Determination by the Committee.* Adjustments under this Article shall be made by the Committee, whose determinations shall be final and binding upon all parties.

ARTICLE VII
GENERAL RESTRICTIONS

7.1 Investment Representations. The Plan Sponsor may require any person to whom an Option is granted, as a condition of exercising the Option, to give written assurances in substance and form satisfactory to the Plan Sponsor and its counsel to the effect that such person is acquiring the Stock for his own account for investment and not with any present intention of selling or otherwise distributing the same, and to such other effects as the Plan Sponsor deems necessary or appropriate in order to comply with Federal and applicable state securities laws. Legends evidencing such restrictions may be placed on the Stock certificates.

7.2 Compliance with Securities Laws. Each Option grant shall be subject to the requirement that, if at any time counsel to the Plan Sponsor shall determine that the listing, registration, or qualification of the shares subject to such Option grant upon any securities exchange, automated quotation system, or under any state or federal law, or the consent or approval of any governmental or regulatory body, is necessary as a condition of, or in connection with, the issuance or purchase of shares thereunder, such Option grant may not be accepted or exercised in whole or in part unless such listing, registration, qualification, consent or approval shall have been effected or obtained on conditions acceptable to the Committee. Nothing herein shall be deemed to require the Plan Sponsor to apply for or to obtain such listing, registration or qualification.

7.3 Changes in Accounting Rules. Except as provided otherwise at the time an Award is granted, notwithstanding any other provision of the Plan to the contrary, if, during the term of the Plan, any changes in the financial or tax accounting rules applicable to Options shall occur which, in the sole judgment of the Committee, may have a material adverse effect on the reported earnings, assets or liabilities of the Plan Sponsor, the Committee shall have the right and power to modify as necessary, any then outstanding and unexercised Options as to which the applicable services or other restrictions have not been satisfied.

7.4 Shareholders' Agreement. Upon demand by the Plan Sponsor the Option shall execute and deliver to the Plan Sponsor a Shareholders' Agreement in such form and substance as the Company may provide at the time of exercise of the Option. The Shareholders' Agreement may include, without limitation, restrictions upon the Option Holder's right to transfer shares, including the creation of an irrevocable right of first refusal in the Plan Sponsor and its designees, and provisions requiring the Option Holder to transfer the shares to the Plan Sponsor or the Plan Sponsor's designees upon a termination of employment. Upon such demand, execution of the Shareholders' Agreement by the Option Holder prior to the transfer or delivery of any shares and prior to the expiration of the option period shall be a condition precedent to the right to purchase such shares, unless such condition is expressly waived in writing by the Plan Sponsor.

ARTICLE VIII
REQUIREMENTS OF LAW

8.1 Requirements of Law. The issuance of Stock and the payment of cash pursuant to the Plan shall be subject to all applicable laws, rules and regulations.

8.2 Federal Securities Law Requirements. If a Participant is an officer or director of the Plan Sponsor within the meaning of Section 16 of the 1934 Act, Awards granted hereunder shall be subject to all conditions required under Rule 16(b)(3), or any successor rule promulgated under the 1934 Act, to qualify the Award for any exception from the provisions of Section 16(b) of the 1934 Act available under that Rule. Such conditions shall be set forth in the agreement with the Participant which describes the Award or other document evidencing or accompanying the Award.

8.3 Governing Law. The Plan and all agreements hereunder shall be construed in accordance with and governed by the laws of the State of Nevada.

ARTICLE IX
DURATION OF THE PLAN

Unless sooner terminated by the Board of Directors, the Plan shall terminate at the close of business on December 31, 2001, and no Option shall be granted after such termination. Options outstanding at the time of the Plan termination may continue to be exercised, or become free of restrictions, in accordance with their terms.

ARTICLE X
PLAN AMENDMENT, MODIFICATION, AND TERMINATION

The Board may at any time terminate, and from time to time may amend or modify the Plan provided, however, that no amendment or modification may become effective without approval of the amendment or modification by the shareholders if shareholder approval is required to enable the Plan to satisfy any applicable statutory requirement or if the Plan Sponsor, on the advice of counsel, determines that shareholder approval is otherwise necessary or desirable.

No amendment, modification or termination of the Plan shall in any manner adversely affect any Options previously granted under the Plan, without the consent of the Participant holding such Options.

ARTICLE XI
MISCELLANEOUS

11.1 *Gender and Number.* Except when otherwise indicated by the context, the masculine gender shall also include the feminine gender, and the definition of any term herein in the singular shall also include the plural.

11.2 *No Right to Continued Employment.* Nothing contained in the Plan or in any Award granted under the Plan shall confer upon any Participant any right with respect to the continuation of his employment by, or consulting relationship with, the Company, or interfere in any way with the right of the Company, subject to the terms of any separate employment agreement or other contract to the contrary, at any time to terminate such services or to increase or decrease the compensation of the Participant from the rate in existence at the time of the grant of an Award. Nothing in this Plan shall limit or impair the Company's right to terminate the employment of any employee, to terminate the consulting services of any consultant, or to terminate the services of any director. Whether an authorized leave of absence, or absence in military or government service, shall constitute a termination of service shall be determined by the Committee at the time.

11.3 *Nontransferability.* Except as provided otherwise at the time of grant, no right or interest of any Participant in an Option granted pursuant to the Plan shall be assignable or transferable during the lifetime of the Participant, either voluntarily or involuntarily, or subjected to any lien, directly or indirectly, by operation of law, or otherwise, including execution, levy, garnishment, attachment, pledge or bankruptcy. In the event of a Participant's death, a Participant's rights and interests in Options shall, to the extent provided in the Plan, be transferable by will or the laws of descent and distribution, and payment of any amounts due under the Plan shall be made to, and exercise of any Options may be made by, the Participant's legal representatives, heirs, or legatees. Notwithstanding the foregoing, the Option Holder may not transfer an Incentive Option during the Option Holder's lifetime. If in the opinion of the Committee a person entitled to payments or to exercise rights with respect to the Plan is disabled from caring for his affairs because of mental condition, physical condition or age, payment due such person may be made to, and such rights shall be exercised by, such person's guardian, conservator, or other legal personal representative upon furnishing the Committee with evidence satisfactory to the Committee of such status.

11.4 **No Plan Funding.** Obligations to Participants under the Plan will not be funded, trusted, insured or secured in any manner. The Participants under the Plan shall have no security interest in any assets of the Company, and shall be only general creditors of the Company.

11.5 **Other Employee Benefits.** The amount of any compensation deemed to be received by a Participant as a result of the exercise of an Option or the sale of shares received upon such exercise shall not constitute "earnings" or "compensation" with respect to which any other employee benefits of such employee are determined, including without limitation benefits under any pension, profit sharing, 401(k), life insurance or salary continuation plan.

11.6 **No Liability to Failure to Receive Tax Benefits.** Neither the Plan Sponsor or any Affiliated Corporation, Company, nor any of their directors, officers, employees or shareholders, nor the Committee, shall have any liability if any Option Holder or Participant fails to receive the tax benefits of an incentive stock option.

QRX, INC.
Plan Sponsor

By: _____

Title: _____

Date: _____

STOCK OPTION AGREEMENT

OPTION HOLDER:

DATE OF GRANT:

This Agreement between QRX , Inc. (the "Company"), and the Option Holder ("Option Holder"), an employee, of the Company, shall be effective as of the Date of Grant. The Company and Option Holder agree as follows:

1. **Grant of Option.** Option Holder is hereby granted an Incentive Stock Option, within the meaning of Section 422 of the Internal Revenue Code of 1986, as amended (the "Option"), to purchase Common Stock of the Company pursuant to the QRX , Inc. Stock Option Plan. The Option and this Agreement are subject to and shall be construed in accordance with the terms and conditions of the Plan, as now or hereinafter in effect. Any terms which are used in this Agreement without being defined and which are defined in the Plan shall have the meaning specified in the Plan.

2. **Date of Grant.** The date of the grant of the Option shall be the date of the action by the Committee which administers the Plan (the "Committee") in granting the Option, and shall be the Date of Grant set forth above.

3. **Number and Price of Shares.** The number of shares as to which the Option is granted is _____. The purchase price per share is $_____.

4. **Expiration Date.** Unless previously terminated as provided in the Plan, the Option shall expire and terminate on _____, and in no event shall the Option be exercisable after that date.

5. **Manner of Exercise.** Except as provided in this Agreement, the Option shall be exercisable, in whole or in part, from time to time, in the manner provided in the Plan.

6. **Time of Exercise.** The Option granted hereby shall become vested in and exercisable by Option Holder as set forth in the following schedule:

Date	Number of Shares That Become Exercisable
_____	_____
_____	_____
_____	_____
_____	_____
_____	

In order to be in accordance with the schedule, the Option Holder must have been continuously employed (to the extent required by Code 422[a]) by the Company from the Date of Grant of the Option until the date specified.

7. **Shareholders' Agreement.** Upon exercise of the Option, the Option Holder shall execute and deliver to the Company a Shareholders' Agreement in substantially the form attached to this Agreement as Exhibit A. Execution and delivery of the Shareholders' Agreement prior to the transfer or delivery of any shares and prior to the expiration of the option period shall be a condition precedent to the right to purchase such shares.

8. **Nontransferability of Option.** The Option is not transferable by Option Holder other than by Will or the laws of descent and distribution, and the Option shall be exercisable during Option Holder. Upon any attempt to transfer, assign, pledge, hypothecate or otherwise dispose of the Option contrary to the provisions hereof, or upon the levy of any attachment or similar process upon the Option, the Option shall immediately become null and void.

9. **Withholding, for Taxes.** The Company shall have the right to deduct from Option Holder's salary any federal or state taxes required by law to be withheld with respect to the exercise of the Option or any disqualifying disposition of the Common Stock acquired upon exercise of the Option.

10. **Legends.** Certificates representing Common Stock acquired upon exercise of this Option may contain such legends and transfer restrictions as the Company shall deem reasonably necessary or desirable, including, without limitation, legends restricting transfer of the Common Stock until there has been compliance with federal and state securities laws and until Option Holder or any other holder of the Common Stock has paid the Company such amounts as may be necessary in order to satisfy any withholding tax liability of the Company resulting from a disqualifying disposition described in Code 422(a). The sole purpose of legends relating to compliance with federal and state securities law is to ensure compliance with such laws.

11. **Employee Benefits.** Option Holder agrees that the grant and vesting of the Option and the receipt of shares of Common Stock upon exercise of the Option will constitute special incentive compensation that will not be taken into account as "salary" or "compensation" or "bonus" in determining the amount of any payment under any pension, retirement, profit sharing or other remuneration plan of the Company.

12. **Amendment.** Subject to the terms and conditions of the Plan, the Committee may modify, extend, or renew the Option, or accept the surrender of the Option to the extent not theretofore exercised and authorize the granting of new Options in substitution theretofore, except that no such action shall diminish or impair the rights under the Option without the consent of the Option Holder.

13. **Interpretation.** The interpretations and constructions of any provision of and determinations on any question arising under the Plan or this Agreement shall be made by the Committee, and all such interpretations, constructions, and determinations shall be final and conclusive as to all parties.

14. **Receipt of Plan.** By entering into this Agreement, Option Holder acknowledges (i) that he or she has received and read a copy of the Plan and (ii) that this Agreement is subject to and shall be construed in accordance with the terms and conditions of the Plan, as now or hereinafter in effect.

15. **Governing Law.** This Agreement shall be construed and shall take effect in accordance with the laws of the State of Nevada, without regard to the conflicts of laws of such State.

16. **Miscellaneous.** This Agreement constitutes the entire understanding and agreement of the parties with respect to the subject matter hereof and supersedes all prior and contemporaneous agreements or understandings, inducements or conditions, express or implied, written or oral, between the parties with respect hereto. If any provision of this Agreement, or the application thereof, shall for any reason and to any extent be invalid or unenforceable, the remainder of this Agreement and the application of such provision to other circumstances shall be interpreted so as best to reasonably effect the intent of the parties hereto. All notices or other communications which are required to be given or may be given to either party pursuant to the terms of this Agreement shall be in writing and shall be delivered personally or by registered or certified mail, postage prepaid, to the address of the parties as set forth following the signature of such party. Notice shall be deemed given on the date of delivery in the case of personal delivery or on the delivery or refusal date as specified on the return receipt in the case of registered or certified mail. Either party may change its address for such communications by giving notice thereof to the other party in conformity with the Plan.

IN WITNESS WHEREOF, the Company by a duly authorized officer of the Company and Option Holder have executed this Agreement, effective as of the date of grant.

QRX, INC.

By: _____

Title: _____

Date: _____

OPTION HOLDER

By: _____

Title: _____

Address: _____

QRX, INC.

MARKET STANDOFF AGREEMENT

THIS MARKET STANDOFF AGREEMENT (the "Agreement") is made and entered into _____, 2000, by and between QRX , Inc., a Nevada corporation (the "Company"), and _____ ("Shareholder").

RECITALS

A. Shareholder owns or has the right to acquire as of the date hereof shares of Common Stock (the "Shares") of the Company. The term "Shares" refers to such shares presently held by the Shareholder and to all securities received in addition thereto or in replacement thereof, pursuant to or in consequence of any stock dividend, stock split, recapitalization, merger, reorganization, exchange of shares, or other similar event.

B. In order to provide assurance to persons who may purchase shares of stock of the Company in the future and thereby to assist in the equity financing of the Company, Shareholder is willing to enter into this Agreement for the benefit of the Company and any person or entity who holds stock of the Company from time to time.

THE PARTIES AGREE AS FOLLOWS:

1. **Market Standoff.** Shareholder hereby agrees that if so requested by the Company or any representative of the underwriters in connection with any registration of the offering of any securities of the Company under the Securities Act of 1933, as amended (the "Act"), the Shareholder shall not sell or otherwise transfer any Shares or other securities of the Company during the 180-day period following the effective date of a registration statement of the Company filed under the Act. The Company may impose stop-transfer instructions with respect to securities subject to the foregoing restrictions until the end of such 180-day period.

2. **Stock Certificate Restrictive Legend.** Shareholder agrees that the certificate(s) representing the Shares shall bear the following legend:

   "THE SECURITIES REPRESENTED HEREBY ARE SUBJECT TO RESTRICTIONS ON TRANSFER FOR A PERIOD OF 180 DAYS FOLLOWING THE EFFECTIVE DATE OF A REGISTRATION STATEMENT UNDER THE SECURITIES ACT OF 1933) FOR AN OFFERING OF THE COMPANY'S SECURITIES AS MORE FULLY PROVIDED IN A MARKET STANDOFF AGREEMENT BETWEEN THE COMPANY AND THE ORIGINAL PURCHASER OF SUCH SECURITIES."

3. **Binding Effect.** Subject to the limitations set forth in this Agreement, this Agreement shall be binding upon, and inure to the benefit of, the executors, administrators, heirs, legal representatives, successors, and assigns of the parties hereto.

4. **Damages.** Shareholder shall be liable to the Company for all costs and damages, including incidental and consequential damages, resulting from a disposition of Shares which is not in conformity with the provisions of this Agreement.

5. **Governing Law.** This Agreement shall be governed by and construed in accordance with the laws of the State of Nevada applicable to contacts entered into and wholly to be performed within the State of Nevada by Nevada residents. The parties agree that the exclusive jurisdiction and venue of any action with respect to this Agreement shall be Nevada and the state and federal courts within Nevada, and each of the parties hereby submits itself to the exclusive jurisdiction and venue of such courts for the purpose of such action. The parties agree that service of process in any such action may be effected by delivery of the summons to the parties in the manner provided for delivery of notices set forth in Section 6.

6. **Notices.** All notices and other communications under this Agreement shall be in writing. Unless and until Shareholder is notified in writing to the contrary, all notices, communications and documents directed to the company and related to the Agreement, if not delivered by hand, shall be mailed, addressed as follows:

_____

_____

_____

Unless and until the Company is notified in writing to the contrary, all notices, communications and documents intended for Shareholder and related to this Agreement, if not delivered by hand, shall be mailed to Shareholder's last known address as shown on the Company's books. Notices and communications shall be mailed by registered or certified mail, return receipt requested, postage prepaid. All mailings and deliveries related to this Agreement shall be deemed received only when actually received.

IN WITNESS WHEREOF, the parties hereto have executed this Market Standoff Agreement as of the date and year first above written.

Company: **QRX , INC.**

a Nevada Corporation

By: _____

Shareholder hereby accepts and agrees to be bound by all of the terms and conditions of this Agreement.

_____

Shareholder

Shareholder's spouse indicates by the execution of this Agreement his or her consent to be bound by the terms herein as to his or her interests, whether as community property or otherwise, if any, in the Shares.

_____

Shareholder's Spouse

QRX   **Confidential Information, Non-Solicitation**
                                                          And Inventions Agreement

This agreement is between QRX ("QRX"), and _____ (such
individual, whether an employee, consultant, or contractor being hereafter called
"Employee").

1. **Protection of Trade Secrets and Confidential Information**

    (a) **Definition of "Confidential Information."** "Confidential Information" means
    all nonpublic information concerning or arising from QRX's business, including
    particularly but not by way of limitation trade secrets used, developed or
    acquired by QRX in connection with its business; information concerning the
    manner and details of QRX's operation, organization and management; financial
    information and/or documents and nonpublic policies, procedures and other
    printed or written material generated or used in connection with QRX's business;
    QRX's business plans and strategies; the identities of QRX's customers and the
    specific individual customer representatives with whom QRX works; the details
    of QRX's relationship with such customers and customer representatives; the
    identities of distributors, contractors and vendors utilized in QRX's business; the
    details of QRX's relationship with such distributors, contractors and vendors; the
    nature of fees and charges made to QRX's customers, nonpublic forms, contracts,
    and other documents used in QRX's business; the nature and content of computer
    software used in QRX's business, whether proprietary to QRX or used by QRX
    under license from a third party; and all other information concerning QRX's con-
    cepts, prospects, customers, employees, contractors, earnings, products, services,
    equipment, systems, and/or prospective and executed contracts and other busi-
    ness arrangements.

    (b) **Employee's Use of Confidential Information.** Except in connection with and
    in furtherance of Employee's work on QRX's behalf, Employee shall not, without
    QRX's prior written consent, at any time, directly or indirectly, use, disclose, or
    otherwise communicate any Confidential Information to any person or entity.

    (c) **Acknowledgments.** Employee acknowledges that during the period of
    Employee's relationship with QRX (the "term of this agreement"), Employee will
    have access to Confidential Information, all of which shall be made accessible to
    Employee only in strict confidence; that unauthorized disclosure of Confidential
    Information will damage QRX's business; that Confidential Information would be
    susceptible to immediate use by a competitor of QRX's; that QRX's business is
    substantially dependent on access to and the continuing secrecy of Confidential
    Information; that Confidential Information is unique to QRX and known only to
    Employee, QRX and certain key employees and contractors of QRX; that QRX
    shall at all times retain ownership and control of all Confidential Information;
    and that the restrictions contained in this paragraph are reasonable and neces-
    sary for the protection of QRX's business.

    (d) **Records Containing Confidential Information.** All documents or other
    records containing or reflecting Confidential Information ("Confidential Docu-
    ments") prepared by or provided to Employee are and shall remain QRX's prop-
    erty. Except with QRX's prior written consent, Employee shall not copy or use
    any Confidential Document for any purpose not relating directly to Employee's
    work on QRX's behalf, or use, disclose or sell any Confidential Document to any
    party other than QRX. Upon the termination of Employee's employment or upon
    QRX's request, Employee shall immediately deliver to QRX or its designee (and
    shall not keep in Employee's possession or deliver to anyone else) all Confidential
    Documents and all other property belonging to QRX. This paragraph shall not
    bar Employee from complying with any subpoena or court order, provided that
    Employee shall at the earliest practicable date provide a copy of the subpoena or
    court order to QRX's President.

(e) **Third-Parties' Confidential Information.** Employee acknowledges that QRX has received and in the future will receive from third parties confidential or proprietary information, and that QRX must maintain the confidentiality of such information and use it only for proper purposes. Employee shall not use or disclose any such information except as permitted by QRX or the third party to whom the information belongs.

(f) **Employee's Former Employers' Confidential Information.** Employee shall not, during Employee's employment with QRX, improperly use or disclose to QRX any proprietary information or trade secrets belonging to any former employer or any third party as to whom Employee owes a duty of nondisclosure.

2. **Non-Solicitation**

(a) For purposes of this paragraph, "Nonsolicitation Period" shall include: (i) the period during which Employee serves an employee, consultant, or contractor to QRX or any affiliate; and (ii) if but only if Employee voluntarily resigns his or her employment with QRX or QRX involuntarily terminates Employee's employment with just cause, then the period of twelve (12) months after termination of Employee's employment with QRX.

(b) During the Nonsolicitation Period, Employee shall not without QRX's prior written consent, directly or indirectly:

(i) cause or attempt to cause any employee, agent or contractor of QRX or any QRX affiliate, to terminate his or her employment, agency, or contractor relationship with QRX or any QRX affiliate; interfere or attempt to interfere with the relationship between QRX and any employee, contractor, or agent of QRX; or hire, attempt to hire, or encourage or assist any third party in attempting to hire, any employee, agent, or contractor of QRX or any QRX affiliate.

(ii) solicit business from any customer or client served by QRX at any point during the term of this agreement; or interfere or attempt to interfere with any transaction, agreement, or business relationship in which QRX or any affiliate was involved at any point during the term of this agreement.

3. **Inventions**

(a) **Disclosure.** Upon QRX's request, Employee shall promptly disclose to QRX, in a manner specified by QRX in its sole discretion, all ideas, processes, trademarks and service marks, inventions, discoveries, and improvements to any of the foregoing, that Employee learns of, conceives, develops, or creates alone or with others during the term of this agreement (whether or not conceived, developed or created during regular working hours) that directly or indirectly arises from or relates to: (i) QRX's business, (ii) work performed for QRX by Employee or any other QRX employee, (iii) the use of QRX's property or time, or (iv) access to QRX's Confidential Information and/or Confidential Documents.

(b) **Assignment.** Employee hereby assigns to QRX, without further consideration, Employee's entire right to any concept, idea, or invention described in the preceding subparagraph, which shall be the sole and exclusive property of QRX whether or not subject to patent, copyright, trademark, or trade secret protection under applicable law. Employee also acknowledges that all original works of authorship which are made by Employee (solely or jointly with others), within the scope of Employee's employment, and which are protectable by copyright, are "works made for hire," as that term is defined in the United States Copyright Act (17 U.S.C. 101). To the extent that any such works, by operation of law, cannot be "works made for hire," Employee assigns to QRX all right, title, and interest in and to such works and to any related copyrights.

(c) **Additional Instruments.** Employee shall promptly sign and deliver to QRX all additional documents deemed at any time by QRX in its sole discretion to be necessary to carry out the intentions of this paragraph.

4. **Survival.** Employee's obligations to this agreement shall survive the termination of Employee's employment and shall thereafter be enforceable whether or not such termination is later claimed or found to be wrongful or to constitute or result in a breach of any contract or of any other duty owed or claimed to be owed by QRX to Employee.

5. **Remedies.** Employee acknowledges that upon a breach of any obligation under this agreement, QRX will suffer immediate and irreparable harm and damage for which money alone cannot fully compensate QRX. Employee therefore agrees that upon such breach or threatened breach of any obligation under this agreement, QRX shall be entitled to, and Employee shall not oppose entry of, a temporary restraining order, preliminary injunction, permanent injunction or other injunctive relief, without posting any bond or other security, barring Employee from violating any such provision. This paragraph shall not be construed as an election of any remedy, or as a waiver of any right available to QRX under this agreement or the law, including the right to seek damages from Employee for a breach of any provision of this agreement, nor shall this paragraph be construed to limit the rights or remedies available under Nevada law for any violation of any provision of this agreement.

6. **Conflicts With Other Agreements and Publications.** In the event of any conflict between any term of this agreement and any QRX contract, policy, procedure, guideline or other publication, the terms of this agreement shall control.

7. **Non assistance.** Employee agrees not to assist any third person or company in contesting or attacking QRX's rights in and/or to any copyright, patent, trademark or other trade secret or confidential or proprietary information, except pursuant to subpoena or court order.

8. **Miscellaneous. (a) Heirs and Assigns.** This agreement shall be binding upon Employee's heirs, executors, administrators or other legal representatives, shall inure to the benefit of QRX, its successors or assigns, and shall be freely assignable by QRX, but not by Employee. **(b) Governing Law.** This agreement and all disputes arising from or relating in any way, directly or indirectly, to this agreement or the protection of QRX's trade secrets and/or confidential and proprietary information shall be governed by federal law and the internal laws of the State of Nevada, irrespective of the choice of law rules of any jurisdiction. **(c) Severability.** If any court of competent jurisdiction declares any provision of this agreement invalid or unenforceable, the remainder of the agreement shall remain fully enforceable. To the extent that any court concludes that any provision of this agreement is void or voidable, the court shall reform such provision(s) to render the provision(s) enforceable, but only to the extent absolutely necessary to render the provision(s) enforceable and only in view of the parties' express desire that QRX be protected to the greatest extent possible under applicable law from improper competition and/or the misuse or disclosure of trade secrets, Confidential Documents, and/or Confidential Information. **(d) Disputes.** Any action arising from or relating in any way, directly or indirectly, to this agreement and/or the protection of QRX's trade secrets and/or confidential and proprietary information, shall be tried only in the state or federal courts situated in Nevada. The parties consent to jurisdiction and venue in those courts. The prevailing party in any action to enforce any provision of this agreement shall recover all costs and attorneys' fees that party incurs in connection with the action.

EXECUTED this _____ day of _____, 20__.

Sign: Witness:

_____   _____

Print Name: _____   Print Name: _____

SSN: _____

APPENDIX 5

PUBLIC COMPANY
[TIME VESTED]
GHI, INC.
2002 STOCK OPTION PLAN

1. Purpose of Plan

The purpose of this 2002 Stock Option Plan (the "Plan") is to provide additional incentive to officers, other key employees, and directors of, and important consultants to, GHI, Inc., a Pennsylvania corporation (the "Company"), and each present or future parent or subsidiary corporation, by encouraging them to invest in shares of the Company's common stock, no par value ("Common Stock"), and thereby acquire a proprietary interest in the Company and an increased personal interest in the Company's continued success and progress.

2. Aggregate Number of Shares

200,000 shares of the Company's Common Stock shall be the aggregate number of shares which may be issued under this Plan. Notwithstanding the foregoing, in the event of any change in the outstanding shares of the Common Stock of the Company by reason of a stock dividend, stock split, combination of shares, recapitalization, merger, consolidation, transfer of assets, reorganization, conversion, or what the Committee (defined in Section 4[a]), deems in its sole discretion to be similar circumstances, the aggregate number and kind of shares which may be issued under this Plan shall be appropriately adjusted in a manner determined in the sole discretion of the Committee. Reacquired shares of the Company's Common Stock, as well as unissued shares, may be used for the purpose of this Plan. Common Stock of the Company subject to options which have terminated unexercised, either in whole or in part, shall be available for future options granted under this Plan.

3. Class of Persons Eligible to Receive Options

All officers and key employees of the Company and of any present or future Company parent or subsidiary corporation are eligible to receive an option or options under this Plan. All directors of, and important consultants to, the Company and of any present or future Company parent or subsidiary corporation are also eligible to receive an option or options under this Plan. The individuals who shall, in fact, receive an option or options shall be selected by the Committee, in its sole discretion, except as otherwise specified in Section 4 hereof. No individual may receive options under this Plan for more than 80 percent of the total number of shares of the Company's Common Stock authorized for issuance under this Plan.

4. Administration of Plan

(a) This Plan shall be administered by the Company's Board of Directors or by an Option Committee ("Committee") appointed by the Company's Board of Directors. The Committee shall consist of a minimum of two and a maximum of five members of the Board of Directors, each of whom shall be a "Non-Employee Director" within the meaning of Rule 16(b)(3) under the Securities Exchange Act of 1934, as amended, or any future corresponding rule, except that the failure of the Committee for any reason to be composed solely of Non-Employee Directors shall not prevent an option from being considered granted under this Plan. The Committee shall, in addition to its other authority and subject to the provisions of this Plan, determine which individuals shall in fact be granted an option or options, whether the option shall be an Incentive Stock Option or a Non-Qualified Stock Option (as such terms are defined in Section 5[a]), the number of shares to be subject to each of the options, the time or times at which the options shall be granted, the rate of option exercisability, and, subject to Section 5 hereof, the price at which each of the options is exercisable and the duration of the option. The term "Committee," as used in this Plan and the options granted hereunder, refers to either the Board of Directors or to the Committee, whichever is then administering this Plan.

(b) The Committee shall adopt such rules for the conduct of its business and administration of this Plan as it considers desirable. A majority of the members of the Committee shall constitute a quorum for all purposes. The vote or written consent of a majority of the members of the Committee on a particular matter shall constitute the act of the Committee on such matter. The Committee shall have the right to construe the Plan and the options issued pursuant to it, to correct defects and omissions and to reconcile inconsistencies to the extent necessary to effectuate the Plan and the options issued pursuant to it, and such action shall be final, binding and conclusive upon all parties concerned. No member of the Committee or the Board of Directors shall be liable for any act or omission (whether or not negligent) taken or omitted in good faith, or for the exercise of an authority or discretion granted in connection with the Plan to a Committee or the Board of Directors, or for the acts or omissions of any other members of a Committee or the Board of Directors. Subject to the numerical limitations on Committee membership set forth in Section 4(a) hereof, the Board of Directors may at any time appoint additional members of the Committee and may at any time remove any member of the Committee with or without cause. Vacancies in the Committee, however caused, may be filled by the Board of Directors, if it so desires.

5. Incentive Stock Options and Non-Qualified Stock Options

(a) Options issued pursuant to this Plan may be either Incentive Stock Options granted pursuant to Section 5(b) hereof or Non-Qualified Stock Options granted pursuant to Section 5(c) hereof, as determined by the Committee. An "Incentive Stock Option" is an option which satisfies all of the requirements of Section 422(b) of the Internal Revenue Code of 1986, as amended (the "Code") and the regulations thereunder, and a "Non-Qualified Stock Option" is an option which either does not satisfy all of those requirements or the terms of the option provide that it will not be treated as an Incentive Stock Option. The Committee may grant both an Incentive Stock Option and a Non-Qualified Stock Option to the same person, or more than one of each type of option to the same person. The option price for options issued under this Plan shall be equal at least to the fair market value (as defined below) of the Company's Common Stock on the date of the grant of the option. The fair market value of the Company's Common Stock on any particular date shall mean the last reported sale price of a share of the Company's Common Stock on any stock exchange on which such stock is then listed or admitted to trading, or on the NASDAQ National Market System or Small Cap NASDAQ, on such date, or if no sale took place on such day, the last such date on which a sale took place, or if the Common Stock is not then quoted on the NASDAQ National Market System or Small Cap NASDAQ, or listed or admitted to trading on any stock exchange, the average of the bid and asked prices in the over-the-counter market on such date, or if none of the foregoing, a price determined in good faith by the Committee to equal the fair market value per share of the Common Stock.

(b) Subject to the authority of the Committee set forth in Section 4(a) hereof, Incentive Stock Options issued pursuant to this Plan shall be issued substantially in the form set forth in Appendix I hereof, which form is hereby incorporated by reference and made a part hereof, and shall contain substantially the terms and conditions set forth therein. Incentive Stock Options shall not be exercisable after the expiration of ten years from the date such options are granted, unless terminated earlier under the terms of the option, except that options granted to individuals described in Section 422(b)(6) of the Code shall conform to the provisions of Section 422(c)(5) of the Code. At the time of the grant of an Incentive Stock Option hereunder, the Committee may, in its discretion, amend or supplement any of the option terms contained in Appendix I for any particular optionee, provided that the option as amended or supplemented satisfies the requirements of Section 422(b) of the Code and the regulations thereunder. Each of the options granted pursuant to this Section 5(b) is intended, if possible, to be an "Incentive Stock Option" as that term is defined in Section 422(b) of the Code and the regulations thereunder. In the event this Plan or any option granted pursuant to this Section 5(b) is in any way inconsistent with the applicable legal requirements of the Code or the regulations thereunder for an Incentive Stock Option, this Plan and such option shall be deemed automatically amended as of the date hereof to conform to such legal requirements, if such conformity may be achieved by amendment.

(c) Subject to the authority of the Committee set forth in Section 4(a) hereof, Non-Qualified Stock Options issued to officers and other key employees pursuant to this Plan shall be issued substantially in the form set forth in Appendix II hereof, which form is hereby incorporated by reference and made a part hereof, and shall contain substantially the terms and conditions set forth therein. Subject to the authority of the Committee set forth in Section 4(a) hereof, Non-Qualified Stock Options issued to directors and important consultants pursuant to this Plan shall be issued substantially in the form set forth in Appendix III hereof, which form is hereby incorporated by reference and made a part hereof, and shall contain substantially the terms and conditions set forth therein. Non-Qualified Stock Options shall expire ten years after the date they are granted, unless terminated earlier under the option terms. At the time of granting a Non-Qualified Stock Option hereunder, the Committee may, in its discretion, amend or supplement any of the option terms contained in Appendix II or Appendix III for any particular optionee.

(d) Neither the Company nor any of its current or future parent, subsidiaries or affiliates, nor their officers, directors, shareholders, stock option plan committees, employees or agents shall have any liability to any optionee in the event (i) an option granted pursuant to Section 5(b) hereof does not qualify as an "Incentive Stock Option" as that term is used in Section 422(b) of the Code and the regulations thereunder; (ii) any optionee does not obtain the tax treatment pertaining to an Incentive Stock Option; or (iii) any option granted pursuant to Section 5(c) hereof is an "Incentive Stock Option."

6. Amendment, Supplement, Suspension, and Termination

Options shall not be granted pursuant to this Plan after the expiration of ten years from the date the Plan is adopted by the Board of Directors of the Company. The Board of Directors reserves the right at any time, and from time to time, to amend or supplement this Plan in any way, or to suspend or terminate it, effective as of such date, which date may be either before or after the taking of such action, as may be specified by the Board of Directors; provided, however, that such action shall not, without the consent of the optionee, affect options granted under the Plan prior to the actual date on which such action occurred. If an amendment or supplement of this Plan is required by the Code or the regulations thereunder to be approved by the shareholders of the Company in order to permit the granting of "Incentive Stock Options" (as that term is defined in Section 422(b) of the Code and regulations thereunder) pursuant to the amended or supplemented Plan, such amendment or supplement shall also be approved by the shareholders of the Company in such manner as is prescribed by the Code and the regulations thereunder. If the Board of Directors voluntarily submits a proposed amendment, supplement, suspension or termination for shareholder approval, such submission shall not require any future amendments, supplements, suspensions or terminations (whether or not relating to the same provision or subject matter) to be similarly submitted for shareholder approval.

7. Effectiveness of Plan

This Plan shall become effective on the date of its adoption by the Company's Board of Directors, subject however to approval by the holders of the Company's Common Stock in the manner as prescribed in the Code and the regulations thereunder. Options may be granted under this Plan prior to obtaining shareholder approval, provided such options shall not be exercisable until shareholder approval is obtained.

8. General Conditions

(a) Nothing contained in this Plan or any option granted pursuant to this Plan shall confer upon any employee the right to continue in the employ of the Company or any affiliated or subsidiary corporation or interfere in any way with the rights of the Company or any affiliated or subsidiary corporation to terminate his employment in any way.

(b) Nothing contained in this Plan or any option granted pursuant to this Plan shall confer upon any director or consultant the right to continue as a director of, or consultant to, the Company or any affiliated or subsidiary corporation or interfere in any way with the rights of the Company or any affiliated or subsidiary corporation, or their respective shareholders, to terminate the directorship of any such director or the consultancy relationship of any such consultant.

(c) Corporate action constituting an offer of stock for sale to any person under the terms of the options to be granted hereunder shall be deemed complete as of the date when the Committee authorizes the grant of the option to such person, regardless of when the option is actually delivered to such person or acknowledged or agreed to by him.

(d) The terms "parent corporation" and "subsidiary corporation" as used throughout this Plan, and the options granted pursuant to this Plan, shall (except as otherwise provided in the option form) have the meaning that is ascribed to that term when contained in Section 422(b) of the Code and the regulations thereunder, and the Company shall be deemed to be the grantor corporation for purposes of applying such meaning.

(e) References in this Plan to the Code shall be deemed to also refer to the corresponding provisions of any future United States revenue law.

(f) The use of the masculine pronoun shall include the feminine gender whenever appropriate.

APPENDIX I

INCENTIVE STOCK OPTION

To: _____
         Name

      _____
         Address

Date of Grant: _____

You are hereby granted an option, effective as of the date hereof, to purchase _____ shares of common stock, no par value ("Common Stock"), of GHI, Inc., a Pennsylvania corporation (the "Company"), at a price of $____ per share pursuant to the Company's Stock Option Plan (the "Plan").

This option shall terminate and is not exercisable after ten years from the date of its grant (the "Scheduled Termination Date"), except if terminated earlier as hereafter provided.

Your option may first be exercised on and after one year from the date of grant, but not before that time. On and after one year and prior to two years from the date of grant, your option may be exercised for up to $33^1/_3$ percent of the total number of shares subject to the option minus the number of shares previously purchased by exercise of the option (as adjusted for any change in the outstanding shares of the Common Stock of the Company by reason of a stock dividend, stock split, combination of shares, recapitalization, merger, consolidation, transfer of assets, reorganization, conversion or what the Committee deems in its sole discretion to be similar circumstances). Each succeeding year thereafter your option may be exercised for up to an additional $33^1/_3$ percent of the total number of shares subject to the option minus the number of shares previously purchased by exercise of the option (as adjusted for any change in the outstanding shares of the Common Stock of the Company by reason of a stock dividend, stock split, combination of shares, recapitalization, merger, consolidation, transfer of assets, reorganization, conversion or what the Committee deems in its sole discretion to be similar circumstances). Thus, this option is fully exercisable on and after three years after the date of grant, except if terminated earlier as provided herein.

In the event of a "Change of Control" (as defined below) of the Company, your option may, from and after the date which is six months after the Change of Control, and notwithstanding the immediately preceding paragraph, be exercised for up to 100% of the total number of shares then subject to the option minus the number of shares previously purchased upon exercise of the option (as adjusted for any change in the outstanding shares of the Common Stock of the Company by reason of a stock dividend, stock split, combination of shares, recapitalization, merger, consolidation, transfer of assets, reorganization, conversion or what the Committee deems in its sole discretion to be similar circumstances) and your vesting date will accelerate accordingly. A "Change of Control" shall be deemed to have occurred upon the happening of any of the following events:

1. A change within a twelve-month period in the holders of more than 50 percent of the outstanding voting stock of the Company; or

2. Any other event deemed to constitute a "Change of Control" by the Committee.

You may exercise your option by giving written notice to the Secretary of the Company on forms supplied by the Company at its then principal executive office, accompanied by payment of the option price for the total number of shares you specify that you wish to purchase. The payment may be in any of the following forms: (a) cash, which may be evidenced by a check and includes cash received from a stock brokerage firm in a so-called "cashless exercise"; (b) (unless prohibited by the Committee) certificates representing shares of Common Stock of the Company, which will be valued by the Secretary of the

Company at the fair market value per share of the Company's Common Stock (as determined in accordance with the Plan) on the date of delivery of such certificates to the Company, accompanied by an assignment of the stock to the Company; or (c) (unless prohibited by the Committee) any combination of cash and Common Stock of the Company valued as provided in clause (b). The use of the so-called "attestation procedure" to exercise a stock option may be permitted by the Committee. Any assignment of stock shall be in a form and substance satisfactory to the Secretary of the Company, including guarantees of signature(s) and payment of all transfer taxes if the Secretary deems such guarantees necessary or desirable.

Your option will, to the extent not previously exercised by you, terminate three months after the date on which your employment by the Company or a Company subsidiary corporation is terminated (whether such termination be voluntary or involuntary) other than by reason of disability as defined in Section 22(e)(3) of the Internal Revenue Code of 1986, as amended (the "Code"), and the regulations thereunder, or death, in which case your option will terminate one year from the date of termination of employment due to disability or death (but in no event later than the Scheduled Termination Date). After the date your employment is terminated, as aforesaid, you may exercise this option only for the number of shares which you had a right to purchase and did not purchase on the date your employment terminated. If you are employed by a Company subsidiary corporation, your employment shall be deemed to have terminated on the date your employer ceases to be a Company subsidiary corporation, unless you are on that date transferred to the Company or another Company subsidiary corporation. Your employment shall not be deemed to have terminated if you are transferred from the Company to a Company subsidiary corporation, or vice versa, or from one Company subsidiary corporation to another Company subsidiary corporation.

If you die while employed by the Company or a Company subsidiary corporation, your executor or administrator, as the case may be, may, at any time within one year after the date of your death (but in no event later than the Scheduled Termination Date), exercise the option as to any shares which you had a right to purchase and did not purchase during your lifetime. If your employment with the Company or a Company parent or subsidiary corporation is terminated by reason of your becoming disabled (within the meaning of Section 22[e][3] of the Code and the regulations thereunder), you or your legal guardian or custodian may at any time within one year after the date of such termination (but in no event later than the Scheduled Termination Date), exercise the option as to any shares which you had a right to purchase and did not purchase prior to such termination. Your executor, administrator, guardian, or custodian must present proof of his authority satisfactory to the Company prior to being allowed to exercise this option.

In the event of any change in the outstanding shares of the Common Stock of the Company by reason of a stock dividend, stock split, combination of shares, recapitalization, merger, consolidation, transfer of assets, reorganization, conversion, or what the Committee deems in its sole discretion to be similar circumstances, the number and kind of shares subject to this option and the option price of such shares shall be appropriately adjusted in a manner to be determined in the sole discretion of the Committee.

In the event of a liquidation or proposed liquidation of the Company, including (but not limited to) a transfer of assets followed by a liquidation of the Company, or in the event of a Change of Control (as previously defined) or proposed Change of Control, the Committee shall have the right to require you to exercise this option upon thirty (30) days prior written notice to you. If at the time such written notice is given this option is not otherwise exercisable, the written notice will set forth your right to exercise this option even though it is not otherwise exercisable. In the event this option is not exercised by you within the thirty (30) day period set forth in such written notice, this option shall terminate on the last day of such thirty (30) day period, notwithstanding anything to the contrary contained in this option.

This option is not transferable otherwise than by will or the laws of descent and distribution, and is exercisable during your lifetime only by you, including, for this purpose, your legal guardian or custodian in the event of disability. Until the option price has been paid in full pursuant to due exercise of this option and the purchased shares are delivered to you, you do not have any rights as a shareholder of the Company. The Company reserves the right not to deliver to you the shares purchased by virtue of the exercise of this option during any period of time in which the Company deems, in its sole discretion, that such delivery would violate a federal, state, local, or securities exchange rule, regulation, or law.

Notwithstanding anything to the contrary contained herein, this option is not exercisable until all the following events occur and during the following periods of time:

(a) Until the Plan pursuant to which this option is granted is approved by the shareholders of the Company in the manner prescribed by the Code and the regulations thereunder;

(b) Until this option and the optioned shares are approved and/or registered with such federal, state, and local regulatory bodies or agencies and securities exchanges as the Company may deem necessary or desirable; or

(c) During any period of time in which the Company deems that the exercisability of this option, the offer to sell the shares optioned hereunder, or the sale thereof, may violate a federal, state, local, or securities exchange rule, regulation, or law, or may cause the Company to be legally obligated to issue or sell more shares than the Company is legally entitled to issue or sell.

(d) Until you have paid or made suitable arrangements to pay (which may include payment through the surrender of Common Stock, unless prohibited by the Committee) (i) all federal, state and local income tax withholding required to be withheld by the Company in connection with the option exercise and (ii) the employee's portion of other federal, state and local payroll and other taxes due in connection with the option exercise.

The following two paragraphs shall be applicable if, on the date of exercise of this option, the Common Stock to be purchased pursuant to such exercise has not been registered under the Securities Act of 1933, as amended, and under applicable state securities laws, and shall continue to be applicable for so long as such registration has not occurred:

(a) The optionee hereby agrees, warrants and represents that he will acquire the Common Stock to be issued hereunder for his own account for investment purposes only, and not with a view to, or in connection with, any resale or other distribution of any of such shares, except as hereafter permitted. The optionee further agrees that he will not at any time make any offer, sale, transfer, pledge, or other disposition of such Common Stock to be issued hereunder without an effective registration statement under the Securities Act of 1933, as amended, and under any applicable state securities laws or an opinion of counsel acceptable to the Company to the effect that the proposed transaction will be exempt from such registration. The optionee shall execute such instruments, representations, acknowledgments, and agreements as the Company may, in its sole discretion, deem advisable to avoid any violation of federal, state, local, or securities exchange rule, regulation or law.

(b) The certificates for Common Stock to be issued to the optionee hereunder shall bear the following legend:

> "The shares represented by this certificate have not been registered under the Securities Act of 1933, as amended, or under applicable state securities laws. The shares have been acquired for investment and may not be offered, sold, transferred, pledged, or otherwise disposed of without an effective registration statement under the Securities Act of 1933, as amended, and under any applicable state securities laws or an opinion of counsel acceptable to the Company that the proposed transaction will be exempt from such registration."

The foregoing legend shall be removed upon registration of the legended shares under the Securities Act of 1933, as amended, and under any applicable state laws or upon receipt of any opinion of counsel acceptable to the Company that said registration is no longer required.

The sole purpose of the agreements, warranties, representations and legend set forth in the two immediately preceding paragraphs is to prevent violations of the Securities Act of 1933, as amended, and any applicable state securities laws.

It is the intention of the Company and you that this option shall, if possible, be an "Incentive Stock Option" as that term is used in Section 422(b) of the Code and the regulations thereunder. In the event this option is in any way inconsistent with the legal requirements of the Code or the regulations thereunder for an "Incentive Stock Option," this option shall be deemed automatically amended as of the date hereof to conform to such legal requirements, if such conformity may be achieved by amendment. To the extent that the number of shares subject to this option which are exercisable for the first time exceed the $100,000 limitation contained in Section 422(d) of the Code, this option will not be considered an Incentive Stock Option.

Nothing herein shall modify your status as an at-will employee of the Company. Further, nothing herein guarantees you employment for any specified period of time. This means that either you or the Company may terminate your employment at any time for any reason, with or without cause, or for no reason. You recognize that, for instance, you may terminate your employment or the Company may terminate your employment prior to the date on which your option becomes vested or exercisable.

Any dispute or disagreement between you and the Company with respect to any portion of this option (excluding Attachment A hereto) or its validity, construction, meaning, performance, or your rights hereunder shall be settled by arbitration in accordance with the Commercial Arbitration Rules of the American Arbitration Association or its successor, as amended from time to time. However, prior to submission to arbitration you will attempt to resolve any disputes or disagreements with the Company over this option amicably and informally, in good faith, for a period not to exceed two weeks. Thereafter, the dispute or disagreement will be submitted to arbitration. At any time prior to a decision from the arbitrator(s) being rendered, you and the Company may resolve the dispute by settlement. You and the Company shall equally share the costs charged by the American Arbitration Association or its successor, but you and the Company shall otherwise be solely responsible for your own respective counsel fees and expenses. The decision of the arbitrator(s) shall be made in writing, setting forth the award, the reasons for the decision and award and shall be binding and conclusive on you and the Company. Further, neither you nor the Company shall appeal any such award. Judgment of a court of competent jurisdiction may be entered upon the award and may be enforced as such in accordance with the provisions of the award.

This option shall be subject to the terms of the Plan in effect on the date this option is granted, which terms are hereby incorporated herein by reference and made a part hereof. In the event of any conflict between the terms of this option and the terms of the Plan in effect on the date of this option, the terms of the Plan shall govern. This option constitutes the entire understanding between the Company and you with respect to the subject matter hereof and no amendment, supplement, or waiver of this option, in whole or in part, shall be binding upon the Company unless in writing and signed by the President of the Company. This option and the performances of the parties hereunder shall be construed in accordance with and governed by the laws of the State of Pennsylvania.

In consideration of the grant to you of this option, you hereby agree to the confidentiality and noninterference provisions set forth in Attachment A hereto.

Please sign the copy of this option and return it to the Company's Secretary, thereby indicating your understanding of and agreement with its terms and conditions, **including Attachment A hereto.**

GHI, Inc.

By:

_____

I hereby acknowledge receipt of a copy of the foregoing stock option and the Plan, and having read them hereby signify my understanding of, and my agreement with, their terms and conditions, **including Attachment A hereto.** I accept this option in full satisfaction of any previous written or verbal promises made to me by the Company with respect to option grants.

_____   _____

(Signature)   (Date)

Attachment A to Stock Option

Confidentiality and Noninterference

(a) You covenant and agree that, in consideration of the grant to you of this stock option, you will not, during your employment with the Company or at any time thereafter, except with the express prior written consent of the Company or pursuant to the lawful order of any judicial or administrative agency of government, directly or indirectly, disclose, communicate or divulge to any individual or entity, or use for the benefit of any individual or entity, any knowledge or information with respect to the conduct or details of the Company's business which you, acting reasonably, believe or should believe to be of a confidential nature and the disclosure of which not to be in the Company's interest.

(b) You covenant and agree that, in consideration of the grant to you of this stock option, you will not, during your employment with the Company and for a period of two years thereafter, except with the express prior written consent of the Company, directly or indirectly, whether as employee, owner, partner, consultant, agent, director, officer, shareholder or in any other capacity, engage in or assist any individual or entity to engage in any act or action which you, acting reasonably, believe or should believe would be harmful or inimical to the interests of the Company.

(c) You covenant and agree that, in consideration of the grant to you of this stock option, you will not, for a period of two years after your employment with the Company ceases for any reason whatsoever (whether voluntary or not), except with the express prior written consent of the Company, directly or indirectly, whether as employee, owner, partner, consultant, agent, director, officer, shareholder or in any other capacity, for your own account or for the benefit of any individual or entity, (i) solicit any customer of the Company for business which would result in such customer terminating their relationship with the Company; or (ii) solicit or induce any individual or entity which is an employee of the Company to leave the Company or to otherwise terminate their relationship with the Company.

(d) The parties agree that any breach by you of any of the covenants or agreements contained in this Attachment A will result in irreparable injury to the Company for which money damages could not adequately compensate the Company and therefore, in the event of any such breach, the Company shall be entitled (in addition to any other rights and remedies which it may have at law or in equity) to have an injunction issued by any competent court enjoining and restraining you and/or any other individual or entity involved therein from continuing such breach. The existence of any claim or cause of action which you may have against the Company or any other individual or entity shall not constitute a defense or bar to the enforcement of such covenants. If the Company is obliged to resort to the courts for the enforcement of any of the covenants or agreements contained in this Attachment A, or if such covenants or agreements are otherwise the subject of litigation between the parties, and the Company prevails in such enforcement or litigation, then the term of such covenants and agreements shall be extended for a period of time equal to the period of such breach, which extension shall commence on the later of (a) the date on which the original (unextended) term of such covenants and agreements is scheduled to terminate or (b) the date of the final court order (without further right of appeal) enforcing such covenant or agreement.

(e) If any portion of the covenants or agreements contained in this Attachment A, or the application hereof, is construed to be invalid or unenforceable, the other portions of such covenant(s) or agreement(s) or the application thereof shall not be affected and shall be given full force and effect without regard to the invalid or enforceable portions to the fullest extent possible. If any covenant or agreement in this Attachment A is held unenforceable because of the area covered, the duration thereof, or the scope thereof, then the court making such determination shall have the power to reduce the area and/or duration and/or limit the scope thereof, and the covenant or agreement shall then be enforceable in its reduced form.

(f) For purposes of this Attachment A, the term "the Company" shall include the Company, any successor to the Company and all present and future direct and indirect subsidiaries and affiliates of the Company.

APPENDIX II

NON-QUALIFIED STOCK OPTION FOR
OFFICERS AND OTHER KEY EMPLOYEES

To: _____
          Name

_____
          Address

Date of Grant: _____

You are hereby granted an option, effective as of the date hereof, to purchase _____ shares of common stock, no par value ("Common Stock"), of GHI, Inc., a Pennsylvania corporation (the "Company"), at a price of $____ per share pursuant to the Company's Stock Option Plan (the "Plan").

This option shall terminate and is not exercisable after ten years from the date of its grant (the "Scheduled Termination Date"), except if terminated earlier as hereafter provided.

Your option may first be exercised on and after one year from the date of grant, but not before that time. On and after one year and prior to two years from the date of grant, your option may be exercised for up to 33 1/3 percent of the total number of shares subject to the option minus the number of shares previously purchased by exercise of the option (as adjusted for any change in the outstanding shares of the Common Stock of the Company by reason of a stock dividend, stock split, combination of shares, recapitalization, merger, consolidation, transfer of assets, reorganization, conversion or what the Committee deems in its sole discretion to be similar circumstances). Each succeeding year thereafter your option may be exercised for up to an additional 33 1/3 percent of the total number of shares subject to the option minus the number of shares previously purchased by exercise of the option (as adjusted for any change in the outstanding shares of the Common Stock of the Company by reason of a stock dividend, stock split, combination of shares, recapitalization, merger, consolidation, transfer of assets, reorganization, conversion or what the Committee deems in its sole discretion to be similar circumstances). Thus, this option is fully exercisable on and after three years after the date of grant, except if terminated earlier as provided herein.

In the event of a "Change of Control" (as defined below) of the Company, your option may, from and after the date which is six months after the Change of Control, and notwithstanding the immediately preceding paragraph, be exercised for up to 100% of the total number of shares then subject to the option minus the number of shares previously purchased upon exercise of the option (as adjusted for any change in the outstanding shares of the Common Stock of the Company by reason of a stock dividend, stock split, combination of shares, recapitalization, merger, consolidation, transfer of assets, reorganization, conversion or what the Committee deems in its sole discretion to be similar circumstances) and your vesting date will accelerate accordingly. A "Change of Control" shall be deemed to have occurred upon the happening of any of the following events:

1. A change within a twelve-month period in the holders of more than 50 percent of the outstanding voting stock of the Company; or

2. Any other event deemed to constitute a "Change of Control" by the Committee.

You may exercise your option by giving written notice to the Secretary of the Company on forms supplied by the Company at its then principal executive office, accompanied by payment of the option price for the total number of shares you specify that you wish to purchase. The payment may be in any of the following forms: (a) cash, which may be evidenced by a check and includes cash received from a stock brokerage firm in a so-called "cashless exercise"; (b) (unless prohibited by the Committee) certificates representing shares of Common Stock of the Company, which will be valued by the Secretary of the Company at the fair market value per share of the Company's Common Stock (as determined in accordance with the Plan) on the date of delivery of such certificates to the Company, accompanied by an assignment of the stock to the Company; or (c) (unless prohibited by the Committee) any combination of cash and Common Stock of the Company valued as provided in clause (b). The use of the so-called "attestation procedure" to exercise a stock option may be permitted by the Committee. Any assignment of stock shall be in a form and substance satisfactory to the Secretary of the Company, including guarantees of signature(s) and payment of all transfer taxes if the Secretary deems such guarantees necessary or desirable.

Your option will, to the extent not previously exercised by you, terminate three months after the date on which your employment by the Company or a Company subsidiary corporation is terminated (whether such termination be voluntary or involuntary) other than by reason of disability as defined in Section 22(e)(3) of the Internal Revenue Code of 1986, as amended (the "Code"), and the regulations thereunder, or death, in which case your option will terminate one year from the date of termination of employment due to disability or death (but in no event later than the Scheduled Termination Date). After the date your employment is terminated, as aforesaid, you may exercise this option only for the number of shares which you had a right to purchase and did not purchase on the date your employment terminated. If you are employed by a Company subsidiary corporation, your employment shall be deemed to have terminated on the date your employer ceases to be a Company subsidiary corporation, unless you are on that date transferred to the Company or another Company subsidiary corporation. Your employment shall not be deemed to have terminated if you are transferred from the Company to a Company subsidiary corporation, or vice versa, or from one Company subsidiary corporation to another Company subsidiary corporation.

If you die while employed by the Company or a Company subsidiary corporation, your executor or administrator, as the case may be, may, at any time within one year after the date of your death (but in no event later than the Scheduled Termination Date), exercise the option as to any shares which you had a right to purchase and did not purchase during your lifetime. If your employment with the Company or a Company parent or subsidiary corporation is terminated by reason of your becoming disabled (within the meaning of Section 22[e][3] of the Code and the regulations thereunder), you or your legal guardian or custodian may at any time within one year after the date of such termination (but in no event later than the Scheduled Termination Date), exercise the option as to any shares which you had a right to purchase and did not purchase prior to such termination. Your executor, administrator, guardian, or custodian must present proof of his authority satisfactory to the Company prior to being allowed to exercise this option.

In the event of any change in the outstanding shares of the Common Stock of the Company by reason of a stock dividend, stock split, combination of shares, recapitalization, merger, consolidation, transfer of assets, reorganization, conversion, or what the Committee deems in its sole discretion to be similar circumstances, the number and kind of shares subject to this option and the option price of such shares shall be appropriately adjusted in a manner to be determined in the sole discretion of the Committee.

In the event of a liquidation or proposed liquidation of the Company, including (but not limited to) a transfer of assets followed by a liquidation of the Company, or in the event of a Change of Control (as previously defined) or proposed Change of Control, the Committee shall have the right to require you to exercise this option upon thirty (30) days prior written notice to you. If at the time such written notice is given this option is not otherwise exercisable, the written notice will set forth your right to exercise this option even though it is not otherwise exercisable. In the event this option is not exercised by you within the thirty (30) day period set forth in such written notice, this option shall terminate on the last day of such thirty (30) day period, notwithstanding anything to the contrary contained in this option.

This option is not transferable otherwise than by will or the laws of descent and distribution, and is exercisable during your lifetime only by you, including, for this purpose, your legal guardian or custodian in the event of disability. Until the option price has been paid in full pursuant to due exercise of this option and the purchased shares are delivered to you, you do not have any rights as a shareholder of the Company. The Company reserves the right not to deliver to you the shares purchased by virtue of the exercise of this option during any period of time in which the Company deems, in its sole discretion, that such delivery would violate a federal, state, local, or securities exchange rule, regulation, or law.

Notwithstanding anything to the contrary contained herein, this option is not exercisable until all the following events occur and during the following periods of time:

(a) Until the Plan pursuant to which this option is granted is approved by the shareholders of the Company in the manner prescribed by the Code and the regulations thereunder;

(b) Until this option and the optioned shares are approved and/or registered with such federal, state, and local regulatory bodies or agencies and securities exchanges as the Company may deem necessary or desirable; or

(c) During any period of time in which the Company deems that the exercisability of this option, the offer to sell the shares optioned hereunder, or the sale thereof, may violate a federal, state, local, or securities exchange rule, regulation, or law, or may cause the Company to be legally obligated to issue or sell more shares than the Company is legally entitled to issue or sell.

(d) Until you have paid or made suitable arrangements to pay (which may include payment through the surrender of Common Stock, unless prohibited by the Committee) (i) all federal, state and local income tax withholding required to be withheld by the Company in connection with the option exercise and (ii) the employee's portion of other federal, state and local payroll and other taxes due in connection with the option exercise.

The following two paragraphs shall be applicable if, on the date of exercise of this option, the Common Stock to be purchased pursuant to such exercise has not been registered under the Securities Act of 1933, as amended, and under applicable state securities laws, and shall continue to be applicable for so long as such registration has not occurred:

(a) The optionee hereby agrees, warrants and represents that he will acquire the Common Stock to be issued hereunder for his own account for investment purposes only, and not with a view to, or in connection with, any resale or other distribution of any of such shares, except as hereafter permitted. The optionee further agrees that he will not at any time make any offer, sale, transfer, pledge, or other disposition of such Common Stock to be issued hereunder without an effective registration statement under the Securities Act of 1933, as amended, and under any applicable state securities laws or an opinion of counsel acceptable to the Company to the effect that the proposed transaction will be exempt from such registration. The optionee shall execute such instruments, representations, acknowledgements, and agreements as the Company may, in its sole discretion, deem advisable to avoid any violation of federal, state, local, or securities exchange rule, regulation or law.

(b) The certificates for Common Stock to be issued to the optionee hereunder shall bear the following legend:

> "The shares represented by this certificate have not been registered under the Securities Act of 1933, as amended, or under applicable state securities laws. The shares have been acquired for investment and may not be offered, sold, transferred, pledged, or otherwise disposed of without an effective registration statement under the Securities Act of 1933, as amended, and under any applicable state securities laws or an opinion of counsel acceptable to the Company that the proposed transaction will be exempt from such registration."

The foregoing legend shall be removed upon registration of the legended shares under the Securities Act of 1933, as amended, and under any applicable state laws or upon receipt of any opinion of counsel acceptable to the Company that said registration is no longer required.

The sole purpose of the agreements, warranties, representations and legend set forth in the two immediately preceding paragraphs is to prevent violations of the Securities Act of 1933, as amended, and any applicable state securities laws.

It is the intention of the Company and you that this option shall not be an "Incentive Stock Option" as that term is used in Section 422(b) of the Code and the regulations thereunder.

Nothing herein shall modify your status as an at-will employee of the Company. Further, nothing herein guarantees you employment for any specified period of time. This means that either you or the Company may terminate your employment at any time for any reason, with or without cause, or for no reason. You recognize that, for instance, you may terminate your employment or the Company may terminate your employment prior to the date on which your option becomes vested or exercisable.

Any dispute or disagreement between you and the Company with respect to any portion of this option (excluding Attachment A hereto) or its validity, construction, meaning, performance, or your rights hereunder shall be settled by arbitration in accordance with the Commercial Arbitration Rules of the American Arbitration Association or its successor, as amended from time to time. However, prior to submission to arbitration you will attempt to resolve any disputes or disagreements with the Company over this option amicably and informally, in good faith, for a period not to exceed two weeks. Thereafter, the dispute or disagreement will be submitted to arbitration. At any time prior to a decision from the arbitrator(s) being rendered, you and the Company may resolve the dispute by settlement. You and the Company shall equally share the costs charged by the American Arbitration Association or its successor, but you and the Company shall otherwise be solely responsible for your own respective counsel fees and expenses. The decision of the arbitrator(s) shall be made in writing, setting forth the award, the reasons for the decision and award and shall be binding and conclusive on you and the Company. Further, neither you nor the Company shall appeal any such award. Judgment of a court of competent jurisdiction may be entered upon the award and may be enforced as such in accordance with the provisions of the award.

This option shall be subject to the terms of the Plan in effect on the date this option is granted, which terms are hereby incorporated herein by reference and made a part hereof. In the event of any conflict between the terms of this option and the terms of the Plan in effect on the date of this option, the terms of the Plan shall govern. This option constitutes the entire understanding between the Company and you with respect to the subject matter hereof and no amendment, supplement, or waiver of this option, in whole or in part, shall be binding upon the Company unless in writing and signed by the President of the Company. This option and the performances of the parties hereunder shall be construed in accordance with and governed by the laws of the State of Pennsylvania.

In consideration of the grant to you of this option, you hereby agree to the confidentiality and noninterference provisions set forth in Attachment A hereto.

Please sign the copy of this option and return it to the Company's Secretary, thereby indicating your understanding of and agreement with its terms and conditions, **including Attachment A hereto.**

GHI, Inc.

By:_____

I hereby acknowledge receipt of a copy of the foregoing stock option and, having read it, hereby signify my understanding of, and my agreement with, its terms and conditions, **including Attachment A hereto.**

_____   _____

(Signature)   (Date)

Attachment A to Stock Option

Confidentiality and Noninterference

(a) You covenant and agree that, in consideration of the grant to you of this stock option, you will not, during your employment with the Company or at any time thereafter, except with the express prior written consent of the Company or pursuant to the lawful order of any judicial or administrative agency of government, directly or indirectly, disclose, communicate or divulge to any individual or entity, or use for the benefit of any individual or entity, any knowledge or information with respect to the conduct or details of the Company's business which you, acting reasonably, believe or should believe to be of a confidential nature and the disclosure of which not to be in the Company's interest.

(b) You covenant and agree that, in consideration of the grant to you of this stock option, you will not, during your employment with the Company and for a period of two years thereafter, except with the express prior written consent of the Company, directly or indirectly, whether as employee, owner, partner, consultant, agent, director, officer, shareholder or in any other capacity, engage in or assist any individual or entity to engage in any act or action which you, acting reasonably, believe or should believe would be harmful or inimical to the interests of the Company.

(c) You covenant and agree that, in consideration of the grant to you of this stock option, you will not, for a period of two years after your employment with the Company ceases for any reason whatsoever (whether voluntary or not), except with the express prior written consent of the Company, directly or indirectly, whether as employee, owner, partner, consultant, agent, director, officer, shareholder or in any other capacity, for your own account or for the benefit of any individual or entity, (i) solicit any customer of the Company for business which would result in such customer terminating their relationship with the Company; or (ii) solicit or induce any individual or entity which is an employee of the Company to leave the Company or to otherwise terminate their relationship with the Company.

(d) The parties agree that any breach by you of any of the covenants or agreements contained in this Attachment A will result in irreparable injury to the Company for which money damages could not adequately compensate the Company and therefore, in the event of any such breach, the Company shall be entitled (in addition to any other rights and remedies which it may have at law or in equity) to have an injunction issued by any competent court enjoining and restraining you and/or any other individual or entity involved therein from continuing such breach. The existence of any claim or cause of action which you may have against the Company or any other individual or entity shall not constitute a defense or bar to the enforcement of such covenants. If the Company is obliged to resort to the courts for the enforcement of any of the covenants or agreements contained in this Attachment A, or if such covenants or agreements are otherwise the subject of litigation between the parties, and the Company prevails in such enforcement or litigation, then the term of such covenants and agreements shall be extended for a period of time equal to the period of such breach, which extension shall commence on the later of (a) the date on which the original (unextended) term of such covenants and agreements is scheduled to terminate or (b) the date of the final court order (without further right of appeal) enforcing such covenant or agreement.

(e) If any portion of the covenants or agreements contained in this Attachment A, or the application hereof, is construed to be invalid or unenforceable, the other portions of such covenant(s) or agreement(s) or the application thereof shall not be affected and shall be given full force and effect without regard to the invalid or enforceable portions to the fullest extent possible. If any covenant or agreement in this Attachment A is held unenforceable because of the area covered, the duration thereof, or the scope thereof, then the court making such determination shall have the power to reduce the area and/or duration and/or limit the scope thereof, and the covenant or agreement shall then be enforceable in its reduced form.

(f) For purposes of this Attachment A, the term "the Company" shall include the Company, any successor to the Company and all present and future direct and indirect subsidiaries and affiliates of the Company.

APPENDIX III

NON-QUALIFIED STOCK OPTION FOR
DIRECTORS AND IMPORTANT CONSULTANTS

To: _____
                Name

        _____
                Address

Date of Grant: _____

You are hereby granted an option, effective as of the date hereof, to purchase _____ shares of common stock, no par value ("Common Stock"), of GHI, Inc., a Pennsylvania corporation (the "Company"), at a price of $____ per share pursuant to the Company's Stock Option Plan (the "Plan").

This option shall terminate and is not exercisable after ten years from the date of its grant (the "Scheduled Termination Date"), except if terminated earlier as hereafter provided.

Your option may first be exercised on and after one year from the date of grant, but not before that time. On and after one year and prior to two years from the date of grant, your option may be exercised for up to 33⅓ percent of the total number of shares subject to the option minus the number of shares previously purchased by exercise of the option (as adjusted for any change in the outstanding shares of the Common Stock of the Company by reason of a stock dividend, stock split, combination of shares, recapitalization, merger, consolidation, transfer of assets, reorganization, conversion or what the Committee deems in its sole discretion to be similar circumstances). Each succeeding year thereafter your option may be exercised for up to an additional 33⅓ percent of the total number of shares subject to the option minus the number of shares previously purchased by exercise of the option (as adjusted for any change in the outstanding shares of the Common Stock of the Company by reason of a stock dividend, stock split, combination of shares, recapitalization, merger, consolidation, transfer of assets, reorganization, conversion or what the Committee deems in its sole discretion to be similar circumstances). Thus, this option is fully exercisable on and after three years after the date of grant, except if terminated earlier as provided herein.

In the event of a "Change of Control" (as defined below) of the Company, your option may, from and after the date which is six months after the Change of Control, and notwithstanding the immediately preceding paragraph, be exercised for up to 100% of the total number of shares then subject to the option minus the number of shares previously purchased upon exercise of the option (as adjusted for any change in the outstanding shares of the Common Stock of the Company by reason of a stock dividend, stock split, combination of shares, recapitalization, merger, consolidation, transfer of assets, reorganization, conversion or what the Committee deems in its sole discretion to be similar circumstances) and your vesting date will accelerate accordingly. A "Change of Control" shall be deemed to have occurred upon the happening of any of the following events:

1.   A change within a twelve-month period in the holders of more than 50 percent of the outstanding voting stock of the Company; or

2.   Any other event deemed to constitute a "Change of Control" by the Committee.

You may exercise your option by giving written notice to the Secretary of the Company on forms supplied by the Company at its then principal executive office, accompanied by payment of the option price for the total number of shares you specify that you wish to purchase. The payment may be in any of the following forms: (a) cash, which may be evidenced by a check and includes cash received from a stock brokerage firm in a so-called "cashless exercise"; (b) (unless prohibited by the Committee) certificates representing shares of Common Stock of the Company, which will be valued by the Secretary of the Company at the fair market value per share of the Company's Common Stock (as determined in accordance with the Plan) on the date of delivery of such certificates to the Company, accompanied by an assignment of the stock to the Company; or (c) (unless prohibited by the Committee) any combination of cash and Common Stock of the Company valued as provided in clause (b). The use of the so-called "attestation procedure" to exercise a stock option may be permitted by the Committee. Any assignment of stock shall be in a form and substance satisfactory to the Secretary of the Company, including guarantees of signature(s) and payment of all transfer taxes if the Secretary deems such guarantees necessary or desirable.

Your option will, to the extent not previously exercised by you, terminate three months after the date on which you cease for any reason to be a director of, or consultant to, the Company or a subsidiary corporation (whether by death, disability, resignation, removal, failure to be reappointed, reelected or otherwise, or the expiration of any consulting arrangement, and regardless of whether the failure to continue as a director or consultant was for cause or without cause or otherwise), but in no event later than ten years from the date this option is granted. After the date you cease to be a director or consultant, you may exercise this option only for the number of shares which you had a right to purchase and did not purchase on the date you ceased to be a director or consultant. If you are a director of, or consultant to, a subsidiary corporation, your directorship or consultancy shall be deemed to have terminated on the date such company ceases to be a subsidiary corporation, unless you are also a director of, or consultant to, the Company or another subsidiary corporation, or on that date became a director of, or consultant to, the Company or another subsidiary corporation. Your directorship or consultancy shall not be deemed to have terminated if you cease being a director of, or consultant to, the Company or a subsidiary corporation but are or concurrently therewith become a director of, or consultant to, the Company or another subsidiary corporation.

In the event of any change in the outstanding shares of the Common Stock of the Company by reason of a stock dividend, stock split, combination of shares, recapitalization, merger, consolidation, transfer of assets, reorganization, conversion, or what the Committee deems in its sole discretion to be similar circumstances, the number and kind of shares subject to this option and the option price of such shares shall be appropriately adjusted in a manner to be determined in the sole discretion of the Committee.

In the event of a liquidation or proposed liquidation of the Company, including (but not limited to) a transfer of assets followed by a liquidation of the Company, or in the event of a Change of Control (as previously defined) or proposed Change of Control, the Committee shall have the right to require you to exercise this option upon thirty (30) days prior written notice to you. If at the time such written notice is given this option is not otherwise exercisable, the written notice will set forth your right to exercise this option even though it is not otherwise exercisable. In the event this option is not exercised by you within the thirty (30) day period set forth in such written notice, this option shall terminate on the last day of such thirty (30) day period, notwithstanding anything to the contrary contained in this option.

This option is not transferable otherwise than by will or the laws of descent and distribution, and is exercisable during your lifetime only by you, including, for this purpose, your legal guardian or custodian in the event of disability. Until the option price has been paid in full pursuant to due exercise of this option and the purchased shares are delivered to you, you do not have any rights as a shareholder of the Company. The Company reserves the right not to deliver to you the shares purchased by virtue of the exercise of this option during any period of time in which the Company deems, in its sole discretion, that such delivery would violate a federal, state, local, or securities exchange rule, regulation, or law.

Notwithstanding anything to the contrary contained herein, this option is not exercisable until all the following events occur and during the following periods of time:

(a) Until the Plan pursuant to which this option is granted is approved by the shareholders of the Company in the manner prescribed by the Code and the regulations thereunder;

(b) Until this option and the optioned shares are approved and/or registered with such federal, state, and local regulatory bodies or agencies and securities exchanges as the Company may deem necessary or desirable; or

(c) During any period of time in which the Company deems that the exercisability of this option, the offer to sell the shares optioned hereunder, or the sale thereof, may violate a federal, state, local, or securities exchange rule, regulation, or law, or may cause the Company to be legally obligated to issue or sell more shares than the Company is legally entitled to issue or sell.

(d) Until you have paid or made suitable arrangements to pay (which may include payment through the surrender of Common Stock, unless prohibited by the Committee) (i) all federal, state and local income tax withholding required to be withheld by the Company in connection with the option exercise and (ii) the employee's portion of other federal, state and local payroll and other taxes due in connection with the option exercise.

The following two paragraphs shall be applicable if, on the date of exercise of this option, the Common Stock to be purchased pursuant to such exercise has not been registered under the Securities Act of 1933, as amended, and under applicable state securities laws, and shall continue to be applicable for so long as such registration has not occurred:

(a) The optionee hereby agrees, warrants and represents that he will acquire the Common Stock to be issued hereunder for his own account for investment purposes only, and not with a view to, or in connection with, any resale or other distribution of any of such shares, except as hereafter permitted. The optionee further agrees that he will not at any time make any offer, sale, transfer, pledge, or other disposition of such Common Stock to be issued hereunder without an effective registration statement under the Securities Act of 1933, as amended, and under any applicable state securities laws or an opinion of counsel acceptable to the Company to the effect that the proposed transaction will be exempt from such registration. The optionee shall execute such instruments, representations, acknowledgments, and agreements as the Company may, in its sole discretion, deem advisable to avoid any violation of federal, state, local, or securities exchange rule, regulation or law.

(b) The certificates for Common Stock to be issued to the optionee hereunder shall bear the following legend:

"The shares represented by this certificate have not been registered under the Securities Act of 1933, as amended, or under applicable state securities laws. The shares have been acquired for investment and may not be offered, sold, transferred, pledged, or otherwise disposed of without an effective registration statement under the Securities Act of 1933, as amended, and under any applicable state securities laws or an opinion of counsel acceptable to the Company that the proposed transaction will be exempt from such registration."

The foregoing legend shall be removed upon registration of the legended shares under the Securities Act of 1933, as amended, and under any applicable state laws or upon receipt of any opinion of counsel acceptable to the Company that said registration is no longer required.

The sole purpose of the agreements, warranties, representations and legend set forth in the two immediately preceding paragraphs is to prevent violations of the Securities Act of 1933, as amended, and any applicable state securities laws.

It is the intention of the Company and you that this option shall not be an "Incentive Stock Option" as that term is used in Section 422(b) of the Code and the regulations thereunder.

Nothing herein guarantees your term as a director of, or consultant to, the Company for any specified period of time. This means that either you or the Company may terminate your relationship with the Company at any time for

any reason, with or without cause, or for no reason. You recognize that, for instance, the Company may terminate your relationship with the Company prior to the date on which your option becomes vested or exercisable.

Any dispute or disagreement between you and the Company with respect to any portion of this option (excluding Attachment A hereto) or its validity, construction, meaning, performance, or your rights hereunder shall be settled by arbitration in accordance with the Commercial Arbitration Rules of the American Arbitration Association or its successor, as amended from time to time. However, prior to submission to arbitration you will attempt to resolve any disputes or disagreements with the Company over this option amicably and informally, in good faith, for a period not to exceed two weeks. Thereafter, the dispute or disagreement will be submitted to arbitration. At any time prior to a decision from the arbitrator(s) being rendered, you and the Company may resolve the dispute by settlement. You and the Company shall equally share the costs charged by the American Arbitration Association or its successor, but you and the Company shall otherwise be solely responsible for your own respective counsel fees and expenses. The decision of the arbitrator(s) shall be made in writing, setting forth the award, the reasons for the decision and award and shall be binding and conclusive on you and the Company. Further, neither you nor the Company shall appeal any such award. Judgment of a court of competent jurisdiction may be entered upon the award and may be enforced as such in accordance with the provisions of the award.

This option shall be subject to the terms of the Plan in effect on the date this option is granted, which terms are hereby incorporated herein by reference and made a part hereof. In the event of any conflict between the terms of this option and the terms of the Plan in effect on the date of this option, the terms of the Plan shall govern. This option constitutes the entire understanding between the Company and you with respect to the subject matter hereof and no amendment, supplement, or waiver of this option, in whole or in part, shall be binding upon the Company unless in writing and signed by the President of the Company. This option and the performances of the parties hereunder shall be construed in accordance with and governed by the laws of the State of Pennsylvania.

In consideration of the grant to you of this option, you hereby agree to the confidentiality and noninterference provisions set forth in Attachment A hereto.

Please sign the copy of this option and return it to the Company's Secretary, thereby indicating your understanding of and agreement with its terms and conditions, **including Attachment A hereto.**

GHI, Inc.

By: _____

I hereby acknowledge receipt of a copy of the foregoing stock option and, having read it, hereby signify my understanding of, and my agreement with, its terms and conditions, **including Attachment A hereto.**

_____   _____

(Signature)   (Date)

Attachment A to Stock Option

Confidentiality and Noninterference

(a) You covenant and agree that, in consideration of the grant to you of this stock option, you will not, during your term as a director of, or a consultant to, the Company or at any time thereafter, except with the express prior written consent of the Company or pursuant to the lawful order of any judicial or administrative agency of government, directly or indirectly, disclose, communicate or divulge to any individual or entity, or use for the benefit of any individual or entity, any knowledge or information with respect to the conduct or details of the Company's business which you, acting reasonably, believe or should believe to be of a confidential nature and the disclosure of which not to be in the Company's interest.

(b) You covenant and agree that, in consideration of the grant to you of this stock option, you will not, during your term as a director of, or a consultant to, the Company and for a period of two years thereafter, except with the express prior written consent of the Company, directly or indirectly, whether as employee, owner, partner, consultant, agent, director, officer, shareholder or in any other capacity, engage in or assist any individual or entity to engage in any act or action which you, acting reasonably, believe or should believe would be harmful or inimical to the interests of the Company.

(c) You covenant and agree that, in consideration of the grant to you of this stock option, you will not, for a period of two years after your term as a director of, or a consultant to, the Company ceases for any reason whatsoever (whether voluntary or not), except with the express prior written consent of the Company, directly or indirectly, whether as employee, owner, partner, consultant, agent, director, officer, shareholder or in any other capacity, for your own account or for the benefit of any individual or entity, (i) solicit any customer of the Company for business which would result in such customer terminating their relationship with the Company; or (ii) solicit or induce any individual or entity which is an employee of the Company to leave the Company or to otherwise terminate their relationship with the Company.

(d) The parties agree that any breach by you of any of the covenants or agreements contained in this Attachment A will result in irreparable injury to the Company for which money damages could not adequately compensate the Company and therefore, in the event of any such breach, the Company shall be entitled (in addition to any other rights and remedies which it may have at law or in equity) to have an injunction issued by any competent court enjoining and restraining you and/or any other individual or entity involved therein from continuing such breach. The existence of any claim or cause of action which you may have against the Company or any other individual or entity shall not constitute a defense or bar to the enforcement of such covenants. If the Company is obliged to resort to the courts for the enforcement of any of the covenants or agreements contained in this Attachment A, or if such covenants or agreements are otherwise the subject of litigation between the parties, and the Company prevails in such enforcement or litigation, then the term of such covenants and agreements shall be extended for a period of time equal to the period of such breach, which extension shall commence on the later of (a) the date on which the original (unextended) term of such covenants and agreements is scheduled to terminate or (b) the date of the final court order (without further right of appeal) enforcing such covenant or agreement.

(e) If any portion of the covenants or agreements contained in this Attachment A, or the application hereof, is construed to be invalid or unenforceable, the other portions of such covenant(s) or agreement(s) or the application thereof shall not be affected and shall be given full force and effect without regard to the invalid or enforceable portions to the fullest extent possible. If any covenant or agreement in this Attachment A is held unenforceable because of the area covered, the duration thereof, or the scope thereof, then the court making such determination shall have the power to reduce the area and/or duration and/or limit the scope thereof, and the covenant or agreement shall then be enforceable in its reduced form.

(f) For purposes of this Attachment A, the term "the Company" shall include the Company, any successor to the Company and all present and future direct and indirect subsidiaries and affiliates of the Company.

APPENDIX 6

SECTIONS 421 THROUGH 424 OF THE INTERNAL REVENUE CODE

SECTION 421

Section 421. General Rules

(a) Effect of qualifying transfer

If a share of stock is transferred to an individual in a transfer in respect of which the requirements of section 422(a) or 423(a) are met—

(1) no income shall result at the time of the transfer of such share to the individual upon his exercise of the option with respect to such share;

(2) no deduction under section 162 (relating to trade or business expenses) shall be allowable at any time to the employer corporation, a parent or subsidiary corporation of such corporation, or a corporation issuing or assuming a stock option in a transaction to which section 424(a) applies, with respect to the share so transferred; and

(3) no amount other than the price paid under the option shall be considered as received by any of such corporations for the share so transferred.

(b) Effect of disqualifying disposition

If the transfer of a share of stock to an individual pursuant to his exercise of an option would otherwise meet the requirements of section 422(a) or 423(a) except that there is a failure to meet any of the holding period requirements of section 422(a)(1) or 423(a)(1), then any increase in the income of such individual or deduction from the income of his employer corporation for the taxable year in which such exercise occurred attributable to such disposition, shall be treated as an increase in income or a deduction from income in the taxable year of such individual or of such employer corporation in which such disposition occurred.

(c) Exercise by estate

(1) In general if an option to which this part applies is exercised after the death of the employee by the estate of the decedent, or by a person who acquired the right to exercise such option by bequest or inheritance or by reason of the death of the decedent, the provisions of subsection (a) shall apply to the same extent as if the option had been exercised by the decedent, except that—

    (A) the holding period and employment requirements of sections 422(a) and 423(a) shall not apply, and

    (B) any transfer by the estate of stock acquired shall be considered a disposition of such stock for purposes of section 423(c).

(2) Deduction for estate tax. If an amount is required to be included under section 423(c) in gross income of the estate of the deceased employee or of a person described in paragraph (1), there shall be allowed to the estate or such person a deduction with respect to the estate tax attributable to the inclusion in the taxable estate of the deceased employee of the net value for estate tax purposes of the option. For this purpose, the deduction shall be determined under section 691(c) as if the option acquired from the deceased employee were an item of gross income in respect of the decedent under section 691 and as if the amount includible in gross income under section 423(c) were an amount included in gross income under section 691 in respect of such item of gross income.

(3) Basis of shares acquired. In the case of a share of stock acquired by the exercise of an option to which paragraph (1) applies—

    (A) the basis of such share shall include so much of the basis of the option as is attributable to such share; except that the basis of such share shall be reduced by the excess (if any) of (i) the amount which would have been includible in gross income under section 423(c) if the employee had exercised the option on the date of his death and had held the share acquired pursuant to such exercise at the time of his death, over (ii) the amount which is includible in gross income under such section; and

(B) the last sentence of section 423(c) shall apply only to the extent that the amount includible in gross income under such section exceeds so much of the basis of the option as is attributable to such share.

SECTION 422

Section 422. Incentive stock options

(a) In general

Section 421(a) shall apply with respect to the transfer of a share of stock to an individual pursuant to his exercise of an incentive stock option if—

(1) no disposition of such share is made by him within 2 years from the date of the granting of the option nor within 1 year after the transfer of such share to him, and

(2) at all times during the period beginning on the date of the granting of the option and ending on the day 3 months before the date of such exercise, such individual was an employee of either the corporation granting such option, a parent or subsidiary corporation of such corporation, or a corporation or a parent or subsidiary corporation of such corporation issuing or assuming a stock option in a transaction to which section 424(a) applies.

(b) Incentive stock option

For purposes of this part, the term "incentive stock option" means an option granted to an individual for any reason connected with his employment by a corporation, if granted by the employer corporation or its parent or subsidiary corporation, to purchase stock of any of such corporations, but only if—

(1) the option is granted pursuant to a plan which includes the aggregate number of shares which may be issued under options and the employees (or class of employees) eligible to receive options, and which is approved by the stockholders of the granting corporation within 12 months before or after the date such plan is adopted;

(2) such option is granted within 10 years from the date such plan is adopted, or the date such plan is approved by the stockholders, whichever is earlier;

(3) such option by its terms is not exercisable after the expiration of 10 years from the date such option is granted;

(4) the option price is not less than the fair market value of the stock at the time such option is granted;

(5) such option by its terms is not transferable by such individual otherwise than by will or the laws of descent and distribution, and is exercisable, during his lifetime, only by him; and

(6) such individual, at the time the option is granted, does not own stock possessing more than 10 percent of the total combined voting power of all classes of stock of the employer corporation or of its parent or subsidiary corporation. Such term shall not include any option if (as of the time the option is granted) the terms of such option provide that it will not be treated as an incentive stock option.

(c) Special rules

(1) Good faith efforts to value of stock. If a share of stock is transferred pursuant to the exercise by an individual of an option which would fail to qualify as an incen-

tive stock option under subsection (b) because there was a failure in an attempt, made in good faith, to meet the requirement of subsection (b)(4), the requirement of subsection (b)(4) shall be considered to have been met. To the extent provided in regulations by the Secretary, a similar rule shall apply for purposes of subsection (d).

(2) Certain disqualifying dispositions where amount realized is less than value at exercise If—

    (A) an individual who has acquired a share of stock by the exercise of an incentive stock option makes a disposition of such share within either of the periods described in subsection (a)(1), and

    (B) such disposition is a sale or exchange with respect to which a loss (if sustained) would be recognized to such individual, then the amount which is includible in the gross income of such individual, and the amount which is deductible from the income of his employer corporation, as compensation attributable to the exercise of such option shall not exceed the excess (if any) of the amount realized on such sale or exchange over the adjusted basis of such share.

(3) Certain transfers by insolvent individuals. If an insolvent individual holds a share of stock acquired pursuant to his exercise of an incentive stock option, and if such share is transferred to a trustee, receiver, or other similar fiduciary in any proceeding under title 11 or any other similar insolvency proceeding, neither such transfer, nor any other transfer of such share for the benefit of his creditors in such proceeding, shall constitute a disposition of such share for purposes of subsection (a)(1).

(4) Permissible provisions

An option which meets the requirements of subsection (b) shall be treated as an incentive stock option even if—

    (A) the employee may pay for the stock with stock of the corporation granting the option,

    (B) the employee has a right to receive property at the time of exercise of the option, or

    (C) the option is subject to any condition not inconsistent with the provisions of subsection (b). Subparagraph (B) shall apply to a transfer of property (other than cash) only if section 83 applies to the property so transferred.

(5) 10-percent shareholder rule

Subsection (b)(6) shall not apply if at the time such option is granted the option price is at least 110 percent of the fair market value of the stock subject to the option and such option by its terms is not exercisable after the expiration of 5 years from the date such option is granted.

(6) Special rule when disabled

For purposes of subsection (a)(2), in the case of an employee who is disabled (within the meaning of section 22[e][3]), the 3-month period of subsection (a)(2) shall be 1 year.

(7) Fair market value

For purposes of this section, the fair market value of stock shall be determined without regard to any restriction other than a restriction which, by its terms, will never lapse.

(d) $100,000 per year limitation

(1) In general

To the extent that the aggregate fair market value of stock with respect to which incentive stock options (determined without regard to this subsection) are exercisable for the 1st time by any individual during any calendar year (under all plans of the individual's employer corporation and its parent and subsidiary corporations) exceeds $100,000, such options shall be treated as options which are not incentive stock options.

(2) Ordering rule

Paragraph (1) shall be applied by taking options into account in the order in which they were granted.

(3) Determination of fair market value

For purposes of paragraph (1), the fair market value of any stock shall be determined as of the time the option with respect to such stock is granted.

SECTION 423

Section 423. Employee stock purchase plans

(a) General rule

Section 421(a) shall apply with respect to the transfer of a share of stock to an individual pursuant to his exercise of an option granted after December 31, 1963, under an employee stock purchase plan (as defined in subsection [b]) if—(1) no disposition of such share is made by him within 2 years after the date of the granting of the option nor within 1 year after the transfer of such share to him; and (2) at all times during the period beginning with the date of the granting of the option and ending on the day 3 months before the date of such exercise, he is an employee of the corporation granting such option, a parent or subsidiary corporation of such corporation, or a corporation or a parent or subsidiary corporation of such corporation issuing or assuming a stock option in a transaction to which section 424(a) applies.

(b) Employee stock purchase plan

For purposes of this part, the term "employee stock purchase plan" means a plan which meets the following requirements:

(1) the plan provides that options are to be granted only to employees of the employer corporation or of its parent or subsidiary corporation to purchase stock in any such corporation;

(2) such plan is approved by the stockholders of the granting corporation within 12 months before or after the date such plan is adopted;

(3) under the terms of the plan, no employee can be granted an option if such employee, immediately after the option is granted, owns stock possessing 5 percent or more of the total combined voting power or value of all classes of stock of the employer corporation or of its parent or subsidiary corporation. For purposes of this paragraph, the rules of section 424(d) shall apply in determining the stock ownership of an individual, and stock which the employee may purchase under outstanding options shall be treated as stock owned by the employee;

(4) under the terms of the plan, options are to be granted to all employees of any corporation whose employees are granted any of such options by reason of their employment by such corporation, except that there may be excluded—

(A) employees who have been employed less than 2 years,

(B) employees whose customary employment is 20 hours or less per week,

(C) employees whose customary employment is for not more than 5 months in any calendar year, and

(D) highly compensated employees (within the meaning of section 414[q]).

(5) under the terms of the plan, all employees granted such options shall have the same rights and privileges, except that the amount of stock which may be purchased by any employee under such option may bear a uniform relationship to the total compensation, or the basic or regular rate of compensation, of employees, and the plan may provide that no employee may purchase more than a maximum amount of stock fixed under the plan;

(6) under the terms of the plan, the option price is not less than the lesser of—

(A) an amount equal to 85 percent of the fair market value of the stock at the time such option is granted, or

(B) an amount which under the terms of the option may not be less than 85 percent of the fair market value of the stock at the time such option is exercised;

(7) under the terms of the plan, such option cannot be exercised after the expiration of—

(A) 5 years from the date such option is granted if, under the terms of such plan, the option price is to be not less than 85 percent of the fair market value of such stock at the time of the exercise of the option, or

(B) 27 months from the date such option is granted, if the option price is not determinable in the manner described in subparagraph (A)

(8) under the terms of the plan, no employee may be granted an option which permits his rights to purchase stock under all such plans of his employer corporation and its parent and subsidiary corporations to accrue at a rate which exceeds $25,000 of fair market value of such stock (determined at the time such option is granted) for each calendar year in which such option is outstanding at any time. For purposes of this paragraph—

(A) the right to purchase stock under an option accrues when the option (or any portion thereof) first becomes exercisable during the calendar year;

(B) the right to purchase stock under an option accrues at the rate provided in the option, but in no case may such rate exceed $25,000 of fair market value of such stock (determined at the time such option is granted) for any one calendar year; and

(C) a right to purchase stock which has accrued under one option granted pursuant to the plan may not be carried over to any other option; and

(9) under the terms of the plan, such option is not transferable by such individual otherwise than by will or the laws of descent and distribution, and is exercisable, during his lifetime, only by him.

For purposes of paragraphs (3) to (9), inclusive, where additional terms are contained in an offering made under a plan, such additional terms shall, with respect to options exercised under such offering, be treated as a part of the terms of such plan.

(c) Special rule where option price is between 85 percent and 100 percent of value of stock

If the option price of a share of stock acquired by an individual pursuant to a transfer to which subsection (a) applies was less than 100 percent of the fair market value of such share at the time such option was granted, then, in the event of any disposition of such share by him which meets the holding period requirements of subsection (a), or in the event of his death (whenever occurring) while owning such share, there shall be included as compensation (and not as gain upon the sale or exchange of a capital asset) in his gross income, for the taxable year in which falls the date of such disposition or for the taxable year closing with his death, whichever applies, an amount equal to the lesser of—

(1) the excess of the fair market value of the share at the time of such disposition or death over the amount paid for the share under the option, or

(2) the excess of the fair market value of the share at the time the option was granted over the option price. If the option price is not fixed or determinable at the time the option is granted, then for purposes of this subsection, the option price shall be determined as if the option were exercised at such time. In the case of the disposition of such share by the individual, the basis of the share in his hands at the time of such disposition shall be increased by an amount equal to the amount so includible in his gross income.

SECTION 424

Section 424.   Definitions and special rules

(a) Corporate reorganizations, liquidations, etc. For purposes of this part, the term "issuing or assuming a stock option in a transaction to which section 424(a) applies" means a substitution of a new option for the old option, or an assumption of the old option, by an employer corporation, or a parent or subsidiary of such corporation, by reason of a corporate merger, consolidation, acquisition of property or stock, separation, reorganization, or liquidation, if—

(1) the excess of the aggregate fair market value of the shares subject to the option immediately after the substitution or assumption over the aggregate option price of such shares is not more than the excess of the aggregate fair market value of all shares subject to the option immediately before such substitution or assumption over the aggregate option price of such shares, and

(2) the new option or the assumption of the old option does not give the employee additional benefits which he did not have under the old option. For purposes of this subsection, the parent-subsidiary relationship shall be determined at the time of any such transaction under this subsection.

(b) Acquisition of new stock

For purposes of this part, if stock is received by an individual in a distribution to which section 305, 354, 355, 356, or 1036 (or so much of section 1031 as relates to section 1036) applies, and such distribution was made with respect to stock transferred to him upon his exercise of the option, such stock shall be considered as having been transferred to him on his exercise of such option. A similar rule shall be applied in the case of a series of such distributions.

(c) Disposition

(1) In general

Except as provided in paragraphs (2), (3), and (4), for purposes of this part, the term "disposition" includes a sale, exchange, gift, or a transfer of legal title, but does not include—

(A) a transfer from a decedent to an estate or a transfer by request or inheritance;

(B) an exchange to which section 354, 355, 356, or 1036 (or so much of section 1031 as relates to section 1036) applies; or

(C) a mere pledge or hypothecation.

(2) Joint tenancy. The acquisition of a share of stock in the name of the employee and another jointly with the right of survivorship or a subsequent transfer of a share of stock into such joint ownership shall not be deemed a disposition, but a termination of such joint tenancy (except to the extent such employee acquires ownership of such stock) shall be treated as a disposition by him occurring at the time such joint tenancy is terminated.

(3) Special rule where incentive stock is acquired through use of other statutory option stock

(A) Nonrecognition sections not to apply If—

(i) there is a transfer of statutory option stock in connection with the exercise of any incentive stock option, and

(ii) the applicable holding period requirements (under section 422(a)(1) or 423(a)(1)) are not met before such transfer, then no section referred to in subparagraph (B) of paragraph (1) shall apply to such transfer.

(B) Statutory option stock

For purpose of subparagraph (A), the term "statutory option stock" means any stock acquired through the exercise of an incentive stock option or an option granted under an employee stock purchase plan.

(4) Transfers between spouses or incident to divorce

In the case of any transfer described in subsection (a) of section 1041—

(A) such transfer shall not be treated as a disposition for purposes of this part, and

(B) the same tax treatment under this part with respect to the transferred property shall apply to the transferee as would have applied to the transferor.

(d) Attribution of stock ownership

For purposes of this part, in applying the percentage limitations of sections 422(b)(6) and 423(b)(3)—

(1) the individual with respect to whom such limitation is being determined shall be considered as owning the stock owned, directly or indirectly, by or for his brothers and sisters (whether by the whole or half blood), spouse, ancestors, and lineal descendants; and

(2) stock owned, directly or indirectly, by or for a corporation, partnership, estate, or trust, shall be considered as being owned proportionately by or for its shareholders, partners, or beneficiaries.

(e) Parent corporation

For purposes of this part, the term "parent corporation" means any corporation (other than the employer corporation) in an unbroken chain of corporations ending with the employer corporation if, at the time of the granting of the option, each of the corporations other than the employer corporation owns stock possessing 50 percent or more of the total combined voting power of all classes of stock in one of the other corporations in such chain.

(f) Subsidiary corporation

For purposes of this part, the term "subsidiary corporation" means any corporation (other than the employer corporation) in an unbroken chain of corporations beginning with the employer corporation if, at the time of the granting of the option, each of the corporations other than the last corporation in the unbroken chain owns stock possessing 50 percent or more of the total combined voting power of all classes of stock in one of the other corporations in such chain.

(g) Special rule for applying subsections (e) and (f)

In applying subsections (e) and (f) for purposes of sections 422(a)(2) and 423(a)(2), there shall be substituted for the term "employer corporation" wherever it appears in subsections (e) and (f) the term "grantor corporation" or the term "corporation issuing or assuming a stock option in a transaction to which section 424(a) applies" as the case may be.

(h) Modification, extension, or renewal of option

(1) **In general**

For purposes of this part, if the terms of any option to purchase stock are modified, extended, or renewed, such modification, extension, or renewal shall be considered as the granting of a new option.

(2) **Special rule for section 423 options**

In the case of the transfer of stock pursuant to the exercise of an option to which section 423 applies and which has been so modified, extended, or renewed, the fair market value of such stock at the time of the granting of the option shall be considered as whichever of the following is the highest—

(A) the fair market value of such stock on the date of the original granting of the option,

(B) the fair market value of such stock on the date of the making of such modification, extension, or renewal, or

(C) the fair market value of such stock at the time of the making of any intervening modification, extension, or renewal.

(3) **Definition of modification**

The term "modification" means any change in the terms of the option which gives the employee additional benefits under the option, but such term shall not include a change in the terms of the option—

(A) attributable to the issuance or assumption of an option under subsection (a);

(B) to permit the option to qualify under section 423(b)(9); or

(C) in the case of an option not immediately exercisable in full, to accelerate the time at which the option may be exercised.

(i) Stockholder approval

For purposes of this part, if the grant of an option is subject to approval by stockholders, the date of grant of the option shall be determined as if the option had not been subject to such approval.

(j) Cross references

For provisions requiring the reporting of certain acts with respect to a qualified stock option, an incentive stock option, options granted under employer stock purchase plans, or a restricted stock option, see section 6039.

APPENDIX 7

INTERNAL REVENUE SERVICE (I.R.S.) PRIVATE LETTER RULING ISSUE: JULY 19, 1996 APRIL 24, 1996

Section 83—Property Transferred in Connection With Performance of Services

   83.00-00 Property Transferred in Connection With Performance of Services

   83.11-00 Nonqualified Stock Options

Section 421—Stock Options—General Rules

   421.00-00 Stock Options—General Rules

   421.02-00 Disqualifying Dispositions

Section 422—Qualified Stock Options

   422.00-00 Qualified Stock Options

Section 424—Restricted Stock Options

   424.00-00 Restricted Stock Options

   424.01-00 Holding Period

Section 1036—Stock for Stock of Same Corporation (Recognition v. Nonrecognition)

   1036.00-00 Stock for Stock of Same Corporation (Recognition v. Nonrecognition)

TR-31-2741-95 / CC:EBEO:4

Legend:

Company =

Dear ***

This is in response to a letter dated December 5, 1995, submitted on behalf of the Company, requesting rulings concerning certain stock option plans maintained by the Company and certain of its subsidiaries.

The Company is a corporation that currently maintains three stock option plans (collectively referred to as the "Plans"). Options granted under the Plans may be either incentive stock options ("ISOs") or nonqualified stock options ("NQSOs"). No option granted under the Plans is assignable or transferrable, except by will or the laws of descent and distribution. No option granted under the Plans is exercisable during an option holder's lifetime except by the option holder.

The Plans expressly provide that options may be exercised, in whole or in part, by the surrender (or delivery) to the Company of previously acquired shares of its common stock. The Company, through the Compensation Committee of its Board of Directors, has officially interpreted the Plans to allow employees to exercise options granted under the Plans by constructively surrendering previously acquired Company stock in payment for the shares to be received under the option exercise. Consistent with this interpretation, the Company proposes to allow employees, in connection with the exercise of an option that permits payment with shares of Company stock, to make a constructive exchange of Company shares already owned ("Payment Shares"), in lieu of actually tendering such Company stock to the Company. If the Payment Shares are held by a registered securities broker for the optionee in "street name," the optionee would provide the Company with a notarized statement attesting to the number of shares owned that are intended to serve as Payment Shares. If the Company stock certificates are actually held by the optionee, he would provide the Company with their certificate numbers. Upon receipt of a notarized statement regarding ownership of the Payment Shares, or upon confirmation of ownership of the Payment Shares by reference to Company records, the Company would treat the Payment Shares as being constructively exchanged, and therefore issue to the employee a certificate for a net number of shares: the number of shares subject to the option exercise less the number of Payment Shares.

Section 83(a) of the Internal Revenue Code generally provides that if, in connection with the performance of services, property is transferred to any person other than the person for whom the services were performed, the excess of the fair market value of the property over the amount paid for the property is included in the service provider's gross income in the first taxable year in which the rights of the service provider in the property are transferable or are not subject to a substantial risk of forfeiture.

Pursuant to section 83(e) of the Code and section 1.83-7(a) of the Income Tax Regulations, an individual only recognizes income under section 83(a), with respect to an option that does not have a readily ascertainable fair market value, upon the transfer of stock at the time the option is exercised.

Section 1.83-7(b) of the regulations provides that an option does not have a readily ascertainable fair market value if it is not traded on an established market and it is not transferable.

Section 421(a) of the Code provides that, if an individual receives stock by exercising an ISO and the requirements of Section 422(a) are met, the individual will not recognize any income at the time of the transfer.

Section 421(b) of the Code provides that a "disqualifying disposition" occurs when an individual "disposes" of stock received pursuant to an ISO before meeting the holding period requirements of section 422(a) and that the disposition results in the individual's recognizing compensation income attributable to the disposition.

Section 1.422A-1(b)(3), Example (3) of the proposed regulations states that, upon a disqualifying disposition, an individual recognizes as ordinary income the difference between the exercise price of the option and the fair market value of the acquired stock when the option was exercised and recognizes as capital gain the difference between the fair market value of the acquired stock when the option was exercised and the amount realized upon the disqualifying disposition.

To satisfy the holding period requirements of section 422(a) of the Code, an optionee cannot dispose of stock received pursuant to an ISO within the two-year period after the ISO is granted or within the one-year period following the date the stock is transferred to the optionee.

Section 422(c)(4) of the Code provides that an employee may pay for stock pursuant to an ISO with stock of the corporation granting the option.

Section 1.422A-2(i)(1)(iii)(A) and (B) of the proposed regulations state, in part, that, if an individual exercises an ISO solely with previously acquired stock and section 1036(a) of the Code applies, the individual's basis in the acquired shares, up to the number of exchanged shares, will be equal to the individual's basis in the exchanged shares, and, except for purposes of section 422(a)(1), the holding period of such stock will be determined under section 1223, whereas the individual's basis in acquired shares exceeding the number of exchanged shares will be zero, and the holding period of such stock will begin on the date of the transfer.

Section 424(c)(1) of the Code defines a disposition for purposes of sections 421–424 as a "sale, exchange, gift, or transfer of legal title." Section 424(c)(1)(B) excludes from this definition a stock for stock exchange to which section 1036(a) applies.

Section 424(c)(3) of the Code provides that the nonrecognition rules of Section 1036(a) do not apply to a "transfer" of stock that was previously acquired through the exercise of an ISO in connection with the exercise of any ISO if the previously acquired stock has not met the holding period requirements of section 422(a)(1).

Section 424(h) of the Code provides that a "modification" of the terms of an ISO is considered the granting of a new option and defines "modification" as any change in the terms of an ISO that gives the employee additional benefits under the ISO.

Section 1.425-1(e)(5)(i) of the proposed regulations explains that a modification includes a change that provides more favorable terms for payment for the stock purchased under the ISO, such as the right to tender previously acquired stock.

Section 1012 of the Code provides that property has a basis equal to its cost.

Section 1031(d) of the Code provides that the basis of stock received in a stock for stock exchange to which section 1036(a) applies is the same as the basis of the stock exchanged.

Section 1036(a) of the Code provides that no gain or loss is recognized when common stock of a corporation is exchanged for common stock of that same corporation.

Section 1223(1) of the Code provides that the capital asset holding period of stock acquired in exchange for stock includes the period for which the exchanged stock was held, if the acquired stock has the same basis as the exchanged stock.

Rev. Rul. 80-244, 1980-2 C.B. 234, concludes that, when stock acquired pursuant to the exercise of a qualified stock option is used (to the extent of its fair market value) to pay the full exercise price of a nonqualified stock option at a point in time when the stock acquired pursuant to the exercise of the qualified option had not met the holding period requirements, (i) the basis in the shares of stock received on the exercise of the nonqualified stock option that are equal in number to the shares of stock used as payment is the same as the basis in the stock used as payment, (ii) a "disposition" of the stock acquired pursuant to the exercise of the qualified options does not occur and (iii) the fair market value of any additional shares received will be includible in income as compensation. The adjusted basis of those shares would then be the amount included in income. Also see section 1.422A-2(i)(4), example 4, of the proposed regulations.

In this case, an option holder will be permitted to pay the option exercise price by a certification procedure that eliminates the need to physically deliver previously acquired shares to the Company. Under the certification procedure, an option holder will provide the Company with either a notarized statement attesting to the number of shares owned that are intended as Payment Shares, or the certificate numbers of the Payment Shares.

Based upon the information submitted, we conclude that the Company's certification procedure, which eliminates the need to physically deliver Payment Shares to the Company, will be deemed a constructive delivery of such shares for Federal income tax purposes, and accordingly provide the following rulings:

(1) An optionee who constructively pays the exercise price of an ISO with Payment Shares that (i) were previously acquired through the exercise of an ISO and that have satisfied the holding requirements of Section 422(a) of the Code ("Mature ISO Stock") or (ii) that were acquired by some other means such as through the exercise of an NQSO ("NQSO Stock") or purchased on the open market would receive the same tax treatment as if the optionee had physically surrendered shares that had satisfied the holding period, if applicable, specifically:

  (a) The optionee will not recognize income upon the exercise of the ISO. Sections 421(a)(1), 422(c)(4)(A), 424(c)(1)(B), 424(c)(3). Furthermore, the optionee will not recognize capital gain or loss on the constructive surrender of previously owned shares. See section 1036(a).

  (b) The optionee will have a carryover basis with respect to those shares of stock deemed to be received that are equal in number to the Payment Shares. The basis in any stock actually received will be the cash, if any, paid on the transfer. Sections 1012 and 1031(d).

(c) For purposes of section 1223(1), the optionee will have a carryover holding period with respect to those shares of stock deemed to be received that are equal in number to the Payment Shares, whereas the holding period of any additional shares of stock actually received will begin on the date that the new ISO is exercised. For purposes of section 422(a)(1), the holding period of all shares, including those shares deemed to be received and those actually received, will begin on the date the new ISO is exercised.

(2) An optionee who constructively pays the exercise price of an ISO with Payment Shares that were previously acquired through the exercise of an ISO but that have not satisfied the holding requirements of Section 422(a) of the Code ("Immature ISO Stock") would receive the same tax treatment as if the optionee had physically surrendered shares that had not satisfied the holding period, specifically:

(a) The constructive surrender of the Payment Shares is a disqualified disposition of those shares that will result in the recognition of compensation income under the rules of section 421(b) and 422(c)(2). See also section 424(c)(3). Any additional appreciation in the value of the stock that is not taxed as compensation income under the disqualified disposition rules is subject to the nonrecognition rules of section 1036.

(b) The basis of the shares deemed to be received that are equal in number to the Payment Shares will be the basis of the Payment Shares increased by any reported compensation income as a result of the disqualified disposition. Any additional shares actually received will have a basis equal to the amount of cash paid, if any, to exercise the new ISO. Sections 424(c)(3) and 1012.

(c) The optionee will not recognize income upon receiving the new shares of stock as a result of the exercise of the ISO. Section 422(c)(4)(A).

(d) For purposes of section 1223(1), the optionee will have a carryover holding period with respect to those shares of stock deemed to be received that are equal in number to the Payment Shares, whereas the holding period of any additional shares of stock received will begin on the date that the new ISO is exercised. For purposes of section 422(a)(1), the holding period of all shares, including those shares deemed to be received and those actually received, will begin on the date the new ISO is exercised.

(3) An optionee who constructively pays the exercise price of an NQSO with Payment Shares that are Mature ISO Stock, Immature ISO Stock, NQSO Stock, or stock that was purchased on the open market would receive the same tax treatment as if the optionee had physically surrendered the shares, specifically:

(a) The optionee will recognize as compensation income the fair market value of the shares that exceed the number Payment Shares used to exercise the NQSO, less cash, if any, paid on the transfer. Section 83 and section 1.83-7 of the regulations;

(b) The optionee will not recognize income upon the constructive exchange of the Payment Shares for those shares of stock received that are equal in number to the Payment Shares. Section 1036(a), example 4 of section 1.422A- 2(i)(4) of the proposed regulations, and Rev. Rul. 80-244;

(c) The optionee will have a carryover basis with respect to those shares of stock received that are equal in number to the Payment Shares and a basis in any additional stock equal to the difference between the fair market value of the shares received pursuant to the NQSO and the exercise price of the NQSO, plus any cash actually paid. Sections 1012 and 1031(d), Rev. Rul. 80-244, Ruling 2; and

(d) The optionee will have a carryover holding period with respect to those shares of stock received that are equal in number to the Payment Shares, whereas the holding period of any additional shares of stock received will begin on the date that the NQSO is exercised. Section 1223(1).

(4) The Company's interpretation of the Plans to permit an optionee to use the certification procedure outlined above to exercise an ISO through constructive surrender of Payment Shares is not a "modification, extension, or renewal" of the ISO. Section 424(h).

(5) Neither the Code nor applicable regulations require the Company to amend the Plans before instituting the certification procedure described above. Section 1.422A-2(b)(1) of the proposed regulations.

This ruling is directed only to the taxpayer who requested it. Section 6110(j)(3) of the Code provides that it may not be used or cited as precedent. No opinion is expressed as to the Federal tax consequences of the above transaction under any other provision of the Code.

Temporary or final regulations pertaining to one or more of the issues addressed in this ruling have not been adopted. Therefore, this ruling will be modified or revoked by adoption of temporary or final regulations to the extent that the regulations are inconsistent with any conclusion in the ruling. However, when the criteria in section 11.05 of Rev. Proc. 96-1, 1996-1 I.R.B. 8, are satisfied, a ruling is not revoked or modified retroactively, except in rare or unusual circumstances.

Sincerely yours,

CHARLES T. DELIEE
Assistant Chief, Branch 4
Office of the Associate Chief Counsel
(Employee Benefits and Exempt Organizations)

Enclosure: Copy for section 6110 purposes

This document may not be used or cited as precedent. Section 6110(j)(3) of the Internal Revenue Code.

PLR 9629,028, 1996 WL 404756 (IRS PLR)

APPENDIX 8

ALL PROFESSIONAL PERSONNEL ACCOUNTING FOR CERTAIN TRANSACTIONS INVOLVING STOCK COMPENSATION

The FASB has released Interpretation 44, *Accounting for Certain Transactions Involving Stock Compensation,* which addresses—in question-and-answer form—certain practice issues related to APB 25, *Accounting for Stock Issued to Employees.* The Interpretation applies only to companies that have chosen not to adopt SFAS 123, *Accounting for Stock-Based Compensation,* for transactions with employees.

Our January 2000 *Financial Reporting Letter,* "Year in Review—Significant 1999 Financial Reporting Developments," discussed the rules as they had been proposed earlier in the exposure process. However, some of the final rules are substantially different, as a result of further FASB deliberations.

The sections that follow provide a summary of certain of the final rules, while the appendix lists all of the issues raised in the Interpretation, along with their related paragraph numbers, for ease of reference.

This *Assurance Comments* is more detailed than usual because issues involving stock-based compensation affect a large number of our clients and have been among the most common subjects for internal consultations. However, this *Assurance Comments* does not cover every issue in the new Interpretation and, therefore, is not a substitute for a thorough reading of the Interpretation.

Given the complexity of the accounting issues and the detailed record-keeping for stock options issued to employees, clients may wish to consider purchasing specially developed computer software, available from such companies as E-Trade Business Solutions and Corporate Management Solutions. If we tell the client about such software, we need to be clear that we are neither endorsing it nor vouching for any claims that might be made by the developer.

DEFINITION OF EMPLOYEE

The common law definition of employee should generally be used for purposes of applying APB 25. Therefore, independent contractors would not qualify.

OPTIONS GRANTED TO DIRECTORS

An exception to the common law employee definition has been made for options or awards granted to a nonemployee member of the board of directors for services provided as a director if the director (a) was elected by the shareholders or (b) was appointed to a position on the board that will be filled by a shareholder election when the existing term for that position expires.

However, SFAS 123 continues to apply to options or awards granted to individuals for advisory or consulting services in a nonelected capacity or to nonemployee directors for services outside their role as a director, such as legal advice, investment banking advice, or loan guarantees. Accordingly, the fair value of such options or awards should initially be charged to deferred compensation cost (assuming a vesting requirement) with a corresponding credit to stockholders' equity. The deferred compensation cost would then be amortized to earnings, as compensation expense, over the vesting period.

MODIFICATIONS TO A FIXED STOCK OPTION OR AWARD

There are accounting consequences for a modification to a fixed stock option or award that:

> renews or extends the award's life (e.g., acceleration of vesting) or provides for a renewal or extension if a specified future separation from employment (e.g., death or disability) occurs, reduces the award's exercise price (commonly called "repricing") or increases the number of shares to be issued under an award, including the addition of a feature that provides for a new award to be granted automatically when an existing award is exercised if specified conditions are met (commonly called a reload feature).

RENEWALS OR EXTENSIONS OF THE AWARD'S LIFE

A modification that renews or extends the award's life results in a new measurement of compensation cost as if the award were newly granted. More specifically:

> A modification, including a modification that depends on a specified *future* separation from employment, that extends the award's maximum contractual life results in a new measurement of compensation cost at the modification date. For any employee who could benefit from the modification, any intrinsic value at the modification date that exceeds the amount measured at the original measurement date is reported as compensation cost either over the remaining future service period if the award is unvested, or immediately if the award is vested.

Example Involving Modification That Extends the Maximum Contractual Life

On January 1, 2004, Company W grants 100 fixed stock options each to Employee A and Employee B. The options have an exercise price equal to the market price at the grant date and a 10-year life. Under the original terms of the plan, an employee who retires after reaching age 65 has the lesser of 90 days or the remaining period of the 10-year life to exercise vested options.

On January 1, 2007, Company W modifies the awards to provide that, upon retirement after age 65, a retiree will have 2 years to exercise vested options, not limited by the original 10-year option life. At the modification date, the intrinsic value is $15 per option. As a result of the modification, the maximum contractual life of the option has been extended beyond 10 years for any employee eligible for retirement at age 65 within the original 10-year option life.

At January 1, 2007, Employee A is 30 years old and Employee B is 61 years old. The effects of the modification on each employee's option award are as follows:

Employee A: No effect, because Employee A is not eligible for retirement (as defined in the option agreement) within the remaining period of the 10-year option life and, accordingly, Employee A cannot benefit from the modification.

Employee B: The maximum contractual life of Employee B's options has been extended to 12 years (if Employee B retires at the end of the original 10-year option life) because Employee B will be eligible to retire within the remaining life of the options and receive the extended exercise period. Regardless of when in the future Employee B retires, Company W must measure and recognize (over any future vesting period, or immediately if the options are vested) compensation cost of $1,500, representing the additional intrinsic value of the options at the modification date.

A modification that increases the award's life upon separation from employment, but not beyond the original maximum contractual life, results in an extension of that award at the date of separation. In this case,

- the award's intrinsic value is measured at the modification date and

- any intrinsic value at that date that exceeds the amount measured at the original measurement date is reported as compensation cost upon the occurrence of the separation event, unless the award vests and is exercised before the separation event.

Example Involving Modification That Extends the Life, But Not Beyond the Original Maximum Contractual Life

Assume the same facts as in the preceding example, except that on January 1, 2007, Company W modifies the awards to provide that an employee who retires after reaching age 65 will have the lesser of 2 years or the remaining period of the 10-year option life to exercise vested awards.

In this case, the modification does not extend the award's maximum contractual life beyond 10 years. However, the modification extends the life of any award at the date an employee retires and obtains, as a result of the modification, a remaining exercise period for that award in excess of the 90 days provided in the original terms of the award. Therefore, Company W must measure additional compensation cost equal to the intrinsic value of the modified option awards held by Employee B at the modification date and will recognize that compensation cost if Employee B retires and receives, as a result of the modification, a period in excess of 90 days to exercise the awards. (Assuming that Company W is unable to estimate whether Employee B will retire and receive an extension of the award's life as a result of the modification, no estimate of additional compensation cost would be recognized prior to Employee B's retirement.)

A modification that accelerates an award's vesting or provides for acceleration if certain conditions are met effectively results in that award's renewal if the modification enables an employee to vest in an award that, under the original terms, would have expired. In this case, the award's intrinsic value is measured at the modification date and any intrinsic value at that date that exceeds the amount measured at the original measurement date is recognized as compensation cost if, had it not been for the acceleration, the award would have expired.

Example Involving Modification That Accelerates Vesting

Company R grants 100 fixed stock options to each of its 200 employees. Each option has an exercise price equal to the stock's quoted market price at the date of grant. The options "cliff vest" at the end of five years. Two years after the grant date, Company R modifies the awards to immediately vest the options. At the modification date, each option has an intrinsic value of $40. Based on historical employee turnover rates and Company R's best estimate of future employee separation, Company R estimates that 70 employees will terminate employment before the original vesting date.

At the modification date, Company R recognizes, as compensation cost, the intrinsic value measured at the modification date ($40) in excess of the original intrinsic value ($0) for the estimated number of awards that, had it not been for the modification, would have expired unexercisable. Compensation cost is recognized immediately as future vesting has been eliminated. Accordingly, $280,000 of compensation cost is recognized at the modification date based on Company R's estimate of employee turnover in the next 3 years (70 employees, 100 options per employee with incremental intrinsic value of $40 each).

The estimate of $280,000 will require adjustment in future periods for actual experience. For example, assume 1 year after the modification, 50 employees with modified awards have terminated employment and Company R now estimates that an additional 50 employees will terminate in the next 2 years (i.e., before the original 5-year cliff vesting date). Company R recognizes an additional $120,000 of compensation cost as an adjustment to the earlier estimate (30 employees, 100 options per employee with an incremental intrinsic value of $40 each).

REDUCTIONS IN THE EXERCISE PRICE

If a modification directly or indirectly reduces an award's exercise price, the award is accounted for as variable from the modification date until the date the award is exercised, is forfeited, or expires unexercised.

For this purpose, exercise price is considered reduced if the fair value of the consideration required to be remitted by the grantee upon exercise is less than, or potentially less than, the fair value of the consideration required to be remitted under the award's original terms. Following are examples in which the exercise price is considered reduced:

Grantor provides grantee with a cash bonus arrangement that vests (is paid) only if the option award is exercised.

Grantor allows the grantee to exercise the option award with a full-recourse note that does not bear a market interest rate.

Grantor agrees to reduce the exercise price if a certain earnings target or stock price is achieved in the future.

Grantor cancels or settles for cash or other consideration an outstanding option award, while also granting a replacement award at a lower exercise price, either before or after the cancellation (settlement). Variable accounting, as discussed below, applies if such a replacement award is granted within the following periods:

The period prior to the date of cancellation (settlement) that is the shorter of (1) six months or (2) the period from grant date of the canceled (settled) option.

The period ending six months after the cancellation (settlement) date.

Because of the onerous effect of variable accounting, few companies are expected to reprice options in a simple manner, unless there is a substantial business reason for doing so (e.g. retaining key employees). However, a company may avoid variable accounting when it reprices options if it:

Cancels existing stock options and issues new ones at least six months and one day later with an exercise price equal to the stock's fair/market value on the date the new award is issued or makes a commitment to the employee to issue a certain number of options at that later date. (Variable accounting would be required, however, if the employer agrees to protect the employee against any increases in the stock's fair/market value between the dates of cancellation and issuance of new options, regardless of the length of time between those two dates.)

Issues new stock options at the then current market price, leaving the existing out-of-the-money stock options outstanding and, then, cancels the old stock options at least six months and a day later. (Variable accounting would be required, however, if [a] the employees agree to surrender their existing stock options when the new stock options are granted or [b] the employer, within six months of issuing the new options, increases the old option's exercise price or takes any other actions that make it likely that the employees would be able to exercise the old options.)

Cancels existing stock options and issues restricted stock (effectively an award having a zero exercise price, which makes future reductions in exercise price impossible). Of course, there would be a fixed compensation charge for the value of the restricted stock.

As noted earlier, if any options were granted during the "look back" period with exercise prices lower than those of cancelled options, variable accounting is required. If, however, the number of options granted within the "look back" period exceeds the number of options cancelled, variable award accounting would not apply to the excess.

Example Involving Modification to Reduce Exercise Price

Company S grants fixed stock options to its employees. The exercise price of each option equals the quoted market price of the stock on the grant date. All options "cliff vest" at the end of 4 years and have a maximum life of 10 years. Information about the stock options granted to Employee A on January 1, 2000, follows:

Options granted	1,000
Stock price	$20 per share
Exercise price	$20 per option

On January 1, 2002, the quoted market price of Company S's stock has decreased to $15 per share. Company S modifies the award held by Employee A to reduce the award's exercise price to $15 per option. Variable accounting is required for the 1,000 options from January 1, 2002 (the date of the modification), until the date the options are exercised, are forfeited, or expire unexercised.

INCREASE IN THE NUMBER OF SHARES TO BE ISSUED

If a modification increases the number of shares to be issued, including the addition of a reload feature, the award is accounted for as variable from the modification date to the date the award is exercised, is forfeited, or expires unexercised.

RECOGNITION AND MEASUREMENT OF COMPENSATION COST

Compensation cost is recognized and measured as follows:

If a fixed stock option or award is canceled or modified such that a new measurement of compensation cost or variable accounting is required, total compensation cost is measured as the sum of

- any intrinsic value of the award at the original measurement date and

- the amount by which the intrinsic value of the modified (or variable) award exceeds the lesser of (1) the intrinsic value of the award at the original measurement date or (2) the intrinsic value immediately prior to the modification.

The total compensation cost is reported over the remaining vesting (service) period, unless the award is fully vested at the modification date, in which case the total compensation cost is reported immediately. Compensation cost for an unvested award that is forfeited because an employee failed to fulfill an obligation to exercise the award is reduced to zero, by decreasing compensation cost, in the period of the forfeiture.

Additional compensation, measured as of the modification date, is reported for all awards that were modified to accelerate vesting or extend the award's life upon a specified future separation from employment (but not beyond the award's original maximum contractual life). Estimates and adjustments of such estimates in subsequent periods may be required.

If a modification (including a modification through a cancellation and a replacement grant) requires variable accounting for the modified (replacement) award, compensation cost should be adjusted for changes in the intrinsic value of the modified (replacement) award in subsequent periods until that award is exercised, is forfeited, or expires unexercised. However, compensation cost should not be adjusted below intrinsic value of the modified stock option or award at the original measurement date, unless the award is forfeited because the employee fails to fulfill an obligation.

If cash is paid to an employee to settle an outstanding stock option, to settle an earlier grant of a stock award within six months after vesting, or to repurchase shares within six months after an option is exercised or the shares are issued, total compensation cost is measured as the sum of

- any intrinsic value of the stock option or award at the original measurement date and

- the amount of cash paid to the employee (reduced by any amount paid by the employee to acquire the shares) that exceeds the lesser of (1) the intrinsic value of the award at the original measurement date or (2) the intrinsic value immediately prior to the cash settlement.

Example Involving Cash Settlement

Company M grants fixed stock options to employees on January 1, 2003. Relevant information on those awards is as follows:

Options granted:	10,000
Expiration:	10 years from grant date
Vesting:	100 percent at the end of 20X6 (4-year cliff vesting)
Stock price at grant date:	$10
Option exercise price:	$10

The quoted market price per share of Company M's stock at December 31 of subsequent years is:

2003 = $14; 2004 = $6; 2005 = $20; 2006 = $10; 2007 = $5; and 2008 = $18

Company M settles the original January 1, 2003 grant of options for cash at December 31, 2004. Company M pays $2 per option and recognizes additional compensation cost for the cash settlement. As the original intrinsic value of the option awards was zero, $2 of compensation cost per option ($20,000) is recognized at the date of the cash settlement.

SHARE REPURCHASE FEATURES

The accounting for share repurchase features (e.g., a put, a call or a right of first refusal) generally depends on whether the company is publicly held or nonpublic.

Publicly Held Companies

The accounting by publicly held companies is as follows:

- Except for shares expected to be repurchased at fair value on option exercise or share issuance only to meet tax withholding requirements, variable accounting applies to a stock option or award with a share repurchase feature in the following circumstances:

  - the shares are expected to be repurchased within six months after the option is exercised or the shares are issued ("six-month period");

  - the repurchase feature gives the employee the right to sell the shares back to the company and the right can be exercised within the six-month period; or

  - the repurchase feature gives the employee the right to sell the shares back to the company (after the option is exercised or shares are issued) for a premium that is not fixed and determinable over the then-current stock price, even if the shares cannot be sold back within the six-month period.

- If a share repurchase feature gives the employee the right to sell the shares back to the company for a fixed-dollar amount over the stock price, but not within the six-month period, the premium is recognized as additional compensation cost over the vesting period.

- A subsequent repurchase of shares by the company beyond the six-month period is accounted for as treasury stock, rather than as part of the original option or award.

- A subsequent repurchase of shares by the company within the six-month period that had not been expected by the company is accounted for as a cash settlement of an earlier grant, which is discussed in the immediately preceding section.

NONPUBLIC COMPANIES

Nonpublic companies are *not* required to apply variable accounting for a stock option or award with the following share repurchase features:

- The stated share repurchase price equals the fair value of the shares at the date of repurchase, the employee cannot require the company to repurchase the shares within six months of option exercise or share issuance, and the shares are not expected to be repurchased within six months after exercise or share issuance.

- The stated share repurchase price is other than the fair value of the shares at the date of repurchase (e.g., under a book value plan), but the employee has made a substantial investment and must bear risks and rewards normally associated with share ownership for a reasonable period (at least six months).

- Shares expected to be repurchased are only to meet tax withholding requirements.

For purposes of an award that contains a repurchase feature at other than fair value, an employee is considered to have made a substantial investment when the employee invests (in a form other than services rendered to the company) an amount equal to 100 percent of the stated share repurchase price calculated at the grant date. Accordingly, if the award is an option, a substantial investment cannot exist before that option is exercised, and compensation cost is recognized (as the award is variable) for any intrinsic value of the option from the grant date to the date a substantial investment has been made.

BUSINESS COMBINATIONS

There are no accounting consequences for an exchange of stock options in a business combination accounted for under the pooling-of-interests method, provided: (1) the aggregate intrinsic value of the options immediately after the exchange is not greater than the intrinsic value immediately before the exchange and (2) the ratio of the exercise price per option to the market value per share is not reduced.

In a purchase business combination, the fair value of options granted by the acquirer in exchange for outstanding options of the target company should be included as part of the consideration paid to acquire the target company. However, to the extent that service is required after the consummation date to vest in the awards, a portion of the intrinsic value of the unvested awards should be (1) deducted from the fair value of the awards included in the purchase price, (2) allocated to unearned compensation, and (3) recognized as compensation cost over the remaining future vesting (service) period.

Example Involving Exchange of Options in a Purchase Business Combination

On July 1, 2006, Company A acquires Company B in a purchase business combination in which Company A exchanges 10,000 options with a fair value of $100,000 for 5,000 options held by the employees of Company B. The options previously held by Company B employees had been granted on June 30, 2002, and provided for "cliff vesting" on June 30, 2007. Company A options granted in the exchange vest according to the vesting schedule of the previous Company B options (cliff vest on June 30, 2007). The intrinsic value of the Company A options granted at the date of the exchange is $4 per option.

The $100,000 fair value of the options granted in the exchange is part of the purchase price paid for Company B. However, $8,000 is allocated to unearned compensation and is deducted from the cost of Company B in allocating the purchase price to the other assets acquired. The unearned compensation ($8,000) is determined as the total intrinsic value of the granted awards of $40,000 ($4 × 10,000 options) multiplied by the fraction (1/5) that is the remaining vesting period over the total vesting period.

GRANT DATE

Awards made under a plan that is subject to shareholder approval should not be deemed granted until that approval is obtained, unless the approval is essentially a formality (e.g., if management and the members of the board of directors control enough votes to approve the plan).

DEFERRED TAX ASSETS

Deferred tax assets recognized for a temporary difference related to a stock option or award accounted for under APB 25 should not be adjusted for a subsequent decline in the stock price.

Such deferred tax assets should be determined by reference to the compensation expense recognized for financial reporting rather than to the expected future tax deduction (which would be estimated using the current intrinsic value of the award). A valuation allowance to reduce the carrying amount of those deferred tax assets would be established only if the company expects future taxable income to be insufficient to recover the deferred tax assets in the periods in which the deduction would otherwise be recognized for tax purposes.

EFFECTIVE DATE AND TRANSITION

The new rules are effective July 1, 2000 and, except as noted in the following two paragraphs, are to be applied prospectively to new awards, exchanges of awards in a business combination, modifications to existing awards and changes in grantee status that occur on or after that date. While the Interpretation is silent on whether it may be adopted early, we have been informed by an FASB staff member that early adoption is not permitted.

The new rules for determining who meets the definition of an employee and for modifications to directly or indirectly reduce an award's exercise price apply to new awards or modifications after December 15, 1998. The new rules for modifications of existing awards to add a reload option feature apply to modifications after January 12, 2000. If any of these events occur before July 1, 2000, no adjustments are to be made to financial statements for periods before that date. Additional compensation cost measured on initial application that is attributable to periods before July 1, 2000 should not be recognized.

In addition, the initial application of the new rules for existing awards to the nonemployee members of a company's board of directors, if previously accounted for as awards to nonemployees under SFAS 123, should be reported as a cumulative effect of a change in accounting principle, as described in APB 20, Accounting Changes.

Example Involving Change in Accounting for Existing Awards to Nonemployee Directors

On January 1, 1998, Company A, a calendar-year, publicly held company, issued stock options with a fair value of $400,000 to non-employee members of its board of directors. The options are earned ratably over 4 years and are exercisable on December 31, 2001. The options were accounted for as awards to nonemployees under SFAS 123. The exercise price equaled the market price at the date of grant and, accordingly, no compensation expense would have been recognized under APB 25. Company A adopts Interpretation 44 on its effective date (July 1, 2000). The following summarize the reporting requirements under SFAS 3, Reporting Accounting Changes in Interim Financial Statements. For purposes of this example, tax effects have been ignored.

a. This is a cumulative effect type accounting change that is being made in other than the first interim period of Company A's fiscal year. Accordingly, the cumulative effect of the change is not included in net income for the quarter ending September 30, 2000. Instead, the change is made as of the first day of Company A's fiscal year (January 1, 2000) and its previously reported net income for the first and second quarters of 2000 is restated in the quarterly data footnote in Form 10-K or, for small business issuers, the next time Form 10-Q is filed for those periods. However, the originally filed Forms 10-Q need not be amended. The cumulative effect of the change as of January 1, 2000 is $200,000, which is the amount of compensation expense that had been previously recognized for 1998 and 1999 under SFAS 123.

b. The restated net income for the first and second quarters of 2000 would reflect the effects of reversing $25,000 per quarter of compensation expense (i.e., amortization of deferred compensation) that had been previously recognized under SFAS 123.

c. The following disclosures would be required in Company A's interim financial statements:

    –   In financial reports for the third quarter, disclose the nature of and justification for the change.

- In financial reports for the third quarter, disclose the effect of the change on income from continuing operations, net income, and related per share amounts for the quarter (and year-to-date). In addition, since the change is made in other than the first quarter, financial reports for the third quarter should also disclose (i) the effect of the change on income from continuing operations, net income, and related per share amounts for each pre-change interim period of 2000 and (ii) income from continuing operations, net income, and related per share amounts for each prechange interim period as restated.

- In financial reports for the third quarter, disclose income from continuing operations, net income, and related per share amounts computed on a pro forma basis for that quarter (and year-to-date) and the comparable periods of the prior years presented. In all cases, the pro forma amounts are to be computed and presented in conformity with the applicable paragraphs of APB 20 (i.e., paragraphs 19, 21, 22, and 25) as if the new principle had been applied during all periods.

- In financial reports for a subsequent (post-change) interim period of Company A's current fiscal year, disclose the effect of the change on income from continuing operations, net income, and related per share amounts for that post-change interim period.

See appendix A of SFAS 3 for an illustrative footnote for an accounting change.

Additionally, the following examples illustrate how the Interpretation applies to certain events that occur after December 15, 1998 but before the July 1, 2000 effective date.

Example Involving Modification That Reduces the Exercise Price on December 15, 1998

On December 15, 1998, an employee's fixed stock option award is modified to reduce the exercise price to the then-current stock price. Interpretation 44 only applies to modifications to reduce the exercise price of fixed option awards that occur after December 15, 1998 (on or after December 16, 1998). Because the modification was made before December 16, 1998, the accounting for the modified option award is not covered by this Interpretation.

Example Involving Modification to Reduce the Exercise Price After December 15, 1998, and Award Is Exercised Before July 1, 2000

On December 16, 1998, a vested fixed stock option award held by an employee is modified to reduce the exercise price to the then-current stock price of $10. Before July 1, 2000, the stock price increases to $50 and the employee exercises the award. Interpretation 44 applies to modifications to reduce the exercise price of fixed stock option awards that are made after December 15, 1998, but only on a prospective basis from the July 1, 2000 effective date. Because the option award was exercised before that effective date, there is no accounting for the modified option award under the Interpretation.

Example Involving Modification to Reduce the Exercise Price After December 15, 1998, and the Award Is *Not* Exercised Prior to July 1, 2000

On December 16, 1998, a vested fixed stock option award held by an employee is modified to reduce the exercise price to the then-current stock price of $10. The stock price at July 1, 2000 (the Interpretation's effective date), is $25. Because the option was modified to reduce its exercise price after December 15, 1998, it is covered by this Interpretation. Accordingly, commencing July 1, 2000, the option award is accounted for as variable until the date the award is exercised, is forfeited, or expires unexercised. Compensation cost is recognized after July 1, 2000, only to the extent that the stock price exceeds the stock price on July 1, 2000 ($25). No compensation cost is recognized for the $15 intrinsic value of the award at July 1, 2000. Correspondingly, no credit (reversal of compensation cost) would be recognized for a subsequent decrease in the stock price below $25. However, because the option is vested, any increase in the stock price above $25 after July 1, 2000, is recognized immediately as compensation cost.

Example Involving Modification to Reduce the Exercise Price Award After December 15, 1998

Assume the same facts as in the preceding example except that the options have a six-year cliff vesting requirement and two years of service have been rendered as of July 1, 2000. Because the option award was modified after December 15, 1998, the modified award is covered by Interpretation 44. Accordingly, the option award is accounted for as variable until the date it is exercised, is forfeited, or expires unexercised. The portion of the award's intrinsic value measured at July 1, 2000 (the effective date of the Interpretation), that is attributable to the remaining vesting (service) period, i.e., $10 (2/3 of $15), is recognized over that future period. However, if the stock price subsequently declines below the stock price at the effective date, compensation cost is adjusted (reduced) proportionately. Additional compensation cost is measured for the full amount of any increases in stock price after the effective date and is recognized over the remaining vesting (service) period. Any adjustment to compensation cost for further changes in stock price after the award vests is recognized immediately.

APPENDIX

Following is a list of all the issues raised in Interpretation 44, by category, along with their related paragraph numbers for ease of reference.

Question Number	Question	Related Paragraphs
Scope of APB 25		
1(a)	Does APB 25 apply to the accounting by a grantor for stock compensation granted to independent contractors or other service providers who are not employees of the grantor?	2–3
1(b)	What is the definition of *employee* for purposes of applying APB 25?	4–6
2	Does APB 25 apply to stock compensation granted to independent members of the grantor's board of directors?	7–8
Awards Granted to Employees of Another Entity		
3	Does APB 25 apply to the accounting by a grantor for stock compensation granted to a nonemployee for employee services the grantee provides to another entity?	9–11
Awards Granted to Employees Based on the Stock of Another Entity		
4	Does APB 25 apply to the accounting by an employer for stock compensation granted to its employees (a) by another entity based on that entity's stock (e.g., an investee's accounting for investor stock awards granted by the investor to the investee's employees) or (b) by the employer based on the stock of another entity?	12–14
Changes in Grantee Status		
5(a)	What is the accounting consequence to a grantor if a grantee (who continues to provide services) changes status to or from that of an employee under APB 25 and an outstanding stock option or award is retained by the grantee without modification to the award's term?	15–17
5(b)	What is the accounting consequence to a grantor if a grantee (who continues to provide services) changes status to or from that of an employee under APB 25 and the change in status is accompanied by a modification to a stock option or award that is retained by the grantee?	18–21

Question Number	Question	Related Paragraphs
5(c)	What is the accounting consequence to a grantor of a change in status of a grantee from that of an employee to a nonemployee as a result of a spin-off transaction?	22–23

Noncompensatory Plans

6	Paragraph 7(d) of APB 25 provides as one criterion for determining whether a plan is noncompensatory that "the discount from the market price of the stock is no greater than would be reasonable in an offer of stock to stockholders or others." Does a purchase discount of up to 15 percent meet that criterion?	24–25
7	In determining whether a plan is noncompensatory, may the stock price at the date of grant of a stock option be used as the basis for determining whether "the discount from the market price of the stock is no greater than would be reasonable in an offer of stock to stockholders or others"?	26–27
8	May a plan with a *look-back option* qualify as a noncompensatory plan?	28–29

Modifications to a Fixed Stock Option or Award

9	Is there an accounting consequence under APB 25 if the terms of a fixed stock option or award are modified after the original measurement date?	30–31

Modifications That Renew or Increase Life

10	What is the accounting consequence of a modification that renews or extends the life of a fixed award (e.g., acceleration of vesting) or provides for an extension or renewal if a specified future separation from employment occurs?	32–37

Modifications That Reduce Exercise Price

11(a)	What is the accounting consequence of a modification that reduces the exercise price of a fixed stock option award (commonly referred to as repricing)?	38–48
11(b)	What is the accounting consequence of a cancellation (settlement) of a fixed stock option award and the grant of stock ?	49–51
11(c)	What is the accounting consequence of a change to the exercise price, the number of shares, or both, of a fixed stock option or award that occurs as a direct result of an equity restructuring?	52–54

Question Number	Question	Related Paragraphs
Modifications That Increase the Number of Shares to Be Issued		
12(a)	What is the accounting consequence of a modification that increases the number of shares to be issued under a fixed stock option award?	55–56
12(b)	What is the accounting consequence of a modification to a fixed stock option award to add a reload feature?	57–59
Recognition and Measurement of Compensation Cost		
13	How should compensation cost be measured and recognized if a fixed stock option or award is canceled or if a new measurement of compensation cost or variable accounting is required as a result of a modification to the award?	60–64
14	How should compensation cost be measured if cash is paid to settle a stock option or (unvested) stock award or to repurchase shares within six months after option exercise or issuance of the repurchased shares?	65–66
Share Repurchase (and Tax Withholding) Features		
15(a)	Is variable accounting required for a stock option or award with a share repurchase feature (e.g., put, call, or right of first refusal)?	67–72
15(b)	For nonpublic entities with awards containing repurchase features at other than fair value, such as a book value stock purchase plan, when is an employee considered to have made a substantial investment?	73–74
15(c)	Consistent with paragraph 11(g) of APB 25, for public and nonpublic entities, variable accounting is not required for shares expected to be repurchased (at fair value) upon option exercise or share issuance only to meet required tax withholding. What is the definition of required tax withholding?	75–76
15(d)	Is variable accounting required for stock options granted with terms in the award or plan that permit share repurchases upon exercise in excess of the number necessary to satisfy the employer's required tax withholding?	77–80

Question Number	Question	Related Paragraphs
Business Combinations		
16	What is the accounting consequence, if any, for changes to the exercise price or the number of shares as a result of an exchange of fixed stock option awards in a business combination accounted for as a pooling of interests?	81–82
17	Should an exchange of employee stock options or awards in a purchase business combination be accounted for by the acquirer under APB 25 as employee stock compensation or under APB Opinion No. 16, *Business Combinations,* as part of the consideration paid for the acquiree?	83–85
Grant Date		
18	If a plan is subject to shareholder approval, can the grant date ever be deemed to occur prior to obtaining that approval?	86–87
Deferred Tax Assets		
19	Should the carrying amount of a deferred tax asset recognized for a temporary difference related to a stock option or award accounted for under APB 25 be adjusted for a subsequent decline in the stock price?	88–89
Cash Bonus Plan Linked to a Stock Compensation Award		
20	When should a cash bonus and a stock option or award be accounted for under APB 25 as a combined award?	90–92

Appendix 9

Limited Liability Company Agreement of XYZ Company LLC (A Delaware Limited Liability Company) Dated As of February 1, 2001

TABLE OF CONTENTS

**LIMITED LIABILITY COMPANY AGREEMENT OF
XYZ COMPANY LLC**

This Limited Liability Company Agreement of XYZ Company LLC (the "Company") is made as of February 1, 2001, among the Members of the Company, and the Persons who become Members of the Company in accordance with the provisions hereof, and whose names are set forth as Members on Schedule A hereto.

WHEREAS, the Company was formed on February 1, 2001, pursuant to the Delaware Act, by filing a Certificate of Formation of the Company with the office of the Secretary of State of the State of Delaware; and

WHEREAS, the Members desire to become Members of the Company and to conduct the business of the Company as a limited liability company under the Delaware Act.

NOW THEREFORE, in consideration of the agreements and obligations set forth herein and for other good and valuable consideration, the receipt and sufficiency of which are hereby acknowledged, the Members, intending to be legally bound hereby, do mutually covenant and agree as follows:

ARTICLE I
DEFINED TERMS

Section 1.1 Definitions. Unless the context otherwise requires, the terms defined in this Article I shall, for the purposes of this Agreement, have the meanings herein specified.

"ABC Company" means, collectively, ABC & Co., L.P., a Delaware limited partnership, ABC & Co. Associates II, L.P., a Delaware limited partnership and any ABC Permitted Transferee.

"ABC Permitted Transferee" means with respect to ABC, any partnership with the same controlling general partner as ABC and any of the partners of ABC which receive Units upon a distribution to any such partners by ABC .

"Additional Members" has the meaning set forth in Section 12.1 hereof.

"Additional Units" has the meaning set forth in Section 12.1 hereof.

"Adjusted Capital Account Deficit" shall mean, with respect to any Member, the deficit balance, if any, in such Member's Capital Account as of the end of the applicable Fiscal Year after (i) crediting thereto any amounts which such Member is, or is deemed to be, obligated to restore pursuant to Treasury Regulations § 1.704-2(g)(1) and § 1.704-2(i)(5) and (ii) debiting such Capital Account by the amount of the items described in Treasury Regulations § 1.704-1(b)(2)(ii)(d)(4), (5) and (6). The foregoing definition of Adjusted Capital Account Deficit is intended to comply with the provisions of Treasury Regulation section 1.704-1(b)(2)(ii)(d) and shall be interpreted consistently therewith.

"Admission Event" means the:

(a) execution of this Agreement or any other writing evidencing intent to become a Member; and

(b) the making of a Capital Contribution.

"Affiliate" means with respect to a specified Person, any Person that directly or indirectly controls, is controlled by, or is under common control with the specified Person. As used in this definition, the term "control" means the possession, directly or indirectly, of the power to direct or cause the direction of the management and policies of a Person, whether through ownership of voting securities, by contract or otherwise.

"Agreement" means this Limited Liability Company Agreement of XYZ Company LLC, as amended, modified, supplemented or restated from time to time.

"Applicable Percentage" means, with respect to a distribution pursuant to Section 8.3(iv), the percentage set forth on Exhibit X hereto opposite the cumulative return on investment targets set forth therein which have actually been met by the Class A Holders (or will be met) after giving effect to all distributions through the date of the distribution for which the Applicable Percentage is being calculated to the Class A Holders in accordance with Section 8.3 with respect to all investments made by the Class A Holders in the Company through the date of the distribution for which the Applicable Percentage is being calculated.

"Assignee" means any Person who is an assignee of a Member's interest in the Company, or part thereof, and who does not become a Member pursuant to Section 13.3 hereof.

"Available Cash" means all cash (including the net proceeds from capital transactions and sale of assets not in the ordinary course of business) held and owned by the Company less any reserve for the working capital and other foreseeable future needs of the Company, as determined by the Board in its sole discretion.

"Board" has the meaning set forth in Section 6.1.

"Capital Account" means, for each Member, the sum of Capital Contributions made by such Member pursuant to Section 4.1 hereof and such adjustments made pursuant to Section 43 hereof.

"Capital Contribution" means, with respect to any Member, the aggregate amount of money and the Fair Asset Value of any property (other than money) contributed to the Company pursuant to Section 4.1 hereof with respect to the Units held by such Member. In the case of a Member who acquires an interest in the Company by virtue of an assignment in accordance with the terms of this Agreement, "Capital Contribution" has the meaning set forth in Section 4.3(b) hereof.

"Cause" means (i) embezzlement, theft or other misappropriation of any property of the Company or any Affiliate, (ii) gross or willful misconduct resulting in substantial loss to the Company or any Affiliate or substantial damage to the reputation of the Company or any Affiliate, (iii) any act involving moral turpitude which results in a conviction for a felony involving moral turpitude, fraud or misrepresentation, (iv) gross neglect of his assigned duties to the Company or any Affiliate, (v) gross breach of his fiduciary obligations to the Company or any Affiliate, or (vi) any chemical dependence which materially affects the performance of his duties and responsibilities to the Company or any Affiliate; provided that in the case of the misconduct set forth in clauses (iv), (v) and (vi) above, such misconduct shall continue for a period of 30 days following written notice specifying such misconduct by the Company to the Holder; and provided further that "Cause" shall not mean the failure to renew or extend an employment agreement of the employee unless such failure was a result of misconduct referred to in clauses (i)-(vi) above (including the immediately preceding proviso).

"Certificate" means the Certificate of Formation and any and all amendments thereto and restatements thereof filed on behalf of the Company with the office of the Secretary of State of the State of Delaware pursuant to the Delaware Act.

"Change of Control" means a transaction or series of related transactions (other than by the Company or any Subsidiary thereof with any other Subsidiary of the Company) to effect any of the following:

(i)   a sale, redemption, exchange or other disposition of shares (including by way of merger or consolidation) of the Common Stock of ABC Company, Inc. (or any successor thereto), par value $.01 per share, or options or warrants to acquire such Common Stock, after which the holders of Class A Units immediately prior to such event hold directly or indirectly 50% or less of the then outstanding shares of such Common Stock after such event;

(ii) a sale, redemption, exchange or other disposition of Class A Units (including by way of merger or consolidation), or options or warrants to acquire Class A Units, after which the holders of Class A Units immediately prior to such event hold 50% or less of the number of outstanding Class A Units after such event;

(iii) a sale of all or substantially all of the assets of the Company or ABC Company; or

(iv) a liquidation, dissolution, or other winding up of the affairs of the Company, whether voluntary or involuntary.

"Class A Holder" means any Person listed on Schedule A hereto as a holder of Class A Units.

"Class A Units" means the outstanding Class A Units, each of which shall have the rights, powers and preferences set forth in Section 4.6 hereof.

"Class B Holder" means any Person listed on Schedule A hereto as a holder of Class B Units.

"Class B Units" means the outstanding Class B Units, each of which shall have the rights, powers and preferences set forth in Section 4.6 hereof. Each Class B Unit shall be evidenced by a non-negotiable certificate of Class B limited liability company interest in the Company, substantially in the form set forth on Schedule C hereto.

"Class C Holder" means any Person listed on Schedule A hereto as a holder of Class C Units; provided that a Class C Holder must also be an Outside Manager upon the initial issuance of such Class C Units.

"Class C Unit Percentage" means ____%, being the percentage of the Company's Available Cash to which each Class C Unit shall be entitled upon a distribution pursuant to Section 8.3(iv) hereof.

"Class C Units" means the outstanding Class C Units, each of which shall have the rights, powers and preferences set forth in Section 4.6 hereof.

"Class D Holder" means any Person listed on Schedule A hereto as a holder of Class D Units.

"Class D Units" means the outstanding Class D Units, each of which shall have the rights, powers and preferences set forth in Section 4.6 hereof. Each Class D Unit shall be evidenced by a non-negotiable certificate of Class D limited liability company interest in the Company, substantially in the form set forth on Schedule C hereto.

"Code" means the Internal Revenue Code of 1986, as amended from time to time, or any corresponding federal tax statute enacted after the date of this Agreement. A reference to a specific section (§) of the Code refers not only to such specific section but also to any corresponding provision of any federal tax statute enacted after the date of this Agreement, as such specific section or corresponding provision is in effect on the date of application of the provisions of this Agreement containing such reference.

"Company" means XYZ Company LLC, the limited liability company formed under and pursuant to the Delaware Act and this Agreement.

"Company Minimum Gain" shall have the meaning given the term "partnership minimum gain" in Treasury Regulations Sections 1.704-2(b)(2) and 1.704-2(d).

"Covered Person" means a Member, a Manager, an Officer, any Affiliate of a Member, Manager or Officer, any officers, directors, shareholders, partners, employees, representatives or agents of a Member, a Manager, an Officer or their respective Affiliates, or any employee or agent of the Company or its Affiliates.

"Delaware Act" means the Delaware Limited Liability Company Act, 6 Del. C. § 18- 10 1, *et seq.*, as amended from time to time.

"Depreciation" means, for each Fiscal Year or other period, an amount equal to the depreciation, amortization or other cost recovery deduction allowable with respect to an asset for such Fiscal Year or other period; provided, however, that if the Gross Asset Value of an asset differs from its adjusted basis for federal income tax purposes at the beginning of such Fiscal Year or other period, Depreciation shall be an amount that bears the same ratio to such beginning Gross Asset Value as the federal income tax depreciation, amortization or other cost recovery deduction with respect to such asset for such Fiscal Year or other period bears to such beginning adjusted tax basis; and provided further, that if the federal income tax depreciation, amortization or other cost recovery deduction for such Fiscal Year or other period is zero, Depreciation shall be determined with reference to such beginning Gross Asset Value using any reasonable method selected by the Board.

"Fair Asset Value" means the amount for which any asset could be sold in an arm's length transaction by one who desires to sell, but is not under any urgent requirement to sell, to a buyer who desires to buy, but is under no urgent necessity to buy, when both have a reasonable knowledge of the facts, all as determined by the Board. Securities which are listed on a national securities exchange shall be valued at the average last sales price during the immediately preceding 15 days on which such securities are traded on such exchange or, with respect to any of such dates on which no sales occurred, at the mean between the high "bid" and low "asked" prices at the close of business on such date.

"Fiscal Year" means (i) the calendar year or (ii) any portion of the period described in clause (i) of this sentence for which the Company is required to allocate Profits, Losses and other items of Company income, gain, loss or deduction pursuant to Article VIII hereof.

"Gross Asset Value" means, with respect to any asset, such asset's adjusted basis for federal income tax purposes, except as follows:

(a) the initial Gross Asset Value of any asset contributed by a Member to the Company shall be the gross fair market value of such asset, as agreed to by the contributing Member and the Board;

(b) the Gross Asset Value of all Company assets shall be adjusted to equal their respective Fair Asset Values, as of the following times: (i) the acquisition of an additional interest in the Company by any new or existing Member in exchange for more than a *de minims* Capital Contribution; (ii) the distribution by the Company to a Member of more than a *de minimis* amount of Company assets as consideration for an interest in the Company; and (iii) the liquidation of the Company within the meaning of Treasury Regulation § 1.704-1(b)(2)(ii)(g); provided, however that adjustments pursuant to clause (i) and clause (ii) of this sentence shall be made only if the Board reasonably determines that such adjustments are necessary or appropriate to reflect the relative economic interests of the Members in the Company; and

(c) the Gross Asset Value of any Company asset distributed to any Member shall be the Fair Asset Value of such asset on the date of distribution, as determined by the distributee Member and the Board.

(d) the Gross Asset Value of an asset has been determined or adjusted pursuant to paragraph (a) or paragraph (b) above, such Gross Asset Value shall thereafter be adjusted by the Depreciation taken into account with respect to such asset for purposes of computing Profits and Losses.

"Liquidating Trustee" has the meaning set forth in Section 15.3 hereof.

"Majority Vote" means the written approval of, or the affirmative vote by, Members holding a majority of the Voting Units held by Members.

"Managers" means the Persons designated in Section 6.1 hereof as the managers of the Company and shall include additional managers and successors appointed pursuant to the provisions of this Agreement. A Manager shall not be deemed to be a "manager" within the meaning of the Delaware Act.

"Member" means any Person named as a member of the Company on Schedule A hereto and includes any Person admitted as an Additional Member or a Substitute Member pursuant to the provisions of this Agreement, and "Members" means two or more of such Persons when acting in their capacities as members of the Company. Except as otherwise provided herein, the Members shall constitute one class or group of members.

"Member Minimum Gain" shall mean an amount, determined in accordance with Treasury Regulations Section 1.704-2(i)(3) with respect to each Member Nonrecourse Debt, equal to the Company Minimum Gain that would result if such Member Nonrecourse Debt were treated as a Nonrecourse Liability.

"Member Nonrecourse Debt" shall have the meaning given the term "partner nonrecourse debt" in Treasury Regulations Section 1.704-2(b)(4).

"Member Nonrecourse Deductions" shall have the meaning given the term "partner nonrecourse deductions" in Treasury Regulations Section 1.704-2(i).

"Non-Public Shareholders" of the Public Company means the stockholders of the Public Company other than any stockholders who acquired their equity securities of the Public Company pursuant to a registration statement filed with the Securities and Exchange Commission under the Securities Act of 1933, as amended, and the rules and regulations thereunder.

"Nonrecourse Deduction" shall have the meaning given such term in Treasury Regulations Section 1.704-2(b)(1).

"Nonrecourse Liability" shall have the meaning given such term in Treasury Regulations Section 1.704-2(b)(3).

"Officers" means officers of the Company appointed by the Board pursuant to Article VI hereof.

"Outside Manager" shall mean any Manager who is neither a partner nor officer of a Member nor an employee of the Company or any of its Subsidiaries.

"Permanent Disability" means, as a result of physical or mental illness or incapacity, the Holder has been unable in the sole determination of the Board to perform his duties to the Company and/or a Subsidiary of the Company for a period of four consecutive months or for an aggregate of more than six months in any 12-month period.

"Permitted Transferees" means the Persons to whom Transfers are permitted to be made under Section 13.2.

"Person" includes any individual, corporation, association, partnership (general or limited), joint venture, trust, estate, limited liability company or other legal entity or organization.

"Profits" and "Losses" means, for each Fiscal Year, an amount equal to the Company's taxable income or loss for such Fiscal Year, determined in accordance with § 703(a) of the Code (but including in taxable income or loss, for this purpose, all items of income, gain, loss or deduction required to be stated separately pursuant to § 703(a)(1) of the Code), with the following adjustments:

(a) any income of the Company exempt from federal income tax and not otherwise taken into account in computing Profits or Losses pursuant to this definition shall be added to such taxable income or loss;

(b) any expenditures of the Company described in § 705(a)(2)(B) of the Code (or treated as expenditures described in § 705(a)(2)(B) of the Code pursuant to Treasury Regulation § 1.704-1(b)(2)(iv)(i)) and not otherwise taken into account in computing Profits or Losses pursuant to this definition shall be subtracted from such taxable income or loss;

(c) in the event the Gross Asset Value of any Company asset is adjusted in accordance with paragraph (b) or paragraph (c) of the definition of "Gross Asset Value" above, the amount of such adjustment shall be taken into account as gain or loss from the disposition of such asset for purposes of computing Profits or Losses;

(d) gain or loss resulting from any disposition of any asset of the Company with respect to which gain or loss is recognized for federal income tax purposes shall be computed by reference to the Gross Asset Value of the asset disposed of, notwithstanding that the adjusted tax basis of such asset differs from its Gross Asset Value; and

(e) in lieu of the depreciation, amortization and other cost recovery deductions taken into account in computing such taxable income or loss, there shall be taken into account Depreciation for such Fiscal Year or other period, computed in accordance with the definition of "Depreciation" above.

"Proportionate Percentage" means, (i) with respect to each Member that elects to exercise its rights under Section 12.2 hereof, a percentage (expressed as a decimal fraction rounded to the nearest one-hundredth) obtained by dividing (x) the number of all Class A Units owned by such electing Member by (y) the aggregate number of Class A Units owned by all Members, (ii) with respect to Section 14.1 hereof, a percentage (expressed as a decimal fraction rounded to the nearest one-hundredth) obtained by dividing (x) the number of all Class A Units proposed to be sold by ABC pursuant to the Transfer giving rise to the Tag-Along Period under Section 14.1 hereof by (y) the aggregate number of Class A Units owned by ABC and (iii) with respect to Section 14.3(a) or 14.3(b) hereof, a percentage (expressed as a decimal fraction rounded to the nearest one-hundredth) obtained by dividing (X) the number of Class B Units or Class D Units, as applicable, proposed to be repurchased pursuant to Section 14.3(a) or 14.3(b) hereof by (y) the aggregate number of Class B Units or Class D Units, as applicable, outstanding.

"Public Company" means the Company or any Subsidiary, or any successor thereto, in each case which intends to effect a Public Offering.

"Public Offering" means (i) the sale to the public by the Public Company for its own account of equity securities issued by such Public Company, and/or (ii) the sale to the public by the Non-Public Shareholders pursuant to a Secondary Sale of equity securities issued by the Public Company and held by the Non-Public Shareholders, in either case pursuant to a registration statement filed with the Securities and Exchange Commission under the Securities Act of 1933, as amended, and the rules and regulations promulgated thereunder.

"Regulatory Allocations" has the meaning set forth in Section 8.11 hereof.

"Secondary Sale" means any sale by one or more Non-Public Shareholders of equity securities issued by the Public Company and held by such Non-Public Shareholders (but not originally issued by the Public Company pursuant to a Public Offering), whether such sale is pursuant to a registered public offering under the Securities Act of 1933, as amended, an exemption from the registration requirements thereof, or otherwise.

"Subsidiary" with respect to any company means any corporation more than 50% of whose stock or equity securities (measured by virtue of voting rights) in the aggregate is owned by such company, by one or more Subsidiaries of such company, or by such company and one or more Subsidiaries of such company.

"Substitute Member" means a Person who is admitted to the Company as a Member pursuant to Section 13.3 hereof, and who is named as a Member on Schedule A to this Agreement.

"Tax Liability Distribution" shall have the meaning given such term in Section 8.2 hereof.

"Tax Matters Member" has the meaning set forth in Section 10.1 hereof.

"Transaction" has the meaning set forth in Section 6.12 hereof.

"Transfer" means (i) as a noun, any transaction (or the consummation of a transaction) which has resulted in a change in the ownership of any Unit, including without limitation, any voluntary or involuntary sale, assignment, transfer, pledge, hypothecation, encumbrance, disposal, loan, gift, attachment or levy of, by or with respect to the Member which owns such Unit which has resulted in a transfer of the voting rights or the rights to distribution with respect to such Unit, and (ii) as a verb, to make any transaction described in (i).

"Treasury Regulations" means the income tax regulations, including temporary regulations, promulgated under the Code, as such regulations may be amended from time to time (including corresponding provisions of succeeding regulations).

"Unit" means any one of the Class A Units, Class B Units, Class C Units or Class D Units. Each Unit represents a limited liability company interest in the Company, with the respective rights, powers and preferences as provided in this Agreement. All issued Units are held by the Members as set forth on the Schedule A hereto. If Additional Units are issued as provided in Article XII, the total number of Units outstanding shall be automatically increased by the number of Additional Units issued. Upon their issuance, all Units shall be owned by the Members holding such Units.

"Unrecouped Capital Contribution" means as to any Member or Assignee the amount of such Member's or Assignee's Capital Contribution with respect to Class A Units held by such Member or Assignee minus the aggregate of all distributions previously made to such Member or Assignee pursuant to Section 8.3(ii) hereof.

"Voting Units" means, collectively, the Class A Units and the Class B Units, which shall vote together as a single class.

Section 1.2 Headings. The headings and subheadings in this Agreement are included for convenience and identification only and are in no way intended to describe, interpret, define or limit the scope, extent or intent of this Agreement or any provision hereof.

ARTICLE II
ORGANIZATION AND TERM

Section 2.1 Organization.

(a) The Members hereby agree to organize the Company as a limited liability company under and pursuant to the provisions of the Delaware Act and agree that the rights, duties and liabilities of the Members and the Managers shall be as provided in the Delaware Act, except as otherwise provided herein.

(b) Any Person listed on Schedule A hereto that performs an Admission Event, and any Person listed on Schedule A hereto whose authorized representative performs an Admission Event, shall be deemed to have evidenced its intent to become a Member, to have complied with the conditions for becoming a Member as set forth in this Agreement, and to have requested that the records of the Company reflect such admission as a Member, and when the records of the Company are amended to reflect the admission of such Person as a Member, such Person shall be admitted to the Company as a Member.

(c) The name and mailing address of each Member shall be listed on the Schedules hereto. The Managers shall update any Schedule from time to time as necessary to accurately reflect the information therein. Any amendment or revision to a Schedule made in accordance with this Agreement shall not be deemed an amendment to this Agreement. Any reference in this Agreement to a Schedule shall be deemed to be a reference to such Schedule as amended and in effect from time to time.

Section 2.2 Name. The name of the Company is XYZ Company LLC. The business of the Company may also be conducted under any other name or names designated by the Board from time to time.

Section 2.3 Term. The term of the Company commenced on the date the Certificate was filed in the office of the Secretary of State of the State of Delaware and shall continue until dissolved in accordance with the provisions of this Agreement. The existence of the Company as a separate legal entity shall continue until the cancellation of the Certificate.

Section 2.4 Registered Agent and Office. The Company's registered agent and office in the State of Delaware shall be [   ]. At any time, the Board may designate another registered agent and/or registered office.

Section 2.5 Principal Place of Business. The principal place of business of the Company shall be at [   ]. Upon 10 days' notice to the Members, the Board may change the location of the Company's principal place of business.

ARTICLE III
PURPOSE AND POWERS OF THE COMPANY

Section 3.1 Purpose. The purpose of the Company is to acquire, hold for investment, sell and dispose of the stock and other securities, directly or indirectly, of any Subsidiary, and to engage in all activities necessary, advisable or incidental thereto, including without limitation engaging in (or causing or permitting any of its Subsidiaries to engage in) any of the transactions identified in Section 6.12 hereof.

Section 3.2 Powers of the Company. Subject to the provisions of Section 3.3, the Company shall have the power and authority to take any and all actions necessary, appropriate, proper, advisable, incidental or convenient to or for the furtherance of the purpose set forth in Section 3.1, including, but not limited to, the power:

(i) to conduct its business, carry on its operations and have and exercise the powers granted to a limited liability company by the Delaware Act in any state, territory, district or possession of the United States, or in any foreign country that may be necessary, convenient or incidental to the accomplishment of the purpose of the Company;

(ii) to acquire by purchase, lease, contribution of property or otherwise, own, hold, operate, maintain, finance, improve, lease, sell, convey, mortgage, transfer or dispose of any real or personal property that may be necessary, convenient or incidental to the accomplishment of the purpose of the Company;

(iii) to enter into, perform and carry out contracts of any kind convenient to or incidental to the accomplishment of the purpose of the Company;

(iv) to lend money for its proper purpose, to invest and reinvest its funds, to take and hold real and personal property for the payment of funds so loaned or invested;

(v) to appoint employees and agents of the Company, and define their duties and fix their compensation;

(vi) to indemnify any Person in accordance with the Delaware Act;

(vii) to cease its activities and cancel its Certificate;

(viii) to negotiate, enter into, renegotiate, extend, renew, terminate, modify, amend, waive, execute, acknowledge or take any other action with respect to any lease, contract or security agreement in respect of any assets of the Company; and

(ix) to guaranty the obligations of any Person and to secure any of the same by a mortgage, pledge or other lien on the assets of the Company.

Section 3.3 Limitations on Actions. Anything in this Agreement to the contrary notwithstanding, the Company shall not hold any investment, incur any indebtedness or otherwise take any action that would cause any Member of the Company (or any Person holding an indirect interest in the Company through an entity or series of entities that are treated as partnerships for U.S. federal income tax purposes) to realize "unrelated business taxable income" as such term is defined in Section 5.12 of the Code.

ARTICLE IV
CAPITAL CONTRIBUTIONS, UNITS, CAPITAL ACCOUNTS, AND ADVANCES

Section 4.1 Capital Contributions

(a) Each Member has contributed to the capital of the Company the amount of cash, if any, set forth opposite the Member's name on Schedule A hereto, and the Company has issued to each Member the number of Units set forth opposite the Member's name on Schedule A hereto.

(b) No Member shall be required to make any additional capital contribution to the Company.

Section 4.2 Status of Capital Contributions

(a) Except as otherwise provided in this Agreement, the amount of a Member's Capital Contributions may be returned to it, in whole or in part, at any time, but only with the consent of all Members.

(b) No Member shall receive any interest, salary or drawing with respect to its Capital Contributions or its Capital Account or for services rendered on behalf of the Company or otherwise in its capacity as a Member, except as otherwise specifically provided in this Agreement.

(c) Except as otherwise provided herein and by applicable state law, the Members shall be liable only to make their Capital Contributions pursuant to Section 4.1 hereof, and no Member or Assignee shall be required to lend any funds to the Company or, after a Member's Capital Contributions has been fully paid pursuant to Section 4.1 hereof, to make any additional capital contributions to the Company. No Member shall have any personal liability for the repayment of any Capital Contribution of any other Member or Assignee.

Section 4.3 Capital Accounts

(a) An individual Capital Account shall be established and maintained for each Member. The Capital Account of each Member shall be maintained in accordance with the rules of Section 704(b) of the Code and the Treasury Regulations (including Section 1.704-1[b][2][iv] thereof) thereunder. Adjustments shall be made to the Capital Accounts for all distributions and allocations as required by the rules of Section 704(b) of the Code and the Treasury Regulations thereunder. In general, a Member's Capital Account shall be increased by (i) the amount of money and the Gross Asset Value of property (net of liabilities secured by such contributed property that the Company is considered to assume or to take subject to under Section 752 of the Code) contributed to the Company by the Member and (ii) allocations to the Member of Profits and decreased by (i) the amount of money distributed to the Member by the Company, (ii) the Gross Asset Value of property distributed to the Member by the Company (net of liabilities secured by such distributed property that such Member is considered to assume or take subject to under Section 752 of the Code), and (iii) allocations to the Member of Losses. In the event the Gross Asset Value of Company assets is adjusted under Article I of this Agreement or pursuant to Section 4.3(c) or 4.3(d), the Capital Accounts of the Members shall be adjusted to reflect the aggregate net adjustment as if the Company recognized Profits or Losses equal to the amount of such aggregate net adjustment and such Profits or Losses were allocated to the Members pursuant to Sections 8.7 and 8.8, or Section 8.9, as the case may be, of this Agreement. The foregoing provisions relating to the maintenance of Capital Accounts are intended to comply with Treasury Regulations Sections 1.704-1(b) and 1.704-2 and shall be applied in a manner consistent with such Treasury Regulations.

(b) The Capital Accounts of the Members shall be adjusted to reflect the provisions of Sections 14.3(a)(iv) and 14.3(b)(v) hereof. Further, the original Capital Account established for any Member or Assignee who acquires an interest in the Company by virtue of a Transfer or an assignment that does not cause a termination of the Company within the meaning of Code Section 708(b)(1)(B) and that is in accordance with the terms of this Agreement shall be in the same amount as, and shall replace, the Capital Account of the transferor or assignor of such interest, and, for purposes of this Agreement, such Member or Assignee shall be deemed to have made the Capital Contributions made by the transferor or assignor of such interest (or made by such transferor's or assignor's predecessor in interest) and have received the distributions and been allocated the allocations received by or allocated to the transferor or assignor of such interest (or received by or allocated to such transferor's or assignor's predecessor in interest). if the Company has a Code Section 754 election in effect, the Capital Account will not be adjusted to reflect any adjustment under Code Section

743. To the extent such Member or Assignee acquires less than the entire interest in the Company of the transferor or assignor of the interest so acquired by such Member or Assignee, the original Capital Account of such Member or Assignee and its Capital Contributions shall be in proportion to the interest it acquires, and the Capital Account of the transferor or assignor who retains a partial interest in the Company, and the amount of its Capital Contributions, shall be reduced in proportion to the interest it retains. If a Transfer or assignment of an interest in the Company causes a termination of the Company within the meaning of Code Section 708(b)(1)(B), the income tax consequences of the deemed contribution of the property to the new limited liability company (which for all other purposes continues to be the Company) shall be governed by the relevant provisions of Subchapter K of Chapter I of the Code and the Regulations promulgated thereunder, and the initial Capital Accounts of the Members and the Assignee in the new limited liability company shall be determined in accordance with the rules of Treasury Regulations Section 1.704-1(b)(2)(iv)(d), (e), (f), (g) and (h) under Code Section 704 and thereafter in accordance with this Section 4.3.

(c) Notwithstanding anything in this Agreement to the contrary, in the event the Company repurchases Class B Units or Class D Units pursuant to Section 14.3(a) or 14.3(b) hereof, the Gross Asset Value of Company assets shall be adjusted to reflect the Fair Asset Value of such assets,

(d) Notwithstanding anything in this Agreement to the contrary, in the event the Company issues additional Class B Units, Class C Units or Class D Units pursuant to Section 12.1 (a) hereof, the Gross Asset Value of Company assets shall be adjusted to reflect the Fair Asset Value of such assets.

Section 4.4 Negative Capital Accounts. At no time during the term of the Company or upon dissolution and liquidation thereof shall a Member with a negative balance in his Capital Account have any obligation to the Company or the other Members to restore such negative balance.

Section 4.5 Advances. If any Member shall advance any funds to the Company in excess of its Capital Contributions, the amount of such advance shall neither increase its Capital Account nor entitle it to any increase in its share of the distributions of the Company. The amount of any such advance shall be a debt obligation of the Company to such Member and shall be repaid to it by the Company with interest at a rate equal to the lesser of (i) such rate as the Board agrees and (ii) the maximum rate permitted by applicable law, and upon such other terms and conditions as shall be mutually determined by such Member and the Board. Any such advance shall be payable and collectible only out of Company assets, and the other Members shall not be personally obligated to repay any part thereof. No Person who makes any nonrecourse loan to the Company shall have or acquire, as a result of making such loan, any direct or indirect interest in the profits, capital or property of the Company, other than as a creditor.

Section 4.6 Units

(a) Distributions. Distributions on Units shall be made in accordance with Article VIII hereof.

(b) Voting. Except as otherwise provided in this Agreement, (i) the Members who are Class A Holders shall be entitled to vote on each matter on which the Members shall be entitled to vote at the rate of one vote for each Class A Unit held by such Member and (ii) the Members who are Class B Holders shall be entitled to one vote on each matter on which the Members shall be entitled to vote at the rate of one vote for each Class B Unit held by such Member.

(c) Class B Units and Class D Units. The Class B Units and the Class D Units shall be subject to repurchase by the Company in accordance with the provisions set forth in Section 14.3 hereof. Class B Units and Class D Units that are repurchased may be reissued (subject to Section 12.1 (a) hereof).

(d) Class C Units. The Class C Units shall be subject to repurchase by the Company in accordance with the provisions set forth in Section 14.4 hereof. Class C Units that are repurchased may be issued (subject to Section 12.1[a] hereof).

ARTICLE V
MEMBERS

Section 5.1 Powers of Members. The Members shall have the power to exercise any and all rights or powers granted to the Members pursuant to the express terms of this Agreement. Except as expressly provided in this Agreement, Members shall have no power as Members to bind the Company.

Section 5.2 Reimbursements. The Company shall reimburse the Members for all reasonable out-of-pocket expenses incurred by the Members on behalf of the Company. The Board's sole determination of which expenses may be reimbursed to a Member and the amount of such expenses shall be conclusive. Such reimbursement shall be treated as an expense of the Company that shall be deducted in computing the Profits and shall not be deemed to constitute a distributive share of Profits or a distribution or return of capital to any Member.

Section 5.3 Partition. Each Member waives any and all rights that it may have to maintain an action for partition of the Company's property.

Section 5.4 Resignations. Other than any resignation by a Member approved by a Majority Vote of the Members and any resignation described in Section 13.3, a Member may not resign from the Company.

ARTICLE VI
BOARD OF MANAGERS AND OFFICERS OF THE COMPANY

Section 6.1 Designation of Board of Managers. The management of the Company's business shall be vested, to the extent provided in this Article VI, in a Board of Managers of the Company (the "Board"). The Members hereby designate the following Persons to serve as the initial Managers on the Board, and such Managers hereby accept and agree to be bound by the terms and conditions of this Agreement: (A) three persons designated by ABC, (B) Bill Jones (for so long as Mr. Jones shall be an officer of the Company), (C) John Smith (for so long as Mr. Smith shall be an officer of the Company) and (D) such other persons designated by ABC.

Section 6.2 Election; Resignation; Removal

(a) Each Manager shall serve from the effective date of his designation until the effective date of his resignation or removal. In the event any Manager ceases to be a Manager of the Company whether by resignation or removal as provided in this Agreement or otherwise, a successor Manager shall be elected by a Majority Vote. The Members agree to vote for the Managers designated in accordance with Section 6.1 hereof. Such successor Manager shall execute an instrument reasonably satisfactory to the Members accepting and agreeing to the terms and conditions of this Agreement.

(b) A Manager may resign from his position as a Manager at any time upon not less than 10 days' prior written notice to all of the Members.

(c) Any Manager may be removed by a Majority Vote. Any removal of a Manager shall become effective on such date as may be specified by the Members voting in favor thereof. Should a Manager that is removed continue to be a Member, such Member shall continue to participate in the Company as a Member and shall share in the Profits, Losses and Available Cash in the same ratios, as provided in Article VIII hereof.

Section 6.3 Officers. The Board may appoint agents and employees of the Company who are designated as officers of the Company. The officers of the Company shall include a Chairman, a President and Chief Executive Officer, a Chief Financial Officer, one or more Senior Vice Presidents, a Secretary and such other officers with such titles as may be approved by the Board. Charles Ayres shall be Chairman until his resignation or removal. Bill Jones shall be President and Chief Executive Officer until his resignation or removal. John Smith shall be Chief Financial Officer and Senior Vice President until his resignation or removal. Joe Smith shall be Vice President and Secretary until his resignation or removal. The Board may remove any officer so appointed at any time, with or without Cause, in its absolute discretion. The Chairman and other officers shall be agents of the Company, authorized to execute and deliver documents and take other actions on behalf of the Company, subject to the direction of the Board, and to have such other duties as may be approved by the Board; provided, that the delegation of any such power and authority to the Chairman and other officers shall not limit in any respect the power and authority of the Managers to take such actions (or any other action) on behalf of the Company as provided in this Agreement. The Secretary shall record the actions of the Board, certify this Agreement and any related document or instrument, certify resolutions of the Board, incumbency and other matters of the Company, and have such other ministerial duties as may be specified by the Board from time to time.

Section 6.4 Board Action. Unless otherwise specified in this Agreement, the Board shall act by majority vote; provided, that so long as ABC holds more than 50% of the voting control of the then outstanding Class A Units, ABC shall have the right, by taking such action as would be required under the Delaware General Corporation law for a majority shareholder to act without a meeting, to increase its number of votes to the number of votes that would constitute a majority of the total votes on the Board.

Section 6.5 Meetings. The Board may hold regular or special meetings upon 48 hours prior notice to all Managers (which notice may be waived), at such places and at such times as the Board may from time to time determine.

Section 6.6 Quorum. At any meeting of the Board, the presence of at least one of the Managers appointed by ABC shall constitute a quorum. Any meeting may be adjourned from time to time by a majority of votes, whether or not a quorum is present, and the meeting may be held as adjourned upon reasonable notice.

Section 6.7 Action by Consent. Any action of the Board may be taken without a meeting if (i) the Managers holding not less than the minimum number of votes that would be required to approve and adopt such action at a meeting consent to the action in writing, signed by such Managers, (ii) notice of the actions to be approved by such Managers is given to all Managers in advance and copies of the written consents are so delivered to all Managers promptly thereafter, and (iii) the written consents are filed with the records of the meetings of the Board. Such actions by consent shall be treated for all purposes as actions taken at a meeting.

Section 6.8 Telephonic Meetings. Managers may participate in a meeting of the Board by means of a conference telephone or similar communications equipment provided all Managers participating in the meeting can hear each other at the same time, and participation by such means shall constitute presence in person at a meeting.

Section 6.9 Managers As Agents. The Managers, to the extent of the powers set forth herein, are agents of the Company for the purpose of the Company's business, and the actions of the Managers taken in accordance with such powers shall bind the Company.

Section 6.10 Powers of the Board; Powers of Officers.

(a) The Board's powers on behalf and in respect of the Company, subject to the provisions of this Agreement requiring the approval of the Members, shall be all powers and privileges permitted to be exercised by members that manage the Company under the Delaware Act, including, without limitation, Section 18-402 of the Delaware Act; provided, nothing herein shall supersede, limit or otherwise invalidate any action, authorization or resolution of the Members set forth in this Agreement.

(b) The Board may delegate any of its powers to the Officers of the Company, or any one of them, except to the extent that this Agreement requires the Board to take an action by voting.

(c) The Board hereby delegates to the Officers of the Company the respective powers delegated to officers of a corporation under the Delaware General Corporation Law, subject to the powers of a board of directors of a corporation under such Delaware law; provided, that the Board reserves the right to rescind the delegation of any such powers at any time in the sole discretion of the Board. Notwithstanding the foregoing, all decisions as to the hiring and terminating the employment of and the compensation of any officer who reports directly to the Chairman or Chief Executive Officer of the Company shall be subject to the approval of the Board.

Section 6.11 Reimbursement. The Company shall reimburse each Manager for all reasonable out-of-pocket expenses incurred by such Manager on behalf of the Company according to such terms as shall be approved by the Board. The Board's sole determination of which expenses may be reimbursed to a Manager and the amount of such expenses shall be conclusive. Such reimbursement shall be treated as an expense of the Company that shall be deducted in computing Profits and shall not be deemed to constitute a distributive share of Profits or a distribution or return of capital to the Manager.

Section 6.12 Required Approvals by the Board

(a) Except for transactions between or among the Company and one or more of its Subsidiaries, or between or among the Company's Subsidiaries themselves, without the approval of the Board, the Company shall neither take nor permit any of its Subsidiaries to take any of the following actions (each event hereinafter described being hereafter referred to as a "Transaction") without the approval of the Board:

  (i)   any sale, Transfer, assignment or other disposition by the Company of any interest in a Subsidiary of the Company, or by any Subsidiary of the Company of any interest in another Subsidiary of the Company;

  (ii) any consolidation or merger of the Company with or into any other limited liability company or other business entity (as defined in Section 18-209[a] of the Delaware Act), or any liquidation, dissolution or winding-up of the Company;

  (iii) (A) any consolidation or merger of any Subsidiary of the Company with or into any business entity (as defined in Section 18-209[a] of the Delaware Act), (B) any sale by any Subsidiary of the Company of all or substantially all of its assets or (C) any liquidation, dissolution or winding-up of any Subsidiary of the Company;

  (iv) any issuance of any equity securities of any Subsidiary of the Company, or any securities convertible into shares of preferred stock or common stock of any Subsidiary of the Company;

  (v)   any acquisition by the Company or any Subsidiary of the Company of any stock or assets of another entity or of capital assets, in a single transaction or a series of related transactions in any 12-month period, for an aggregate purchase price in excess of $2,500,000;

  (vi) any incurrence by the Company or any Subsidiary of the Company of funded debt in a principal amount in excess of $2,500,000;

  (vii) any capital expenditure or commitment therefor in excess of $1,000,000;

  (viii) any approval of the annual budget for any of the Subsidiaries; and

  (ix) any selection of the firm of independent public accountants that will audit the financial statements of the Company or its Subsidiaries.

Section 6.13 Board of Directors of Subsidiaries of the Company

(a) Each Manager agrees to take such action as a Manager as may be necessary to cause a stockholder of any Subsidiary to elect the following persons as members of the Board of Directors of such Subsidiary: (A) three persons designated by ABC, (B) Bill Jones (for so long as he shall be an officer of the Company), (C) John Smith (for so long as he shall be an officer of the Company) and (D) such other persons designated by ABC. Notwithstanding the foregoing, so long as ABC holds more than 50% of the voting control of the then outstanding Class A Units, ABC shall have the right, by taking such action as would be required under the Delaware General Corporation Law (including without limitation Section 228 of the Delaware General Corporation Law) for a majority shareholder to act without a meeting, to designate a number of additional persons for election as members of the Board of Directors of such Subsidiary which, when added to the three persons previously designated by ABC, would constitute a majority of members of the Board of Directors of such Subsidiary.

(b) In the event ABC exercises its rights under this Section 6.13, the Managers agree to take such actions as may be necessary to cause the election of the additional persons designated by ABC as directors of any Subsidiary and to amend the By-Laws of such entity in connection therewith.

ARTICLE VII
AMENDMENTS AND MEETINGS

Section 7.1 Amendments. Except as expressly provided in this Agreement, any amendment to this Agreement (including the Schedules hereto) shall be adopted and be effective as an amendment hereto if it is approved by the affirmative vote of Members holding at least 50% of the outstanding Voting Units. In addition to the foregoing requirement:

(i)   no amendment of this Section 7.1 or of Article VIII hereof (or the definitions used therein) shall be effective without the written approval of Members holding a majority of any class of Units that would be adversely affected by such proposed amendment;

(ii)   no amendment of Section 6.1 or 6.2 regarding the initial Managers or this Section 7.1 (ii) shall be made without the unanimous written consent of such initial Managers;

(iii)   no amendment of Section 4.6(c), Section 14.3 or this Section 7.1 (iii) shall be effective without the prior written approval of Members holding a majority of the Class B Units; and

(iv)   no amendment of Section 4.6(d), Section 14.4 or this Section 7.1 (iv) shall be effective without the prior written approval of Members holding a majority of the Class C Units.

Notwithstanding the foregoing, the officers of the Company may amend Schedule A hereto to reflect new Members or Substitute Members duly admitted in accordance with this Agreement, with such amendment to be effective upon the filing of such amendment with the books and records of the Company.

Section 7.2 Meetings of the Members

(a) Meetings of the Members may be called by the Board and shall be called by the Board upon the written request of the Chairman or of Members holding 25% of the outstanding Voting Units. The call shall state the location of the meeting and the nature of the business to be transacted. Notice of any such meeting shall be given to all Members not less than 10 days nor more than 60 days prior to the date of such meeting. Members may vote in person or by proxy at such meeting. Whenever a vote, consent or approval of Members is permitted or required under this Agreement, such vote, consent or approval may be given at a meeting of Members or may be given in accordance with the procedure prescribed in Section 7.2(e) hereof. Except as otherwise expressly provided in this Agreement, a vote by Members holding a majority of the Voting Units shall be required to constitute the act of the Members.

(b) For the purpose of determining the Members entitled to vote on, or to vote at, any meeting of the Members or any adjournment thereof, the Board or the Members requesting such meeting may fix, in advance, a date as the record date for any such determination. Such date shall be not more than 60 days nor less than 10 days before any such meeting.

(c) Each Member may authorize any Person to act for it by proxy on all matters in which a Member is entitled to participate, including waiving notice of any meeting, or voting or participating at a meeting. Every proxy must be signed by the Member or its attorney-in-fact. No proxy shall be valid after the expiration of 12 months from the date thereof unless otherwise provided in the proxy. Every proxy shall be revocable at the pleasure of the Member executing it.

(d) Each meeting of Members shall be conducted by the Board or Members requesting such meeting or by such other Person that the Board or Members requesting such meeting may designate.

(e) Except as otherwise provided in this Agreement, any action of the Members may be taken without a meeting if

(i)   the Members holding not less than the minimum number of Voting Units that would be required to approve and adopt such action at a meeting consent to the action in writing,

(ii) written notice (delivered in person or by facsimile) of the actions to be approved by such Members is given to all Members, and

(iii) the written consents are filed with the records of the meeting of the Members. Such actions by consent shall be treated for all purposes as actions taken at a meeting.

ARTICLE VIII
DISTRIBUTIONS AND ALLOCATIONS

Section 8.1 General Distribution Rules. Except as provided in Section 8.2 hereof, the Company shall distribute Available Cash pursuant to the terms hereunder to the Members at such times as shall be determined by the Board. For purposes of this Article VIII, the term "Member" shall include an Assignee of a Member and their successors and assigns.

Section 8.2 Tax Liability Distributions. The Board shall make cash distributions on or prior to April 15th of each year to the Members in amounts intended to enable the Members (or any Person whose tax liability is determined by reference to the income of a Member) to discharge their United States federal, state and local income tax liabilities arising from the allocations made pursuant to this Article VIII with respect to the Company's operations in the preceding year (a "Tax Liability Distribution"). The amount of any such Tax Liability Distribution shall be equal to 40% of the amount of net taxable income and gain allocated to each Member pursuant to this Article VIII; provided, however, if any distributions are made pursuant to Section 8.3(i), Section 8.3(iii) or Section 8.3(iv) hereof with respect to the year for which the Tax Liability Distribution is being determined, the amount of the Tax Liability Distribution shall be reduced by the amount of such distributions.

Section 8.3 Other Distributions. Distributions other than Tax Liability Distributions, including without limitation distributions of Available Cash, but not including distributions upon liquidation pursuant to Section 8.4 hereof, shall be made to the Members as follows:

(i)   First, an amount shall be distributed to each Class A Holder, which amount, when added to all prior distributions made to such Class A Holder under Section 8.2 with respect to Class A Units and under this Section 8.3(i) shall produce a return of 10% interest per annum compounded annually on the Unrecouped Capital Contributions of such Class A Holder outstanding from time to time. To the extent the amount of any proposed distribution under this Section 8.3(i) is not sufficient to provide a full distribution of the amount required to be distributed to each Class A Holder by this Section 8.3(i), the amount of such distribution shall be allocated among the Class A Holders in proportion to their Class A Units.

(ii)   Next, an amount shall be distributed to the Class A Holders, which amount, when added to all prior distributions made to such Class A Holders with respect to the Class A Units under this Section 8.3(ii), shall equal the aggregate Capital Contributions of all Class A Holders at the time such distribution is made. Such distribution shall be allocated among the Class A Holders in proportion to their Capital Contributions.

(iii) Next, an amount shall be distributed to the Class A Holders which amount, when added to all prior distributions made to such Class A Holders under this Section 8.3(iii), shall equal the aggregate amount of Profit allocated to such Class A Holders under Section 14.3(a)(iv) and 14.3(b)(v) hereof. Such distribution shall be allocated among the Class A Holders in proportion to their Class A Units.

(iv)   Next, any balance shall be distributed to the Members as follows: (A) twenty percent (20%) of such balance shall be distributed to the Class B Holders in proportion to the number of Class B Units held by each such Class B Holder; (B) the Applicable Percentage of such balance shall be distributed to the Class D Holders, if any, in proportion to the number of Class D Units held by each such Class D Holder; (C) each Class C Holder, if any, shall be distributed a percentage of such balance equal to the number of Class C Units held by such Class C Holder multiplied by the Class C Unit Percentage; and (D) the remainder shall be distributed to the Class A Holders in proportion to the number of Class A Units held by each such Class A Holder.

Section 8.4 Distribution of Proceeds upon Liquidation. Upon liquidation of the Company, any distributions shall be made in accordance with the terms and conditions of Article XV hereof and shall be made by the end of the taxable year in which the liquidation occurs, or, if later, within ninety (90) days after the liquidation.

Section 8.5 Tax Withholding. The Board is authorized to withhold from distributions, or with respect to allocations, to the Members and to pay over to any federal, state or local government any amounts required to be so withheld pursuant to the Code or any provision of any other federal, state or local law and shall allocate such amounts to those Members with respect to which such amounts were withheld. All amounts withheld pursuant to the Code or any provision of any state or local tax law with respect to any payment, distribution or allocation to the Company or the Members shall be treated as amounts distributed to the Members pursuant to this Article VIII for all purposes of this Agreement.

Section 8.6 Limitations on Distribution. Notwithstanding any provision to the contrary contained in this Agreement, the Company shall not make a distribution to any Member on account of its interest in the Company if such distribution would violate Section 18-607 of the Delaware Act or other applicable law.

Section 8.7 Allocation of Profits. Except as provided in Sections 8.9 or 8.10, Profits of the Company for any Fiscal Year shall be allocated in the following order and priority:

(i)   First, among the Members in accordance with and in an amount equal to the cumulative Losses allocated among the Members pursuant to Section 8.8(a)(ii) hereof for all prior periods and not previously taken into account under this clause.

(ii) Next, among the Members in accordance with and in an amount equal to the cumulative Losses allocated among the Members pursuant to Section 8.8(a)(i) hereof for all prior periods and not previously taken into account under this clause.

(iii) Next, among the Class A Holders in proportion to, and in an amount equal to the excess, if any, of (A) the cumulative cash distributions under Section 8.3(i) hereof that have previously been made to the Class A Holders and that each Class A Holder would have received under Section 8.3(i) hereof for the then current Fiscal Year and all prior Fiscal Years had an amount of Available Cash at least equal to such Profits been available for such distribution under such Section over (B) the cumulative allocations previously made to the Class A Holders pursuant to this Section 8.7(iii).

(iv) Next, among the Members in proportion to and in an amount equal to the excess, if any, of (A) the cumulative cash distributions under Section 8.3(iv) hereof that have previously been made to such Members and that such Member would have received under Section 8.3(iv) hereof for the then current Fiscal Year and all prior Fiscal Years had an amount of Available Cash at least equal to such Profits been available for such distribution under such Section over (B) the cumulative allocations previously made to the Members pursuant to this Section 8.7(iv).

For purposes of determining Profits allocations under this Section 8.7, amounts actually distributed under the relevant paragraph of Section 8.3 shall be increased by the amount of the reduction under such paragraph that was made to reflect the Section 8.2 distribution referred to therein.

Section 8.8 Allocation of Losses.

(a) Except as provided in Section 8.8(b), 8.9 or 8.10, Losses of the Company for any Fiscal Year shall be allocated in the following order and priority:

(i) First, to offset any Profits previously allocated under Section 8.7 in the inverse order and priority in which such Profits were allocated; and

(ii) Next, to the Class A Holders to the extent of their Capital Contributions.

(b) Losses allocated to a Member pursuant to Section 8.8(a) shall not exceed the maximum amount of losses that can be allocated without causing a Member to have an Adjusted Capital Account Deficit at the end of any Fiscal Year. In the event that any Member would have an Adjusted Capital Account Deficit as a consequence of an allocation of losses pursuant to Section 8.8(a), the amount of losses that would be allocated to such Member but for the application of this Section 8.8(b) shall be allocated to the other Members that are Class A Holders to the extent that such allocations would not cause such other Members to have an Adjusted Capital Account Deficit and allocated among such other Members in proportion to their Class A Units. Any allocation of items of loss pursuant to this Section 8.8(b) shall be taken into account in computing subsequent allocations pursuant to Section 8.7 and 8.8(a), and prior to any allocation of items in such Sections so that the net amount of any items allocated to each Member pursuant to Section 8.7, Section 8.8(a) and this Section 8.8(b) shall, to the maximum extent practicable, be equal to the net amount that would have been allocated to each Member pursuant to the provisions of Section 8.7, Section 8.8(a) and this Section 8.8(b) if such allocation under this Section 8.8(b) had not occurred.

Section 8.9 Allocation with Respect to Revalued Assets. Except as provided in Section 8.10, upon a revaluation of the Company's assets pursuant to Section 4.3(c) or 4.3(d), any gain or loss inherent in Company assets shall, when realized, be allocated to the Members in the same manner as the Capital Accounts of the Members were adjusted in connection with such revaluation, taking into account any reallocation of Capital Accounts effected pursuant to Section 14.3(a)(iv) or 14.3(b)(v).

Section 8.10 Special Allocations. The following special allocations shall be made in the following order:

(a) If there is a net decrease in Company Minimum Gain during any Fiscal Year, each Member shall be specially allocated items of income for such Fiscal Year (and, if necessary, subsequent Fiscal Years) in an amount equal to such Member's share of the net decrease in Company Minimum Gain, determined in accordance with Treasury Regulations Section 1.704-2(g). Allocations pursuant to the previous sentence shall be made in proportion to the respective amounts required to be allocated to each Member pursuant thereto. The items to be so allocated shall be determined in accordance with Treasury Regulations Sections 1.704-2(f)(6) and 1.704-2(2). This Section 8.10(a) is intended to comply with the minimum gain chargeback requirement in Treasury Regulations Section 1.704-2(f) and shall be interpreted consistently therewith. To the extent permitted by such Treasury Regulations and for purposes of this Section 8.10(a) only, each Member's net decrease in Company Minimum Gain shall be determined prior to any other allocations pursuant to this Article VIII with respect to such Fiscal Year.

(b) Notwithstanding any other provision of this Article VIII except Section 8.10(a), if there is a net decrease in Member Minimum Gain attributable to a Member Nonrecourse Debt during any Fiscal Year, each Member who has a share of the Member Minimum Gain attributable to such Member Nonrecourse Debt, determined in accordance with Treasury Regulations Section 1.704-2(i)(5), shall be specially allocated items of income for such Fiscal Year (and, if necessary, subsequent Fiscal Years) in an amount equal to such Member's share of the net decrease in Member Minimum Gain attributable to such Member Nonrecourse Debt, determined in accordance with Treasury Regulations Section 1.704-2(i)(4). Allocations pursuant to the previous sentence shall be made in proportion to the respective amounts required to be allocated to each Member pursuant thereto. The items to be so allocated shall be determined in accordance with Treasury Regulations Sections 1.704-2(i)(4) and 1.704-2(2)(ii). This Section 8.10(b) is intended to comply with the minimum gain chargeback requirement in Treasury Regulations Section 1.704-2(i)(4) and shall be interpreted consistently therewith. Solely for purposes of this Section 8.10(b), each Member's net decrease in Member Minimum Gain shall be determined prior to any other allocations pursuant to this Article VIII with respect to such Fiscal Year, other than allocations pursuant to Section 8.10(a).

(c) In the event that any Member unexpectedly receives any adjustments, allocations or distributions described in Treasury Regulations Sections 1.704-1(b)(2)(ii)(d)(4), (5), or (6), items of income and gain (including gross income) shall be specifically allocated to each such Member in an amount and manner sufficient to eliminate, to the extent required by the Treasury Regulations, the Adjusted Capital Account Deficit of such Member as quickly as possible, provided that an allocation pursuant to this Section 8.10(c) shall be made if and only to the extent that such Member would have an Adjusted Capital Account Deficit after all other allocations provided for in this Article VIII have been tentatively made as if this Section 8.10(c) were not in this Agreement. The foregoing provision is intended to comply with Treasury Regulations Section 1.704-1(b)(2)(ii)(d) and shall be interpreted and applied in a manner consistent with such Treasury Regulations.

(d) In the event that any Member has an Adjusted Capital Account Deficit at the end of any Fiscal Year, then each such Member shall be specially allocated items of income in the amount of such excess as quickly as possible, provided that an allocation pursuant to this Section 8.10(d) shall be made if and only to the extent that such Member would have an Adjusted Capital Account Deficit in excess of such sum after all other allocations provided for in this Article VIII have been tentatively made as if this Section 8.10(d) and Section 8.10(c) were not in this Agreement.

(e) Any item of Nonrecourse Deduction for any period shall be allocated to the Members in the same manner in which such items would have been allocated pursuant to Section 8.8 (a).

(f) Any Member Nonrecourse Deductions for any Fiscal Year or other period shall be specially allocated to the Member who bears the economic risk of loss with respect to the Member Nonrecourse Debt to which such Member Nonrecourse Deductions are attributable in accordance with Treasury Regulations Section 1.704-2(i).

(g) To the extent an adjustment to the adjusted tax basis of any Company asset is required, pursuant to Treasury Regulations Section 1.704-1(b)(2)(iv)(m), to be taken into account in determining Capital Accounts, the amount of such adjustment to the Capital Account shall be treated as an item of gain (if the adjustment increases the basis of the asset) or loss (if the adjustment decreases such basis), and such gain or loss shall be specially allocated to the Members in a manner consistent with the manner in which their Capital Accounts are required to be adjusted pursuant to such Treasury Regulations Section.

Section 8.11 Curative Allocations. The allocations set forth in Sections 8.8(b) and 8.10 (the "Regulatory Allocations") are intended to comply with certain requirements of the Treasury Regulations. It is the intent of the Members that, to the extent possible, all Regulatory Allocations shall be offset either with other Regulatory Allocations or with special allocations of other items of Profit or Loss pursuant to this Section 8.11. Therefore, notwithstanding any other provision of this Article VIII (other than the Regulatory Allocations), the Board shall make such offsetting special allocations of Profit or Loss in whatever manner it determines appropriate so that, after such offsetting allocations are made, each Member's Capital Account balance is, to the extent possible, equal to the Capital Account balance such Member would have had if the Regulatory Allocations were not part of this Agreement and all Company items were allocated pursuant to Sections 8.7, 8.8(a) and 8.9. In exercising its discretion under this Section 8.11, the Board shall take into account future Regulatory Allocations under Sections 8.10(a) and 8.10(b) that, although not yet made, are likely to offset other Regulatory Allocations previously made under Sections 8.10(e) and 8.10(f).

Section 8.12 Allocation Rules.

(a) In the event Members are admitted to the Company pursuant to this Agreement on different dates, the Profits (or Losses) allocated to the Members for each Fiscal Year during which Members are so admitted shall be allocated among the Members in proportion to the respective Units that each holds from time to time during such Fiscal Year in accordance with § 706 of the Code, using any convention permitted by law and selected by the Board.

(b) For purposes of determining the Profits, Losses or any other items allocable to any period, Profits, Losses and any such other items shall be determined on a daily, monthly or other basis, as determined by the Board using any method that is permissible under § 706 of the Code and the Treasury Regulations thereunder.

(c) Except as otherwise provided in this Agreement, all types of Company income, gain, loss, deduction and any other allocations not otherwise provided for shall be divided among the Members in the same proportions as they share Profits and Losses for the Fiscal Year in question.

Section 8.13 Tax Allocations of Section 704(c) of the Code.

(a) In accordance with § 704(c) of the Code and the Treasury Regulations thereunder, income, gain, loss and deduction with respect to any property contributed to the capital of the Company shall, solely for income tax purposes, be allocated among the Members so as to take account of any variation between the adjusted basis of such property to the Company for federal income tax purposes and its initial Gross Asset Value (computed in accordance with Section 1.1 hereof).

(b) In the event the Gross Asset Value of any Company asset is adjusted pursuant to Paragraph (b) of the definition of "Gross Asset Value" contained in Section 1.1 hereof subsequent allocations of income, gain, loss and deduction with respect to such asset shall take account of any variation between the adjusted basis of such asset for federal income tax purposes and its Gross Asset Value in the same manner as under § 704(c) of the Code and the Treasury Regulations thereunder.

(c) Any elections or other decisions relating to allocations solely for tax purposes under this Article VIII, including the selection of any allocation method permitted under Treasury Regulation § 1.704-3, shall be made by the Board in any manner that reasonably reflects the purpose and intention of this Agreement. Allocations pursuant to this Section 8.13 are solely for purposes of federal, state and local taxes and shall not affect, or in any way be taken into account in computing, any Member's Capital Account or share of Profits, Losses, other items or distributions pursuant to any provision of this Agreement.

(d) The Members are aware of the income tax consequences of the allocations made by this Article VIII and hereby agree to be bound by the provisions of this Article VIII in reporting their shares of Company income and loss for income tax purposes.

ARTICLE IX
BOOKS AND RECORDS

Section 9.1 Books, Records, and Financial Statements. At all times during the continuance of the Company, the Company shall maintain, at its principal place of business, separate books of account for the Company that shall show a true and accurate record of all costs and expenses incurred, all charges made, all credits made and received and all income derived in connection with the operation of the Company business in accordance with generally accepted accounting principles consistently applied, and, to the extent inconsistent therewith, in accordance with this Agreement. Such books of account, together with a copy of this Agreement and of the Certificate, shall at all times be maintained at the principal place of business of the Company and shall be open to inspection and examination at reasonable times by each Member and its duly authorized representative for any purpose reasonably related to such Member's interest in the Company. The books of account and the records of the Company shall be examined by and reported upon as of the end of each Fiscal Year by a firm of independent certified public accountants selected by the Board.

Section 9.2 Accounting Method. The books and records of the Company shall be kept on the accrual method of accounting applied in a consistent manner and shall reflect all Company transactions and be appropriate and adequate for the Company's business.

Section 9.3 Annual Audit. As soon as practical after the end of each Fiscal Year, the financial statements of the Company shall be audited by the independent certified public accountants referred to in Section 9.1 hereof, and such financial statements shall be accompanied by a report of such accountants containing their opinion. The cost of such audits will be an expense of the Company.

ARTICLE X
TAX

Section 10.1 Tax Matters Member.

(a) ABC & Co., L.P. is hereby designated as the initial "Tax Matters Member" of the Company and as the "Tax Matters Partner" for purposes of § 6231(a)(7) of the Code and shall have the power to manage and control, on behalf of the Company, any administrative proceeding at the Company level with the Internal Revenue Service relating to the determination of any item of Company income, gain, loss, deduction or credit for federal income tax purposes. The Tax Matters Member shall not take any action or make any decision that materially affects the Company or the Members (including without limitation with respect to income, loss, deduction or credit of the Company) without the prior written consent of Members by Majority Vote.

(b) The Members may at any time hereafter designate a new Tax Matters Member by a Majority Vote; provided, however, that only a Member may be designated as the Tax Matters Member of the Company.

Section 10.2 Right to Make Section 754 Election. The Board may, in its sole discretion, make or revoke, on behalf of the Company, an election in accordance with § 754 of the Code, so as to adjust the tax basis of Company property in the case of a distribution of property within the meaning of § 734 of the Code, and in the case of a transfer of a Company interest within the meaning of § 743 of the Code. Each of the Members shall, upon request of the Board, supply the information necessary to give effect to such an election.

ARTICLE XI
LIABILITY, EXCULPATION, AND INDEMNIFICATION

Section 11.1 Liability. Except as otherwise provided by the Delaware Act, the debts, obligations and liabilities of the Company, whether arising in contract, tort or otherwise, shall be solely the debts, obligations and liabilities of the Company, and no Covered Person shall be obligated personally for any such debt, obligation or liability of the Company solely by reason of being a Covered Person.

Section 11.2 Exculpation.

(a) No Covered Person shall be liable to the Company or any other Covered Person for any loss, damage or claim incurred by reason of any act or omission performed or omitted by such Covered Person in good faith on behalf of the Company and in a manner reasonably believed to be within the scope of authority conferred on such Covered Person by this Agreement, except that a Covered Person shall be liable for any such loss, damage or claim incurred by reason of such Covered Person's gross negligence or willful misconduct.

(b) A Covered Person shall be fully protected in relying in good faith upon the records of the Company and upon such information, opinions, reports or statements presented to the Company by any Person as to matters the Covered Person reasonably believes are within such other Person's professional or expert competence and who has been selected with reasonable care by or on behalf of the Company, including information, opinions, reports or statements as to the value and amount of the assets, liabilities, Profits, Losses or any other facts pertinent to the existence and amount of assets from which distributions to Members might properly be paid.

Section 11.3 Fiduciary Duty.

(a) To the extent that, at law or in equity, a Covered Person has duties (including fiduciary duties) and liabilities relating thereto to the Company or to any other Covered Person, a Covered Person acting under this Agreement shall not be liable to the Company or to any other Covered Person for its good faith reliance on the provisions of this Agreement. The provisions of this Agreement, to the extent that they restrict the duties and liabilities of a Covered Person otherwise existing at law or in equity, are agreed by the parties hereto to replace such other duties and liabilities of such Covered Person.

(b) Whenever in this Agreement a Covered Person is permitted or required to make a decision

(i) in its "discretion" or under a grant of similar authority or latitude, the Covered Person shall be entitled to consider such interests and factors as it desires, including its own interests, and shall have no duty or obligation to give any consideration to any interest of or factors affecting the Company or any other Person, or

(ii) in its "good faith" or under another express standard, the Covered Person shall act under such express standard and shall not be subject to any other or different standard imposed by this Agreement or other applicable law.

Section 11.4 Indemnification. To the fullest extent permitted by applicable law, a Covered Person shall be entitled to indemnification from the Company for any loss, damage or claim incurred by such Covered Person by reason of any act or omission performed or omitted by such Covered Person in good faith on behalf of the Company and in a manner reasonably believed to be within the scope of authority conferred on such Covered Person by this Agreement, except that no Covered Person shall be entitled to be indemnified in respect of any loss, damage or claim incurred by such Covered Person by reason of gross negligence or willful misconduct with respect to such acts or omissions; provided, however, that any indemnity under this Section 11.4 shall be provided out of and to the extent of Company assets only, and no Covered Person shall have any personal liability on account thereof.

Section 11.5 Expenses. To the fullest extent permitted by applicable law, expenses (including legal fees) incurred by a Covered Person in defending any claim, demand, action, suit or proceeding shall, from time to time, be advanced by the Company prior to the final disposition of such claim, demand, action, suit or proceeding including any claim, demand, action, suit or proceeding with respect to which such Covered Person is alleged to have not met the applicable standard of conduct or is alleged to have committed conduct so that, if true, such Covered Person would not be entitled to indemnification under this Agreement, upon receipt by the Company of an undertaking by or on behalf of the Covered Person to repay such amount if it shall be determined that the Covered Person is not entitled to be indemnified as authorized in Section 11.4 hereof.

ARTICLE XII
ADDITIONAL MEMBERS AND UNITS

Section 12.1 Additional Units.

(a) If approved by a Majority Vote, the Company is authorized to raise additional capital by offering and selling, or causing to be offered and sold, additional limited liability company interests in the Company ("Additional Units") to any Person in such amounts and on such terms as the Board may determine. With respect to any issuance of Class B Units or Class D Units, or reissuance of Class B Units or Class D Units that are repurchased in accordance with Section 14.3, the approval of a Majority Vote of Members shall not be required with respect thereto; provided, that any issuance of Class B Units or Class D Units shall be to such Persons and shall be in such amounts as the Chief Executive Officer of the Company recommends to the Board subject to the approval of the Board. With respect to the issuance of Class C Units, or reissuance of Class C Units that are repurchased in accordance with Section 14.4, the approval of a Majority Vote of Members shall not be required with respect thereto; provided, that any issuance of Class C Units shall be to such Outside Managers and shall be in such amounts as shall be approved by the Board. Each Person who subscribes for any of the Additional Units shall be admitted as an additional member of the Company (each, an "Additional Member" and collectively, the "Additional Members") at the time such Person (i) executes this Agreement or a counterpart of this Agreement and (ii) is named as a Member on the Schedules hereto. The legal fees and expenses associated with such admission may be home by the Company.

(b) If Additional Units are issued pursuant to this Article XII such Additional Units will be treated for all purposes of this Agreement as Units as of the date of issuance.

Section 12.2 Preemptive Rights. In the event that the Company at any time shall propose to issue additional Class A Units or units of any other class of limited liability company interests (other than Class B Units, Class C Units or Class D Units) to ABC or its Affiliates, or any securities convertible into, or exchangeable for, or any rights, warrants or options to purchase, any limited liability company interests in the Company, each Class A Holder shall have the right to purchase up to such Holder's Proportionate Percentage of such Additional Units or such securities being issued.

Section 12.3 Allocations. Additional Units shall not be entitled to any retroactive allocation of the Company's income, gains, losses, deductions, credits or other items; provided that, subject to the restrictions of § 706(d) of the Code, Additional Units shall be entitled to their respective share of the Company's income, gains, losses, deductions, credits and other items arising under contracts entered into before the effective date of the issuance of any Additional Units to the extent that such income, gains, losses, deductions, credits and other items arise after such effective date. To the extent consistent with § 706(d) of the Code and Treasury Regulations promulgated thereunder, the Company's books may be closed at the time Additional Units are issued (as though the Company's Fiscal Year had ended) or the Company may credit to the Additional Units pro rata allocations of the Company's income, gains, losses, deductions, credits and items for that portion of the Company's Fiscal Year after the effective date of the issuance of the Additional Units.

ARTICLE XIII
ASSIGNABILITY AND SUBSTITUTE MEMBERS

Section 13.1 Restrictions on Transfer.

(a) No Member shall sell or otherwise Transfer any of its Units (whether now held or hereafter acquired), except in accordance with the terms of this Agreement. Any attempted Transfer of any of a Member's Units in violation of the terms of this Agreement will be null, void and of no effect, and the proposed transferee shall not be recognized by the Company as the owner or holder of the Units attempted to be Transferred or any rights pertaining thereto (including, without limitation, voting rights and rights to allocations and distributions).

(b) Except as otherwise provided in this Agreement, no Transfer of any Units may be made without the consent of the Board, which may be withheld in its sole discretion.

(c) As a condition precedent to the effectiveness of any Transfer of Units to any Person (other than the Company or a Person that is already a Member and has executed this Agreement), the transferee shall execute a counterpart of this Agreement and deliver it to the Company.

Section 13.2 Permitted Transfers. The rights and obligations under Section 13.1 (a) of this Agreement will not apply to a Transfer:

(a) to a Member's ancestors or descendants or spouse or to a trust, partnership, custodianship or other fiduciary account for his or for their benefit;

(b) if the Member is a partnership or limited liability company, to the respective partners in such partnership or Affiliates of such partners or members of such limited liability company;

(c) to an Affiliate of the Member, provided, that such Affiliate is not being used as a device to avoid the restrictions on Transfer provided in this Agreement;

(d) by ABC to an ABC Permitted Transferee, or by an ABC Permitted Transferee to another ABC Permitted Transferee, provided, that such ABC Permitted Transferee is not being used as a device to avoid the restrictions on Transfer provided in this Agreement;

(e) a Transfer pursuant to Article XIV of this Agreement; or

(f) by ABC to any other Person, so long as ABC shall hold at least 50.1% of the Voting Units after such Transfer.

Section 13.3 Substitute Members. Any Transfer of Units pursuant to this Article XIII or XIV including, but not limited to, a Transfer made pursuant to Section 14.1 hereof, shall, nevertheless, not entitle the transferee to become a Substitute Member or to be entitled to exercise or receive any of the rights, powers or benefits of a Member other than the right to share in such profits and losses, to receive distribution or distributions and to receive such allocation of income, gain, loss, deduction or credit or similar item to which the transferor Member would otherwise be entitled, to the extent assigned, unless the transferor Member designates, in a written instrument delivered to the other Members, its transferee to become a Substitute Member and the non-transferring Members holding a majority of the capital and Profits interests of the Company in their sole and absolute discretion, consent to the admission of such transferee as a Member; and provided further, that such transferee shall not become a Substitute Member without having first executed an instrument reasonably satisfactory to the other Members accepting and agreeing to the terms and conditions of this Agreement, including a counterpart signature page to this Agreement, and without having paid to the Company a fee sufficient to cover all reasonable expenses of the Company in connection with such transferee's admission as a Substitute Member. If a Member Transfers all of its interest in the Company and the transferee of such interest is entitled to become a Substitute Member pursuant to this Section 13.3, such transferee shall be admitted to the Company effective immediately prior to the effective date of the Transfer, and, immediately following such admission, the transferor Member shall automatically resign as a Member of the Company. In such event, the Company shall not dissolve as a result of such resignation, in accordance with Section 15.2 hereof.

Section 13.4 Recognition of Assignment by Company. No Transfer or assignment, or any part thereof, that is in violation of this Article XIII shall be valid or effective, and neither the Company nor the Members shall recognize the same for the purpose of making distributions pursuant to Article VIII hereof with respect to such assigned interest or part thereof. Neither the Company nor the nonassigning Members shall incur any liability as a result of refusing to make any such distributions to the assignee of any such invalid assignment.

Section 13.5 Effective Date of Transfer. Any valid Transfer of a Member's interest in the Company, or part thereof, pursuant to the provisions of this Article XIII shall be effective as of the close of business on the last day of the calendar month in which such Transfer occurs. The Company shall, from the effective date of such assignment, thereafter pay all further distributions on account of the Company interest (or part thereof) so assigned, to the transferee of such interest, or part thereof. As between any Member and its transferee, Profits and Losses for the Fiscal Year of the Company in which such Transfer occurs shall be apportioned for federal income tax purposes in accordance with any convention permitted under § 706(d) of the Code and selected by the Managers.

Section13.6 Indemnification. In the case of a Transfer or assignment or attempted Transfer or assignment of an interest in the Company that has not received the consents required by this Article XIII, the parties engaging or attempting to engage in such Transfer or assignment shall be liable to indemnify and hold harmless the Company and the other Members from all costs, liabilities and damages that any of such indemnified Persons may incur (including, without limitation, incremental tax liability and lawyers' fees and expenses) as a result of such Transfer or assignment or attempted Transfer or assignment and efforts to enforce the indemnity granted hereby.

ARTICLE XIV
TAG-ALONG OPTION AND COME-ALONG
OBLIGATION; REPURCHASE OF UNITS

Section 14.1 Tag-Along Option. Subject to Section 13.1(c) hereof, in the event that ABC intends to voluntarily Transfer to another Person (other than to a Permitted Transferee or pursuant to a Public Offering) (such Person being the "Purchaser") any of its Class A Units, then ABC shall deliver to the Company and each other Member a written notice (the "Tag Notice") stating that it intends to make such a Transfer and setting forth the terms and conditions of such proposed Transfer. During the 30-day period (the "Tag-Along Period") from and after the delivery of such notice to the Company and such other Members, each Member shall have the right to elect to sell to the Purchaser, and the Purchaser shall have the obligation to purchase from such Member such Member's Proportionate Percentage of the Class A Units being proposed to be sold pursuant to the notice on the terms and conditions set forth in the Tag Notice. In addition, if the proposed Transfer will result in a Change of Control, each Member shall have the right to elect to sell to the Purchaser, and the Purchaser shall have the obligation to purchase from such Member, any Class B Units, Class C Units or Class D Units such Member elects to sell to the Purchaser up to such Member's Proportionate Percentage of the Class B Units, Class C Units or Class D Units as the case may be, at the fair market value of such Class B Units, Class C Units or Class D Units as the case may be, as interpolated based on the price of the Class A Units set forth in the Tag Notice, provided that the aggregate price for all such Class B Units, Class C Units and Class D Units which Members shall have a right to sell pursuant to this Section 14.1 shall not exceed that percentage of the value that the Purchaser would have paid for all Class A Units which would have been sold pursuant to this Section 14.1 but for the provisions of this sentence as (x) the fair market value of all Class B Units, Class C Units and Class D Units bears to (y) the fair market value of all Units of all classes, in each case as interpolated based on the value of the Class A Units as set forth in the Tag Notice. In the event that the value of the Class B Units, Class C Units and Class D Units that Members wish to sell exceeds the value that is permitted to be sold pursuant to the preceding sentence, then any such limitation shall be shared by the Members wishing to sell such Class B Units, Class C Units or Class D Units based upon the relative values of the respective Class B Units, Class C Units or Class D Units they wish to sell.

Section 14.2 Come-Along Obligation. If any Person or group of Persons makes an offer to purchase all outstanding Units of the Company from all Members (a "Tender Offer"), then the Members (other than any Members who are Affiliates of the Person making the Tender Offer) who hold 50% or more of the total number of Voting Units held by Members who are not Affiliates of the Persons making the Tender Offer (the "Approving Members") may require all other Members ("Minority Members") to sell their Units pursuant to the Tender Offer. To exercise this right, the Approving Members must deliver a written notice to the Minority Members describing the terms and conditions of the Tender Offer. If such an exercise has been made by the Approving Members, then each Minority Member shall be obligated to sell all of its Units pursuant to the Tender Offer. Any amounts to be received by Members or Assignees in connection with a Transfer of Units under this Section 14.2 shall be allocated in accordance with Section 15.5 hereof.

Section 14.3 Repurchase of Class B Units and Class D Units.

(a) Initial Repurchase Right. Subject to the remaining provisions of this Section 14.3, the Company shall be entitled to repurchase a percentage of a Class B Holder's or his Permitted Transferee's Class B Units or a Class D Holder's or his Permitted Transferee's Class D Units pursuant to the terms set forth in this Section 14.3(a).

(i) For any Class B Units issued to a Class B Holder whose employment with the Company or its Subsidiary has terminated for any reason, the Company may repurchase the following percentage of such Class B Units at the following times:

Date of Termination of Employment on or Before	Percentage Company May Repurchase
first anniversary of date of issuance	80%
second anniversary of date of issuance	60%
third anniversary of date of issuance	40%
fourth anniversary of date of issuance	20%

Upon the repurchase of any Class B Units of a Class B Holder pursuant to this Section 14.3(a), the Company may also repurchase the same percentage of the Class D Units held by such Class D Holder, if any.

(ii) The purchase price to be paid by the Company in connection with a repurchase of Class B Units of a Class B Holder or his Permitted Transferee pursuant to this Section 14.3 (a) shall equal the Proportionate Percentage of such Class B Holder or his Permitted Transferee multiplied by twenty percent (20%) of (x) the accumulated earnings and profits of the Company's Subsidiaries less (y) distributions that have been made to the Class A Holders pursuant to Section 8.3(i) or that would be required to be made to such Class A Holders to meet their 10% preferred return pursuant to Section 8.3(i); provided, however, that the purchase price shall not exceed the Fair Asset Value (without discount for lack of marketability and minority interest) of the repurchased Units at the date of purchase as determined by the Board in good faith.

(iii) The purchase price to be paid by the Company in connection with a repurchase of Class D Units of a Class D Holder or his Permitted Transferee pursuant to this Section 14.3(a) shall equal the Proportionate Percentage of such Class D Holder or his Permitted Transferee multiplied by Applicable Percentage of (x) the accumulated earnings and profits of the Company's Subsidiaries less (y) distributions that have been made to the Class A Holders pursuant to Section 8.3(i) or that would be required to be made to such Class A Holders to meet their 10% preferred return pursuant to Section 8.3(i); provided, however, that the purchase price shall not exceed the Fair Asset Value (without discount for lack of marketability and minority interest) of the repurchased Units at the date of purchase as determined by the Board in good faith.

(iv) The amount of the adjusted Capital Account balance of a Class B Holder or a Class D Holder attributable to a repurchased Class B Unit or Class D Unit that exceeds the purchase price paid by the Company for such Class B Unit or Class D Unit (after revaluing the Capital Accounts of the Members pursuant to Section 4.3[c]) shall be allocated to the Capital Accounts of the Class A Holders in proportion to the number of Class A Units held by each.

(b) Additional Repurchase Rights. In addition to the repurchase rights set forth in Section 14.3(a), Class B Units held by a Class B Holder or his Permitted Transferees and Class D Units held by a Class D Holder or his Permitted Transferee shall be subject to repurchase by the Company as provided below:

(i) In the event a Class B Holder's employment by the Company and/or a Subsidiary of the Company terminates because of discharge or termination by the Company or its Subsidiary with Cause or as a result of the resignation of the Class B Holder within 5 years of the grant of Class B Units to such Class B Holder, then all Class B Units held by such Class B Holder or his Permitted Transferees at the time of such termination shall be subject to repurchase by the Company at a repurchase price equal to the Proportionate Percentage of such Class B Holder multiplied by twenty percent (20%) of (x) the accumulated earnings and profits of the Company's Subsidiaries less (y) distributions that have been made to the Class A Holders pursuant to Section 8.3(i) or that would be required to be made to Class A Holders to meet their 10% preferred return pursuant to Section 8.3(i); provided, however, that the purchase price shall not exceed the Fair Asset Value (without discount for lack of marketability and minority interest) of the repurchased Units at the date of purchase as determined by the Board in good faith.

(ii) In the event a Class B Holder's employment by the Company and/or a Subsidiary of the Company terminates (1) because of discharge or termination by the Company or its Subsidiary without Cause, (2) because of the death or Permanent Disability of the Class B Holder, (3) because of the retirement of the Class B Holder in accordance with the policies of the Company or its Subsidiary or (4) as a result of the resignation of the Class B Holder more than 5 years after the grant of Class B Units to such Class B Holder, then the Class B Units held by such Class B Holder or his Permitted Transferees at the time of such termination shall be subject to repurchase by the Company at a purchase price equal to the Fair Asset Value thereof (without discount for lack of marketability and minority interest) at the date of purchase as determined by the Board in good faith.

(iii) In the event a Class D Holder's employment by the Company and/or a Subsidiary of the Company terminates because of discharge or termination by the Company or its Subsidiary with Cause or as a result of the resignation of the Class D Holder within 5 years of the grant of Class D Units to such Class D Holder, then all Class D Units held by such Class D Holder or his Permitted Transferees at the time of such termination shall be subject to repurchase by the Company at a repurchase price equal to the Proportionate Percentage of such Class D Holder multiplied by the Applicable Percentage of (x) the accumulated earnings and profits of the Company's Subsidiaries less (y) distributions that have been made to the Class A Holders pursuant to Section 8.3(i) or that would be required to be made to Class A Holders to meet their 10% preferred return pursuant to Section 8.3(i); provided, however, that the purchase price shall not exceed the Fair Asset Value (without discount for lack of marketability and minority interest) of the repurchased Units at the date of purchase as determined by the Board in good faith.

(iv) In the event a Class D Holder's employment by the Company and/or a Subsidiary of the Company terminates (1) because of discharge or termination by the Company or its Subsidiary without Cause, (2) because of the death or Permanent Disability of the Class D Holder, (3) because of the retirement of the Class D Holder in accordance with the policies of the Company or its Subsidiary or (4) as a result of the resignation of the Class D Holder more than 5 years after the grant of Class D Units to such Class D Holder, then the Class D Units held by such Class D Holder or his Permitted Transferees at the time of such termination shall be subject to repurchase by the Company at a purchase price equal to the Fair Asset Value thereof (without discount for lack of marketability and minority interest) at the date of purchase as determined by the Board in good faith.

(v) The amount of the adjusted Capital Account balance of a Class B Holder or a Class D Holder attributable to a repurchased Class B Unit or Class D Unit that exceeds the purchase price paid by the Company for such Class B Unit or Class D Unit (after revaluing the Capital Accounts of the Members pursuant to Section 4.3[c]) shall be allocated to the Capital Accounts of the Class A Holders in proportion to the number of Class A Units held by each.

(c) Procedures. To exercise any right to repurchase Class B Units and/or Class D Units pursuant to this Section 14.3, the Company shall deliver a written notice (an "Election Notice") to the Class B Holder, Class D Holder or his respective Permitted Transferee whose Class B Units and/or Class D Units are being repurchased within 45 days following the event giving rise to such right. The Election Notice shall state (i) the number of Class B Units and/or Class D Units being repurchased and (ii) the repurchase price therefor. Such repurchase shall be consummated within 60 days following delivery by the Company of such Election Notice. At the closing of any such purchase, (A) such Class B Holder, Class D Holder or his respective Permitted Transferee shall deliver any documentation reasonably requested by the Company and necessary to Transfer such Class B Units and/or Class D Units to the Company and (B) the Company shall deliver in cash or otherwise in immediately available funds to such Class B Holder, Class D Holder or his respective Permitted Transferee the purchase price being paid by the Company for such Class B Units and/or Class D Units. If the right to repurchase any Class B Units and/or Class D Units pursuant to this Section 14.3 is not exercised by the Company, then ABC shall have the right to repurchase such Class B Units and/or Class D Units on the terms set forth in this Section 14.3.

(d) Public Offering. In the event the Public Company intends to consummate a Public Offering:

(i) the Company's right to repurchase Class B Units and/or Class D Units in accordance with Section 14.3 shall terminate and be of no further force and effect, as of the effective date of such Public Offering;

(ii) the Class B Units and Class D Units shall be valued as if all of the equity securities of the Public Company (including those to be sold pursuant to the Public

Offering) were sold at the price per share at which the equity securities of the Public Company are to be sold pursuant to the Public Offering (which price shall be before underwriter's discounts and before expenses) and the aggregate gross proceeds from such hypothetical sale were distributed pursuant to this Agreement in accordance with Article VIII thereof;

(iii) immediately prior to or simultaneously with the closing of the Public Offering, the Company shall distribute or cause the distribution to the Class B Holder(s) and Class D Holder(s) the aggregate number of shares of capital stock of the Public Company equal in value to the value of the Class B Units and Class D Units as determined in accordance with clause (ii) above; and

(iv) each Class B Holder and Class D Holder shall have the registration rights as are set forth in Schedule B to this Agreement.

Section 14.4 Repurchase of Class C Units.

(a) Repurchase Right. Subject to the remaining provisions of this Section 14.4, the Company shall be entitled to repurchase a percentage of a Class C Holder's or his Permitted Transferee's Class C Units pursuant to the terms set forth in this Section 14.4(a).

(i) For any Class C Units issued to a Class C Holder who has resigned as a Manager of the Company for any reason, the Company may repurchase the following percentage of such Class C Units at the following times:

Date of Termination of Service as a Manager on or Before	Percentage Company May Repurchase
first anniversary of date of issuance	75%
second anniversary of date of issuance	50%
third anniversary of date of issuance	25%

(ii) The purchase price to be paid by the Company in connection with a repurchase of Class C Units of a Class C Holder or his Permitted Transferee pursuant to this Section 14.4(a) shall equal the number of Class C Units being repurchased from such Class C Holder or his Permitted Transferee multiplied by the Class C Unit Percentage of (x) the accumulated earnings and profits of the Company's Subsidiaries less (y) distributions that have been made to the Class A Holders pursuant to Section 8.3(i) or that would be required to be made to such Class A Holders to meet their 10% preferred return pursuant to Section 8.3(i); provided, however, that the purchase price shall not exceed the Fair Asset Value (without discount for lack of marketability and minority interest) of the repurchased Units at the date of repurchase as determined by the Board in good faith,

(b) Procedures. To exercise any right to repurchase Class C Units pursuant to this Section 14.4, the Company shall deliver a written notice (an "Election Notice") to the Class C Holder or his Permitted Transferee whose Class C Units are being repurchased within 45 days following the event giving rise to such right. The Election Notice shall state (i) the number of Class C Units being repurchased and (ii) the purchase price therefor. Such repurchase shall be consummated within 60 days following delivery by the Company of such Election Notice. At the closing of any such purchase, (A) such Class C Holder or his Permitted Transferee shall deliver any documentation reasonably requested by the Company and necessary to Transfer such Class C Units to the Company and (B) the Company shall deliver in cash or otherwise in immediately available funds to such Class C Holder or his Permitted Transferee the purchase price being paid by the Company for such Class C Units. If the right to repurchase any Class C Units pursuant to this Section 14.4 is not exercised by the Company, then ABC shall have the right to repurchase such Class C Units on the terms set forth in this Section 14.4.

(c) Public Offering. In the event the Public Company intends to consummate a Public Offering:

    (i)   the Company's right to repurchase Class C Units in accordance with Section 14.4 shall terminate and be of no further force and effect, as of the effective date of such Public Offering;

    (ii)   the Class C Units shall be valued as if all of the equity securities of the Public Company (including those to be sold pursuant to the Public Offering) were sold at the price per share at which the equity securities of the Public Company are to be sold pursuant to the Public Offering (which price shall be before underwriter's discounts and before expenses) and the aggregate gross proceeds from such hypothetical sale were distributed pursuant to this Agreement in accordance with Article VIII thereof;

    (iii)   immediately prior to or simultaneously with the closing of the Public Offering, the Company shall distribute or cause the distribution to the Class C Holder(s) the aggregate number of shares of capital stock of the Public Company equal in value to the value of the Class C Units as determined in accordance with clause (ii) above; and

    (iv)   each Class C Holder shall have the registration rights as are set forth in Schedule B to this Agreement.

ARTICLE XV
DISSOLUTION, LIQUIDATION, AND TERMINATION

Section 15.1 No Dissolution. The Company shall not be dissolved by the admission of Additional Members or Substitute Members in accordance with the terms of this Agreement.

Section 15.2 Events Causing Dissolution. The Company shall be dissolved and its affairs shall be wound up upon the occurrence of any of the following events:

(a) the expiration of the term of the Company, as provided in Section 2.3 hereof;

(b) the written consent of Members holding at least 66-2/3% of the outstanding Voting Units;

(c) the sale of all or substantially all of the assets of the Company and the expiration of any indemnity period or escrow or the payment of any deferred payment relating to such sale;

(d) immediately prior to the effectiveness of a Public Offering; or

(e) the entry of a decree of judicial dissolution under Section 18-802 of the Delaware Act.

    Notwithstanding anything in this Agreement to the contrary, the death, insanity, bankruptcy, retirement, resignation, expulsion or dissolution of a Member shall not cause the Company to be dissolved and upon the occurrence of such an event the Company shall be continued without dissolution.

Section 15.4 Notice of Dissolution. Upon the dissolution of the Company, the Person or Persons approved by a Majority Vote to carry out the winding up of the Company (the "Liquidating Trustee") shall promptly notify the Members of such dissolution.

Section 15.5 Liquidation. Upon dissolution of the Company, the Liquidating Trustee shall immediately commence to wind up the Company's affairs; provided, however, that a reasonable time shall be allowed for the orderly liquidation of the assets of the Company and the satisfaction of liabilities to creditors so as to enable the Members to minimize the normal losses attendant upon a liquidation. The Members shall continue to share Profits and Losses during liquidation in the same proportions, as specified in Sections 8.7, 8.8, 8.9 and 8.10 hereof, as before liquidation. In applying the provisions of

Section 8.7 to allocate Profits in liquidation, the reference in Section 8.7 to Section 8.3 shall be interpreted so as to apply Section 8.3 without regard to the introductory limitation in Section 8.3 (which refers to distributions upon liquidation pursuant to Section 8.4 hereof). Each Member shall be furnished with a statement prepared by the Company's certified public accountants that shall set forth the assets and liabilities of the Company as of the date of dissolution.

(a) The proceeds of any liquidation (or of any transaction that is deemed to be a liquidation under Section 15.5 hereof) shall be distributed, as realized, in the following order and priority:

    (i) first, to creditors of the Company, including Members who are creditors, to the extent otherwise permitted by law, in satisfaction of the liabilities of the Company (whether by payment or the making of reasonable provision for payment thereof), other than liabilities for distributions to Members; and

    (ii) second, to the Members having positive Capital Account balances (after giving effect to all contributions, distributions and allocations for all periods) proportionately to their respective Capital Account balances (as so adjusted).

(b) If the Liquidating Trustee shall determine that it is not feasible to liquidate all of the assets of the Company, then the Liquidating Trustee shall cause the Fair Asset Value of the assets not so liquidated to be determined. Any unrealized appreciation or depreciation with respect to such assets shall be allocated among the Members in accordance with Article VIII as though the property were sold for its Fair Asset Value and distribution of any such assets in kind to a Member shall be considered a distribution of an amount equal to the assets' Fair Asset Value. Such assets, as so appraised, shall be retained or distributed by the Liquidating Trustee as follows:

    (i) The Liquidating Trustee shall retain assets having a Fair Asset Value equal to the amount by which the net proceeds of liquidated assets are sufficient to satisfy the requirements of paragraph (a)(i) of this Section 15.4. The foregoing notwithstanding, the Liquidating Trustee shall, to the fullest extent permitted by law, have the right to distribute property subject to liens at the value of the Company's equity therein.

    (ii) The remaining assets (including mortgages and other receivables) shall be distributed to the Members in such proportions as shall be equal to the respective amounts to which each Member is entitled pursuant to Section 15.4(a) hereof giving full effect in the calculation thereof to any previous distributions made pursuant to this Section 15.4. If, in the sole and absolute judgment of the Liquidating Trustee, it shall not be feasible to distribute to each Member an aliquot share of each asset, the Liquidating Trustee may allocate and distribute specific assets to one or more Members as tenants-in-common as the Liquidating Trustee shall determine to be fair and equitable.

(c) No Member shall have the right to demand or receive property other than cash upon dissolution and termination of the Company.

Section 15.6 Sale Transactions. Any sale of all or substantially all of the Voting Units in a transaction or series of related transactions, including without limitation pursuant to a Tender Offer, shall be deemed to be a liquidation of the Company, and any amounts to be received by Members of Assignees upon the consummation of any such transaction shall be distributed, as realized, in accordance with Section 15.4(a) hereof.

Section 15.7 Termination. The Company and this Agreement shall terminate when all of the assets of the Company, after payment of or due provision for all debts, liabilities and obligations of the Company, shall have been distributed to the Members in the manner provided for in this Article XV (including without limitation after the sale of Units pursuant to a Tender Offer in accordance with Section 14.2 hereof), and the Certificate shall have been canceled in the manner required by the Delaware Act.

Section 15.8 Claims of the Members. The Members and Assignees shall look solely to the Company's assets for the return of their Capital Contributions, and if the assets of the Company remaining after payment of or due provision for all debts, liabilities and obligations of the Company are insufficient to return such Capital Contributions, the Members and Assignees shall have no recourse against any other Member or the Managers or Officers.

ARTICLE XVI
REGISTRATION RIGHTS

Section 16.1 Registration Rights. In the event the Company or any Subsidiary intends to effect a Public Offering of its equity securities for its own account or for the account of its stockholders in either case pursuant to a registration statement filed with the Securities and Exchange Commission under the Securities Act of 1933, as amended, and the rules and regulations promulgated thereunder, the Members shall have such registration rights set forth in Schedule B attached hereto.

ARTICLE XVII
MISCELLANEOUS

Section 17.1 Notices. All notices provided for in this Agreement shall be in writing, duly signed by the party giving such notice, and shall be delivered in person or by an acknowledged overnight delivery service, telecopied or mailed by registered or certified mail, as follows:

(a) if given to the Company, in care of the President at the Company's mailing address set forth in Section 2.5 hereof,

(b) if given to the Managers, at their mailing addresses set forth on Schedule A attached hereto; or

(c) if given to any Member, at the address set forth opposite its name on Schedule A attached hereto, or at such other address as such Member may hereafter designate by written notice to the Company.

All such notices shall be deemed to have been given when received.

Section 17.2 Failure to Pursue Remedies. The failure of any party to seek redress for violation of, or to insist upon the strict performance of, any provision of this Agreement shall not prevent a subsequent act, which would have originally constituted a violation, from having the effect of an original violation.

Section 17.3 Cumulative Remedies. The rights and remedies provided by this Agreement are cumulative and the use of any one fight or remedy by any party shall not preclude or waive its right to use any or all other remedies. Said rights and remedies are given in addition to any other rights the parties may have by law, statute, ordinance or otherwise.

Section 17.4 Binding Effect. This Agreement shall be binding upon and inure to the benefit of all of the parties and, to the extent permitted by this Agreement, their successors, legal representatives and assigns.

Section 17.5 Interpretation. Throughout this Agreement, nouns, pronouns and verbs shall be construed as masculine, feminine, neuter, singular or plural, whichever shall be applicable. All references herein to "Articles," "Sections" and paragraphs shall refer to corresponding provisions of this Agreement unless otherwise indicated.

Section 17.6 Severability. The invalidity or unenforceability of any particular provision of this Agreement shall not affect the other provisions hereof, and this Agreement shall be construed in all respects as if such invalid or unenforceable provision were omitted.

Section 17.7 Counterparts. This Agreement may be executed in any number of counterparts with the same effect as if all parties hereto had signed the same document. All counterparts shall be construed together and shall constitute one instrument.

Section 17.8 Integration. This Agreement, together with all Schedules hereto, constitutes the entire agreement among the parties hereto pertaining to the subject matter hereof and supersedes all prior agreements and understandings pertaining thereto.

Section 17.9 Governing Law. This Agreement, together with all Schedules hereto and the rights of the parties hereunder shall be interpreted in accordance with the laws of the State of Delaware, and all rights and remedies shall be governed by such laws without regard to principles of conflict of laws.

IN WITNESS WHEREOF, the parties hereto have executed this Agreement as of the date first above stated.

MEMBERS:

ABC & CO., L.P.

By: _____

ABC Management Company, LLC, its general partner

By: _____

Name: _____

Title: _____

ABC & CO. ASSOCIATES, L.P.

By: ABC Management Company II, its general partner

By: _____

Name: _____

Title: _____

By: _____

Name: _____

Title: _____

SCHEDULE A

NAME AND MAILING ADDRESS	CAPITAL CONTRIBUTIONS	NUMBER OF UNITS
Class A Units		
ABC & Co., L.P.	$	
Address		
ABC & Co. Associates, L.P.	$	
Address		
Bill Jones	$	
John Smith	$	

Class B Units

Bill Jones

John Smith

[Others]

Class C Units

[Outside Managers]

Class D Units

Bill Jones

John Smith

[Others]

SCHEDULE B

TO THE LIMITED LIABILITY COMPANY AGREEMENT

OF XYZ COMPANY LLC

REGISTRATION RIGHTS

1. **REGISTRATION RIGHTS.** The Company will perform and comply, and cause each of its Subsidiaries to perform and comply, with such of the following provisions as are applicable to it. Each holder of Units will perform and comply with such of the following provisions as are applicable to such holder. Unless this Schedule B otherwise requires, the term the "Company" shall include Subsidiaries of the Company, as applicable. Capitalized terms used herein but not otherwise defined herein shall have the meanings given such terms in the Limited Liability Company Agreement of XYZ Company LLC, dated as of February 1, 2001, as amended (the "LLC Agreement").

1.1 Piggyback Registration Rights.

1.1.1 Piggyback Registration

(a) General. If the Company at any time proposes to register any of its securities under the Securities Act, for its own account or for the account of any holder of its securities, for a Public Offering, the Company will each such time give notice to all holders of Units (collectively, the "Registrable Securities") of its intention to do so. Any such holder may, by written response delivered to the Company within twenty (20) days after the effectiveness of such notice, request that all or a specified part of the Registrable Securities held by such holder be included in such registration. The Company thereupon will use its commercially reasonable efforts to cause to be included in such registration under the Securities Act all Registrable Securities which the Company has been so requested to register by such holders of Registrable Securities, to the extent required to permit the disposition (in accordance with the intended methods thereof as aforesaid) of the Registrable Securities so to be registered.

(b) Excluded Transactions. The Company shall not be obligated to effect any registration of Registrable Securities under this Section 1.1.1 incidental to the registration of any of its securities in connection with:

(i) Any initial Public Offering.

(ii) Any Public Offering relating to the acquisition or merger after the date hereof by the Company or any of its Subsidiaries of or with any other business.

(iii) Any Public Offering relating to employee benefit plans or dividend reinvestment plans.

1.1.2 Payment of Expenses. The Company shall pay all expenses of holders of Registrable Securities incurred in connection with each registration of Registrable Securities requested pursuant to this Section 1.1, other than underwriting discount and commission, if any, and applicable transfer taxes, if any.

1.1.3 Additional Procedures. Holders of Registrable Securities participating in any Public Offering pursuant to Section 1.1.1 shall take all such actions and execute all such documents and instruments that are reasonably requested by the Company to effect the sale of their Registrable Securities in such Public Offering, including, without limitation, being parties to the underwriting agreement entered into by the Company and any other selling shareholders in connection therewith and being liable in respect of the representations and warranties by, and the other agreements (including customary selling stockholder indemnifications and "lockup" agreements) on the part of, the Company and any other selling shareholders to and for the benefit of the underwriters in such underwriting agreement; provided, however, that (i) with respect to individual representations, warranties and agreements of sellers of Registrable Securities in such Public Offering, the aggregate amount of such liability shall not exceed the lesser of (a) such holder's pro rata portion of any such liability, in accordance with such holder's portion of the total number of Registrable Securities included in the offering or (b) such holder's net proceeds from such offering.

1.2 Certain Other Provisions.

1.2.1 Underwriter's Cutback. Notwithstanding any contrary provision of this Section 1, if, in connection with any registration of Registrable Securities, the underwriter determines that marketing factors (including, without limitation, an adverse effect on the per share offering price) require a limitation of the number of shares to be underwritten, the underwriter may limit the number of Registrable Securities to be included in the registration and underwriting or may exclude Registrable Securities entirely from such registration and underwriting, subject to the terms of this paragraph. The Company shall so advise all holders of the Company's securities that would otherwise be registered and underwritten pursuant hereto, and the number of shares of such securities, including Registrable Securities, that may be included in the registration and underwriting (and thereby sold by Persons other than the Company) shall be allocated so that the number of Registrable Securities that may be included shall be allocated among the holders of Registrable Securities thereof in proportion, as nearly as practicable, to the respective amounts of Registrable Securities held by each such holder at the time of filing the Registration Statement. No securities excluded from the underwriting by reason of the underwriter's marketing limitation shall be included in such registration. If any holder of Registrable Securities disapproves of the terms of the underwriting, it may elect to withdraw therefrom by written notice to the Company and the underwriter. The Registrable Securities so withdrawn shall also be withdrawn from registration.

1.2.2 Other Actions. If and in each case when the Company is required to use its commercially reasonable efforts to effect a registration of any Registrable Securities as provided in this Section 1, the Company shall take appropriate and customary actions in furtherance thereof, including, without limitation: (i) filing with the Securities and Exchange Commission (the "**Commission**") a registration statement and using reasonable efforts to cause such registration statement to become effective, (ii) preparing and filing with the Commission such amendments and supplements to such registration statements as may be required to comply with the Securities Act and to keep such registration statement effective for a period not to exceed 180 days from the date of effectiveness or such earlier time as the Registrable Securities covered by such registration statement have been disposed of in accordance with the intended method of distribution therefor or the expiration of the time when a prospectus relating to such registration is required to be delivered under the Securities Act, (iii) use its commercially reasonable efforts to register or qualify such Registrable Securities under the state securities or "blue sky" laws of such jurisdictions as the sellers shall reasonably request; provided, however, that the Company shall not be obligated to file any general consent to services of process or to qualify as a foreign corporation in any jurisdiction in which it is not so qualified or to subject itself to taxation in respect of doing business in any jurisdiction in which it would not otherwise be so subject; and

(iv) otherwise cooperate reasonably with, and take such customary actions as may reasonably be requested by the holders of Registrable Securities in connection with such registration.

1.2.3 Lockup. For a period of the lesser of (i) 180 days from the effective date of any registration statement filed by the Company, or (ii) the shortest period applicable to any Affiliate (as defined in the Securities Act) of the Company who is a selling shareholder pursuant to such registration statement, each holder of Registrable Securities of the Public Company shall refrain from directly or indirectly selling such securities except pursuant to such registration statement.

1.2.4 Black-Out. Upon receipt of any notice from the Company of the happening of any event of which any prospectus included in such registration statement, as then in effect, includes an untrue statement of material fact or omits to state any material fact required to be stated therein or necessary to make the statements therein, in light of the circumstances under which they were made, not misleading, each holder of Registrable Securities will forthwith discontinue such holder's disposition of Registrable Securities pursuant to the registration statement until such holder receives copies of a supplemental or amended prospectus from the Company and, if so directed by the Company, shall deliver to the Company all copies, other than permanent file copies, then in such holders' possession of the prospectus relating to such Registrable Securities current at the time of receipt of such notice.

1.2.5 Selection of Underwriters and Counsel. The underwriters and legal counsel to be retained in connection with any Public Offering shall be selected by the Board.

1.3 Indemnification and Contribution.

1.3.1 Indemnities of the Company. In the event of any registration of any Registrable Securities or other securities of the Company or any of its Subsidiaries under the Securities Act pursuant to this Section 1 or otherwise, and in connection with any registration statement or any other disclosure document produced by or on behalf of the Company including, without limitation, reports required or other documents filed under the Exchange Act, and other documents pursuant to which securities of the Company are sold (whether or not for the account of the Company), the Company will, and hereby does, and will cause its Subsidiaries, jointly and severally to, indemnify and hold harmless each seller of Registrable Securities, any other holder of securities who is or might be deemed to be a controlling Person of the Company within the meaning of Section 15 of the Securities Act or Section 20 of the Exchange Act, their respective direct and indirect partners, advisory board members, directors, officers and shareholders, and each other Person, if any, who controls any such seller or any such holder within the meaning of Section 15 of the Securities Act or Section 20 of the Exchange Act (each such person being referred to herein as a "**Covered Person**"), against any losses, claims, damages or liabilities, joint or several, to which such Covered Person may be or become subject under the Securities Act, the Exchange Act, state securities or blue sky laws, common law or otherwise, insofar as such losses, claims, damages or liabilities (or actions or proceedings in respect thereof) arise out of or are based upon (i) any untrue statement or alleged untrue statement of any material fact contained or incorporated by reference in any registration statement under the Securities Act, any preliminary prospectus or final prospectus included therein, or any related summary prospectus, or any amendment or supplement thereto, or any document incorporated by reference therein, (ii) any omission or alleged omission to state therein a material fact required to be stated therein or necessary to make the statements therein not misleading, or (iii) any violation or alleged violation by the Company of any federal, state or common law rule or regulation applicable to the Company, and will reimburse such Covered Person for any legal or any other expenses incurred by it in connection with investigating or defending any such loss, claim, damage, liability, action or proceeding; provided, however, that neither the Company nor any of its Subsidiaries shall be liable to any Covered Person in any such case to the extent that any such loss, claim, damage, liability, action or proceeding arises out of or is based upon an untrue statement or alleged untrue statement or omission or alleged omission made in such registration statement, any such preliminary prospectus, final prospectus, summary prospectus, amendment or supplement, incorporated document or other such disclosure document in reliance upon and in conformity with written information furnished to the Company through an instrument duly executed by such Covered Person specifically stating that it is for use in the preparation thereof. The indemnities of the Company and of its Subsidiaries contained in this Section 1.3.1 shall remain in full force and effect regardless of any investigation made by or on behalf of such Covered Person and shall survive any transfer of securities.

1.3.2   Indemnities to the Company. The Company may require, as a condition to including any securities in any registration statement filed pursuant to this Section 1, that the Company shall have received an undertaking satisfactory to it from the prospective seller of such securities, to indemnify and hold harmless the Company, each director of the Company, each officer of the Company who shall sign such registration statement and each other Person (other than such seller), if any, who controls the Company within the meaning of Section 15 of the Securities Act or Section 20 of the Exchange Act (each such person being referred to herein as a "**Covered Person**") with respect to any statement in or omission from such registration statement, any preliminary prospectus or final prospectus included therein, or any amendment or supplement thereto, or any other disclosure document (including, without limitation, reports and other documents filed under the Exchange Act) or any document incorporated therein, if such statement or omission was made in reliance upon and in conformity with written information furnished to the Company through an instrument executed by such seller, specifically stating that it is for use in the preparation of such registration statement, incorporated document, or other disclosure document. Such indemnity shall remain in full force and effect regardless of any investigation made by or on behalf of the Company or any such director, officer or controlling Person and shall survive any transfer of securities.

1.3.3   Indemnification Procedures. Promptly after receipt by a Covered Person of notice of the commencement of any action or proceeding involving a claim of the type referred to in the foregoing provisions of this Section 1.3, such Covered Person will, if a claim in respect thereof is to be made by such Covered Person against any indemnifying party, give written notice to each such indemnifying party of the commencement of such action; provided, however, that the failure of any Covered Person to give notice to such indemnifying party as provided herein shall not relieve any indemnifying party of its obligations under the foregoing provisions of this Section 1.3, except and solely to the extent that such indemnifying party is actually prejudiced by such failure to give notice. In case any such action is brought against a Covered Person, each indemnifying party will be entitled to participate in and to assume the defense thereof, jointly with any other indemnifying party similarly notified, to the extent that it may wish, with counsel reasonably satisfactory to such Covered Person (who shall not, except with the consent of the Covered Person, be counsel to such an indemnifying party), and after notice from an indemnifying party to such Covered Person of its election so to assume the defense thereof, such indemnifying party will not be liable to such Covered Person for any legal or other expenses subsequently incurred by the latter in connection with the defense thereof; provided, however, that (i) if the Covered Person reasonably determines that there may be a conflict between the positions of such indemnifying party and the Covered Person in conducting the defense of such action or if the Covered Person reasonably concludes that representation of both parties by the same counsel would be inappropriate due to actual or potential differing interests between them, then counsel for the Covered Person shall conduct the defense to the extent reasonably determined by such counsel to be necessary to protect the interests of the Covered Person and such indemnifying party shall employ separate counsel for its own defense, (ii) the indemnifying party shall bear the legal expenses incurred in connection with the conduct of, and the participation in, the defense as referred to in clauses (i) and (ii) above. If, within a reasonable time after receipt of the notice, such indemnifying party shall not have elected to assume the defense of the action, such indemnifying party shall be responsible for any legal or other expenses incurred by such Covered Person in connection with the defense of the action, suit, investigation, inquiry or proceeding. No indemnifying party will consent to entry of any judgment or enter into any settlement which does not include as an unconditional term thereof the giving by the claimant or plaintiff to such Covered Person of a release from all liabilities in respect to such claim or litigation.

1.3.4   Contribution. If the indemnification provided for in Sections 1.3.1 or 1.3.2 hereof is unavailable to a party that would have been a Covered Person under any such Section in respect of any losses, claims, damages or liabilities (or actions or proceedings in respect thereof) referred to therein, then each party that would have been an indemnifying party thereunder shall, in lieu of indemnifying such Covered Person, contribute to the amount paid or payable by such Covered Person as a result of such losses, claims, damages or liabilities (or actions or proceedings in respect thereof) in such proportion as is appropriate to reflect the relative fault of such indemnifying party on the one hand and such Covered Person on the other in connection with the statements or omissions which resulted in such losses, claims, damages or liabilities (or actions or proceedings in respect thereof). The relative fault shall be determined by reference to, among other things, whether the untrue or alleged untrue statement of a material fact or the omission or alleged omission to state a material fact relates to information supplied by such indemnifying party or such Covered Person and the parties' relative intent, knowledge, access to information and opportunity to correct or prevent such statement or omission. The parties agree that it would not be just or equitable if contribution pursuant to this Section 1.3.4 were determined by pro rata allocation or by any other method of allocation which does not take account of the equitable considerations referred to in the preceding sentence. The amount paid or payable by a contributing party as a result of the losses, claims, damages or liabilities (or actions or proceedings in respect thereof) referred to above in this Section 1.3.4 shall include any legal or other expenses reasonably incurred by such Covered Person in connection with investigating or defending any such action or claim. No Person guilty of fraudulent misrepresentation (within the meaning of Section 11[f] of the Securities Act) shall be entitled to contribution from any Person who was not guilty of such fraudulent misrepresentation.

1.3.5   Limitation on Liability of Holders of Registrable Securities. The liability of each holder of Registrable Securities in respect of any indemnification or contribution obligation of such holder arising under this Section 1.3 shall not in any event exceed an amount equal to the net proceeds to such holder (after deduction of all underwriters' discounts and commissions and all other expenses paid by such holder in connection with the registration in question) from the disposition of the Registrable Securities disposed of by such holder pursuant to such registration.

1.4 Survival.

1.4.1 Survival. The registration rights set forth in this Section 1 shall survive the dissolution of XYZ Company LLC pursuant to Section 15.2(d) of the LLC Agreement and shall remain binding on the Subsidiaries of XYZ Company LLC.

SCHEDULE C

NON-NEGOTIABLE UNIT CERTIFICATE FOR

UNITS IN XYZ COMPANY LLC

"This Certificate and the Units represented hereby are subject to a certain limited liability company agreement dated as of February 1, 2001, and any amendment thereto, a copy of which agreement is on file at the principal place of business of the Company, and any sale, gift, pledge, assignment, bequest, transfer, transfer in trust, mortgage, alienation, hypothecation, encumbering or disposition of Units in any manner whatsoever, voluntarily or involuntarily, including, without limitation, any attachment, assignment for the benefit of creditors or transfer by operation of law or otherwise, or any transfer as a result of any voluntary or involuntary legal proceedings, execution, sale, bankruptcy, insolvency, or otherwise of this Certificate or the Units represented hereby in violation of said agreement shall be invalid."

Certificate No.   Class [B/D] Membership Interest

                                       _____ Class [B/D] Units

XYZ Company LLC, a Delaware limited liability company (the "Company"), hereby certifies that _____ (the "Holder") is the registered owner of the above referenced Units in the Company. This Certificate is issued pursuant to the Limited Liability Company Agreement of the Company, dated as of _____, _____, as the same may be amended, modified or supplemented from time to time (the "Limited Liability Company Agreement"). The rights, powers, preferences, restrictions and limitations of the Units represented hereby are set forth in, and the Certificate and the Units represented hereby are issued and shall in all respects be subject to, the terms and provisions of, the Limited Liability Company Agreement. THE UNITS REPRESENTED BY THIS CERTIFICATE ARE NONTRANSFERABLE EXCEPT AS EXPRESSLY PROVIDED IN THE LIMITED LIABILITY COMPANY AGREEMENT. By acceptance of this Certificate for the above referenced Units, and as a condition to being entitled to any rights and/or benefits with respect to the Units evidenced hereby, the Holder hereof (including any transferee hereof) is deemed to have agreed, whether or not such Holder is admitted to the Company as a Member of the Company with respect to the Units evidenced hereby, to comply with and be bound by all the terms and conditions of the Limited Liability Company Agreement.

Date: _____   XYZ Company LLC

                                 By: _____

EXHIBIT X

APPLICABLE PERCENTAGE FOR SECTION 8.3(IV) DISTRIBUTIONS

If the ROI to the Class A Holders with respect to the relevant year in which distributions are made equals or exceeds the multiple of all Capital Contributions made by such Class A Holders set forth in the column "ROI," the Applicable Percentage for such distribution shall equal the percentage set forth for such year of distribution that corresponds to the highest ROI so equaled or exceeded.

TIME

ROI*	Year**1	Year 2	Year 3	Year 4	Year 5	Year 6	Year 7	Year 8	Year 9	Year 10
3.000x	5%									
3.500x	6%	5%								
4.000x	7%	6%	5%							
4.500x	8%	7%	6%							
5.000x	9%	8%	7%							
5.500x	10%	9%	8%	1%						
6.000x	10%	10%	9%	2%	1%	1%	1%	1%	1%	1%
6.500x	10%	10%	10%	3%	2%	2%	2%	2%	2%	2%
7.000x	10%	10%	10%	4%	3%	3%	3%	3%	3%	3%
7.500x	10%	10%	10%	5%	4%	4%	4%	4%	4%	4%
8.000x	10%	10%	10%	6%	5%	5%	5%	5%	5%	5%
8.500x	10%	10%	10%	7%	6%	6%	6%	6%	6%	6%
9.000x	10%	10%	10%	8%	7%	7%	7%	7%	7%	7%
9.500x	10%	10%	10%	9%	8%	8%	8%	8%	8%	8%
10.000x	10%	10%	10%	10%	9%	9%	9%	9%	9%	9%
11.000x	10%	10%	10%	10%	10%	10%	10%	10%	10%	10%

* "ROI" shall mean the multiple that the return of and return on Capital Contributions (cash on cash) made to the Company by the Class A Holders bears to the aggregate Capital Contributions made to the Company by the Class A Holders.

** Year with respect to which the Applicable Percentage is being calculated, measured from the date of this Agreement.

APPENDIX 10

SECTION 83(B) ELECTION

This statement is being made under Section 83(b) of the Internal Revenue Code, pursuant to Treas. Reg. Section 1.83-2.

(1) The person who performed the services is:

    Name: _____

    Address: _____

    _____

    Taxpayer Id. No.: _____

    Tax Year: 2000

(2) The property with respect to which the election is being made is _____ shares of common stock of _____ (the "Company").

(3) The stock was transferred on _____, 2000.

(4) The stock is subject to restrictions **[describe restrictions on stock].**

(5) The fair market value at the time of transfer (determined without regard to any restriction other than a restriction which by its terms will never lapse) is $_____ per share.

(6) The amount paid for the stock is $____ per share.

(7) A copy of this statement was furnished to the Company.

(8) This statement is executed as of _____.

_____

Taxpayer

[Code of Federal Regulations]

[Title 26, Volume 2, Part 1 (Sections 1.61 to 1.169)]

[Revised as of April 1, 2000]

From the U.S. Government Printing Office via GPO Access

[CITE: 26CFR1.83-2]

[Pages 302–303]

TITLE 26—INTERNAL REVENUE

COMPUTATION OF TAXABLE INCOME—TABLE OF CONTENTS

Sec. 1.83-2 Election to include in gross income in year of transfer.

(a) <u>In general.</u> If property is transferred (within the meaning of Sec. 1.83-3[a]) in connection with the performance of services, the person performing such services may elect to include in gross income under section 83(b) the excess (if any) of the fair market value of the property at the time of transfer (determined without regard to any lapse restriction, as defined in Sec. 1.83-3[i]) over the amount (if any) paid for such property, as compensation for services. The fact that the transferee has paid full value for the property transferred, realizing no bargain element in the transaction, does not preclude the use of the election as provided for in this section. If this election is made, the substantial vesting rules of section 83(a) and the regulations thereunder do not apply with respect to such property, and except as otherwise provided in section 83(d)(2) and the regulations thereunder (relating to the cancellation of a non-lapse restriction), any subsequent appreciation in the value of the property is not taxable as compensation to the person who performed the services. Thus, property with respect to which this election is made shall be includible in gross income as of the time of transfer, even though such property is substantially nonvested (as defined in Sec. 1.83-3[b]) at the time of transfer, and no compensation will be includible in gross income when such property becomes substantially vested (as defined in Sec. 1.83-3[b]). In computing the gain or loss from the subsequent sale or exchange of such property, its basis shall be the amount paid for the property increased by the amount included in gross income under section 83(b). If property for which a section 83(b) election is in effect is forfeited while substantially nonvested, such forfeiture shall be treated as a sale or exchange upon which there is realized a loss equal to the excess (if any) of—

(1) The amount paid (if any) for such property, over,

(2) The amount realized (if any) upon such forfeiture.

If such property is a capital asset in the hands of the taxpayer, such loss shall be a capital loss. A sale or other disposition of the property that is in substance a forfeiture, or is made in contemplation of a forfeiture, shall be treated as a forfeiture under the two immediately preceding sentences.

(b) Time for making election. Except as provided in the following sentence, the election referred to in paragraph (a) of this section shall be filed not later than 30 days after the date the property was transferred (or, if later, January 29, 1970) and may be filed prior to the date of transfer. Any statement filed before February 15, 1970, which was amended not later than February 16, 1970, in order to make it conform to the requirements of paragraph (e) of this section, shall be deemed a proper election under section 83(b).

(c) Manner of making election. The election referred to in paragraph (a) of this section is made by filing one copy of a written statement with the internal revenue office with whom the person who performed the services files his return. In addition, one copy of such statement shall be submitted with this income tax return for the taxable year in which such property was transferred.

(d) Additional copies. The person who performed the services shall also submit a copy of the statement referred to in paragraph (c) of this section to the person for whom the services are performed. In addition, if the person who performs the services and the transferee of such property are not the same person, the person who performs the services shall submit a copy of such statement to the transferee of the property.

(e) Content of statement. The statement shall be signed by the person making the election and shall indicate that it is being made under section 83(b) of the Code, and shall contain the following information:

(1) The name, address and taxpayer identification number of the taxpayer;

(2) A description of each property with respect to which the election is being made;

(3) The date or dates on which the property is transferred and the taxable year (for example, "calendar year 1970" or "fiscal year ending May 31, 1970") for which such election was made;

(4) The nature of the restriction or restrictions to which the property is subject;

(5) The fair market value at the time of transfer (determined without regard to any lapse restriction, as defined in Sec. 1.83-3[i]) of each property with respect to which the election is being made;

(6) The amount (if any) paid for such property; and

(7) With respect to elections made after July 21, 1978, a statement to the effect that copies have been furnished to other persons as provided in paragraph (d) of this section.

(f) Revocability of election. An election under section 83(b) may not be revoked except with the consent of the Commissioner. Consent will be granted only in the case where the transferee is under a mistake of fact as to the underlying transaction and must be requested within 60 days of the date on which the mistake of fact first became known to the person who made the election. In any event, a mistake as to the value, or decline in the value, of the property with respect to which an election under section 83(b) has been made or a failure to perform an act contemplated at the time of transfer of such property does not constitute a mistake of fact.

[T.D. 7554, 43 FR 31915, July 24, 1978]

APPENDIX 11

UVW, INC.
EMPLOYEE STOCK PURCHASE PLAN

1. Objective

The objective of this Employee Stock Purchase Plan is to advance the interests of UVW, Inc. ("UVW") and its shareholders by encouraging its employees and the employees of its subsidiaries to acquire a stake in its growth and earnings.

It is intended that this Employee Stock Purchase Plan shall be an employee stock purchase plan within the meaning of Section 423 of the Internal Revenue Code of 1986, as amended.

2. Definitions

The following terms used in this Employee Stock Purchase Plan shall have the meanings set forth below:

A. "Base Salary Rate" shall mean the base annual salary rate calculated prior to withholding or deduction for FICA taxes, unemployment taxes or any other taxes routinely withheld with regard to any Eligible Employee. The calculation of an Eligible Employee's Base Salary Rate shall not include overtime or incentive compensation, bonuses or any other special payment paid by the Company or any Subsidiary to any Eligible Employee except as otherwise determined by the Committee. All determinations of Base Salary Rate shall be made by the Committee and such determinations shall be applied uniformly to all Eligible Employees.

B. "Board" shall mean the Board of Directors of UVW.

C. "Code" shall mean the Internal Revenue Code of 1986, as amended, or any successor revenue law of the United States.

D. "Committee" shall mean the Employee Stock Purchase Plan Committee established under this Employee Stock Purchase Plan.

E. "Company" shall mean UVW.

F. "Date of Grant" in respect of any option granted under this Employee Stock Purchase Plan shall mean the date on which that option is granted by the Board.

G. "Date of Exercise" in respect of any option granted under this Employee Stock Purchase Plan shall mean the date on which the Optionee's written notice of exercise is received in the Personnel Department of UVW.

H. "Eligible Employee" shall mean all employees of the Company or any Subsidiary who have been employed for at least one (1) year (counting employment with predecessor and employment with a corporation prior to the date it became a Subsidiary) as of the Date of Grant for any option, except that the Committee may elect to exclude employees whose customary employment is twenty (20) hours or less per week.

I. "Exercise" in respect of an option shall mean the delivery by the Optionee to the Personnel Department of UVW a written notice of exercise in the form specified by the Board, accompanied by payment in full for the shares to be acquired pursuant to such exercise.

J. "Optionee" shall mean a person to whom an option has been granted under this Employee Stock Purchase Plan which has not been exercised or surrendered and which has not expired.

K. "Parent" shall mean any corporation which is at the time in question the parent of the Company for purposes of Section 424(e) of the Code.

L. "Plan" shall mean this Employee Stock Purchase Plan.

M. "Shares" shall mean shares of the $5.00 par value common stock of the Company.

N. "Subsidiary" shall mean any corporation (including, without limitations, any bank or business corporation) which is at the time in question a subsidiary of the Company for purposes of Section 424(f) of the Code.

O. "Total Allocated Shares" shall mean the maximum number of Shares determined by the Committee for which options shall be granted on any Date of Grant.

3. Number of Shares Subject to Option

The maximum number of Shares for which options may be granted under the Plan is 100,000 subject to adjustment in the dividend, stock split, reverse stock split, recapitalization, merger, consolidation, transfer of assets, reorganization, conversion or what the Committee deems in its sole discretion to be similar circumstances. Shares which are subject to an outstanding option and the option price per Share will be similarly adjusted in the event of any such transaction in a manner determined in the sole discretion of the Committee. Shares subject to options which have terminated unexercised, either in whole or in part, may again be optioned pursuant to the Plan.

4. Administration and Interpretation

A. This Plan shall be administered by a Committee appointed by the Board. The Committee shall consist of a minimum of three members of the Board, each of whom shall be a "Non-employee Director" as defined in Rule 16b-3(d)(3) under the Securities Exchange Act of 1934, as amended, of the Securities and Exchange Commission (hereinafter called "SEC") or any future corresponding rule. The Committee shall, in addition to its other authority in its sole discretion, to determine the time or times at which the options shall be granted, the rate of option exercisability, the price at which each of the options is exercisable, and the duration of the option.

B. The Committee shall adopt such rules for the conduct of its business and administration of this Plan as it considers desirable. A majority of the members of the Committee shall constitute a quorum for all purposes. The vote or written consent of a majority of the members of the Committee shall have the exclusive right to construe the Plan and the options issued pursuant to it, correct defects, supply omissions and reconcile inconsistencies to the extent necessary to effectuate the Plan and the options issued pursuant to it, and such action shall be final, binding and conclusive upon all parties concerned. No member of the Committee or the Board shall be liable for any act or omission (whether or not negligent) taken or omitted in good faith, or for the exercise of an authority or discretion granted in connection with this Plan to the Committee or the board, or for the acts or omissions of any other members of the Committee or the Board. Subject to the numerical limitations on Committee membership set forth in Section 4A hereof, the Board may at any time appoint additional members of the Committee and may at any time remove any member of the Committee with or without cause. Vacancies in the Committee, however caused, may be filled by the Board if it so desires.

5. Granting of Options and Limitations Thereon

The Committee is authorized to grant options pursuant to this Plan only to employees of the Company and to employees of its Subsidiaries, subject to the following limitations:

A. Options may be granted only to Eligible Employees on one or more Dates of Grant as may be determined by the Committee. The Committee shall also determine the Total Allocated Shares to be granted on each Date of Grant.

B. When options are granted to Eligible Employees, each Eligible Employee may elect to purchase, through payroll deduction or otherwise, the number of Shares, rounded down to the nearest whole Share, which could be purchased with up to twenty-five percent (25%) of such Eligible Employee's Base Salary

Rate determined as of the Date of Grant; provided, however, that if the total number of whole Shares which is elected to be purchased by all Eligible Employees with regard to any such Date of Grant, exceeds the number of Total Allocated Shares, then each Eligible Employee shall be granted an option for such proportion of the Total Allocated Shares, rounded down to the nearest whole Share, as the amount of Shares elected to be purchased by such Eligible Employee (as determined above) bears to the total Shares elected to be purchased by all Eligible Employees. The actual percentage of Base Salary Rate, up to 25%, which each Eligible Employee may elect to purchase Shares shall be based upon his written election to be made in the manner determined by the Committee. All Eligible Employees to whom options are granted under this Plan shall otherwise have the same rights and privileges. The Committee shall have the right, in its sole discretion, to change the maximum percentage of Base Salary Rate which may be elected by Eligible Employees to be used to purchase Shares; provided, however, that such maximum percentage, as determined by the Committee, shall apply to all Eligible Employees.

C. The number of Shares for which options may be granted to each employee shall be subject to the following limitations:

(i) no option shall be granted to any Eligible Employee who, immediately after the grant, would own stock possessing five percent (5%) or more of the total combined voting power or the value of all classes of stock of the Company, its Parent or any Subsidiary. In computing the stock ownership of any Eligible Employee for purposes of this limitation, the rules of Section 424(d) of the Code shall apply and stock which an Eligible Employee may purchase under outstanding options (whether or not such options are fully vested or entitled to special tax treatment under the Code) shall be treated as stock owned by that Eligible Employee.

(ii) no option shall be granted to any Eligible Employee which, at the Date of Grant, would permit his right to purchase stock under the Plan and all other employee stock purchase plans of the Company, its Parent and Subsidiaries to accrue at a rate exceeding $25,000 of fair market value of such stock (determined at the time such option is granted) for each calendar year in which such option is outstanding at any time, as more fully defined in Section 423(b)(8) of the Code.

D. Subject to the restrictions set forth in paragraph (E), below, the option price shall be not less than the lesser of (i) 85% of the fair market value of the Shares on the Date of Grant, or (ii) 85% of the fair market value of the Shares on the Date of Exercise. Fair market value shall be determined in accordance with the rules established by the Committee.

E. All options granted under the Plan shall expire at such time, not later than five (5) years after the Date of Grant, as the Committee shall determine, provided, however, that options exercised more than twenty-seven (27) months after the Date of Grant must be exercised at an option price equal to 85% of the fair market value of the Shares on the Date of Exercise. No option may be exercised under any circumstances after its expiration date.

6. **Option Terms**

The options granted under the Plan shall be on the terms stated in A through E below. The Committee may specify additional terms inconsistent with the provisions of the Plan by rules of general application or by specific direction in connection with a particular group of options.

A. Options shall not be transferred by the Optionee otherwise than by will or the laws of descent and distribution.

B. During the lifetime of an Optionee, an option shall be exercisable only by him and only if he is an employee of the Company or its parent or a Subsidiary on the Date of Exercise or if he ceased to be an employee of the Company or its Parent or a Subsidiary within the three-month period preceding the Date of Exercise (but not later than the periods set forth in Section 5E hereof), but only to the extent that the option was exercisable at the time of termination of the Optionee's employment.

C. In the event an Optionee dies while employed by the Company or its Parent or a Subsidiary or within three months after ceasing to be so employed (but not later than the periods set forth in Section 5E hereof), any option held by him at the time of his death may be exercised within six (6) months after his death by those entitled to do so under his will or under applicable laws of descent and distribution, but only to the extent that the option was exercisable by him at the time of his death. To the extent an option is not so exercised, it shall expire at the end of this six-month period.

D. If the Company is succeeded by another corporation in a merger or consolidation, or Transfer of substantially all of its assets, or if 100% of its stock is acquired by another corporation, and if an option granted under the Plan is assumed by the successor corporation, such option shall be applicable to stock of the successor corporation, with only such modifications as may be necessary to continue its status as an option granted under an employee stock purchase plan within the meaning of Section 423 of the Code. If an option is not assumed by such successor corporation, such option shall be applicable to stock of the successor corporation, with only such modifications as may be necessary to continue its status as an option granted under an employee stock purchase plan within the meaning of Section 423 of the Code. If an option is not assumed by such successor corporation, such option shall expire if it is not exercised before the effective date of such merger, consolidation, Transfer of assets, or acquisition. To the extent that an option is not exercisable by reason of such merger, consolidation, Transfer of assets, or acquisition.

E. The Board may provide that an option shall be exercisable from time to time as to all or any part of the Shares covered by the option or that an option shall be exercisable in part after the Optionee has been continuously employed by the Company, its Parent or a Subsidiary for specified periods.

7. Exercise; Payroll Deduction; Delivery of Option Shares

A. An option may be exercised by giving written notice to the Treasurer of the Company on forms supplied by the Company at its then principal office, accompanied by payment in cash or check for the total number of shares to be purchased. No fractional shares shall be issued or delivered. Until the option price has been paid in full pursuant to the due exercise of an option granted hereunder and the purchased Shares are delivered to the Optionee, the Optionee has no rights as a shareholder of the Company.

B. The Committee may choose to permit or require payroll deductions to enable the Optionee to accumulate the necessary funds in order to exercise his option, in which case the option may be exercised by applying the accumulated payroll deductions toward the total price of the Shares to be purchased under the option at such time and under such conditions as the Committee shall determine. Prior to the due application of the accumulated payroll deductions to the exercise of an option, the Optionee shall have no interest in the Shares subject to the option. Payroll deductions may be withdrawn by an Optionee by giving written notice to the Treasurer of the Company at any time prior to the application of such funds to the exercise of an option. Payroll deductions credited to an Optionee's account may not be assigned, transferred, pledged or otherwise disposed of by the Optionee and the Company may treat any attempt to do so as an election to withdraw the funds. No interest will be paid or allowed on accumulated payroll deductions or on any other amounts credited to the account of any Optionee hereunder. All payroll deductions received or held by the Company may be used by the Company for any corporate purpose and need not be segregated.

C. Upon the due exercise of an option granted hereunder, the Company shall deliver to the Optionee either authorized but unissued Shares or treasury Shares, at the Company's option. The Company shall be under no obligation to retain unissued any particular number of Shares at any time and no particular Shares shall be identified as those optioned. Notwithstanding anything to the contrary contained herein, no option shall be exercisable until all the following events occur and during the following periods of time:

   (i)   Until this Plan is approved by the shareholders of the Company in the manner prescribed by the Code and the regulations thereunder;

   (ii) Until the Shares subject to option are approved and/or registered with such federal, state and local regulatory bodies or agencies and securities exchanges as the Company may deem necessary or desirable; or

   (iii) During any period of time in which the Company deems that the exercisability of any option, the offer to sell the Shares subject to option, or the sale thereof, may violate a federal, state, local or securities exchange rule, regulation or law, or may cause the Company to be legally obligated to issue or sell more Shares than the Company is legally entitled to issue or sell.

8. Plan and Options Not to Affect Employment

Neither the Plan nor any option granted hereunder shall confer any employees any right to continue in the employ of the Company, its Parent, or any Subsidiary or interfere in any way with the right of the Company, its Parent, or any Subsidiary to terminate his employment in any way.

9. Modification, Amendment, Suspension, and Termination

Options shall not be granted pursuant to this Plan after the expiration of ten years from and after the date of the adoption of the Plan by the Board. The Board reserves the right at any time, and from time to time, to modify or amend this Plan in any way, or to suspend or terminate it, effective as of such date, which date may be either before or after the taking of such action, as may be specified by the Board of Directors; provided, however, that such action shall not affect options granted under the Plan prior to the actual date on which such action occurred. If a modification or amendment of this Plan is required by Code or the regulations thereunder to be approved by the shareholders of the Company in order to permit the granting of option under an "employee stock purchase plan" (as that term is defined in Section 423 of the Code and regulations thereunder) pursuant to the modified or amended Plan, such modification or amendment shall also be approved by the shareholders of the Company in such manner as is prescribed by the Code and the regulations thereunder. If the Board of Directors voluntarily submits a proposed modification, amendment, suspension or termination for stockholder approval, such submission shall not require any future modifications, amendments (whether or not relating to the same provisions or subject matter), suspensions or terminations to be similarly submitted for shareholder approval.

10. Effective Date of Plan

The Plan shall become effective on the date on which it is adopted by the Board, provided the Plan is approved within one (1) year after the Effective Date by the shareholders of the Company. The Board may issue options pursuant to the Plan prior to approval by the shareholders of the Company, provided that all such options are contingent upon shareholder approval of the Plan.

11. General Conditions

A. Corporation action constituting an offer of stock for sale to any employee under the terms of the options to be granted hereunder shall be deemed completed as of the date when the Committee authorizes the grant of the option to the employee, regardless of when the option is actually delivered to the employee or acknowledged or agreed to by him.

B. Each of the options granted pursuant to this Plan is intended, if possible, to be an option granted under an employee stock purchase plan as that term is defined in Section 423 of the Code and the regulations thereunder. In the event this Plan or any option granted pursuant to this Plan is in any way inconsistent with the applicable legal requirements of the Code or the regulations thereunder for an option granted under an employee stock purchase plan, this Plan and such option shall be deemed automatically amended as of the date hereof to conform to such legal requirements, if such conformity may be achieved by amendment.

C. Neither the Company nor any present or future Company affiliated with or subsidiary of the Company, nor any of their officers, directors, stockholders, stock option plan committees, employees or agents, shall have any liability to any Optionee in the event an option granted pursuant to this Plan does not qualify as an option granted under an employee stock purchase plan as that term is used in Section 423 of the Code and the regulations thereunder, or in the event any Optionee does not obtain the tax benefits of such an option granted under an employee stock purchase plan.

D. References in this Plan to the Code shall be deemed to also refer to the corresponding provisions of any future United States revenue law.

E. The use of the masculine pronoun shall include the feminine gender whenever appropriate.

APPENDIX 12

DEF, Inc.
PHANTOM STOCK APPRECIATION RIGHTS PLAN

ARTICLE I—GENERAL

1.1 Purpose

The purpose of the DEF, Inc. Phantom Stock Appreciation Rights Plan (the "Plan") is to provide certain officers and key employees of DEF, Inc. (the "Company") an incentive (a) to remain in the service of the Company, (b) to maximize the value of the Company, and (c) to stimulate a proprietary interest, by providing them with an interest in the increase in the sale value of the Company over its value at December 31, 2000 (computed as set forth herein), payable only if and when there is a Change of Control (as hereafter defined) of the Company.

1.2 Administration

The Company's Board of Directors, or a committee thereof (the "Committee"), shall have the authority to administer this Plan, and to prescribe and amend rules and regulations relating to the Plan, including rules governing its own operations. The Board of Directors or Committee shall determine which individuals shall in fact be granted units (or fractions thereof) of Phantom Stock Appreciation Rights and the number of units (or fractions thereof).

The Board of Directors or Committee shall adopt such rules for the conduct of its business and administration of this Plan as it considers desirable. A majority of the members of the Board of Directors or Committee shall constitute a quorum for all purposes. The vote or written consent of a majority of the members of the Board of Directors or Committee on a particular matter shall constitute the act of the Board of Directors or Committee on such matter. The Board of Directors or Committee shall have the right to construe the Plan and the Phantom Stock Appreciation Rights issued pursuant to it, to correct defects and omissions and to reconcile inconsistencies to the extent necessary to effectuate the Plan, and such action shall be final, binding and conclusive upon all parties concerned. No member of the Board of Directors or Committee shall be liable for any act or omission (whether or not negligent) taken or omitted in good faith, or for the exercise of an authority or discretion granted in connection with the Plan to the Board of Directors or Committee, or for the acts or omissions of any other members of the Board of Directors or Committee. If a Committee is utilized, the Board of Directors may at any time appoint additional members of the Committee and may at any time remove any member of the Committee with or without cause. Vacancies in the Committee, however caused, may be filled by the Board of Directors, if it so desires.

1.3 Persons Eligible for Awards

Awards under the Plan may be made to such officers and key employees of the Company (excluding Owner 1 or Owner 2), including prospective key employees conditioned on their becoming employed, as the Company's Board of Directors or Committee, in their sole discretion, select.

1.4 Type of Awards under the Plan

Awards shall be made under the Plan in the form of units, or a fraction of a unit, of Phantom Stock Appreciation Rights.

1.5 Total Authorized Number of Units Available for Awards

The total number of units, or fractions of a unit, of Phantom Stock Appreciation Rights which may be awarded to participants pursuant to the Plan shall not exceed one hundred thousand (100,000) full units in the aggregate. More than 100,000 full units may be issued under the Plan if authorized by the Company's Board of Directors or Committee and a majority of the holders of outstanding units or fractions of a unit.

1.6 Definition of Certain Terms

The term "cause," when used in connection with termination for a grantee's employment, shall have the meaning set forth in any then effective employment agreement, if any, between the grantee and the Company. In the absence of such an employment agreement, "cause" means: (a) conviction of any crime (whether or not involving the Company) constituting a felony in the jurisdiction involved; (b) engaging in any substantiated act involving moral turpitude; (c) engaging in any act which, in each case, subjects, or if generally known would subject, the Company to public ridicule or embarrassment; (d) serious neglect or misconduct in the performance of the grantee's duties for the Company as determined by the Company's Board of Directors or (e) willful or repeated failure or refusal to perform the grantee's duties for the Company or the instructions of the Board of Directors of the Company as determined by the Company's Board of Directors which determination shall be final; binding and conclusive.

The term "Change in Control" shall mean either one of the following events: (A) the closing date for the merger or consolidation of the Company with another corporation if one or more of the holders of voting shares of the Company immediately prior to the merger or consolidation do not beneficially own, immediately after the merger or consolidation, shares of the corporation issuing cash or securities in the merger or consolidation (or its parent corporation) entitling one or more of such holders to 51% or more of all voting shares of the entity issuing cash or securities in the merger or consolidation, or (B) the closing date for the sale of all or substantially all the assets or stock of the Company if one or more shareholders of the Company do not own 51% or more of the voting shares of the acquiring entity (or its parent corporation).

The term "outstanding," when used with respect to units (or fractions thereof) of Phantom Stock Appreciation Rights, shall refer to units (or fractions thereof) which have been granted and not been forfeited under Section 2.5 of this Plan.

The term "voting shares" shall refer to shares entitled to elect members of the Board of Directors or other similar managing group of a corporation or other entity.

ARTICLE II—AWARDS, REDEMPTIONS, AND FORFEITURES OF UNITS

2.1 Awards

Each unit, or fraction thereof, awarded under the Plan shall be evidenced by an award letter in the form attached hereto or such other form which the Company's Board of Directors may in their sole discretion deem necessary or desirable. By accepting an award pursuant to this Plan, a grantee thereby agrees that the award shall be subject to all of the terms and provisions of the Plan.

2.2 Redemption of Phantom Stock Appreciation Right Units

Each outstanding unit (or fractions thereof) of Phantom Stock Appreciation Rights shall be redeemed within 30 days after the expiration of one year subsequent to the date of a Change of Control for the valuation set forth in Section 2.3., provided that the grantee has continued to be a full-time employee of the Company or its successor for a period of one year subsequent to the date of a Change of Control (or such shorter period as the Company or its successor shall determine in writing) at a compensation level (excluding this Plan) at least equal to what such grantee was paid immediately prior to the date of the Change of Control and within 30 miles of such grantee's primary work location prior to the date of the Change of Control.

2.3 Valuation of Units of Phantom Stock Appreciation Rights

Units of Phantom Stock Appreciation Rights will be valued upon the date of a Change of Control as follows:

(a) Determine the Adjusted EBITDA (as hereafter defined) of the Company for the Calculation Period (as hereafter defined). The term "Adjusted EBITDA" refers to the income of the Company as determined in accordance with generally accepted principles consistently applied after such figure has been adjusted to eliminate the effect of any income taxes, interest, depreciation, amortization, any salaries and fringe benefits paid to Owner 1 or Owner 2, and any payments to Owner 3. The term "Calculation Period" shall refer to the 12 consecutive calendar months ending at the end of the calendar month immediately prior to the date of the written agreement which, if consummated, would result in the Change of Control.

(b) Determine the Adjusted EBITDA of the Company for calendar year 2000, which shall be deemed to equal $4,000,000.

(c) Subtract the result of Clause (b) from the result of Clause (a). If the result of Clause (b) is greater than the result of Clause (a), no value shall be ascribed to the Phantom Stock Appreciation Rights.

(d) If the subtraction of the result of Clause (a) from the result of Clause (b) is a positive figure, multiply such figure by 5.

(e) Adjust the result of Clause (d) by the following:

(i) subtract any capital contribution made by the Company's shareholders to the Company after December 31, 2000, and on or prior to the close of business on the date of the Change of Control, except to the extent that such capital contribution is equal to any capital withdrawal by the shareholder from the Company after December 31, 2000 (other than withdrawals for tax purposes in amounts determined by the independent public accountants for the Company). Any decrease in the annual compensation of Owner 1 or Owner 2 from the annual compensation rate in effect on the date of this Plan shall be deemed a capital contribution by the shareholders of the Company.

(ii) compare the long-term indebtedness of the Company at the close of business on the date of the Change of Control to the long-term indebtedness of the Company at the close of business on December 31, 2000. Any increase in the indebtedness on the date on the Change of Control over the indebtedness at the close of business on December 31, 2000. shall be subtracted from the result of Clause (d). Any decrease in the long-term indebtedness on the date on the Change of Control over the long-term indebtedness on December 31, 2000. shall be added to the result of Clause (d). In computing "long-term indebtedness." any increase in the balance sheet account for split-dollar insurance premium payments for insurance on the lives of either Owner 1 and Owner 2 between December 31, 2000 .and the date of the Change of Control shall be subtracted from long-term indebtedness on the date of the Change of Control and any decrease in such balance sheet account between December 31, 2000. and the date of the Change of Control shall be added to the long-term indebtedness on the date of the Change of Control.

(iii) compare the working capital at the close of business on the date of the Change of Control to the working capital at the close of business on December 31, 2000. Any increase in the working capital at the close of business on the date of the Change of Control over the working capital at the close of business on December 31, 2000, shall be added to the result of Clause (d). Any decrease in the working capital at the close of business on the date of the Change of Control over the working capital at the close of business on December 31, 2000, shall be subtracted from the result of Clause (d).

(iv) the terms "long-term indebtedness" and "working capital," as used herein, shall be interpreted consistently with the definition of similar terms, if any, which are used in the agreement which resulted in the Change of Control.

(f) Determine whichever is the lower figure: (i) the result of Clause (d) without the adjustments by the provisions of Clause (e); or (ii) the result of Clause (d) as adjusted by the provisions of Clause (e). Multiply the lower figure by 25%.

(g) Divide the result of Clause (f) by the number of outstanding units (or fractions thereof) of Phantom Stock Appreciation Rights on the date of the Change of Control.

An example of the calculation of the valuation of a unit is contained in the Appendix hereto; nothing contained in the example shall be deemed to change the provisions of this Plan. Any dispute concerning the valuation of a unit (or fractions thereof) shall be determined by the firm which acted as the independent public accountants for the Company immediately prior to the date of the Change of Control and their determination shall be final, binding and conclusive on all parties.

2.4 Forfeiture of Units

All units (or fractions thereof) of Phantom Stock Appreciation Rights shall automatically be forfeited upon termination of the grantee's employment for any reason (including disability or death), whether voluntarily or involuntarily, except that termination by the Company of the grantee's employment without cause within 6 months prior to the date of a Change of Control shall not result in a termination or forfeiture. Forfeited units (or fractions thereof) shall no longer be considered outstanding units (or fractions thereof) and may be reissued by the Company under this Plan. The Company's Board of Directors may, in its sole judgement, allocate forfeited units (or fractions thereof) to the remaining grantees of Phantom Stock Appreciation Rights if the Company's Board of Directors determines that the remaining grantees can operate as effectively without the grantee whose units (or fractions thereof) were forfeited.

2.5 No Rights as Shareholders

No grantee of a unit or units (or fractions thereof) of Phantom Stock Appreciation Rights shall have any of the rights of a shareholder of the Company, including but not limited to, any right to vote, receive dividends or other distributions or receive shareholder notices.

ARTICLE III—MISCELLANEOUS

3.1 Nonassignability

No unit (or fractions thereof) awarded or right granted to any person under this Plan shall be assignable or transferable.

3.2 Nature of Payments

The units (or fractions thereof) granted under this Plan shall constitute a special incentive payment to the grantee and shall not be taken into account in computing the amount of salary or compensation of the grantee for the purpose of determining any benefits under any other employee benefit plan of the Company now or hereafter adopted life insurance, or other benefit of the Company.

3.3 Non-Uniform Determinations

The determinations of the Board of Directors or Committee under this Plan need not be uniform and may be made by it selectively among persons who receive awards under the Plan (whether or not such persons are similarly situated).

3.4 Other Phantom Stock Appreciation Rights Plans

Nothing contained herein shall prevent the Company from adopting other Phantom Stock Appreciation Rights Plans, subject to such terms and provisions, as the Board of Directors or Committee shall determine in their sole discretion.

3.5 Section Headings

The section headings contained herein are for the purpose of convenience only and are not intended to define or limit the contents of the sections.

3.6 Effective Date of Plan

The Plan was adopted by the Board of Directors of DEF, Inc on _____, 2001.

3.7 Governing Law

All rights and obligations under this Plan shall be construed and interpreted with the laws of the State of New York, without giving effect to principles of conflict of laws.

3.8 Amendments, Supplement, Suspension, or Termination

The Board of Directors or Committee reserves the right at any time, and from time to time, to amend or supplement this Plan in any way, or to suspend or terminate it, effective as of such date, which date may be either before or after the taking of such action, as may be specified by the Board of Directors or Committee; provided, however, that such action shall not affect units (or fractions thereof) granted under the Plan prior to the actual date on which such action occurred.

3.9 General Conditions

(a) Nothing contained in this Plan or any units (or fractions thereof) granted pursuant to this Plan shall confer upon any employee the right to continue in the employ of the Company or any affiliated or subsidiary corporation or interfere in any way with the rights of the Company or any affiliated or subsidiary corporation to terminate his employment in any way.

(b) The use of the masculine pronoun shall include the feminine gender whenever appropriate.

FORM OF AWARD LETTER

John Smith

_____

_____

Dear Mr. Smith:

We are pleased to advise you that you have been selected to receive a grant of _____ unit(s) of Phantom Stock Appreciation Rights pursuant to the Phantom Stock Appreciation Rights Plan (the "Plan") of DEF, Inc. (the "Company"), a copy of which is attached.

Nothing contained herein or in the Plan shall confer upon you any rights as a shareholder of the Company.

Nothing herein shall modify your status as an at-will employee of the Company. Further, nothing herein guarantees you employment for any specified period of time. This means that either you or the Company may terminate your employment at any time for any reason, with or without cause, or for no reason. You recognize that, for instance, you may terminate your employment or the Company may terminate your employment prior to the date on which your unit (or fractions thereof) becomes redeemable or the date of a Change of Control (as defined in the Plan).

Except as set forth in Section 2.3 of the Plan, any dispute or disagreement between you and the Company with respect to any portion of this unit (or fractions thereof) or its validity, construction, meaning, performance or your rights hereunder shall be settled by arbitration in accordance with the Commercial Arbitration Rules of the American Arbitration Association or its successor, as amended from time to time. However, prior to submission to arbitration you will attempt to resolve any disputes or disagreements with the Company over this unit (or fractions thereof) amicably and informally, in good faith, for a period not to exceed two weeks. Thereafter, the dispute or disagreement will be submitted to arbitration. At any time prior to a decision from the arbitrator(s) being rendered, you and the Company may resolve the dispute by settlement. You and the Company shall equally share the costs charged by the American Arbitration Association or its successor, but you and the Company shall otherwise be solely responsible for your own respective counsel fees and expenses. The decision of the arbitrator(s) shall be made in writing, setting forth the award, the reasons for the decision and award, and shall be binding and conclusive on you and the Company. Further, neither you nor the Company shall appeal any such award. Judgment of a court of competent jurisdiction may be entered upon the award and may be enforced as such in accordance with the provisions of the award.

This unit (or fractions thereof) shall be subject to the terms of the Plan in effect on the date this unit (or fractions thereof) is granted, which terms are hereby incorporated herein by reference and made a part hereof. In the event of any conflict between the terms of this unit (or fractions thereof) and the terms of the Plan in effect on the date of this unit (or fractions thereof), the terms of the Plan shall govern. This unit (or fractions thereof) constitutes the entire understanding between the Company and you with respect to the subject matter hereof and no amendment, supplement or waiver of this unit (or fractions thereof), in whole or in part, shall be binding upon the Company unless in writing and signed by the President of the Company. This unit (or fractions thereof) and the performances of the parties hereunder shall be construed in accordance with and governed by the laws of the State of New York.

DEF, Inc.

By: _____

I hereby acknowledge receipt of a copy of the Company's Phantom Stock Agreement Rights Plan and, having read it, hereby signify my understanding of, and my agreement with, its terms and conditions.

_____   _____

(Signature)   (Date)

APPENDIX

Example of Valuation of Units of Phantom Stock Appreciation Rights Plan

Assume the following: (1) the Change of Control occurs on December 1, 2003; (2) the pre-tax accounting income for the twelve month period ended November 30, 2003, amounts to $500,000; and (3) during the period January 1, 2001, through December 1, 2003, the aggregate annual compensation of Owner 1 and Owner 2 has been reduced by $300,000.

Section 2.3(a)				
	Pre-tax accounting income		$ 500,000	
Plus:	Interest		$ 325,000	
	Depreciation and amortization		$ 1,100,000	
	Salaries and fringe benefits of Owner 1 and Owner 2, together with Owner 3 payments		$ 1,964,000	
	Adjusted EBITDA		$ 3,889,000	
2.3(b)	Base Year (2000) Adjusted EBITDA		$ 4,000,000	
2.3(c)	Excess of (a) over (b)		$ 111,000	
2.3(d)	Multiply above by 5		$ 555,000	$ 555,000
2.3(e)	(i) Less: Shareholder Capital Contributions		$ (300,000)	$ (300,000)
	(ii) Long term debt as of December 31, 2000		$ (4,113,000)	
	Long term debt as of November 30, 2003		$ (4,613,000)	
	(Increase)		$ (500,000)	$ (500,000)
	(iii) Working Capital as of December 31, 2000		$ 1,842,900	
	Working Capital as of November 30, 2003		$ 2,843,000	
	Increase		$ 1,000,100	$1,000,100
	Total			$ 755,100
2.3(f)	The lower of 2.3(d) ($555,000) or 2.3(d) as adjusted by 2.3(e) ($755,100) is $555,000, which is multiplied by 25%			$ 138,750
2.3(g)	Value per Unit (Assuming 100,000 units issued and outstanding)			$ 1.38750

INDEX